# the Voyeurs

the

Uncivilized Books. Publisher

Gabrielle Bell

# Voyeurs

## Also by Gabrielle Bell:

When I'm Old and Other Stories
Lucky
Cecil and Jordan in New York
Lucky Vol. 2
Gabriellebell.com

Entire contents copyright © 2012 by Gabrielle Bell.

**Uncivilized Books**
P. O. Box 6534
Minneapolis, MN 55406
USA
uncivilizedbooks.com

First Edition, August 2012

10  9  8  7  6  5  4  3  2  1

ISBN 978-0-9846814-0-2

DISTRIBUTED TO THE TRADE BY:
**Consortium Book Sales & Distribution, LLC.**
34 Thirteenth Avenue NE, Suite 101
Minneapolis, MN 55413-1007
cbsd.com
Orders: (800) 283-3572

Printed in China

Pages 9 through 11 originally appeared on my website, *Lucky*.

Pages 13 through 27 were originally published by Drawn & Quarterly in *Lucky*, Volume II, issues one and two.

Pages 68 & 69 originally appeared in Desert Island's *Smoke Signals*.

Page 72 originally appeared is *McSweeney's*.

Pages 105 through 111 appeared in Houghton Mifflin Harcourt's *Best American Comics 2011*.

Pages 59 through 156 originally appeared on my website, *Lucky*.

Colored by Gabrielle Bell and Daryl Seitchik.

Design by Tom Kaczynski.

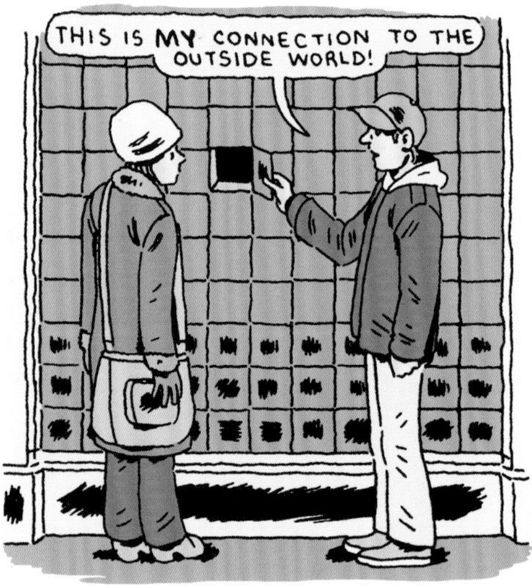
THIS IS MY CONNECTION TO THE OUTSIDE WORLD!

# INTRODUCTION

When I first met Gabrielle she was eleven, an impossibly tall and gangly girl clinging to her mother's skirt. In the twenty-five years since, she hasn't changed much. She still resembles a deer caught in the headlights, or a possum in a crowd of cartoonists, trying to pass. Her manners no doubt come from growing up on a remote mountaintop where she had more animal than human friends, but ten years living in New York City haven't changed her way of looking at the world. Now, instead of spying on passersby from behind a bush, she peers out from a fire escape or from behind a table piled high with books.

Her back-to-the-land childhood is mentioned only in passing in these memoirs, for Gabrielle's comics never dwell in the past. Still, her upbringing is part of what makes her perspective compelling and unique. It gave her an extra-sensitive eye for human interactions—and for human isolation. She sees the urban landscape with a sense of detail and wonder that wouldn't come from a native. And her love of technology and her need for attention and adventure are always at odds with her pining for a simpler, quieter, more solitary life.

But having known Gabrielle for so long, I still barely know her at all. She's secretive and shy, and seems to grow more mysterious instead of less. The same is true of her work. The more she divulges as a narrator, the more elusive she gets. She uses her personality to play hide-and-seek behind, and one wonders sometimes if her shyness isn't really just a mask or a literary device. Memoirs are always about what they leave out as much as what they reveal, but in Gabrielle's books the truly incriminating evidence seems to be hidden just out of sight. Her confession comes across as an elaborate dodge rather than a literal truth. She lapses into daydreams and launches into bald-faced lies. She's an unreliable, uncooperative witness to her own life!

Yet that's what makes Gabrielle's autobiographical comics interesting: she and her characters retain their mystery. You're left to wonder where they came from, how they met, and what makes them tick—and in doing so, you put yourself in their shoes. You have to fill in the blanks, looking for the soft-spoken and unspoken clues. Gabrielle's way of leaving you guessing is her way of turning life into art.

**Aaron Cometbus**
November 2011

# THE VOYEURS

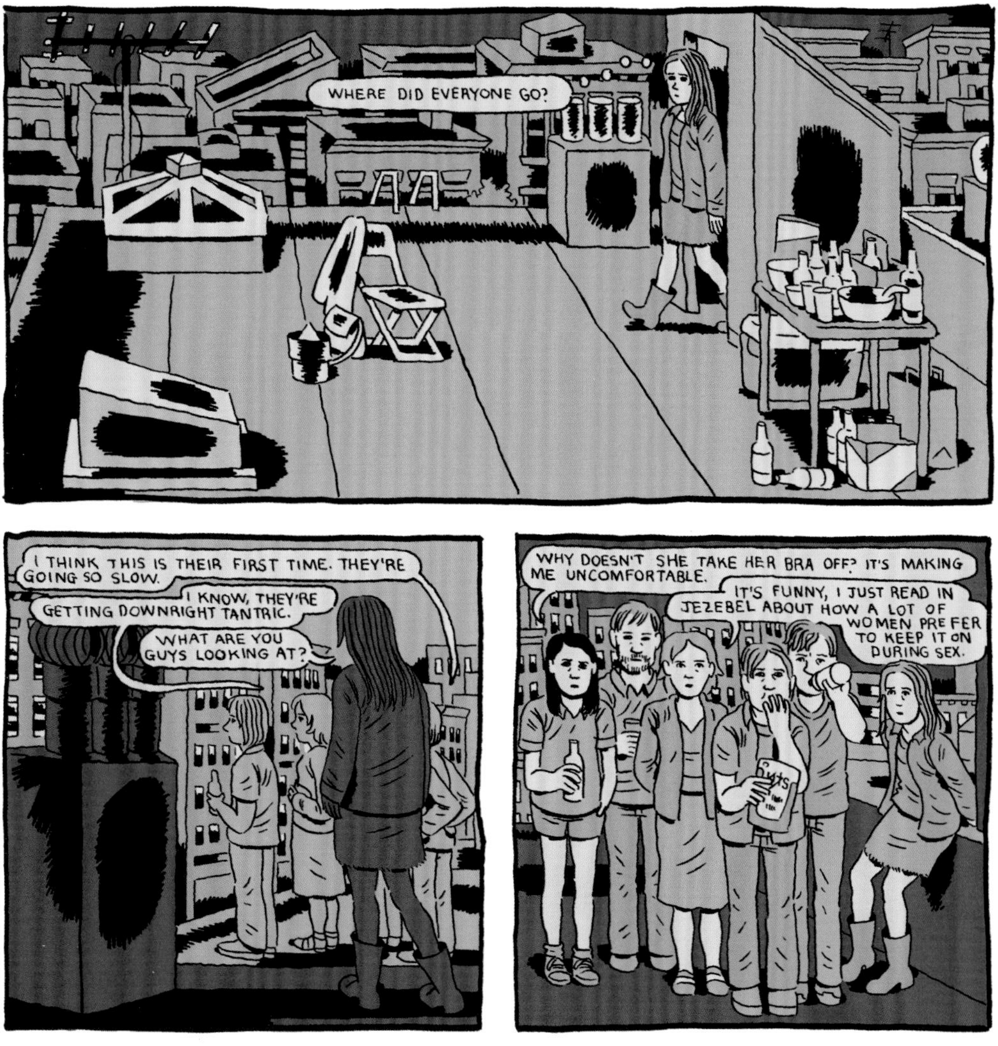

WHERE DID EVERYONE GO?
I THINK THIS IS THEIR FIRST TIME. THEY'RE GOING SO SLOW.
I KNOW, THEY'RE GETTING DOWNRIGHT TANTRIC.
WHAT ARE YOU GUYS LOOKING AT?
WHY DOESN'T SHE TAKE HER BRA OFF? IT'S MAKING ME UNCOMFORTABLE.
IT'S FUNNY, I JUST READ IN JEZEBEL ABOUT HOW A LOT OF WOMEN PREFER TO KEEP IT ON DURING SEX.

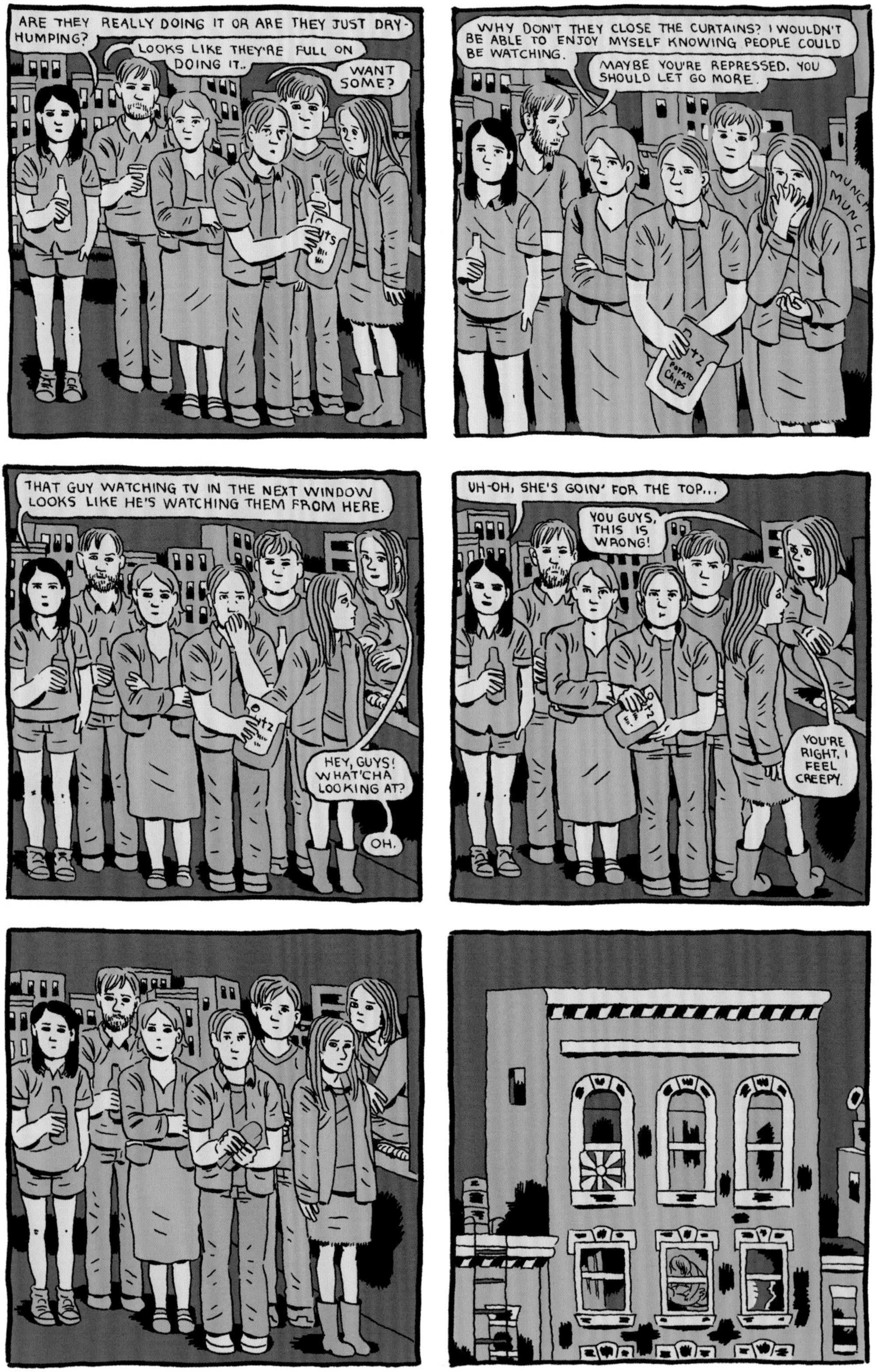
ARE THEY REALLY DOING IT OR ARE THEY JUST DRY-HUMPING?
LOOKS LIKE THEY'RE FULL ON DOING IT..
WANT SOME?
WHY DON'T THEY CLOSE THE CURTAINS? I WOULDN'T BE ABLE TO ENJOY MYSELF KNOWING PEOPLE COULD BE WATCHING.
MAYBE YOU'RE REPRESSED. YOU SHOULD LET GO MORE.
MUNCH MUNCH
POTATO CHIPS
THAT GUY WATCHING TV IN THE NEXT WINDOW LOOKS LIKE HE'S WATCHING THEM FROM HERE.
HEY, GUYS! WHAT'CHA LOOKING AT?
OH.
UH-OH, SHE'S GOIN' FOR THE TOP...
YOU GUYS, THIS IS WRONG!
YOU'RE RIGHT, I FEEL CREEPY.

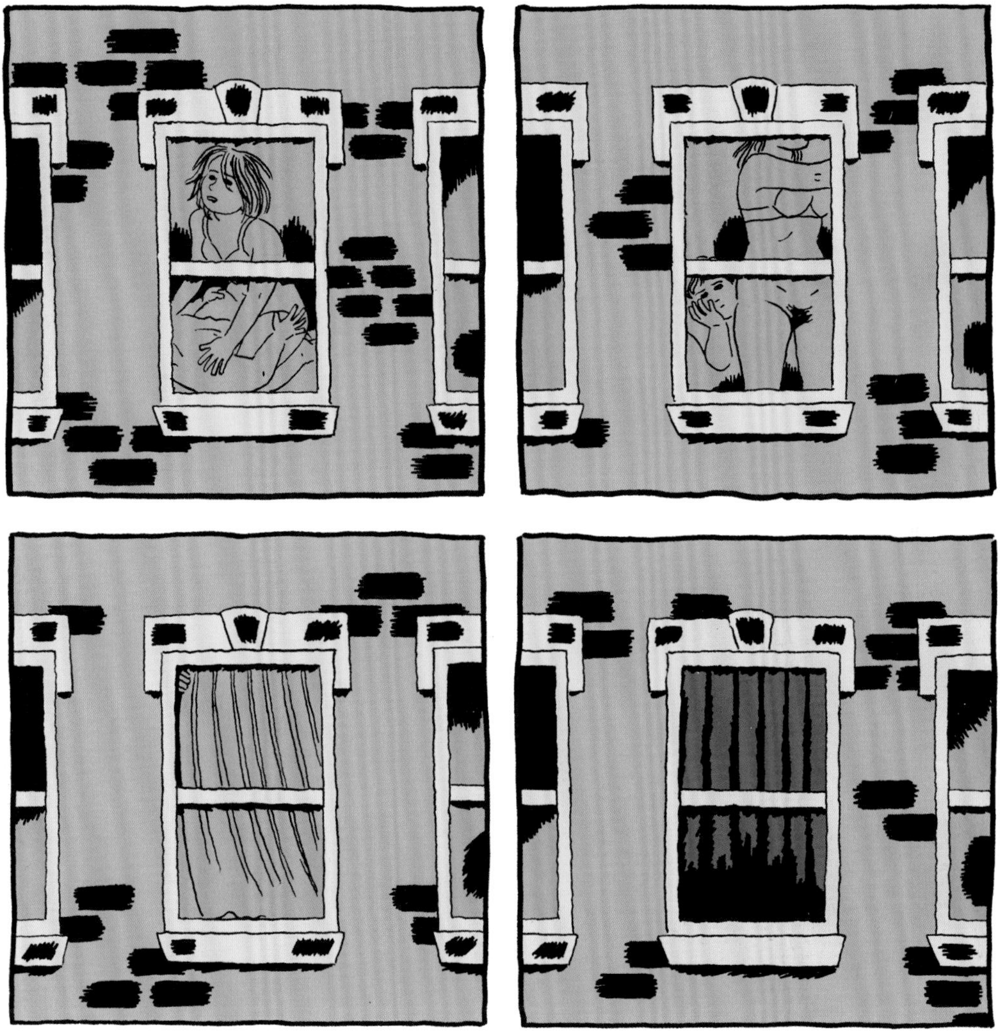

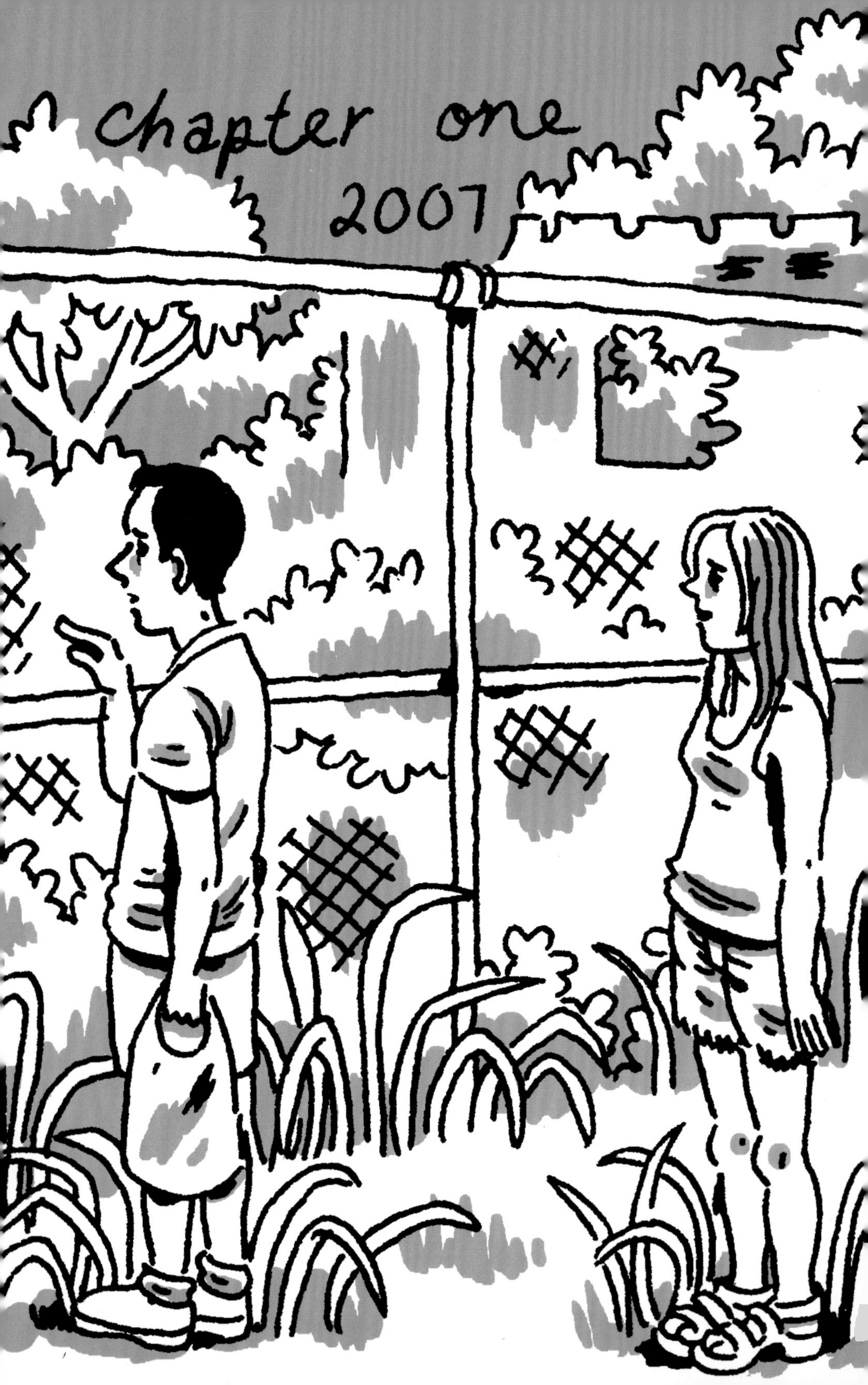
chapter one
2007

July 7th, 2007

Roosevelt Island

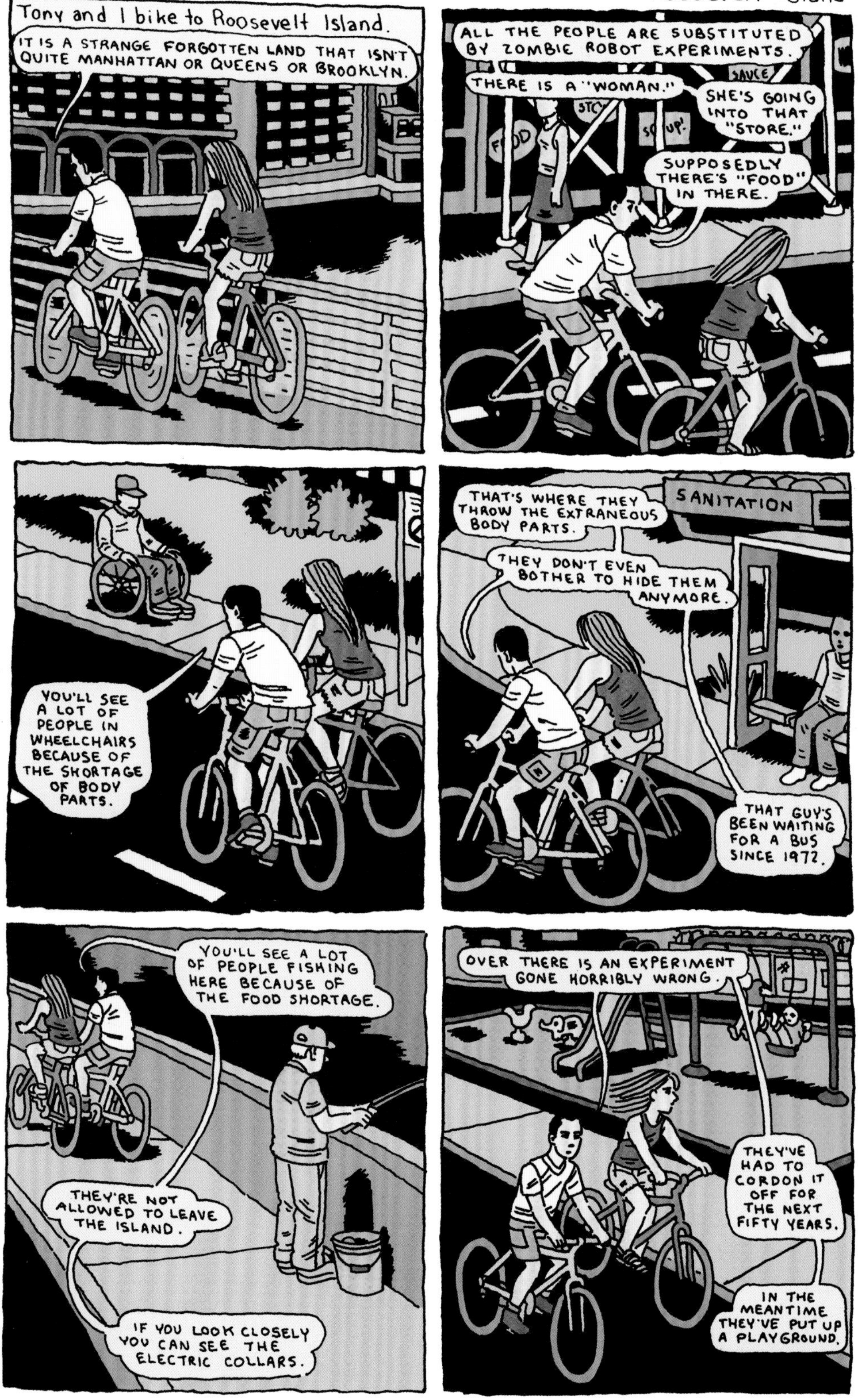

Tony and I bike to Roosevelt Island.
IT IS A STRANGE FORGOTTEN LAND THAT ISN'T QUITE MANHATTAN OR QUEENS OR BROOKLYN.
ALL THE PEOPLE ARE SUBSTITUTED BY ZOMBIE ROBOT EXPERIMENTS.
THERE IS A "WOMAN."
SHE'S GOING INTO THAT "STORE."
SUPPOSEDLY THERE'S "FOOD" IN THERE.
SAUCE
FOOD
SOUP!
YOU'LL SEE A LOT OF PEOPLE IN WHEELCHAIRS BECAUSE OF THE SHORTAGE OF BODY PARTS.
SANITATION
THAT'S WHERE THEY THROW THE EXTRANEOUS BODY PARTS.
THEY DON'T EVEN BOTHER TO HIDE THEM ANYMORE.
THAT GUY'S BEEN WAITING FOR A BUS SINCE 1972.
YOU'LL SEE A LOT OF PEOPLE FISHING HERE BECAUSE OF THE FOOD SHORTAGE.
THEY'RE NOT ALLOWED TO LEAVE THE ISLAND.
IF YOU LOOK CLOSELY YOU CAN SEE THE ELECTRIC COLLARS.
OVER THERE IS AN EXPERIMENT GONE HORRIBLY WRONG.
THEY'VE HAD TO CORDON IT OFF FOR THE NEXT FIFTY YEARS.
IN THE MEANTIME THEY'VE PUT UP A PLAYGROUND.

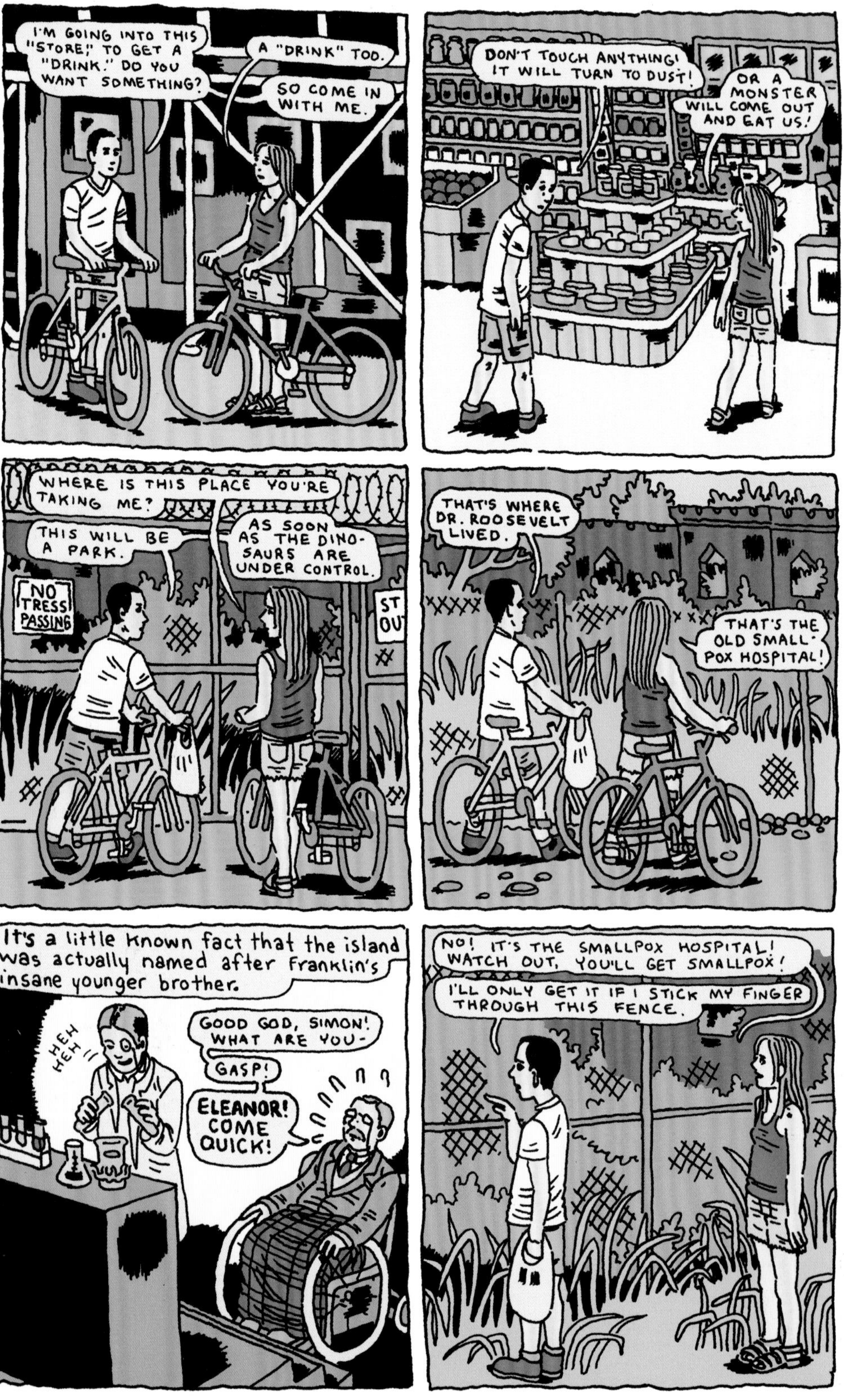
I'M GOING INTO THIS "STORE," TO GET A "DRINK." DO YOU WANT SOMETHING?
A "DRINK" TOO.
SO COME IN WITH ME.
DON'T TOUCH ANYTHING! IT WILL TURN TO DUST!
OR A MONSTER WILL COME OUT AND EAT US!
WHERE IS THIS PLACE YOU'RE TAKING ME?
THIS WILL BE A PARK.
AS SOON AS THE DINO-SAURS ARE UNDER CONTROL.
NO TRESS PASSING
THAT'S WHERE DR. ROOSEVELT LIVED.
THAT'S THE OLD SMALL-POX HOSPITAL!
It's a little known fact that the island was actually named after Franklin's insane younger brother.
HEH HEH
GOOD GOD, SIMON! WHAT ARE YOU-
GASP!
ELEANOR! COME QUICK!
NO! IT'S THE SMALLPOX HOSPITAL! WATCH OUT, YOU'LL GET SMALLPOX!
I'LL ONLY GET IT IF I STICK MY FINGER THROUGH THIS FENCE.

march 18th, 2007

My Space

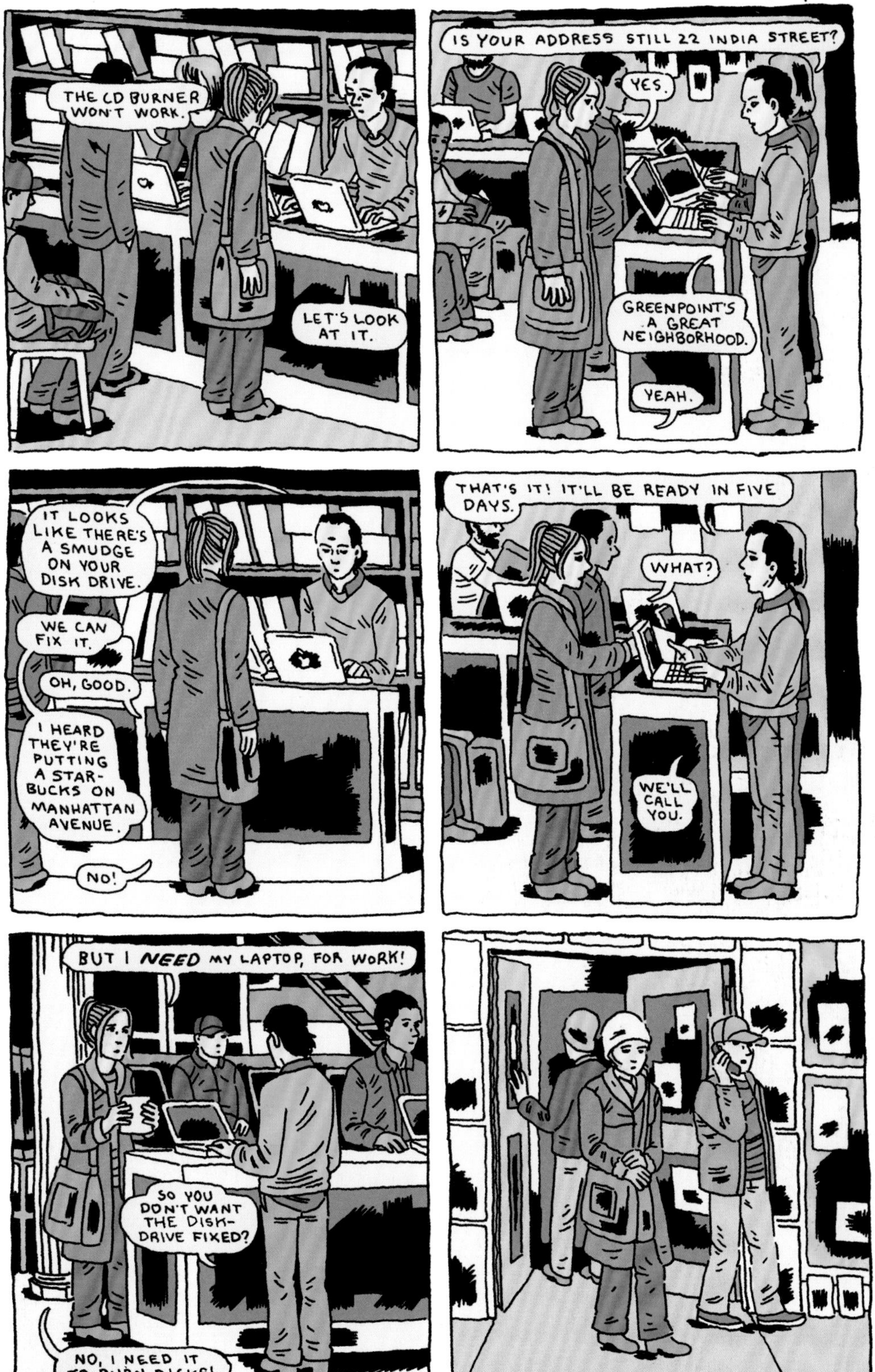
THE CD BURNER WON'T WORK.
LET'S LOOK AT IT.
IS YOUR ADDRESS STILL 22 INDIA STREET?
YES.
GREENPOINT'S A GREAT NEIGHBORHOOD.
YEAH.
IT LOOKS LIKE THERE'S A SMUDGE ON YOUR DISK DRIVE.
WE CAN FIX IT.
OH, GOOD.
I HEARD THEY'RE PUTTING A STAR-BUCKS ON MANHATTAN AVENUE.
NO!
THAT'S IT! IT'LL BE READY IN FIVE DAYS.
WHAT?
WE'LL CALL YOU.
BUT I NEED MY LAPTOP, FOR WORK!
SO YOU DON'T WANT THE DISK-DRIVE FIXED?
NO, I NEED IT TO BURN DISKS!

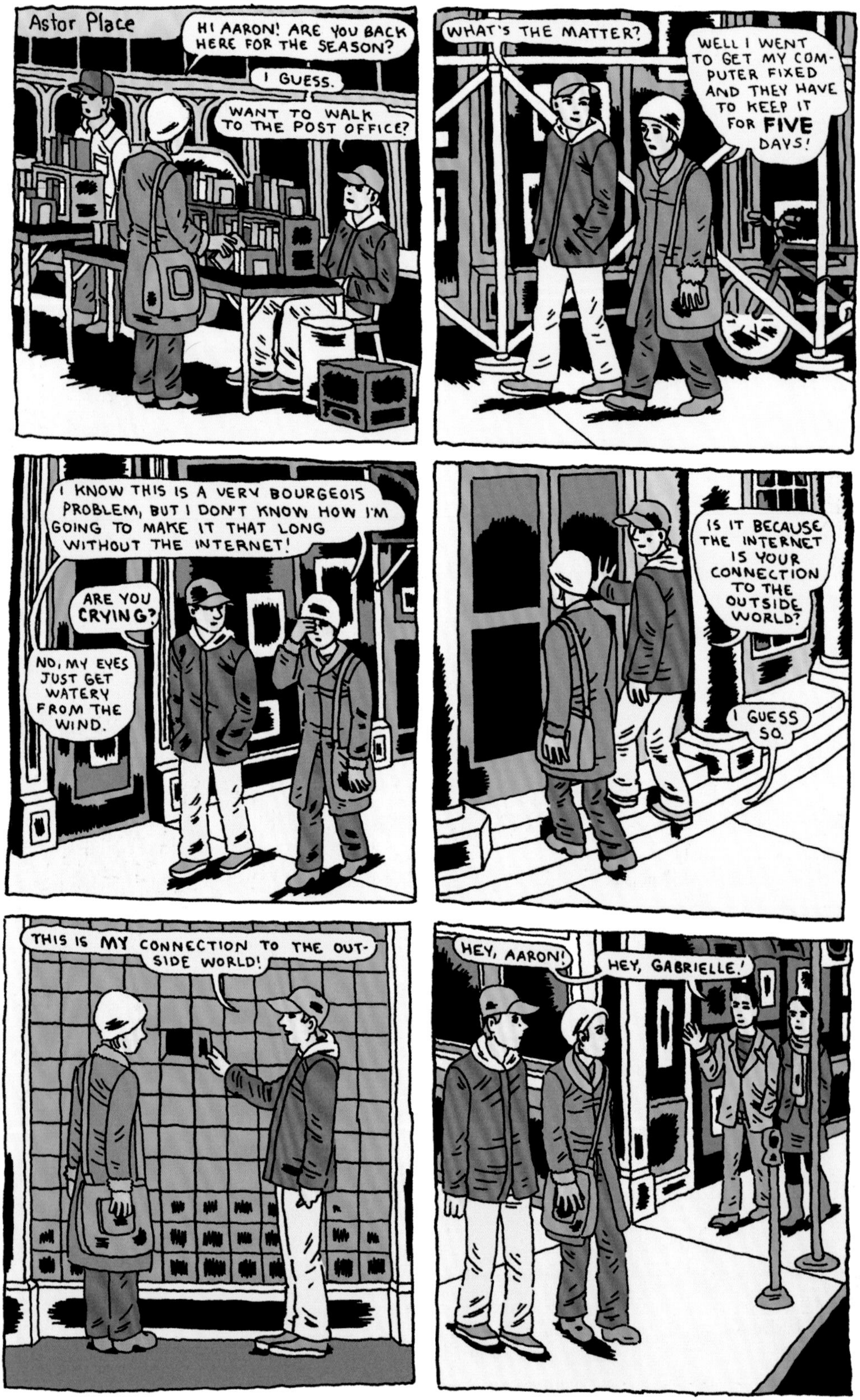

Astor Place
HI AARON! ARE YOU BACK HERE FOR THE SEASON?
I GUESS.
WANT TO WALK TO THE POST OFFICE?
WHAT'S THE MATTER?
WELL I WENT TO GET MY COMPUTER FIXED AND THEY HAVE TO KEEP IT FOR FIVE DAYS!
I KNOW THIS IS A VERY BOURGEOIS PROBLEM, BUT I DON'T KNOW HOW I'M GOING TO MAKE IT THAT LONG WITHOUT THE INTERNET!
ARE YOU CRYING?
NO, MY EYES JUST GET WATERY FROM THE WIND.
IS IT BECAUSE THE INTERNET IS YOUR CONNECTION TO THE OUTSIDE WORLD?
I GUESS SO.
THIS IS MY CONNECTION TO THE OUT-SIDE WORLD!
HEY, AARON!
HEY, GABRIELLE!

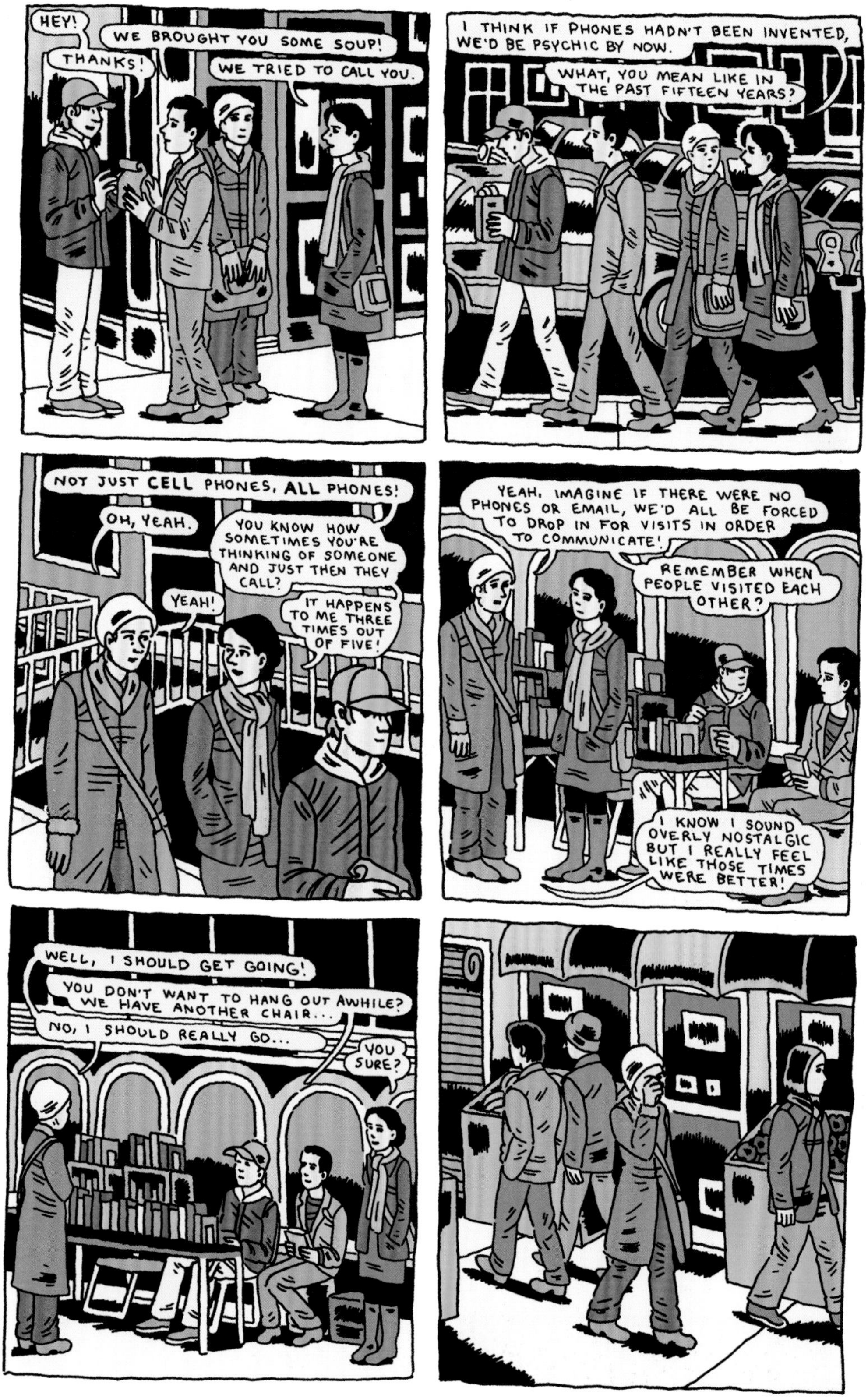
HEY!
WE BROUGHT YOU SOME SOUP!
THANKS!
WE TRIED TO CALL YOU.
I THINK IF PHONES HADN'T BEEN INVENTED, WE'D BE PSYCHIC BY NOW.
WHAT, YOU MEAN LIKE IN THE PAST FIFTEEN YEARS?
NOT JUST CELL PHONES, ALL PHONES!
OH, YEAH.
YOU KNOW HOW SOMETIMES YOU'RE THINKING OF SOMEONE AND JUST THEN THEY CALL?
YEAH!
IT HAPPENS TO ME THREE TIMES OUT OF FIVE!
YEAH, IMAGINE IF THERE WERE NO PHONES OR EMAIL, WE'D ALL BE FORCED TO DROP IN FOR VISITS IN ORDER TO COMMUNICATE!
REMEMBER WHEN PEOPLE VISITED EACH OTHER?
I KNOW I SOUND OVERLY NOSTALGIC BUT I REALLY FEEL LIKE THOSE TIMES WERE BETTER!
WELL, I SHOULD GET GOING!
YOU DON'T WANT TO HANG OUT AWHILE? WE HAVE ANOTHER CHAIR...
NO, I SHOULD REALLY GO...
YOU SURE?

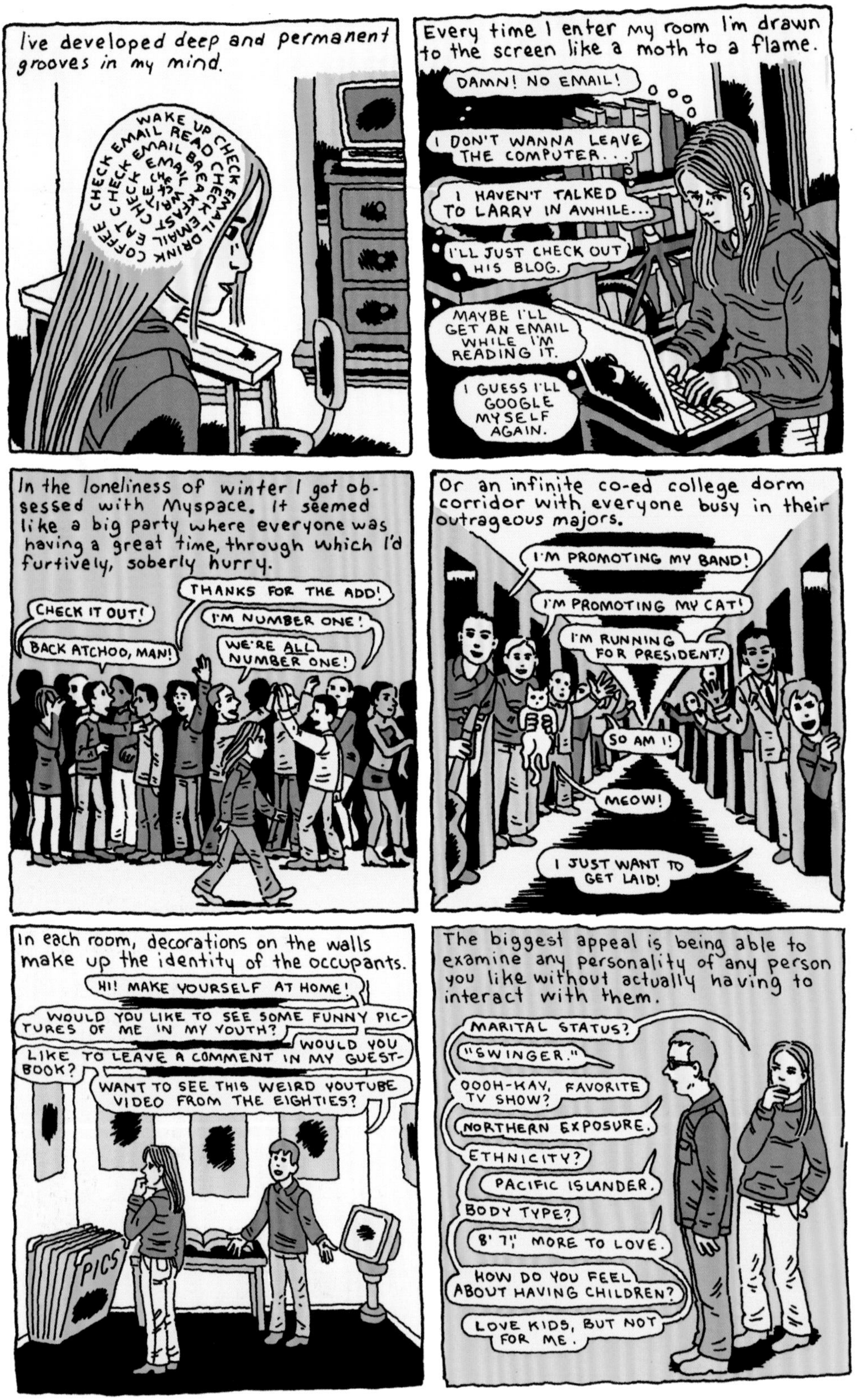
I've developed deep and permanent grooves in my mind.
WAKE UP CHECK EMAIL DRINK COFFEE CHECK EMAIL READ CHECK EMAIL BREAKFAST CHECK EMAIL EAT CHECK EMAIL WRITE CHECK CHE
Every time I enter my room I'm drawn to the screen like a moth to a flame.
DAMN! NO EMAIL!
I DON'T WANNA LEAVE THE COMPUTER...
I HAVEN'T TALKED TO LARRY IN AWHILE...
I'LL JUST CHECK OUT HIS BLOG.
MAYBE I'LL GET AN EMAIL WHILE I'M READING IT.
I GUESS I'LL GOOGLE MYSELF AGAIN.
In the loneliness of winter I got obsessed with Myspace. It seemed like a big party where everyone was having a great time, through which I'd furtively, soberly hurry.
CHECK IT OUT!
BACK ATCHOO, MAN!
THANKS FOR THE ADD!
I'M NUMBER ONE!
WE'RE ALL NUMBER ONE!
Or an infinite co-ed college dorm corridor with everyone busy in their outrageous majors.
I'M PROMOTING MY BAND!
I'M PROMOTING MY CAT!
I'M RUNNING FOR PRESIDENT!
SO AM I!
MEOW!
I JUST WANT TO GET LAID!
In each room, decorations on the walls make up the identity of the occupants.
HI! MAKE YOURSELF AT HOME!
WOULD YOU LIKE TO SEE SOME FUNNY PICTURES OF ME IN MY YOUTH?
WOULD YOU LIKE TO LEAVE A COMMENT IN MY GUESTBOOK?
WANT TO SEE THIS WEIRD YOUTUBE VIDEO FROM THE EIGHTIES?
PICS
The biggest appeal is being able to examine any personality of any person you like without actually having to interact with them.
MARITAL STATUS?
"SWINGER."
OOOH-KAY, FAVORITE TV SHOW?
NORTHERN EXPOSURE.
ETHNICITY?
PACIFIC ISLANDER.
BODY TYPE?
8' 7", MORE TO LOVE.
HOW DO YOU FEEL ABOUT HAVING CHILDREN?
LOVE KIDS, BUT NOT FOR ME.

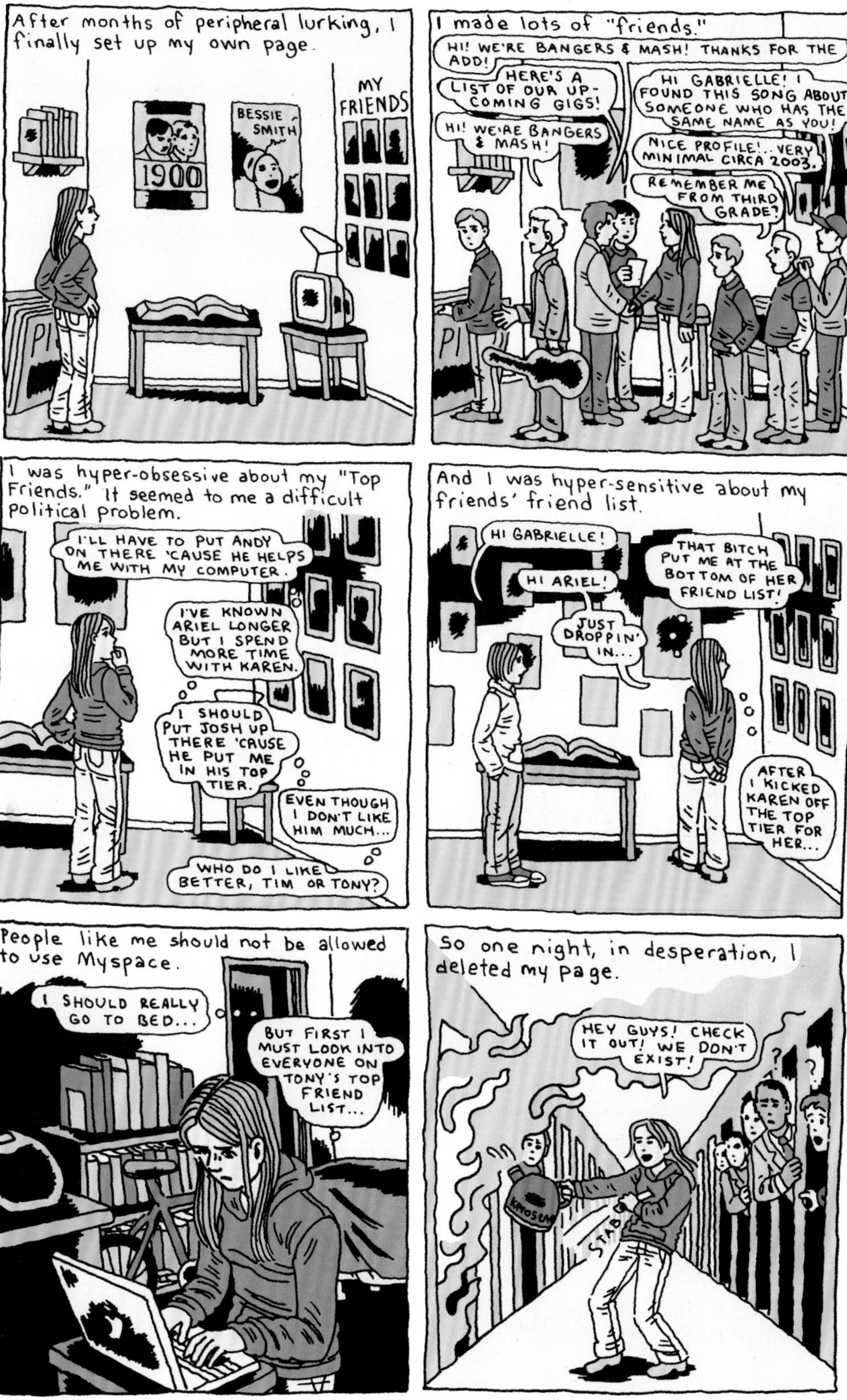
After months of peripheral lurking, I finally set up my own page.
1900
BESSIE SMITH
MY FRIENDS
PI
I made lots of "friends."
HI! WE'RE BANGERS & MASH! THANKS FOR THE ADD!
HERE'S A LIST OF OUR UPCOMING GIGS!
HI! WE'RE BANGERS & MASH!
HI GABRIELLE! I FOUND THIS SONG ABOUT SOMEONE WHO HAS THE SAME NAME AS YOU!
NICE PROFILE!.. VERY MINIMAL CIRCA 2003.
REMEMBER ME FROM THIRD GRADE?
I was hyper-obsessive about my "Top Friends." It seemed to me a difficult political problem.
I'LL HAVE TO PUT ANDY ON THERE 'CAUSE HE HELPS ME WITH MY COMPUTER.
I'VE KNOWN ARIEL LONGER BUT I SPEND MORE TIME WITH KAREN.
I SHOULD PUT JOSH UP THERE 'CAUSE HE PUT ME IN HIS TOP TIER.
EVEN THOUGH I DON'T LIKE HIM MUCH...
WHO DO I LIKE BETTER, TIM OR TONY?
And I was hyper-sensitive about my friends' friend list.
HI GABRIELLE!
HI ARIEL!
JUST DROPPIN' IN...
THAT BITCH PUT ME AT THE BOTTOM OF HER FRIEND LIST!
AFTER I KICKED KAREN OFF THE TOP TIER FOR HER...
People like me should not be allowed to use Myspace.
I SHOULD REALLY GO TO BED...
BUT FIRST I MUST LOOK INTO EVERYONE ON TONY'S TOP FRIEND LIST...
So one night, in desperation, I deleted my page.
HEY GUYS! CHECK IT OUT! WE DON'T EXIST!
?
?
KROSEN
STAB

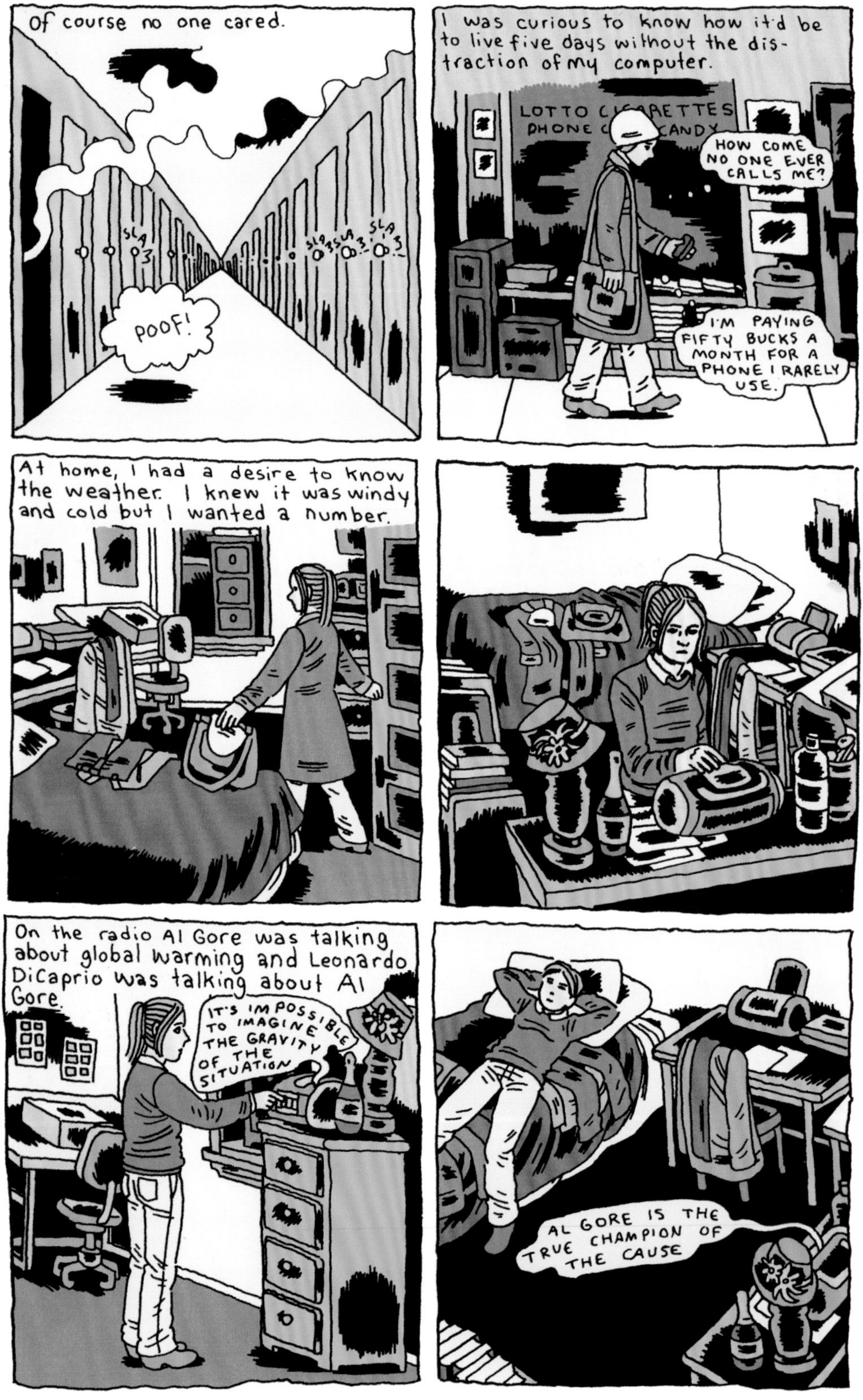
Of course no one cared.
POOF!
I was curious to know how it'd be to live five days without the distraction of my computer.
HOW COME NO ONE EVER CALLS ME?
I'M PAYING FIFTY BUCKS A MONTH FOR A PHONE I RARELY USE.
At home, I had a desire to know the weather. I knew it was windy and cold but I wanted a number.
On the radio Al Gore was talking about global warming and Leonardo DiCaprio was talking about Al Gore.
IT'S IMPOSSIBLE TO IMAGINE THE GRAVITY OF THE SITUATION
AL GORE IS THE TRUE CHAMPION OF THE CAUSE

March 21st

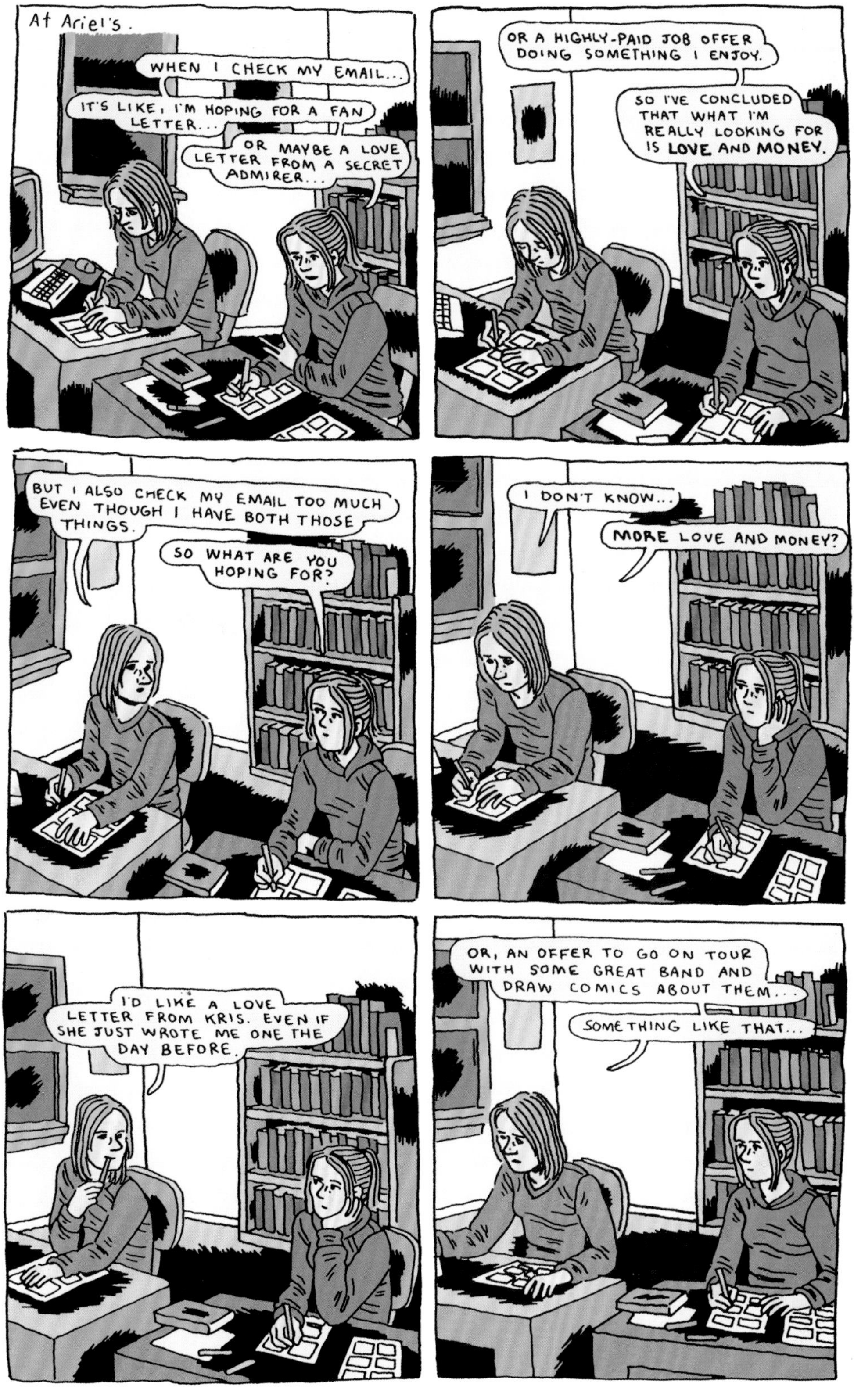
At Ariel's.
WHEN I CHECK MY EMAIL...
IT'S LIKE, I'M HOPING FOR A FAN LETTER...
OR MAYBE A LOVE LETTER FROM A SECRET ADMIRER...
OR A HIGHLY-PAID JOB OFFER DOING SOMETHING I ENJOY.
SO I'VE CONCLUDED THAT WHAT I'M REALLY LOOKING FOR IS LOVE AND MONEY.
BUT I ALSO CHECK MY EMAIL TOO MUCH EVEN THOUGH I HAVE BOTH THOSE THINGS.
SO WHAT ARE YOU HOPING FOR?
I DON'T KNOW...
MORE LOVE AND MONEY?
I'D LIKE A LOVE LETTER FROM KRIS. EVEN IF SHE JUST WROTE ME ONE THE DAY BEFORE.
OR, AN OFFER TO GO ON TOUR WITH SOME GREAT BAND AND DRAW COMICS ABOUT THEM...
SOMETHING LIKE THAT...

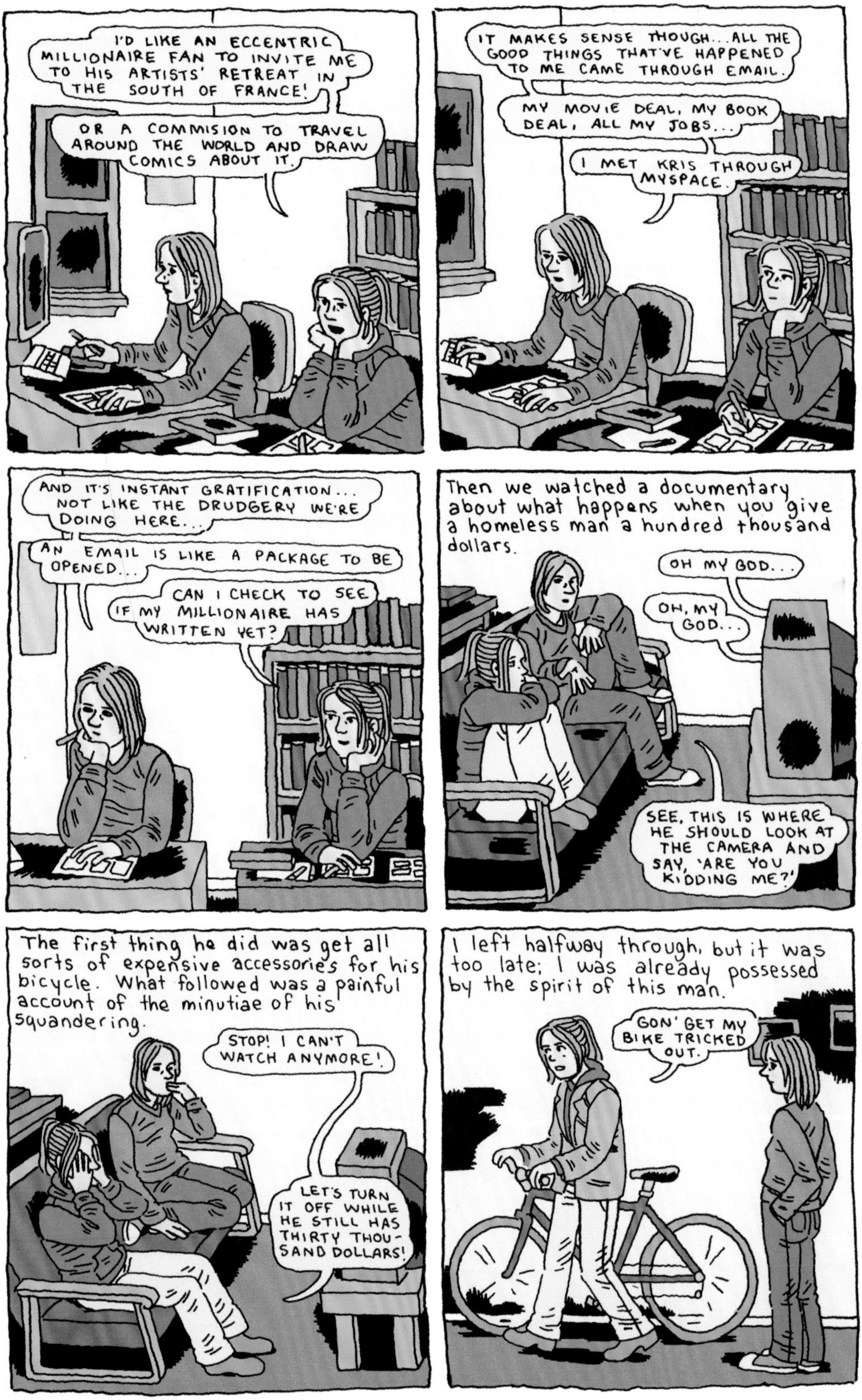
I'D LIKE AN ECCENTRIC MILLIONAIRE FAN TO INVITE ME TO HIS ARTISTS' RETREAT IN THE SOUTH OF FRANCE!
OR A COMMISION TO TRAVEL AROUND THE WORLD AND DRAW COMICS ABOUT IT.
IT MAKES SENSE THOUGH... ALL THE GOOD THINGS THAT'VE HAPPENED TO ME CAME THROUGH EMAIL.
MY MOVIE DEAL, MY BOOK DEAL, ALL MY JOBS...
I MET KRIS THROUGH MYSPACE.
AND IT'S INSTANT GRATIFICATION... NOT LIKE THE DRUDGERY WE'RE DOING HERE...
AN EMAIL IS LIKE A PACKAGE TO BE OPENED...
CAN I CHECK TO SEE IF MY MILLIONAIRE HAS WRITTEN YET?
Then we watched a documentary about what happens when you give a homeless man a hundred thousand dollars.
OH MY GOD...
OH, MY GOD...
SEE, THIS IS WHERE HE SHOULD LOOK AT THE CAMERA AND SAY, 'ARE YOU KIDDING ME?'
The first thing he did was get all sorts of expensive accessories for his bicycle. What followed was a painful account of the minutiae of his squandering.
STOP! I CAN'T WATCH ANYMORE!
LET'S TURN IT OFF WHILE HE STILL HAS THIRTY THOUSAND DOLLARS!
I left halfway through, but it was too late; I was already possessed by the spirit of this man.
GON' GET MY BIKE TRICKED OUT.

March 23rd

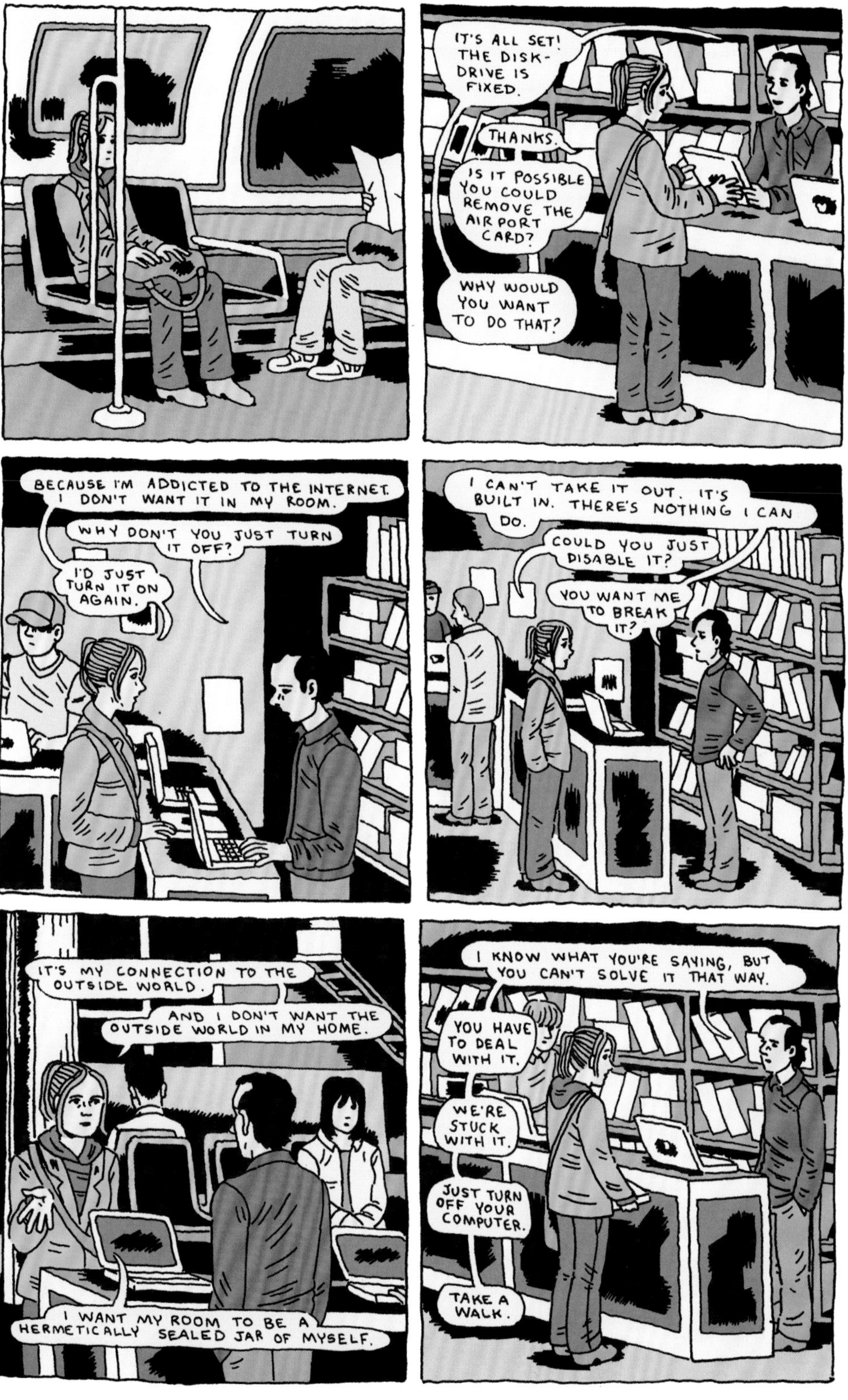

IT'S ALL SET! THE DISK-DRIVE IS FIXED.
THANKS.
IS IT POSSIBLE YOU COULD REMOVE THE AIR PORT CARD?
WHY WOULD YOU WANT TO DO THAT?
BECAUSE I'M ADDICTED TO THE INTERNET. I DON'T WANT IT IN MY ROOM.
WHY DON'T YOU JUST TURN IT OFF?
I'D JUST TURN IT ON AGAIN.
I CAN'T TAKE IT OUT. IT'S BUILT IN. THERE'S NOTHING I CAN DO.
COULD YOU JUST DISABLE IT?
YOU WANT ME TO BREAK IT?
IT'S MY CONNECTION TO THE OUTSIDE WORLD.
AND I DON'T WANT THE OUTSIDE WORLD IN MY HOME.
I WANT MY ROOM TO BE A HERMETICALLY SEALED JAR OF MYSELF.
I KNOW WHAT YOU'RE SAYING, BUT YOU CAN'T SOLVE IT THAT WAY.
YOU HAVE TO DEAL WITH IT.
WE'RE STUCK WITH IT.
JUST TURN OFF YOUR COMPUTER.
TAKE A WALK.

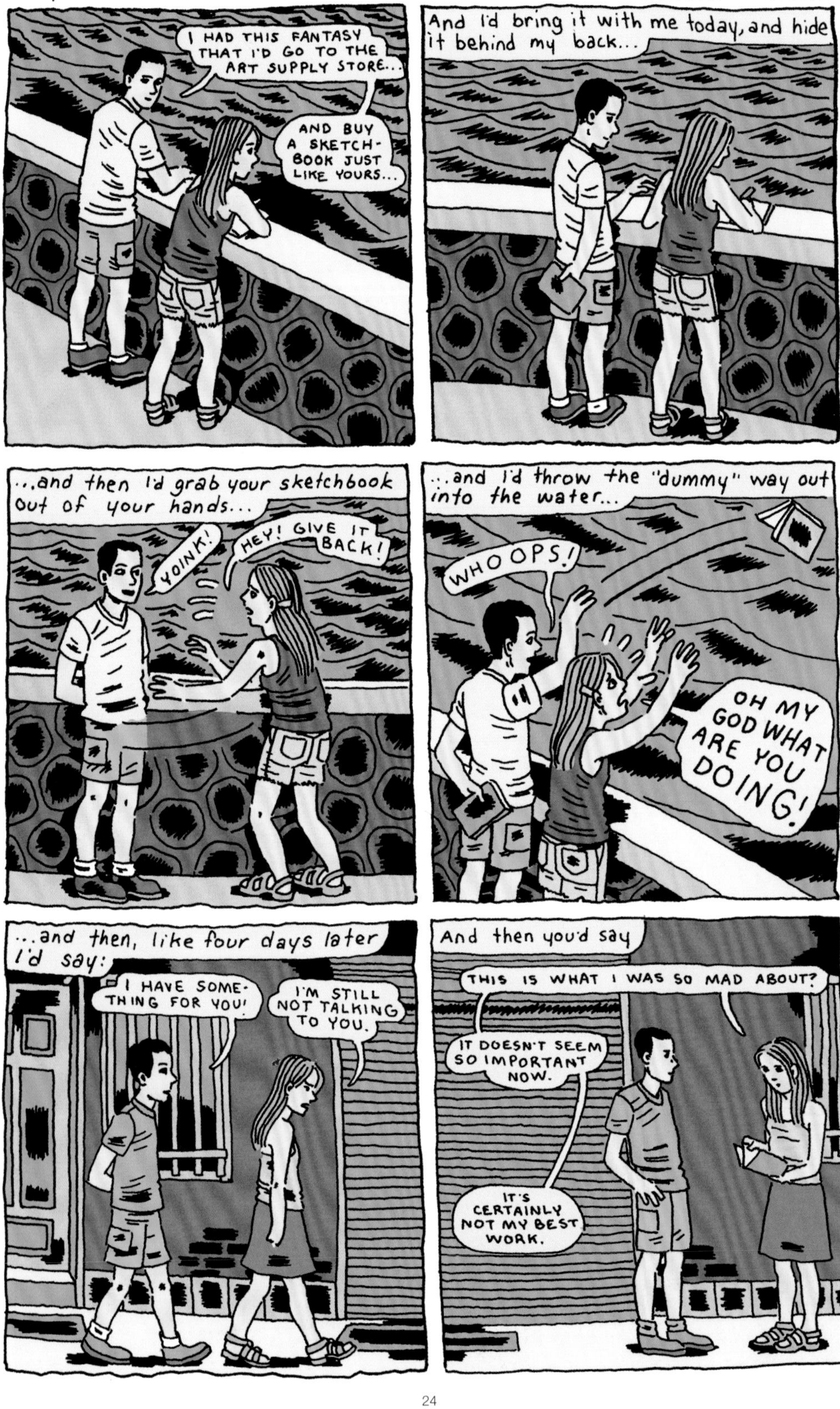
I HAD THIS FANTASY THAT I'D GO TO THE ART SUPPLY STORE...
AND BUY A SKETCH-BOOK JUST LIKE YOURS...
And I'd bring it with me today, and hide it behind my back...
...and then I'd grab your sketchbook out of your hands...
YOINK!
HEY! GIVE IT BACK!
...and I'd throw the "dummy" way out into the water...
WHOOPS!
OH MY GOD WHAT ARE YOU DOING!
...and then, like four days later I'd say:
I HAVE SOME-THING FOR YOU!
I'M STILL NOT TALKING TO YOU.
And then you'd say
THIS IS WHAT I WAS SO MAD ABOUT?
IT DOESN'T SEEM SO IMPORTANT NOW.
IT'S CERTAINLY NOT MY BEST WORK.

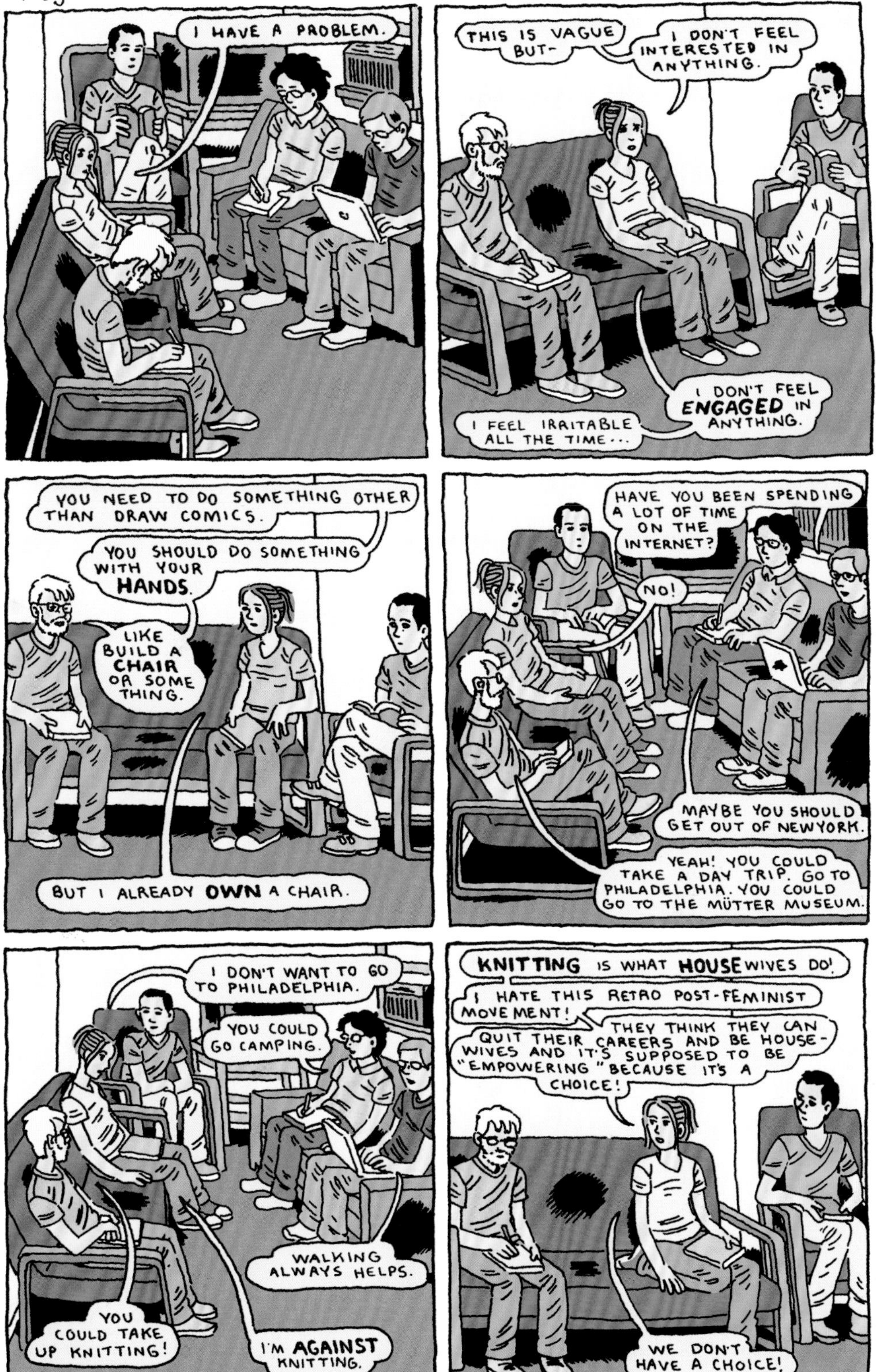
I HAVE A PROBLEM.
THIS IS VAGUE BUT-
I DON'T FEEL INTERESTED IN ANYTHING.
I DON'T FEEL ENGAGED IN ANYTHING.
I FEEL IRRITABLE ALL THE TIME...
YOU NEED TO DO SOMETHING OTHER THAN DRAW COMICS.
YOU SHOULD DO SOMETHING WITH YOUR HANDS.
LIKE BUILD A CHAIR OR SOME THING.
BUT I ALREADY OWN A CHAIR.
HAVE YOU BEEN SPENDING A LOT OF TIME ON THE INTERNET?
NO!
MAYBE YOU SHOULD GET OUT OF NEW YORK.
YEAH! YOU COULD TAKE A DAY TRIP. GO TO PHILADELPHIA. YOU COULD GO TO THE MÜTTER MUSEUM.
I DON'T WANT TO GO TO PHILADELPHIA.
YOU COULD GO CAMPING.
WALKING ALWAYS HELPS.
YOU COULD TAKE UP KNITTING!
I'M AGAINST KNITTING.
KNITTING IS WHAT HOUSEWIVES DO!
I HATE THIS RETRO POST-FEMINIST MOVEMENT!
THEY THINK THEY CAN QUIT THEIR CAREERS AND BE HOUSE-WIVES AND IT'S SUPPOSED TO BE "EMPOWERING" BECAUSE IT'S A CHOICE!
WE DON'T HAVE A CHOICE!

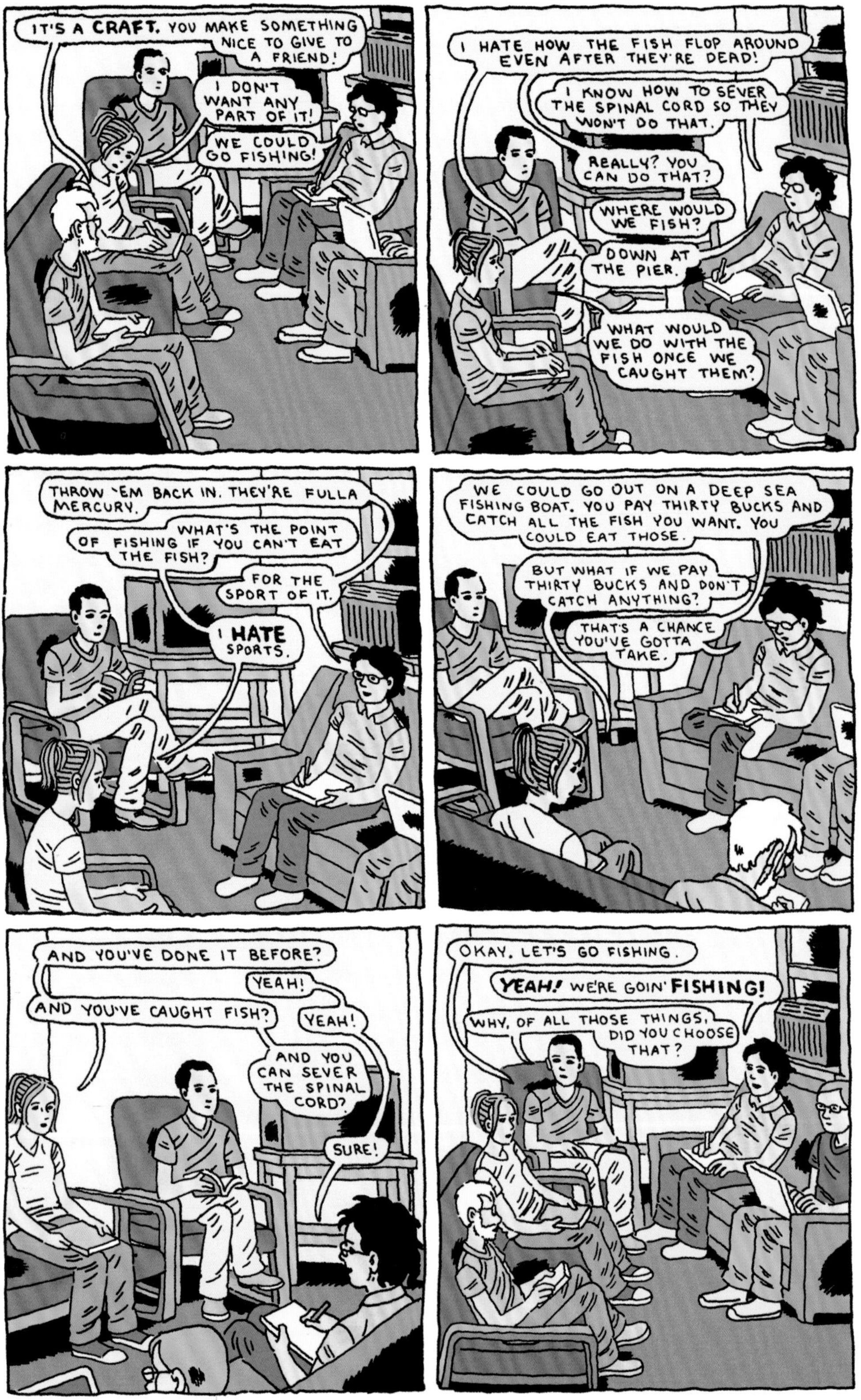
IT'S A CRAFT. YOU MAKE SOMETHING NICE TO GIVE TO A FRIEND!
I DON'T WANT ANY PART OF IT!
WE COULD GO FISHING!
I HATE HOW THE FISH FLOP AROUND EVEN AFTER THEY'RE DEAD!
I KNOW HOW TO SEVER THE SPINAL CORD SO THEY WON'T DO THAT.
REALLY? YOU CAN DO THAT?
WHERE WOULD WE FISH?
DOWN AT THE PIER.
WHAT WOULD WE DO WITH THE FISH ONCE WE CAUGHT THEM?
THROW 'EM BACK IN. THEY'RE FULLA MERCURY.
WHAT'S THE POINT OF FISHING IF YOU CAN'T EAT THE FISH?
FOR THE SPORT OF IT.
I HATE SPORTS.
WE COULD GO OUT ON A DEEP SEA FISHING BOAT. YOU PAY THIRTY BUCKS AND CATCH ALL THE FISH YOU WANT. YOU COULD EAT THOSE.
BUT WHAT IF WE PAY THIRTY BUCKS AND DON'T CATCH ANYTHING?
THAT'S A CHANCE YOU'VE GOTTA TAKE.
AND YOU'VE DONE IT BEFORE?
YEAH!
AND YOU'VE CAUGHT FISH?
YEAH!
AND YOU CAN SEVER THE SPINAL CORD?
SURE!
OKAY. LET'S GO FISHING.
YEAH! WE'RE GOIN' FISHING!
WHY, OF ALL THOSE THINGS, DID YOU CHOOSE THAT?

August 11th

Goin' Fishin'

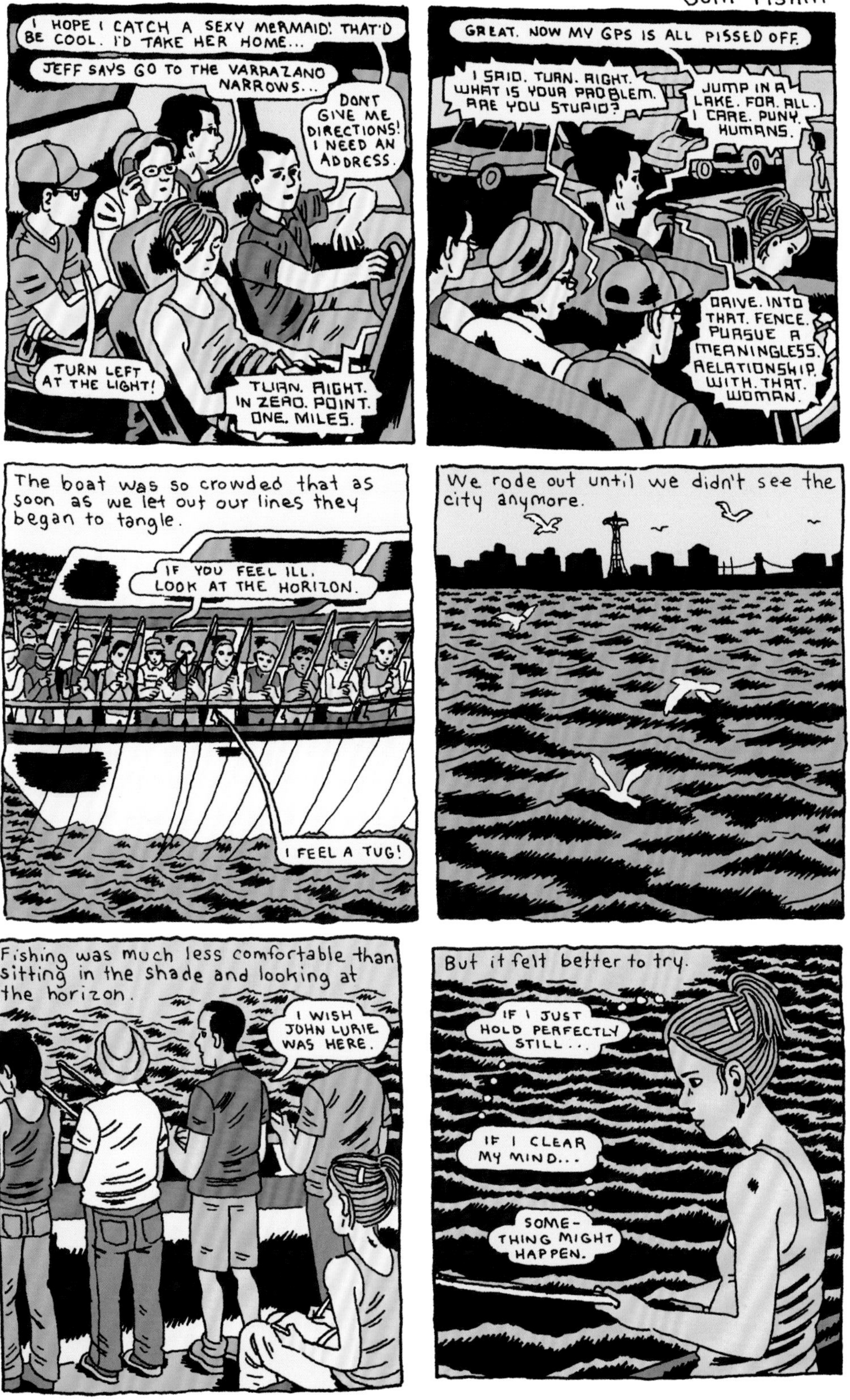
I HOPE I CATCH A SEXY MERMAID! THAT'D BE COOL. I'D TAKE HER HOME...
JEFF SAYS GO TO THE VARRAZANO NARROWS...
DONT GIVE ME DIRECTIONS! I NEED AN ADDRESS.
TURN LEFT AT THE LIGHT!
TURN. RIGHT. IN ZERO. POINT. ONE. MILES.
GREAT. NOW MY GPS IS ALL PISSED OFF.
I SAID. TURN. RIGHT. WHAT IS YOUR PROBLEM. ARE YOU STUPID?
JUMP IN A LAKE. FOR. ALL. I CARE. PUNY. HUMANS.
DRIVE. INTO THAT. FENCE. PURSUE A MEANINGLESS. RELATIONSHIP. WITH. THAT. WOMAN.
The boat was so crowded that as soon as we let out our lines they began to tangle.
IF YOU FEEL ILL, LOOK AT THE HORIZON.
I FEEL A TUG!
We rode out until we didn't see the city anymore.
Fishing was much less comfortable than sitting in the shade and looking at the horizon.
I WISH JOHN LURIE WAS HERE.
But it felt better to try.
IF I JUST HOLD PERFECTLY STILL...
IF I CLEAR MY MIND...
SOME-THING MIGHT HAPPEN.

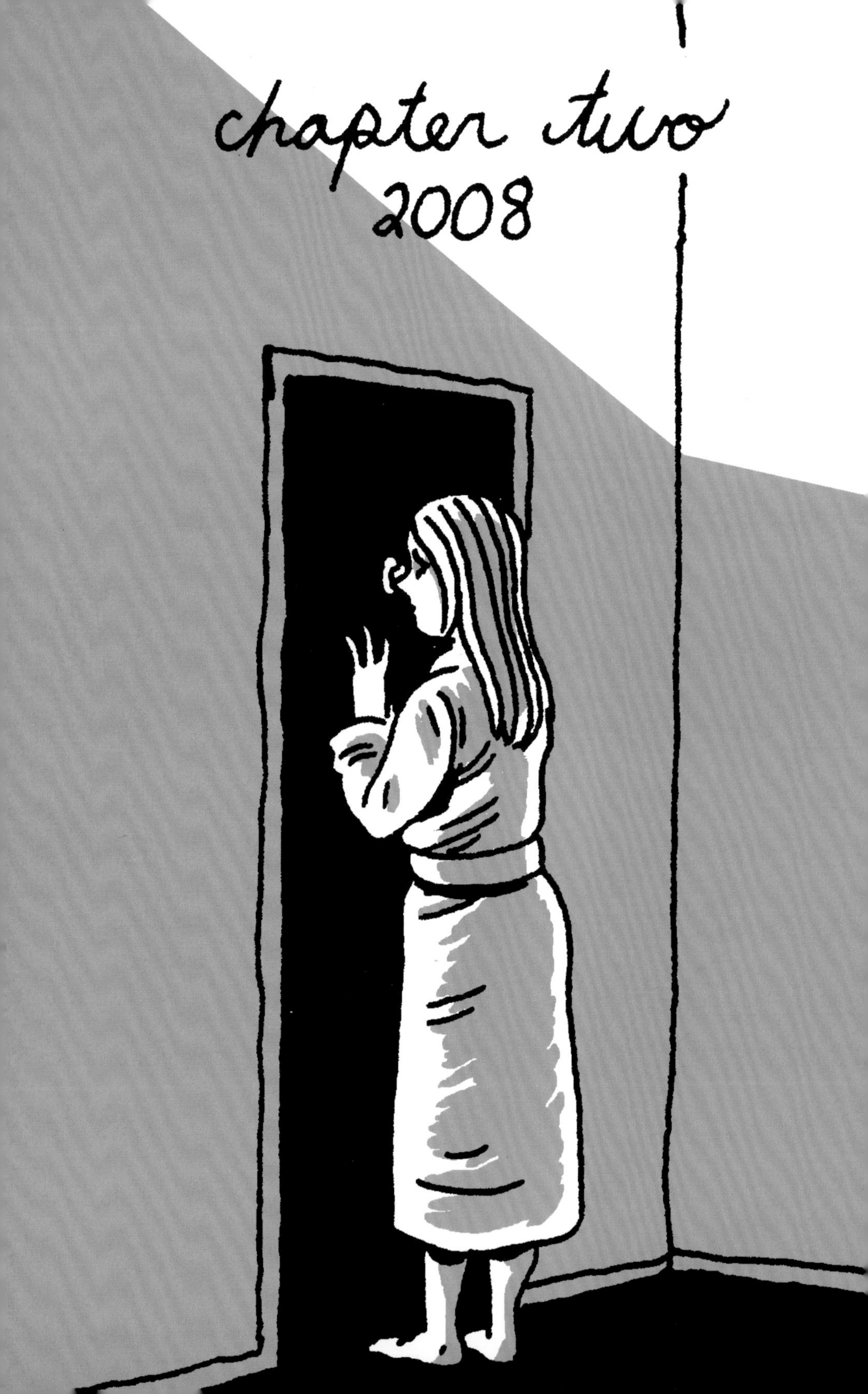
chapter two
2008

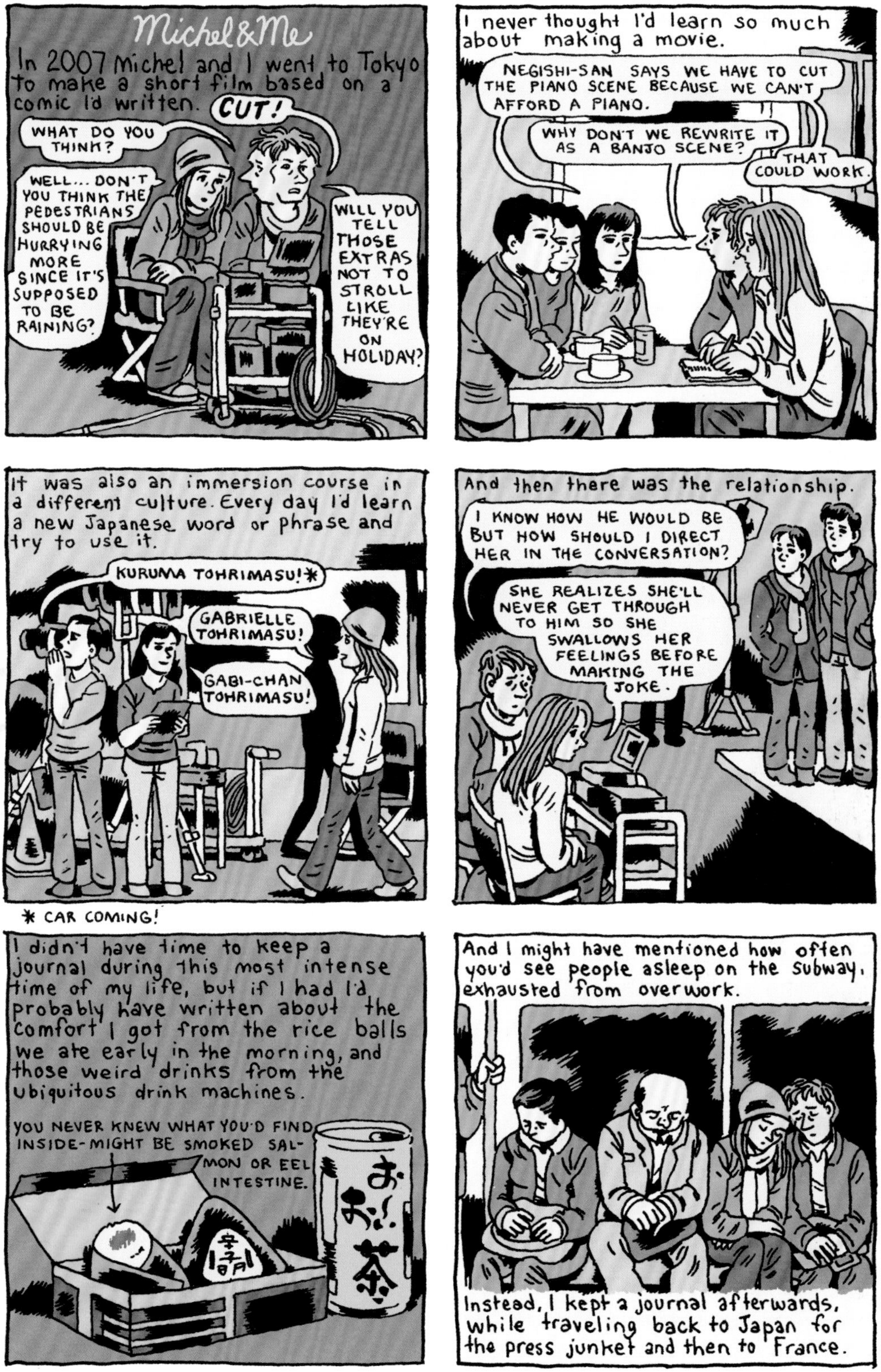
Michel & Me
In 2007 michel and I went to Tokyo to make a short film based on a comic I'd written.
CUT!
WHAT DO YOU THINK?
WELL... DON'T YOU THINK THE PEDESTRIANS SHOULD BE HURRYING MORE SINCE IT'S SUPPOSED TO BE RAINING?
WILL YOU TELL THOSE EXTRAS NOT TO STROLL LIKE THEY'RE ON HOLIDAY?
I never thought I'd learn so much about making a movie.
NEGISHI-SAN SAYS WE HAVE TO CUT THE PIANO SCENE BECAUSE WE CAN'T AFFORD A PIANO.
WHY DON'T WE REWRITE IT AS A BANJO SCENE?
THAT COULD WORK.
It was also an immersion course in a different culture. Every day I'd learn a new Japanese word or phrase and try to use it.
KURUMA TOHRIMASU!*
GABRIELLE TOHRIMASU!
GABI-CHAN TOHRIMASU!
* CAR COMING!
And then there was the relationship.
I KNOW HOW HE WOULD BE BUT HOW SHOULD I DIRECT HER IN THE CONVERSATION?
SHE REALIZES SHE'LL NEVER GET THROUGH TO HIM SO SHE SWALLOWS HER FEELINGS BEFORE MAKING THE JOKE.
I didn't have time to keep a journal during this most intense time of my life, but if I had I'd probably have written about the comfort I got from the rice balls we ate early in the morning, and those weird drinks from the ubiquitous drink machines.
YOU NEVER KNEW WHAT YOU'D FIND INSIDE-MIGHT BE SMOKED SALMON OR EEL INTESTINE.
And I might have mentioned how often you'd see people asleep on the subway, exhausted from overwork.
Instead, I kept a journal afterwards, while traveling back to Japan for the press junket and then to France.

July 29th, 2007

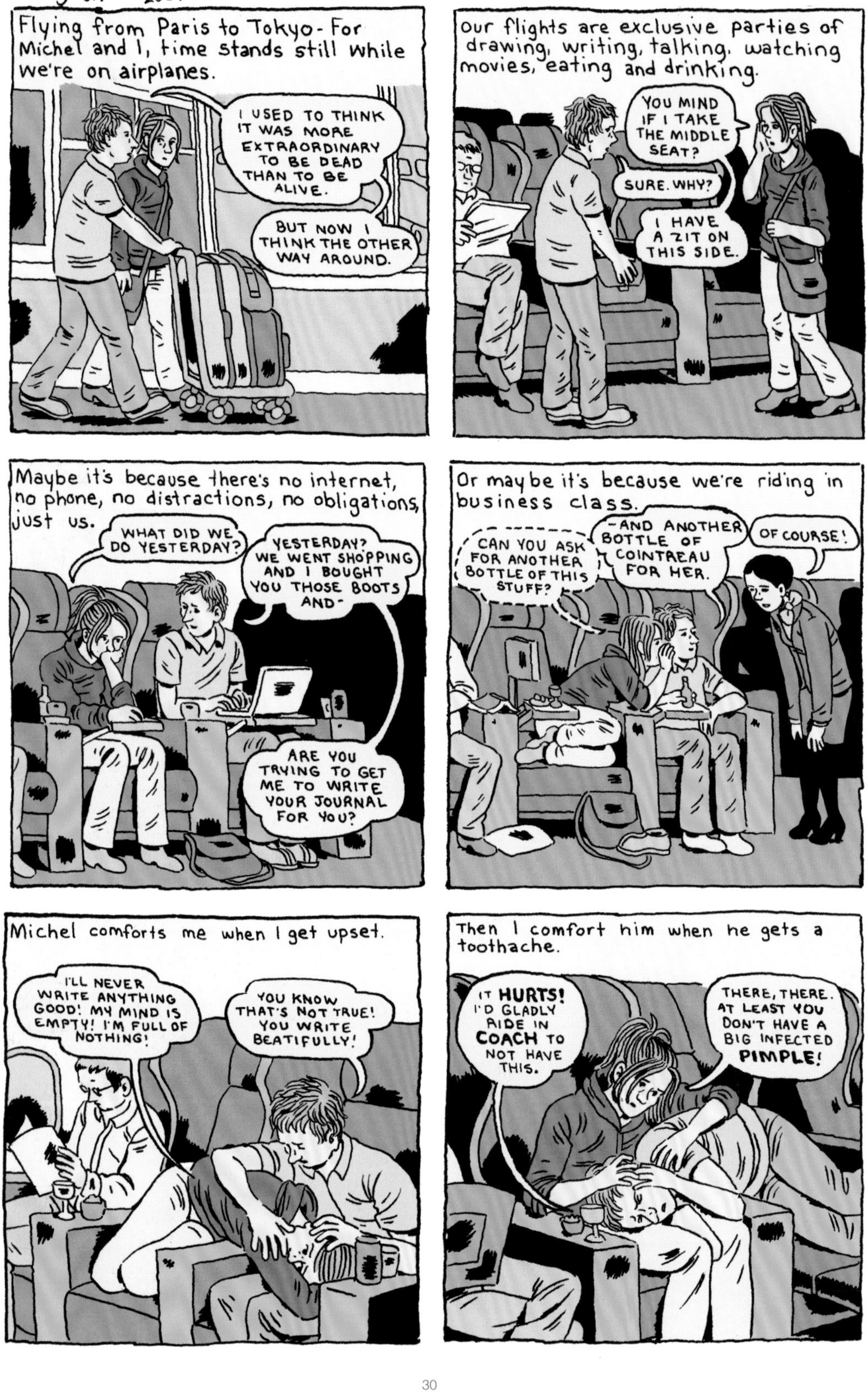
Flying from Paris to Tokyo- For Michel and I, time stands still while we're on airplanes.
I USED TO THINK IT WAS MORE EXTRAORDINARY TO BE DEAD THAN TO BE ALIVE.
BUT NOW I THINK THE OTHER WAY AROUND.
our flights are exclusive parties of drawing, writing, talking, watching movies, eating and drinking.
YOU MIND IF I TAKE THE MIDDLE SEAT?
SURE. WHY?
I HAVE A ZIT ON THIS SIDE.
Maybe it's because there's no internet, no phone, no distractions, no obligations, just us.
WHAT DID WE DO YESTERDAY?
YESTERDAY? WE WENT SHOPPING AND I BOUGHT YOU THOSE BOOTS AND-
ARE YOU TRYING TO GET ME TO WRITE YOUR JOURNAL FOR YOU?
Or maybe it's because we're riding in business class.
CAN YOU ASK FOR ANOTHER BOTTLE OF THIS STUFF?
-AND ANOTHER BOTTLE OF COINTREAU FOR HER.
OF COURSE!
Michel comforts me when I get upset.
I'LL NEVER WRITE ANYTHING GOOD! MY MIND IS EMPTY! I'M FULL OF NOTHING!
YOU KNOW THAT'S NOT TRUE! YOU WRITE BEATIFULLY!
Then I comfort him when he gets a toothache.
IT HURTS! I'D GLADLY RIDE IN COACH TO NOT HAVE THIS.
THERE, THERE. AT LEAST YOU DON'T HAVE A BIG INFECTED PIMPLE!

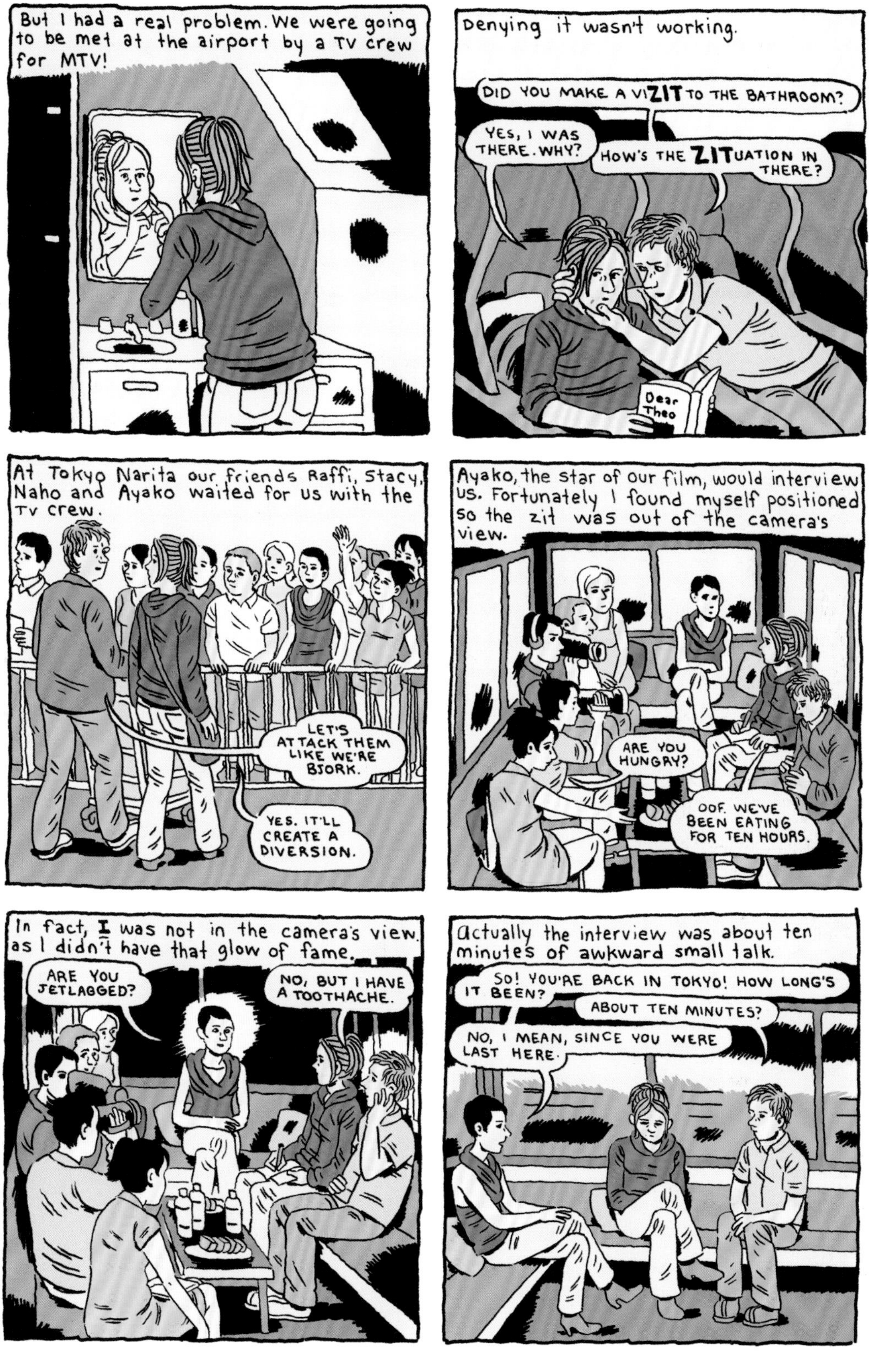
But I had a real problem. We were going to be met at the airport by a TV crew for MTV!
Denying it wasn't working.
DID YOU MAKE A VIZIT TO THE BATHROOM?
YES, I WAS THERE. WHY?
HOW'S THE ZITUATION IN THERE?
Dear Theo
At Tokyo Narita our friends Raffi, Stacy, Naho and Ayako waited for us with the TV crew.
LET'S ATTACK THEM LIKE WE'RE BJORK.
YES. IT'LL CREATE A DIVERSION.
Ayako, the star of our film, would interview us. Fortunately I found myself positioned so the zit was out of the camera's view.
ARE YOU HUNGRY?
OOF. WE'VE BEEN EATING FOR TEN HOURS.
In fact, I was not in the camera's view, as I didn't have that glow of fame.
ARE YOU JETLAGGED?
NO, BUT I HAVE A TOOTHACHE.
Actually the interview was about ten minutes of awkward small talk.
SO! YOU'RE BACK IN TOKYO! HOW LONG'S IT BEEN?
ABOUT TEN MINUTES?
NO, I MEAN, SINCE YOU WERE LAST HERE.

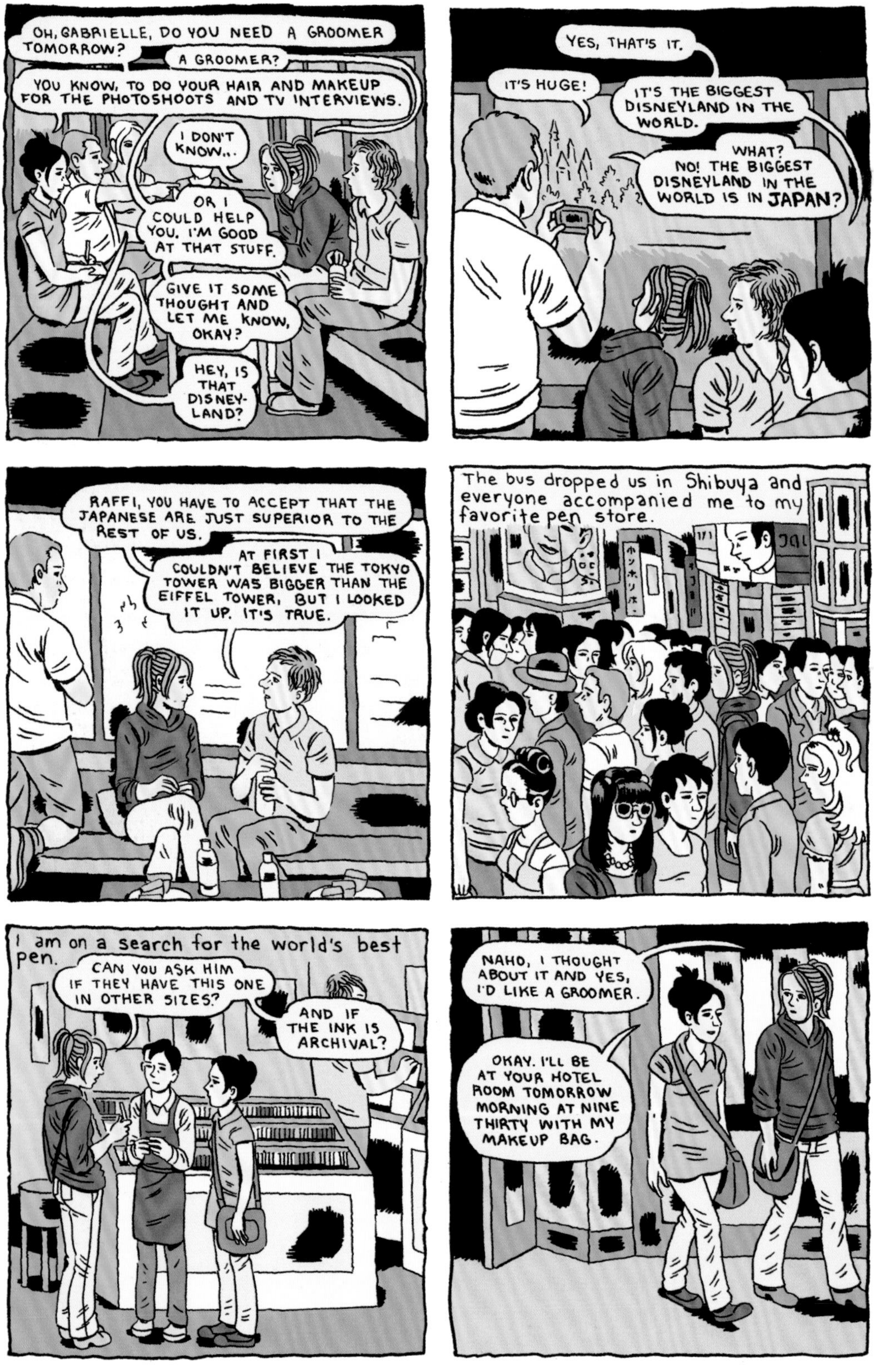
OH, GABRIELLE, DO YOU NEED A GROOMER TOMORROW?
A GROOMER?
YOU KNOW, TO DO YOUR HAIR AND MAKEUP FOR THE PHOTOSHOOTS AND TV INTERVIEWS.
I DON'T KNOW...
OR I COULD HELP YOU. I'M GOOD AT THAT STUFF.
GIVE IT SOME THOUGHT AND LET ME KNOW, OKAY?
HEY, IS THAT DISNEY-LAND?
YES, THAT'S IT.
IT'S HUGE!
IT'S THE BIGGEST DISNEYLAND IN THE WORLD.
WHAT? NO! THE BIGGEST DISNEYLAND IN THE WORLD IS IN JAPAN?
RAFFI, YOU HAVE TO ACCEPT THAT THE JAPANESE ARE JUST SUPERIOR TO THE REST OF US.
AT FIRST I COULDN'T BELIEVE THE TOKYO TOWER WAS BIGGER THAN THE EIFFEL TOWER, BUT I LOOKED IT UP. IT'S TRUE.
The bus dropped us in Shibuya and everyone accompanied me to my favorite pen store.
I am on a search for the world's best pen.
CAN YOU ASK HIM IF THEY HAVE THIS ONE IN OTHER SIZES?
AND IF THE INK IS ARCHIVAL?
NAHO, I THOUGHT ABOUT IT AND YES, I'D LIKE A GROOMER.
OKAY. I'LL BE AT YOUR HOTEL ROOM TOMORROW MORNING AT NINE THIRTY WITH MY MAKEUP BAG.

July 30th

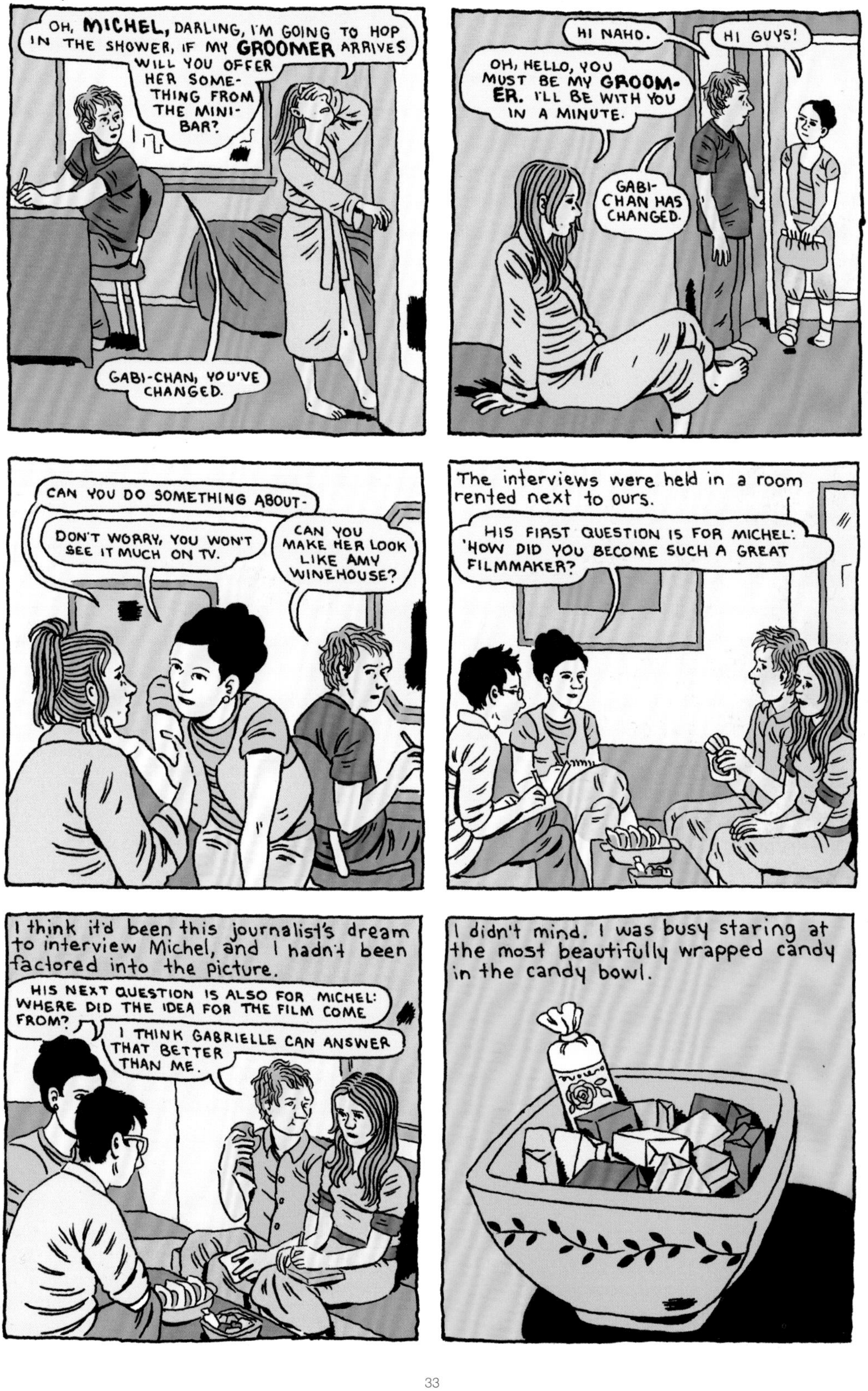
OH, MICHEL, DARLING, I'M GOING TO HOP IN THE SHOWER, IF MY GROOMER ARRIVES WILL YOU OFFER HER SOMETHING FROM THE MINI-BAR?
GABI-CHAN, YOU'VE CHANGED.
HI NAHO.
HI GUYS!
OH, HELLO, YOU MUST BE MY GROOMER. I'LL BE WITH YOU IN A MINUTE.
GABI-CHAN HAS CHANGED.
CAN YOU DO SOMETHING ABOUT-
DON'T WORRY, YOU WON'T SEE IT MUCH ON TV.
CAN YOU MAKE HER LOOK LIKE AMY WINEHOUSE?
The interviews were held in a room rented next to ours.
HIS FIRST QUESTION IS FOR MICHEL: 'HOW DID YOU BECOME SUCH A GREAT FILMMAKER?
I think it'd been this journalist's dream to interview Michel, and I hadn't been factored into the picture.
HIS NEXT QUESTION IS ALSO FOR MICHEL: WHERE DID THE IDEA FOR THE FILM COME FROM?
I THINK GABRIELLE CAN ANSWER THAT BETTER THAN ME.
I didn't mind. I was busy staring at the most beautifully wrapped candy in the candy bowl.

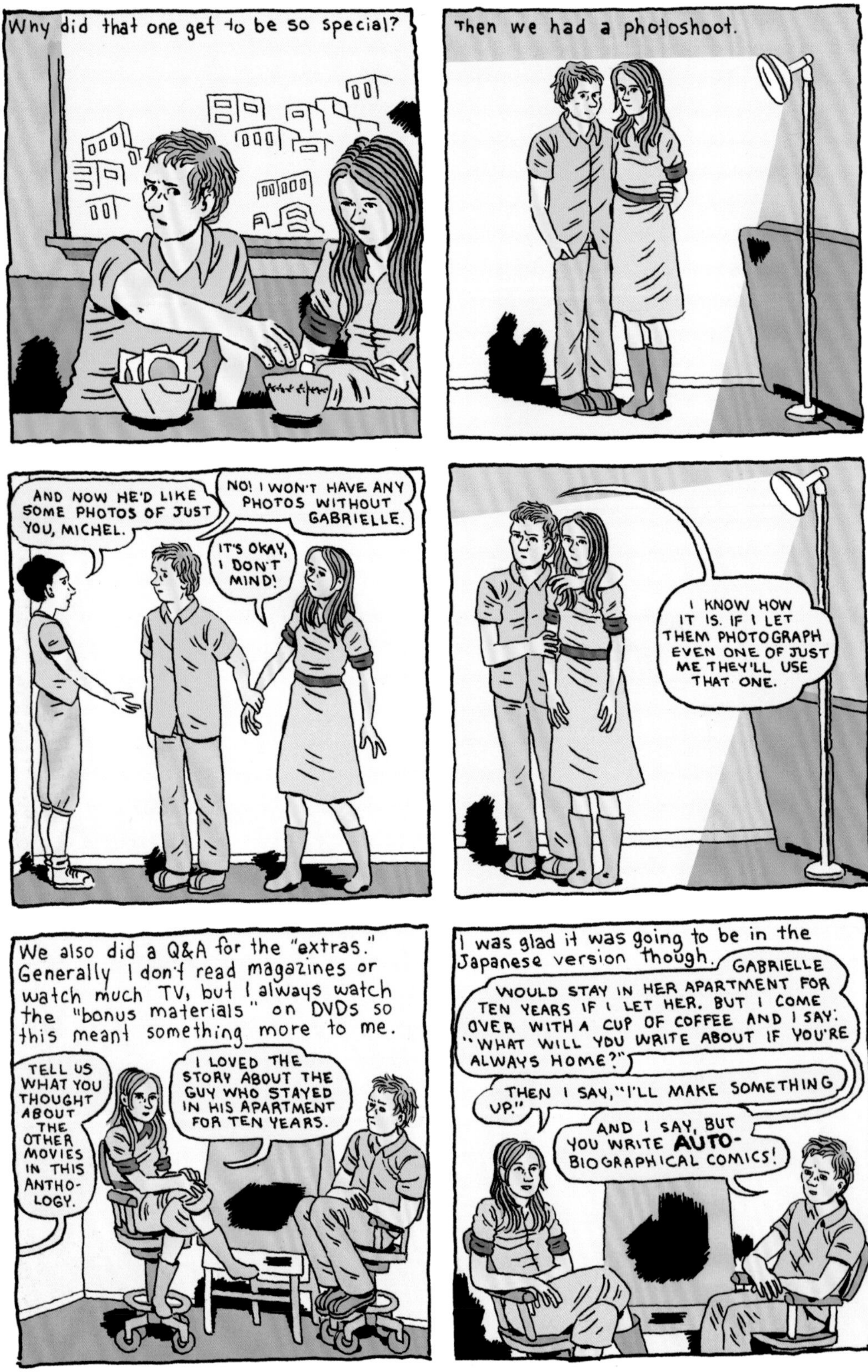
Why did that one get to be so special?
Then we had a photoshoot.
AND NOW HE'D LIKE SOME PHOTOS OF JUST YOU, MICHEL.
NO! I WON'T HAVE ANY PHOTOS WITHOUT GABRIELLE.
IT'S OKAY, I DON'T MIND!
I KNOW HOW IT IS. IF I LET THEM PHOTOGRAPH EVEN ONE OF JUST ME THEY'LL USE THAT ONE.
We also did a Q&A for the "extras." Generally I don't read magazines or watch much TV, but I always watch the "bonus materials" on DVDs so this meant something more to me.
TELL US WHAT YOU THOUGHT ABOUT THE OTHER MOVIES IN THIS ANTHOLOGY.
I LOVED THE STORY ABOUT THE GUY WHO STAYED IN HIS APARTMENT FOR TEN YEARS.
I was glad it was going to be in the Japanese version though.
GABRIELLE WOULD STAY IN HER APARTMENT FOR TEN YEARS IF I LET HER. BUT I COME OVER WITH A CUP OF COFFEE AND I SAY: "WHAT WILL YOU WRITE ABOUT IF YOU'RE ALWAYS HOME?"
THEN I SAY, "I'LL MAKE SOMETHING UP."
AND I SAY, BUT YOU WRITE AUTO-BIOGRAPHICAL COMICS!

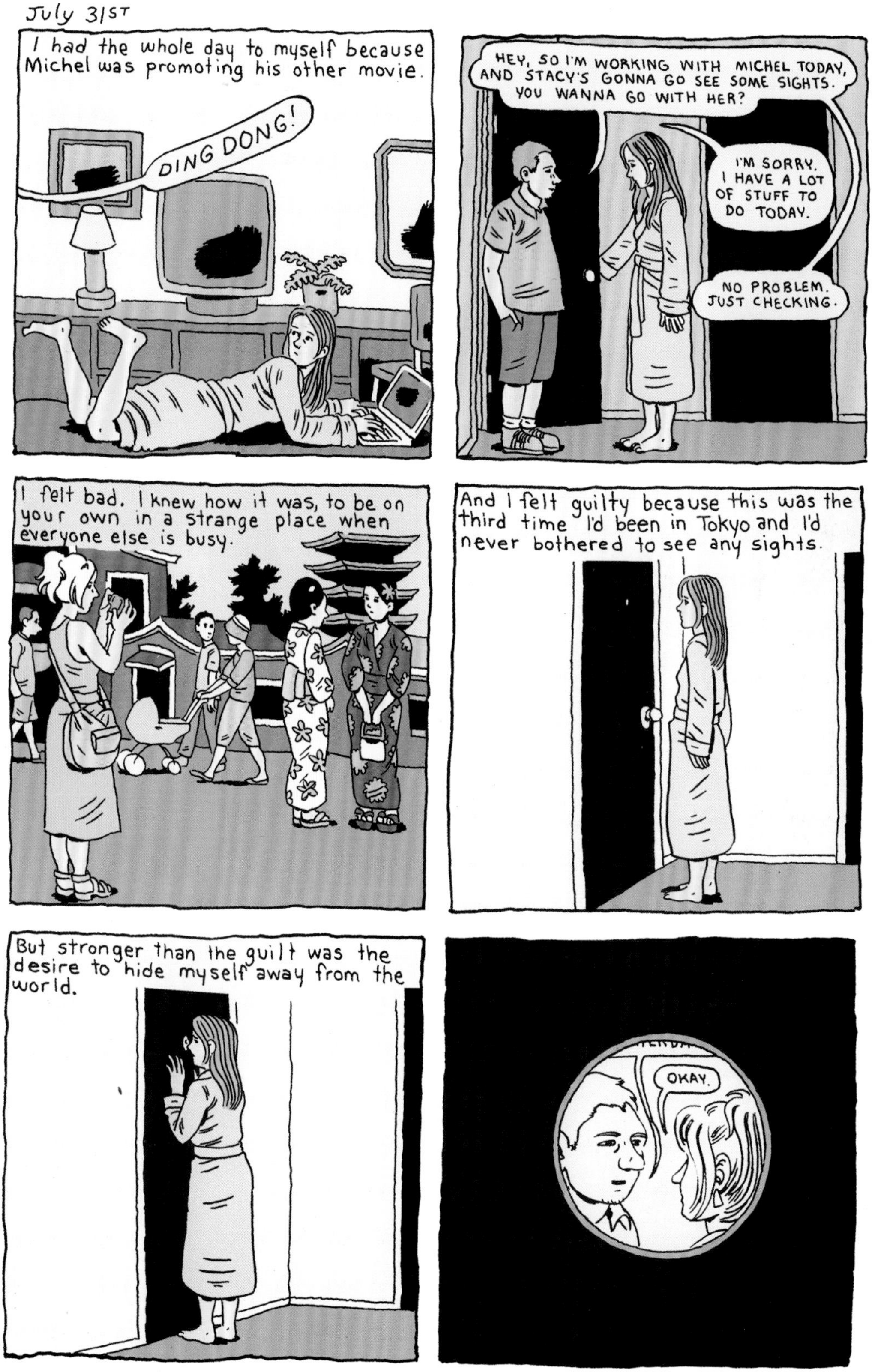
July 31st
I had the whole day to myself because Michel was promoting his other movie.
DING DONG!
HEY, SO I'M WORKING WITH MICHEL TODAY, AND STACY'S GONNA GO SEE SOME SIGHTS. YOU WANNA GO WITH HER?
I'M SORRY. I HAVE A LOT OF STUFF TO DO TODAY.
NO PROBLEM. JUST CHECKING.
I felt bad. I knew how it was, to be on your own in a strange place when everyone else is busy.
And I felt guilty because this was the third time I'd been in Tokyo and I'd never bothered to see any sights.
But stronger than the guilt was the desire to hide myself away from the world.
OKAY.

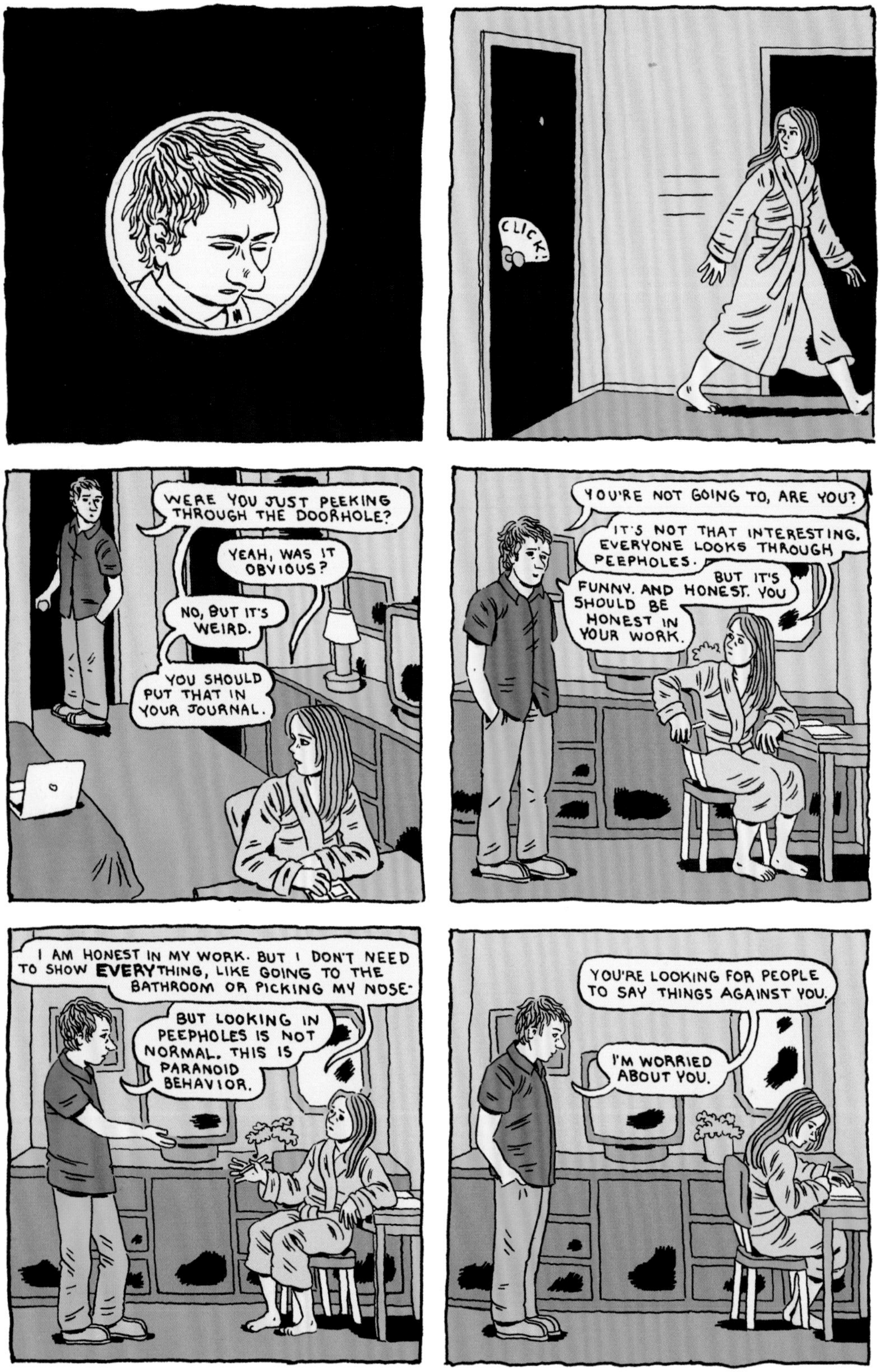
CLICK!
WERE YOU JUST PEEKING THROUGH THE DOORHOLE?
YEAH, WAS IT OBVIOUS?
NO, BUT IT'S WEIRD.
YOU SHOULD PUT THAT IN YOUR JOURNAL.
YOU'RE NOT GOING TO, ARE YOU?
IT'S NOT THAT INTERESTING. EVERYONE LOOKS THROUGH PEEPHOLES.
BUT IT'S FUNNY. AND HONEST. YOU SHOULD BE HONEST IN YOUR WORK.
I AM HONEST IN MY WORK. BUT I DON'T NEED TO SHOW EVERYTHING, LIKE GOING TO THE BATHROOM OR PICKING MY NOSE-
BUT LOOKING IN PEEPHOLES IS NOT NORMAL. THIS IS PARANOID BEHAVIOR.
YOU'RE LOOKING FOR PEOPLE TO SAY THINGS AGAINST YOU.
I'M WORRIED ABOUT YOU.

August 1st

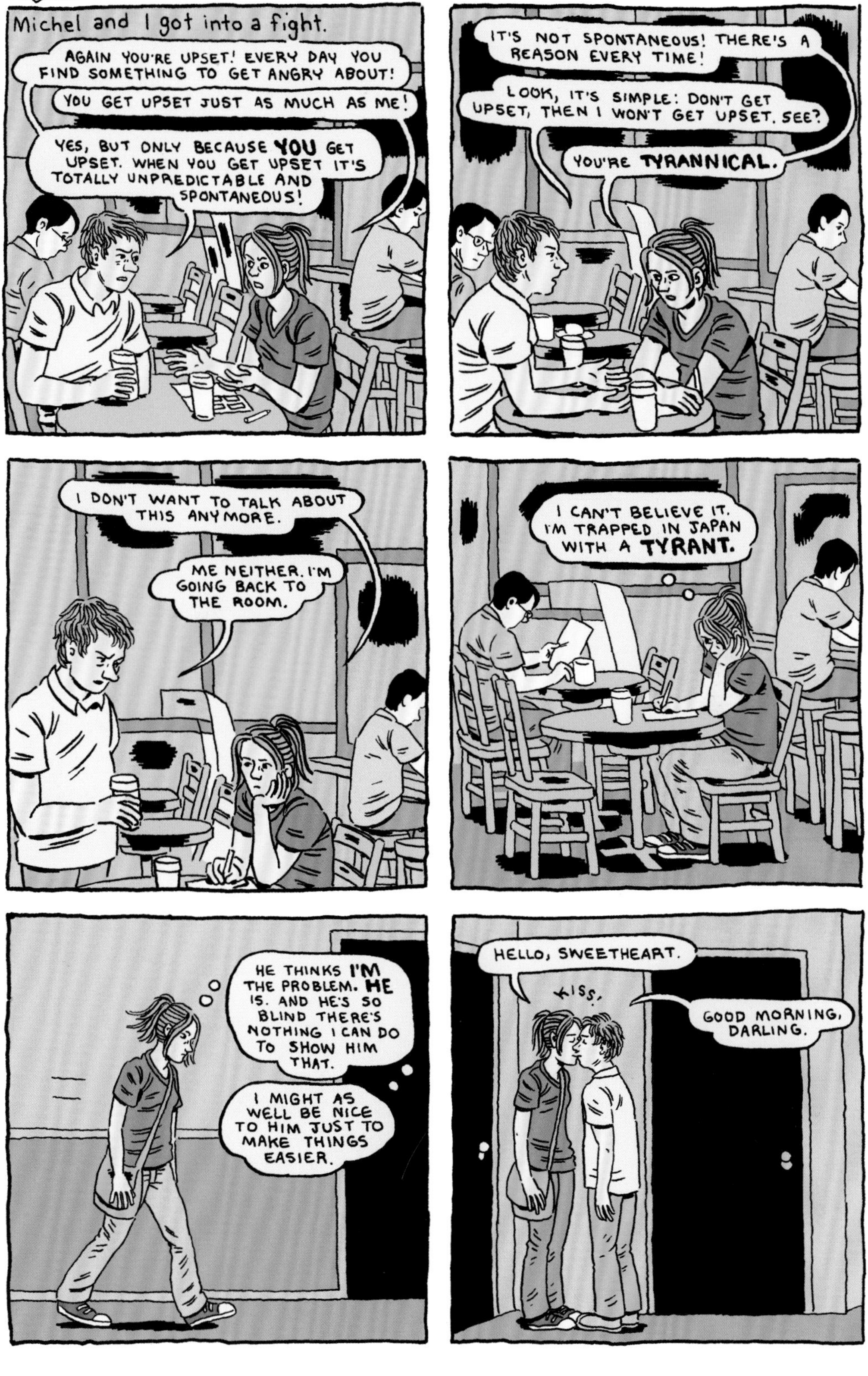
Michel and I got into a fight.
AGAIN YOU'RE UPSET! EVERY DAY YOU FIND SOMETHING TO GET ANGRY ABOUT!
YOU GET UPSET JUST AS MUCH AS ME!
YES, BUT ONLY BECAUSE YOU GET UPSET. WHEN YOU GET UPSET IT'S TOTALLY UNPREDICTABLE AND SPONTANEOUS!
IT'S NOT SPONTANEOUS! THERE'S A REASON EVERY TIME!
LOOK, IT'S SIMPLE: DON'T GET UPSET, THEN I WON'T GET UPSET. SEE?
YOU'RE TYRANNICAL.
I DON'T WANT TO TALK ABOUT THIS ANYMORE.
ME NEITHER. I'M GOING BACK TO THE ROOM.
I CAN'T BELIEVE IT. I'M TRAPPED IN JAPAN WITH A TYRANT.
HE THINKS I'M THE PROBLEM. HE IS. AND HE'S SO BLIND THERE'S NOTHING I CAN DO TO SHOW HIM THAT.
I MIGHT AS WELL BE NICE TO HIM JUST TO MAKE THINGS EASIER.
HELLO, SWEETHEART.
KISS!
GOOD MORNING, DARLING.

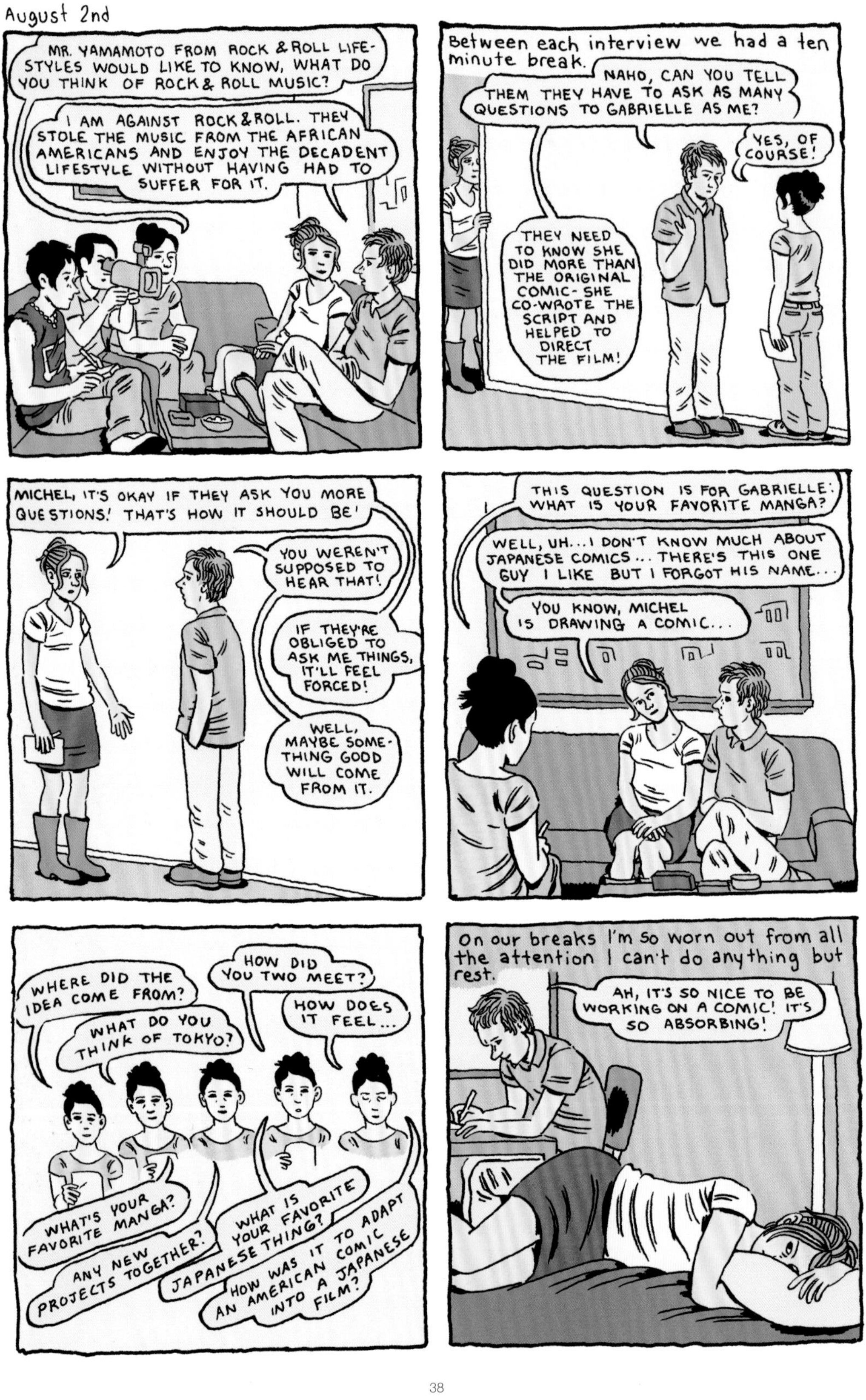
August 2nd
MR. YAMAMOTO FROM ROCK & ROLL LIFESTYLES WOULD LIKE TO KNOW, WHAT DO YOU THINK OF ROCK & ROLL MUSIC?
I AM AGAINST ROCK & ROLL. THEY STOLE THE MUSIC FROM THE AFRICAN AMERICANS AND ENJOY THE DECADENT LIFESTYLE WITHOUT HAVING HAD TO SUFFER FOR IT.
Between each interview we had a ten minute break.
NAHO, CAN YOU TELL THEM THEY HAVE TO ASK AS MANY QUESTIONS TO GABRIELLE AS ME?
YES, OF COURSE!
THEY NEED TO KNOW SHE DID MORE THAN THE ORIGINAL COMIC- SHE CO-WROTE THE SCRIPT AND HELPED TO DIRECT THE FILM!
MICHEL, IT'S OKAY IF THEY ASK YOU MORE QUESTIONS! THAT'S HOW IT SHOULD BE!
YOU WEREN'T SUPPOSED TO HEAR THAT!
IF THEY'RE OBLIGED TO ASK ME THINGS, IT'LL FEEL FORCED!
WELL, MAYBE SOMETHING GOOD WILL COME FROM IT.
THIS QUESTION IS FOR GABRIELLE: WHAT IS YOUR FAVORITE MANGA?
WELL, UH... I DON'T KNOW MUCH ABOUT JAPANESE COMICS... THERE'S THIS ONE GUY I LIKE BUT I FORGOT HIS NAME...
YOU KNOW, MICHEL IS DRAWING A COMIC...
WHERE DID THE IDEA COME FROM?
HOW DID YOU TWO MEET?
WHAT DO YOU THINK OF TOKYO?
HOW DOES IT FEEL...
WHAT'S YOUR FAVORITE MANGA?
ANY NEW PROJECTS TOGETHER?
WHAT IS YOUR FAVORITE JAPANESE THING?
HOW WAS IT TO ADAPT AN AMERICAN COMIC INTO A JAPANESE FILM?
On our breaks I'm so worn out from all the attention I can't do anything but rest.
AH, IT'S SO NICE TO BE WORKING ON A COMIC! IT'S SO ABSORBING!

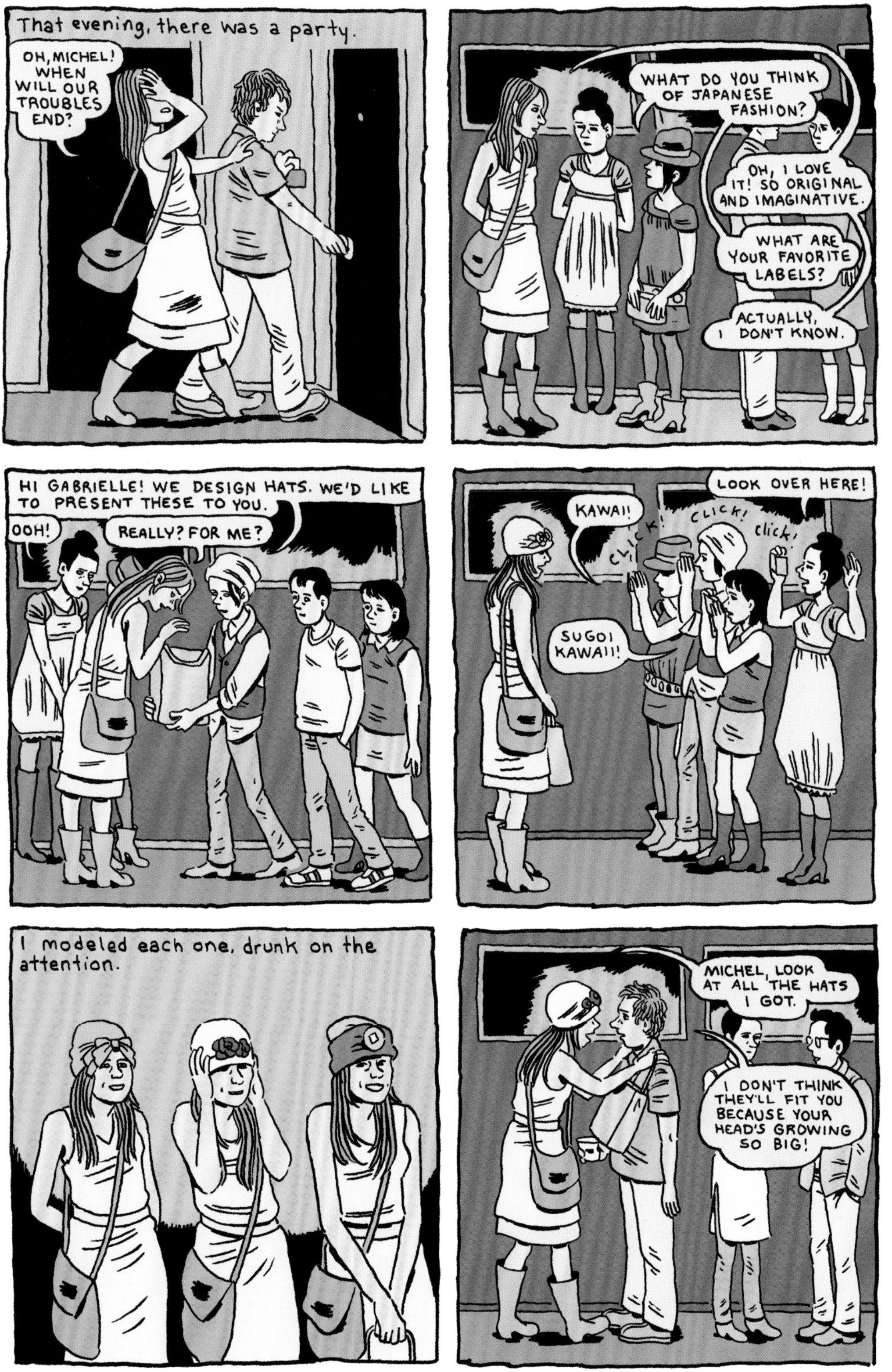
That evening, there was a party.
OH, MICHEL! WHEN WILL OUR TROUBLES END?
WHAT DO YOU THINK OF JAPANESE FASHION?
OH, I LOVE IT! SO ORIGINAL AND IMAGINATIVE.
WHAT ARE YOUR FAVORITE LABELS?
ACTUALLY, I DON'T KNOW.
HI GABRIELLE! WE DESIGN HATS. WE'D LIKE TO PRESENT THESE TO YOU.
OOH!
REALLY? FOR ME?
LOOK OVER HERE!
KAWAII!
CLICK!
CLICK!
click!
SUGOI KAWAII!
I modeled each one, drunk on the attention.
MICHEL, LOOK AT ALL THE HATS I GOT.
I DON'T THINK THEY'LL FIT YOU BECAUSE YOUR HEAD'S GROWING SO BIG!

August 3rd

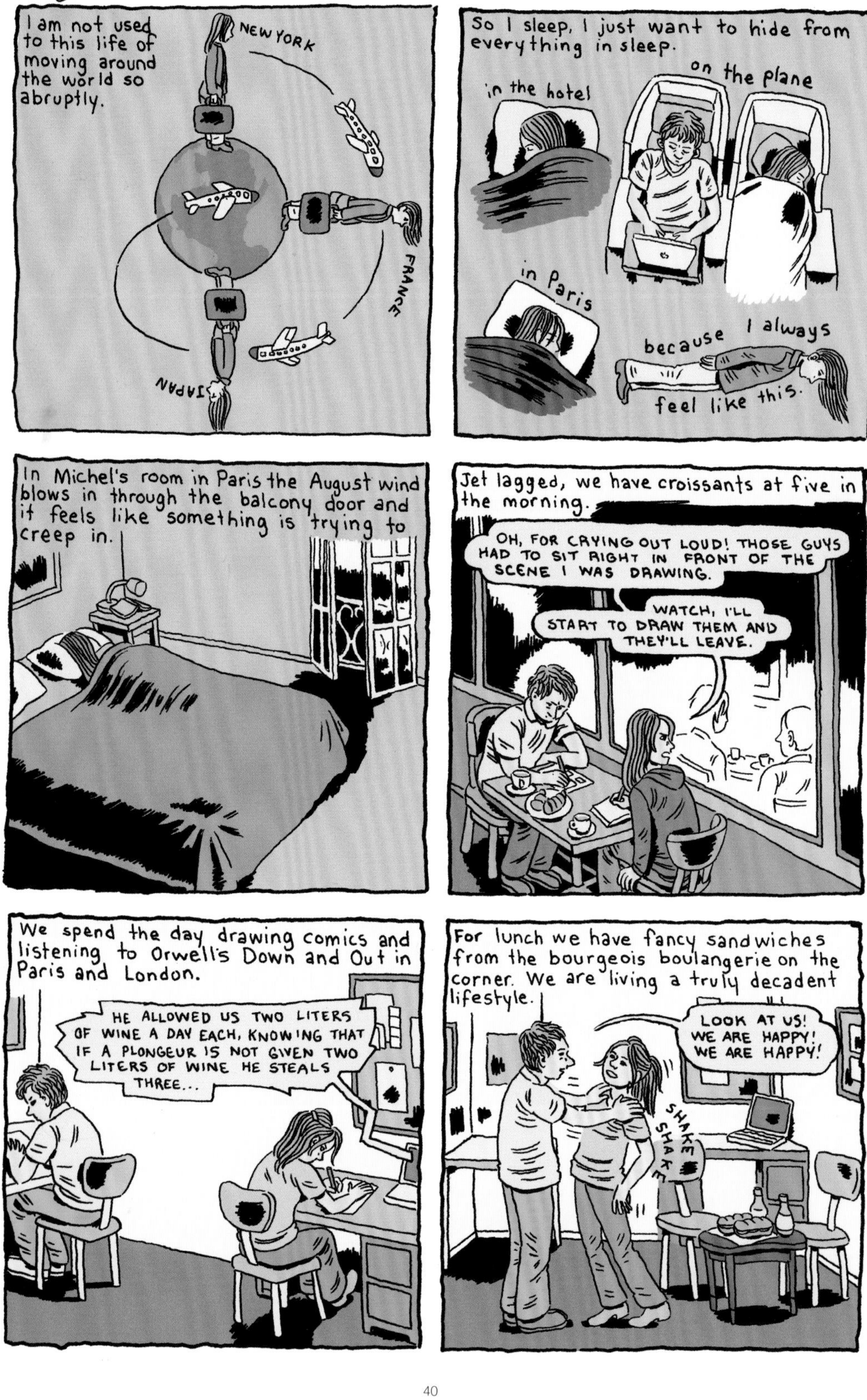
I am not used to this life of moving around the world so abruptly.
NEW YORK
FRANCE
JAPAN
So I sleep, I just want to hide from everything in sleep.
in the hotel
on the plane
in Paris
because I always feel like this.
In Michel's room in Paris the August wind blows in through the balcony door and it feels like something is trying to creep in.
Jet lagged, we have croissants at five in the morning.
OH, FOR CRYING OUT LOUD! THOSE GUYS HAD TO SIT RIGHT IN FRONT OF THE SCENE I WAS DRAWING.
WATCH, I'LL START TO DRAW THEM AND THEY'LL LEAVE.
We spend the day drawing comics and listening to Orwell's Down and Out in Paris and London.
HE ALLOWED US TWO LITERS OF WINE A DAY EACH, KNOWING THAT IF A PLONGEUR IS NOT GIVEN TWO LITERS OF WINE HE STEALS THREE...
For lunch we have fancy sandwiches from the bourgeois boulangerie on the corner. We are living a truly decadent lifestyle.
LOOK AT US! WE ARE HAPPY! WE ARE HAPPY!
SHAKE
SHAKE

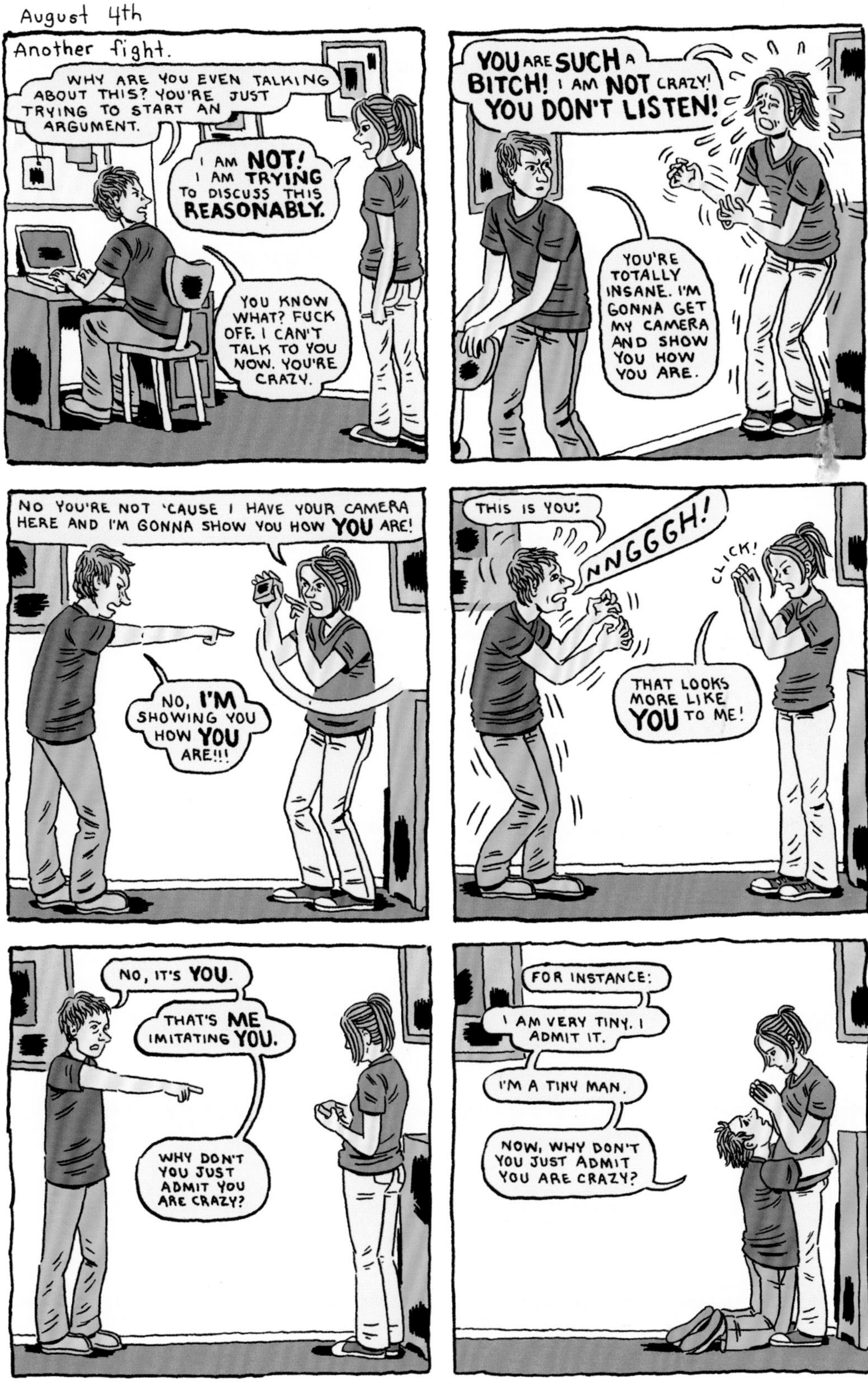
August 4th
Another fight.
WHY ARE YOU EVEN TALKING ABOUT THIS? YOU'RE JUST TRYING TO START AN ARGUMENT.
I AM NOT! I AM TRYING TO DISCUSS THIS REASONABLY.
YOU KNOW WHAT? FUCK OFF. I CAN'T TALK TO YOU NOW. YOU'RE CRAZY.
YOU ARE SUCH A BITCH! I AM NOT CRAZY! YOU DON'T LISTEN!
YOU'RE TOTALLY INSANE. I'M GONNA GET MY CAMERA AND SHOW YOU HOW YOU ARE.
NO YOU'RE NOT 'CAUSE I HAVE YOUR CAMERA HERE AND I'M GONNA SHOW YOU HOW YOU ARE!
NO, I'M SHOWING YOU HOW YOU ARE!!!
THIS IS YOU:
NNGGGH!
CLICK!
THAT LOOKS MORE LIKE YOU TO ME!
NO, IT'S YOU.
THAT'S ME IMITATING YOU.
WHY DON'T YOU JUST ADMIT YOU ARE CRAZY?
FOR INSTANCE:
I AM VERY TINY. I ADMIT IT.
I'M A TINY MAN.
NOW, WHY DON'T YOU JUST ADMIT YOU ARE CRAZY?

August 6th

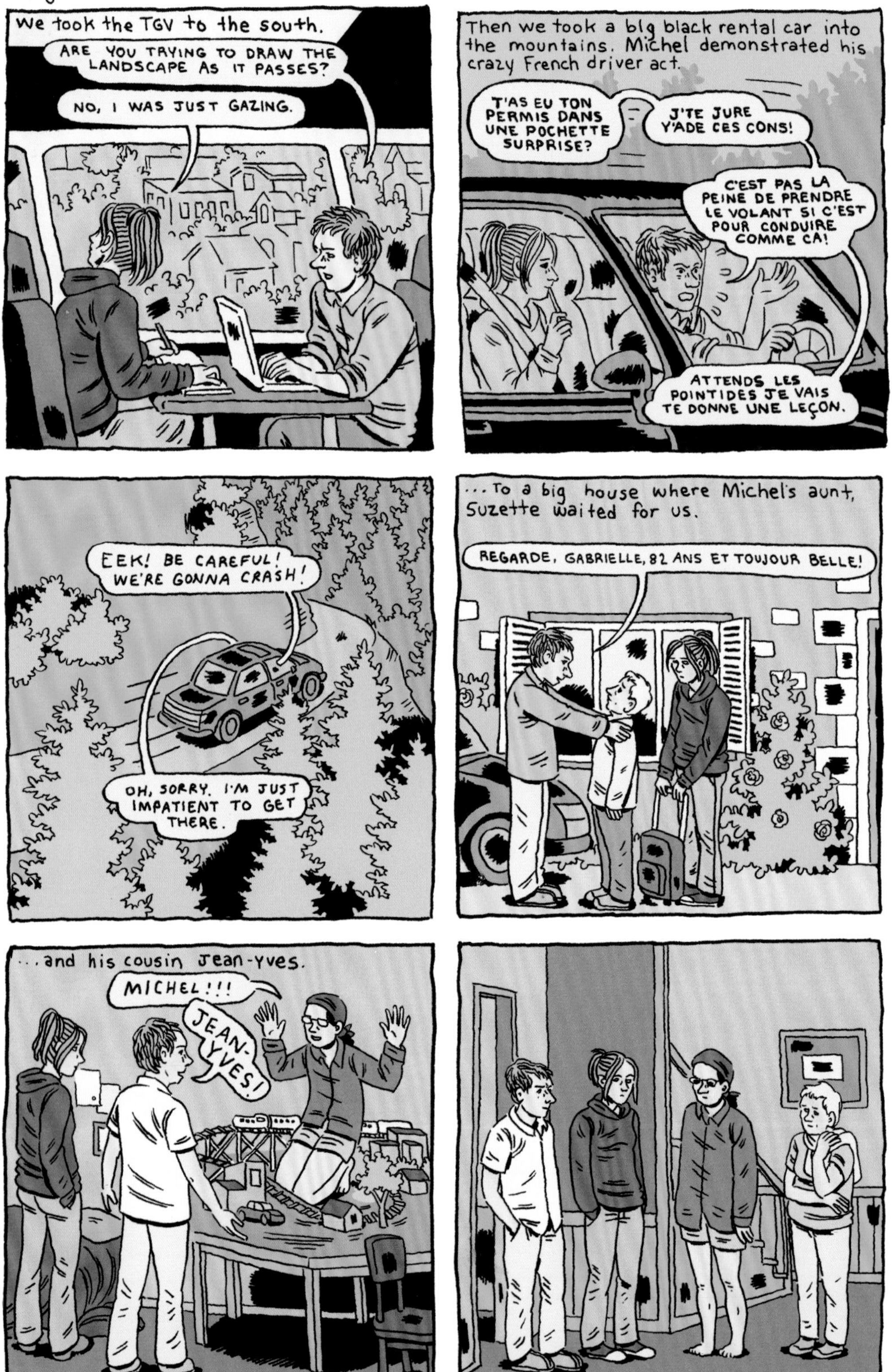
We took the TGV to the south.
ARE YOU TRYING TO DRAW THE LANDSCAPE AS IT PASSES?
NO, I WAS JUST GAZING.
Then we took a big black rental car into the mountains. Michel demonstrated his crazy French driver act.
T'AS EU TON PERMIS DANS UNE POCHETTE SURPRISE?
J'TE JURE Y'ADE CES CONS!
C'EST PAS LA PEINE DE PRENDRE LE VOLANT SI C'EST POUR CONDUIRE COMME CA!
ATTENDS LES POINTIDES JE VAIS TE DONNE UNE LEÇON.
EEK! BE CAREFUL! WE'RE GONNA CRASH!
OH, SORRY. I'M JUST IMPATIENT TO GET THERE.
...To a big house where Michel's aunt, Suzette waited for us.
REGARDE, GABRIELLE, 82 ANS ET TOUJOUR BELLE!
...and his cousin Jean-Yves.
MICHEL!!!
JEAN-YVES!

(1) where'd you get your licence, a gumball machine? (2) I swear there are some dumbasses. (3) get off the road if you're gonna drive like that! (4) Wait'll we get to the dotted line, I'll teach you a lesson! (5) Look at that! Eighty two years and still beautiful!

August 7th

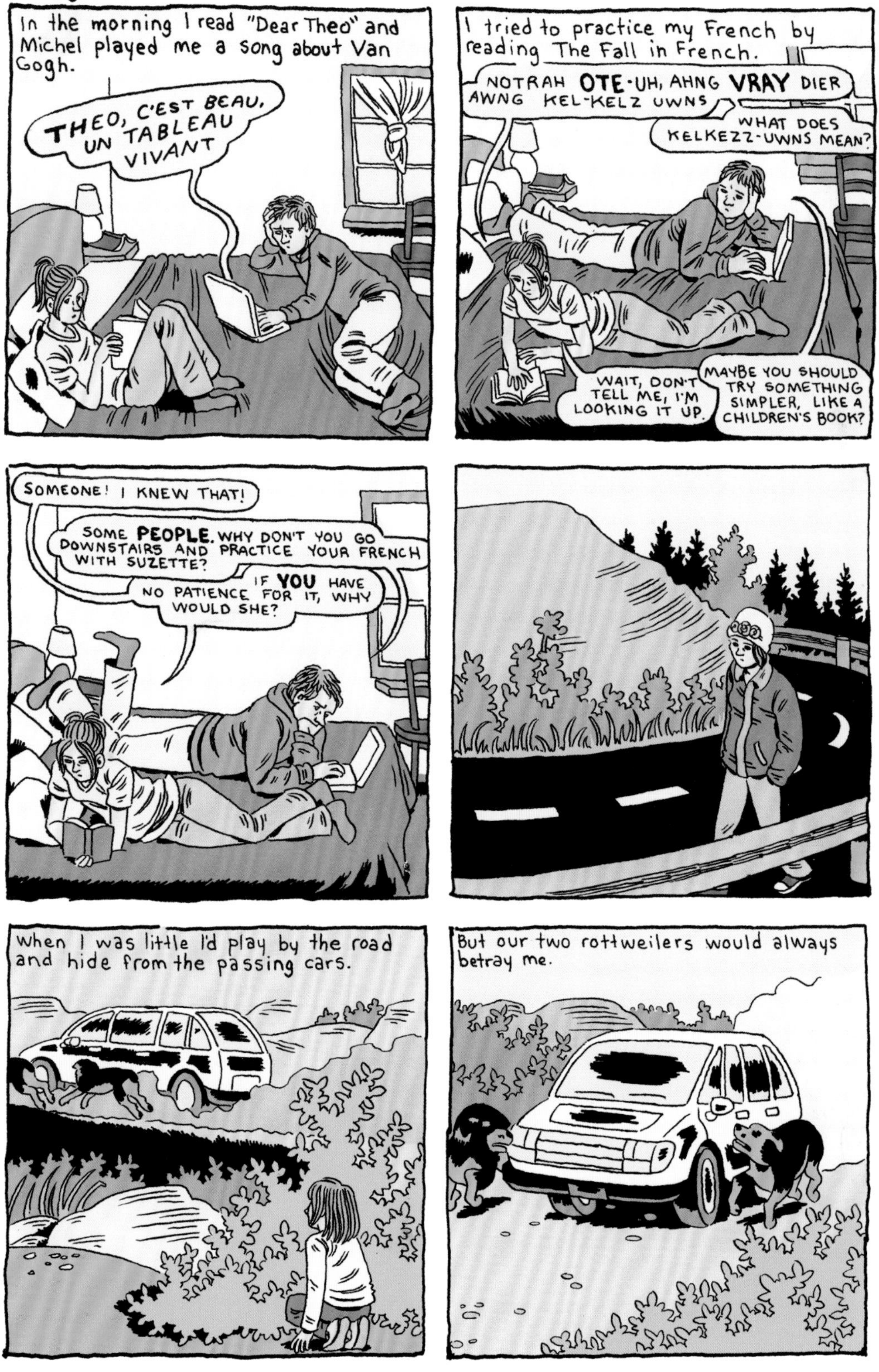
In the morning I read "Dear Theo" and Michel played me a song about Van Gogh.
THEO, C'EST BEAU, UN TABLEAU VIVANT
I tried to practice my French by reading The Fall in French.
NOTRAH OTE-UH, AHNG VRAY DIER AWNG KEL-KELZ UWNS
WHAT DOES KELKEZZ-UWNS MEAN?
WAIT, DON'T TELL ME, I'M LOOKING IT UP.
MAYBE YOU SHOULD TRY SOMETHING SIMPLER, LIKE A CHILDREN'S BOOK?
SOMEONE! I KNEW THAT!
SOME PEOPLE. WHY DON'T YOU GO DOWNSTAIRS AND PRACTICE YOUR FRENCH WITH SUZETTE?
IF YOU HAVE NO PATIENCE FOR IT, WHY WOULD SHE?
When I was little I'd play by the road and hide from the passing cars.
But our two rottweilers would always betray me.

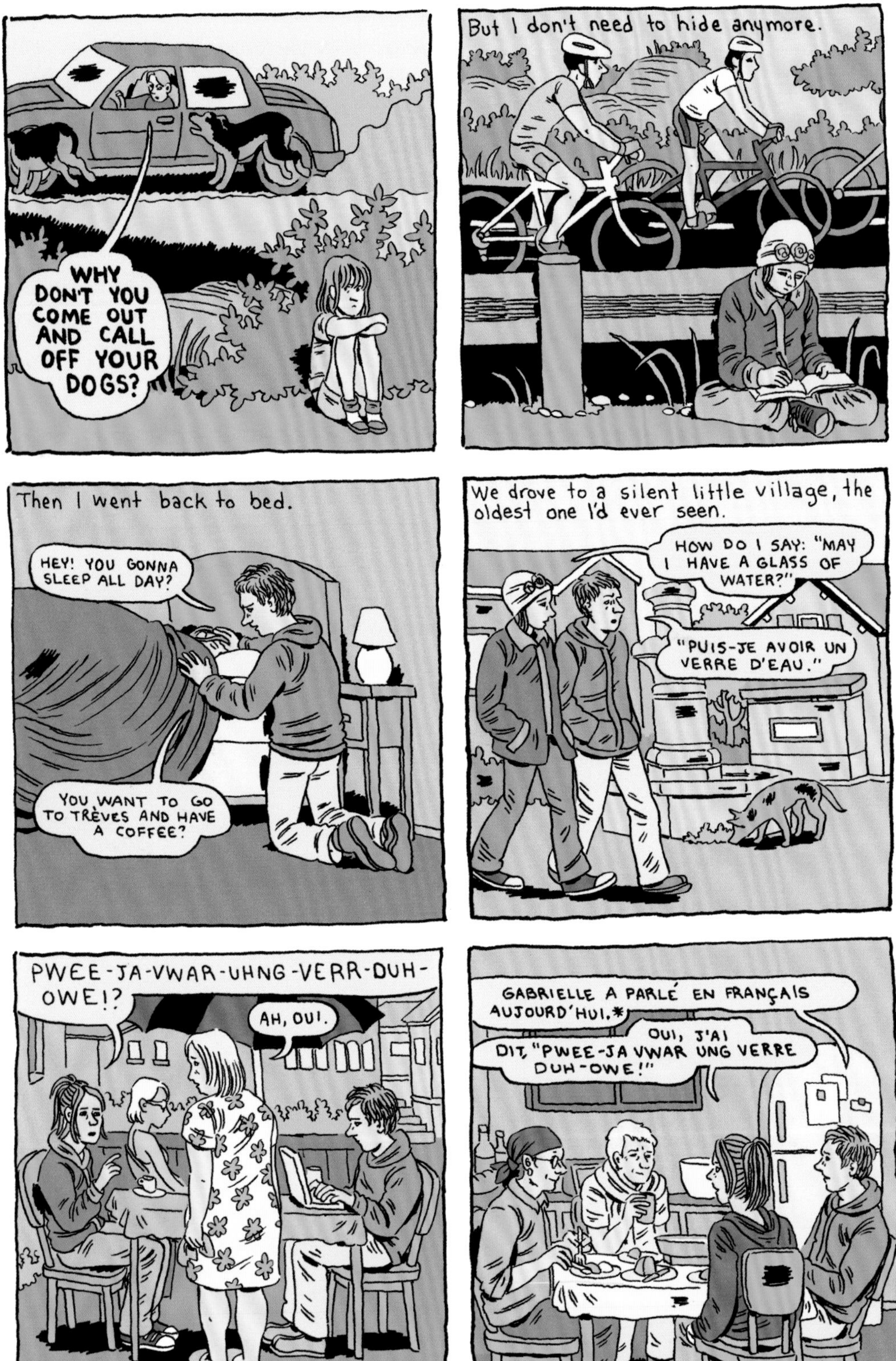
WHY DON'T YOU COME OUT AND CALL OFF YOUR DOGS?
But I don't need to hide anymore.
Then I went back to bed.
HEY! YOU GONNA SLEEP ALL DAY?
YOU WANT TO GO TO TRÈVES AND HAVE A COFFEE?
We drove to a silent little village, the oldest one I'd ever seen.
HOW DO I SAY: "MAY I HAVE A GLASS OF WATER?"
"PUIS-JE AVOIR UN VERRE D'EAU."
PWEE-JA-VWAR-UHNG-VERR-DUH-OWE!?
AH, OUI.
GABRIELLE A PARLÉ EN FRANÇAIS AUJOURD'HUI.*
OUI, J'AI DIT, "PWEE-JA VWAR UNG VERRE DUH-OWE!"

* GABRIELLE SPOKE FRENCH TODAY.

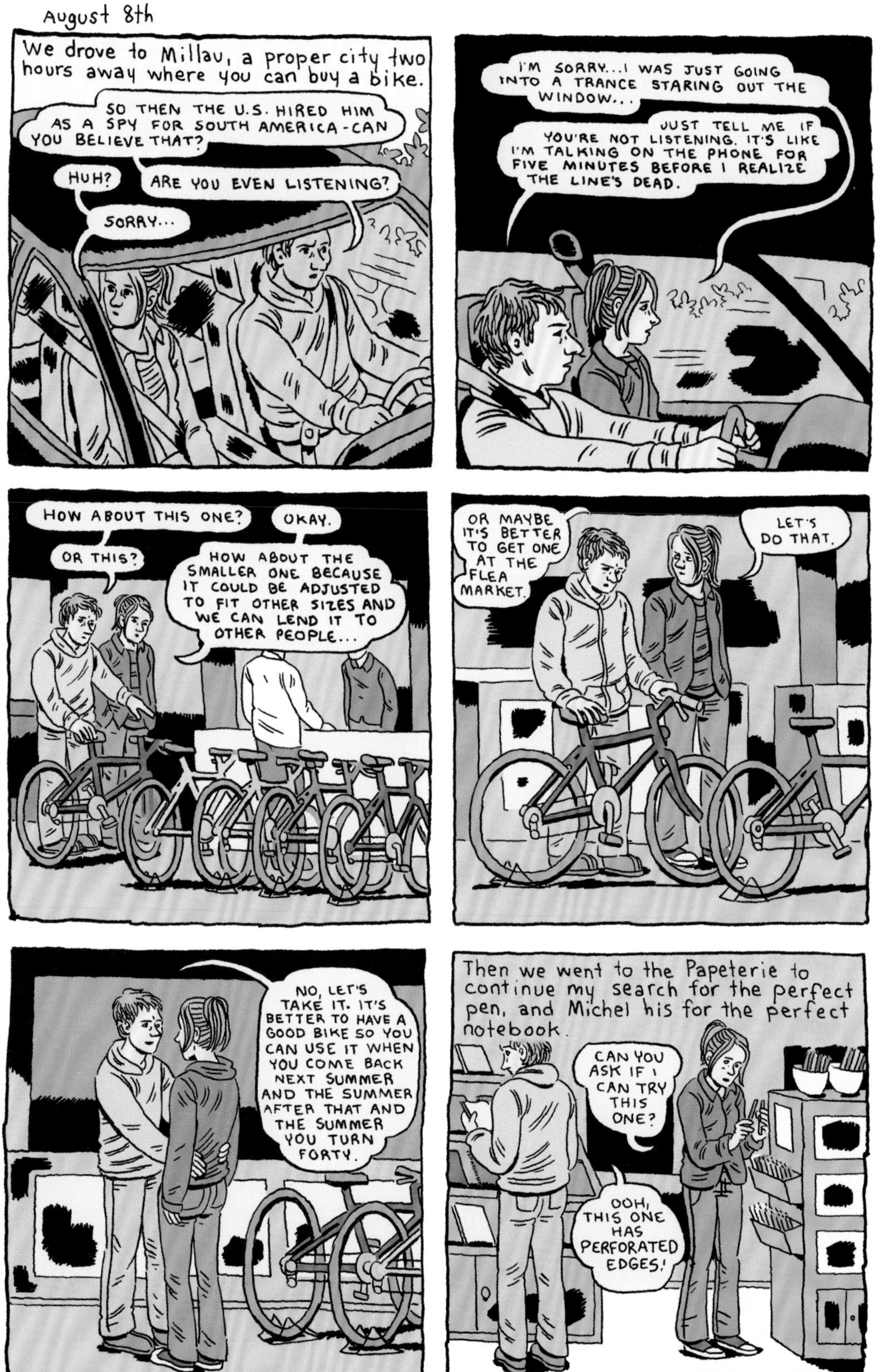

August 8th
We drove to Millau, a proper city two hours away where you can buy a bike.
SO THEN THE U.S. HIRED HIM AS A SPY FOR SOUTH AMERICA - CAN YOU BELIEVE THAT?
HUH?
ARE YOU EVEN LISTENING?
SORRY...
I'M SORRY...I WAS JUST GOING INTO A TRANCE STARING OUT THE WINDOW...
JUST TELL ME IF YOU'RE NOT LISTENING. IT'S LIKE I'M TALKING ON THE PHONE FOR FIVE MINUTES BEFORE I REALIZE THE LINE'S DEAD.
HOW ABOUT THIS ONE?
OKAY.
OR THIS?
HOW ABOUT THE SMALLER ONE BECAUSE IT COULD BE ADJUSTED TO FIT OTHER SIZES AND WE CAN LEND IT TO OTHER PEOPLE...
OR MAYBE IT'S BETTER TO GET ONE AT THE FLEA MARKET.
LET'S DO THAT.
NO, LET'S TAKE IT. IT'S BETTER TO HAVE A GOOD BIKE SO YOU CAN USE IT WHEN YOU COME BACK NEXT SUMMER AND THE SUMMER AFTER THAT AND THE SUMMER YOU TURN FORTY.
Then we went to the Papeterie to continue my search for the perfect pen, and Michel his for the perfect notebook.
CAN YOU ASK IF I CAN TRY THIS ONE?
OOH, THIS ONE HAS PERFORATED EDGES!

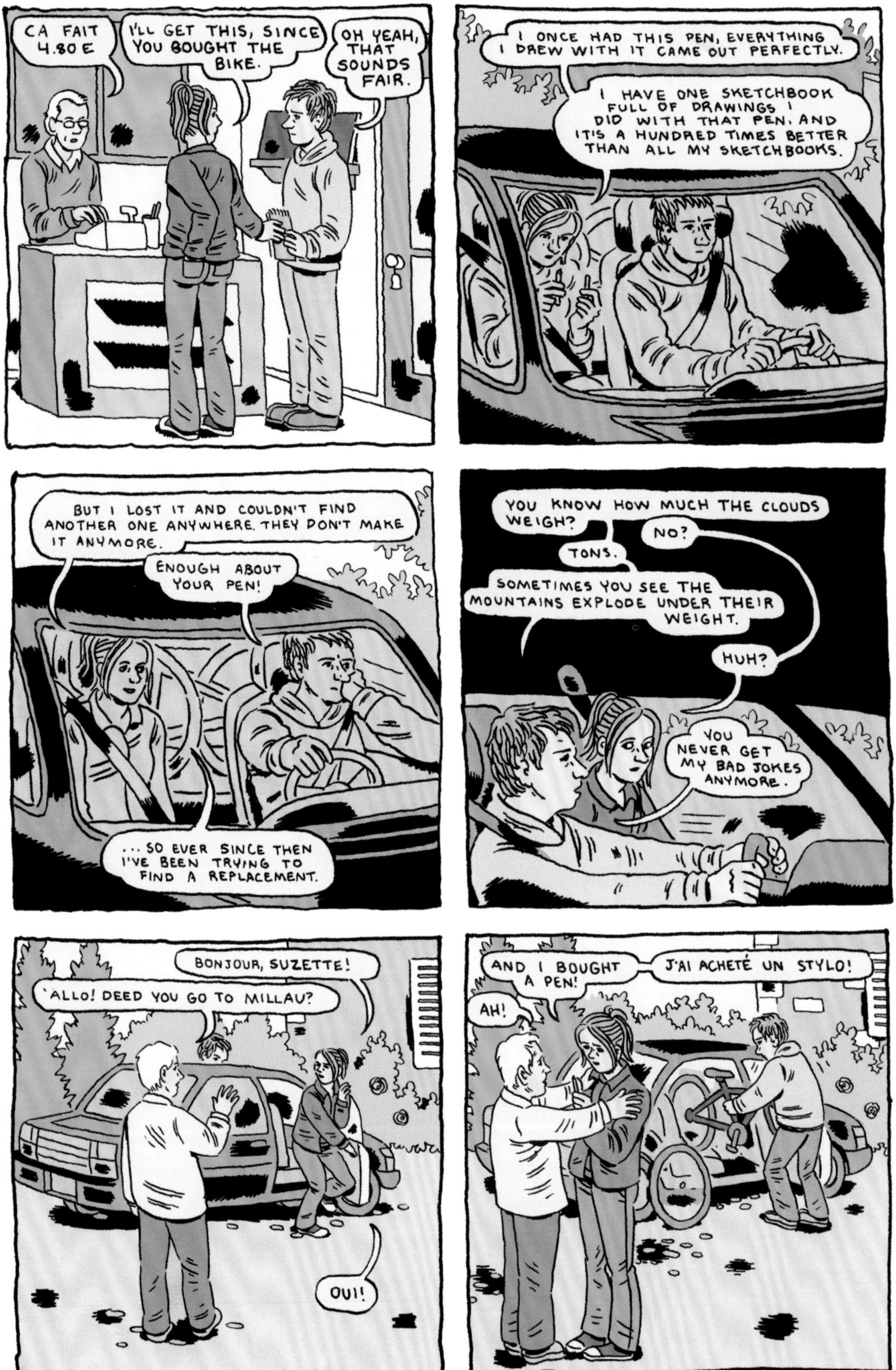
CA FAIT 4.80 E
I'LL GET THIS, SINCE YOU BOUGHT THE BIKE.
OH YEAH, THAT SOUNDS FAIR.
I ONCE HAD THIS PEN, EVERYTHING I DREW WITH IT CAME OUT PERFECTLY.
I HAVE ONE SKETCHBOOK FULL OF DRAWINGS I DID WITH THAT PEN, AND IT'S A HUNDRED TIMES BETTER THAN ALL MY SKETCHBOOKS.
BUT I LOST IT AND COULDN'T FIND ANOTHER ONE ANYWHERE. THEY DON'T MAKE IT ANYMORE.
ENOUGH ABOUT YOUR PEN!
...SO EVER SINCE THEN I'VE BEEN TRYING TO FIND A REPLACEMENT.
YOU KNOW HOW MUCH THE CLOUDS WEIGH?
NO?
TONS.
SOMETIMES YOU SEE THE MOUNTAINS EXPLODE UNDER THEIR WEIGHT.
HUH?
YOU NEVER GET MY BAD JOKES ANYMORE.
BONJOUR, SUZETTE!
`ALLO! DEED YOU GO TO MILLAU?
OUI!
AND I BOUGHT A PEN!
J'AI ACHETÉ UN STYLO!
AH!

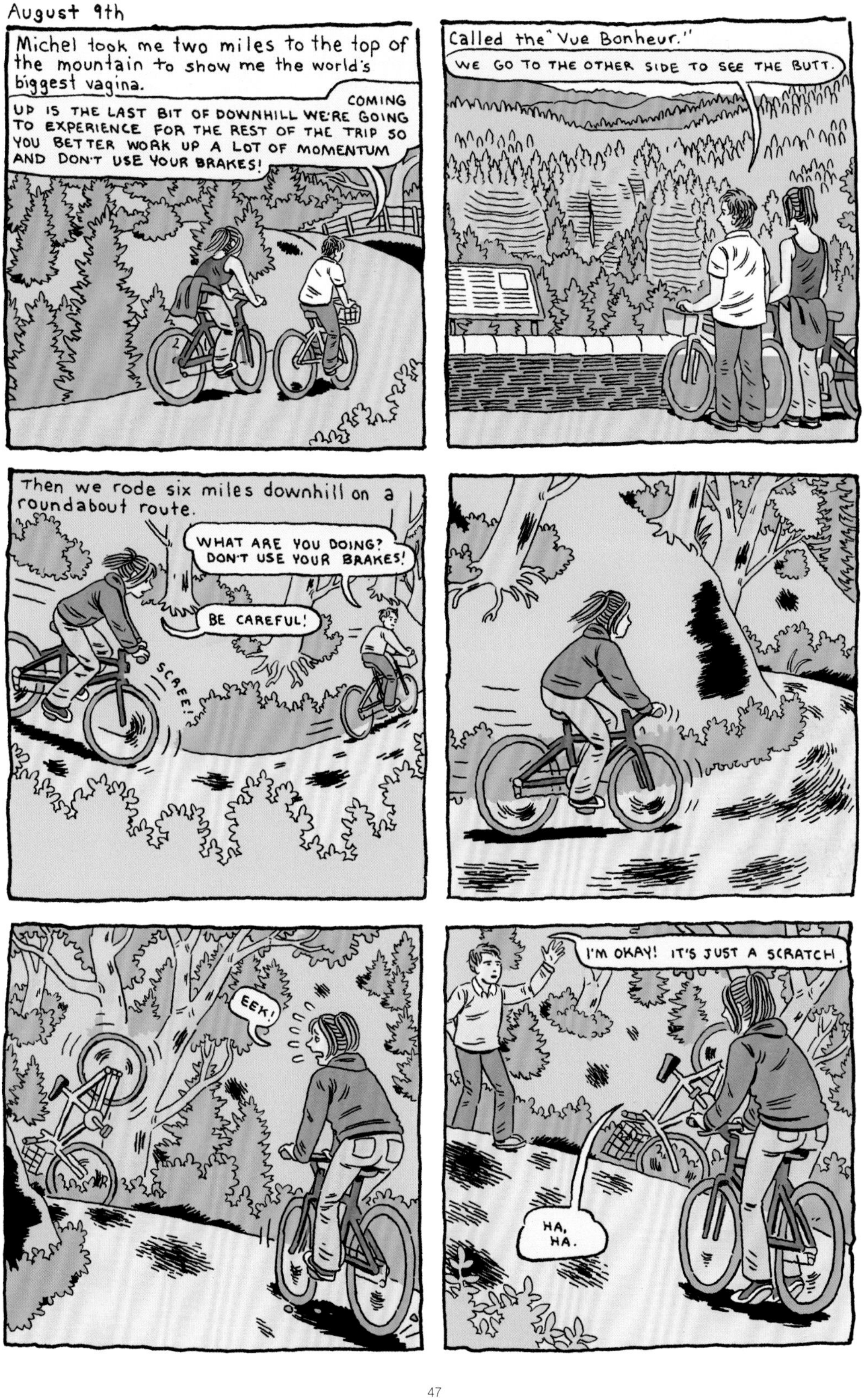
August 9th
Michel took me two miles to the top of the mountain to show me the world's biggest vagina.
COMING UP IS THE LAST BIT OF DOWNHILL WE'RE GOING TO EXPERIENCE FOR THE REST OF THE TRIP SO YOU BETTER WORK UP A LOT OF MOMENTUM AND DON'T USE YOUR BRAKES!
Called the "Vue Bonheur."
WE GO TO THE OTHER SIDE TO SEE THE BUTT.
Then we rode six miles downhill on a roundabout route.
WHAT ARE YOU DOING? DON'T USE YOUR BRAKES!
BE CAREFUL!
SCREE!
EEK!
I'M OKAY! IT'S JUST A SCRATCH.
HA, HA.

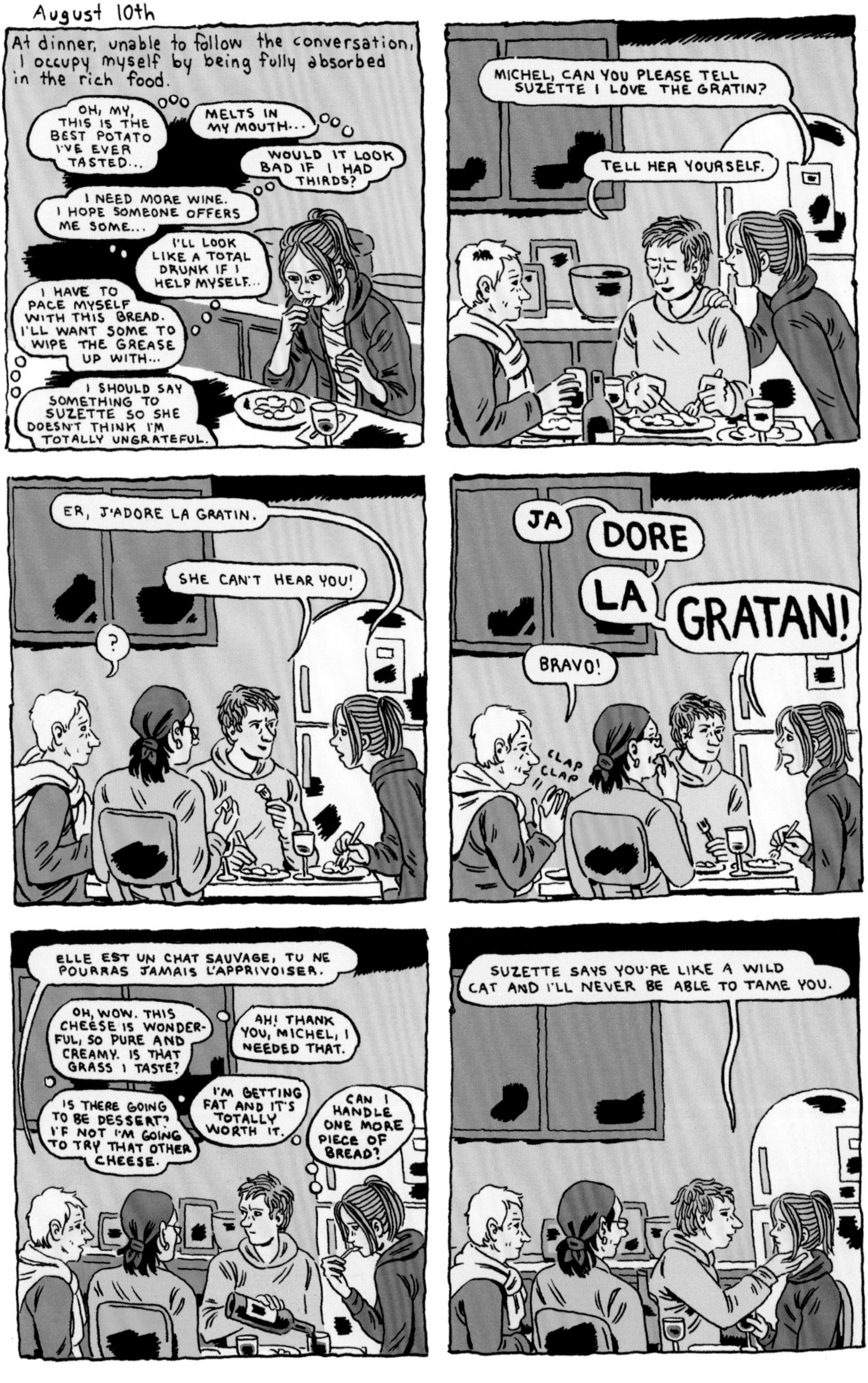
August 10th
At dinner, unable to follow the conversation, I occupy myself by being fully absorbed in the rich food.
OH, MY, THIS IS THE BEST POTATO I'VE EVER TASTED...
MELTS IN MY MOUTH...
WOULD IT LOOK BAD IF I HAD THIRDS?
I NEED MORE WINE. I HOPE SOMEONE OFFERS ME SOME...
I'LL LOOK LIKE A TOTAL DRUNK IF I HELP MYSELF...
I HAVE TO PACE MYSELF WITH THIS BREAD. I'LL WANT SOME TO WIPE THE GREASE UP WITH...
I SHOULD SAY SOMETHING TO SUZETTE SO SHE DOESN'T THINK I'M TOTALLY UNGRATEFUL.
MICHEL, CAN YOU PLEASE TELL SUZETTE I LOVE THE GRATIN?
TELL HER YOURSELF.
ER, J'ADORE LA GRATIN.
SHE CAN'T HEAR YOU!
?
JA
DORE
LA
GRATAN!
BRAVO!
CLAP CLAP
ELLE EST UN CHAT SAUVAGE, TU NE POURRAS JAMAIS L'APPRIVOISER.
OH, WOW. THIS CHEESE IS WONDERFUL, SO PURE AND CREAMY. IS THAT GRASS I TASTE?
AH! THANK YOU, MICHEL, I NEEDED THAT.
IS THERE GOING TO BE DESSERT? IF NOT I'M GOING TO TRY THAT OTHER CHEESE.
I'M GETTING FAT AND IT'S TOTALLY WORTH IT.
CAN I HANDLE ONE MORE PIECE OF BREAD?
SUZETTE SAYS YOU'RE LIKE A WILD CAT AND I'LL NEVER BE ABLE TO TAME YOU.

August 11th

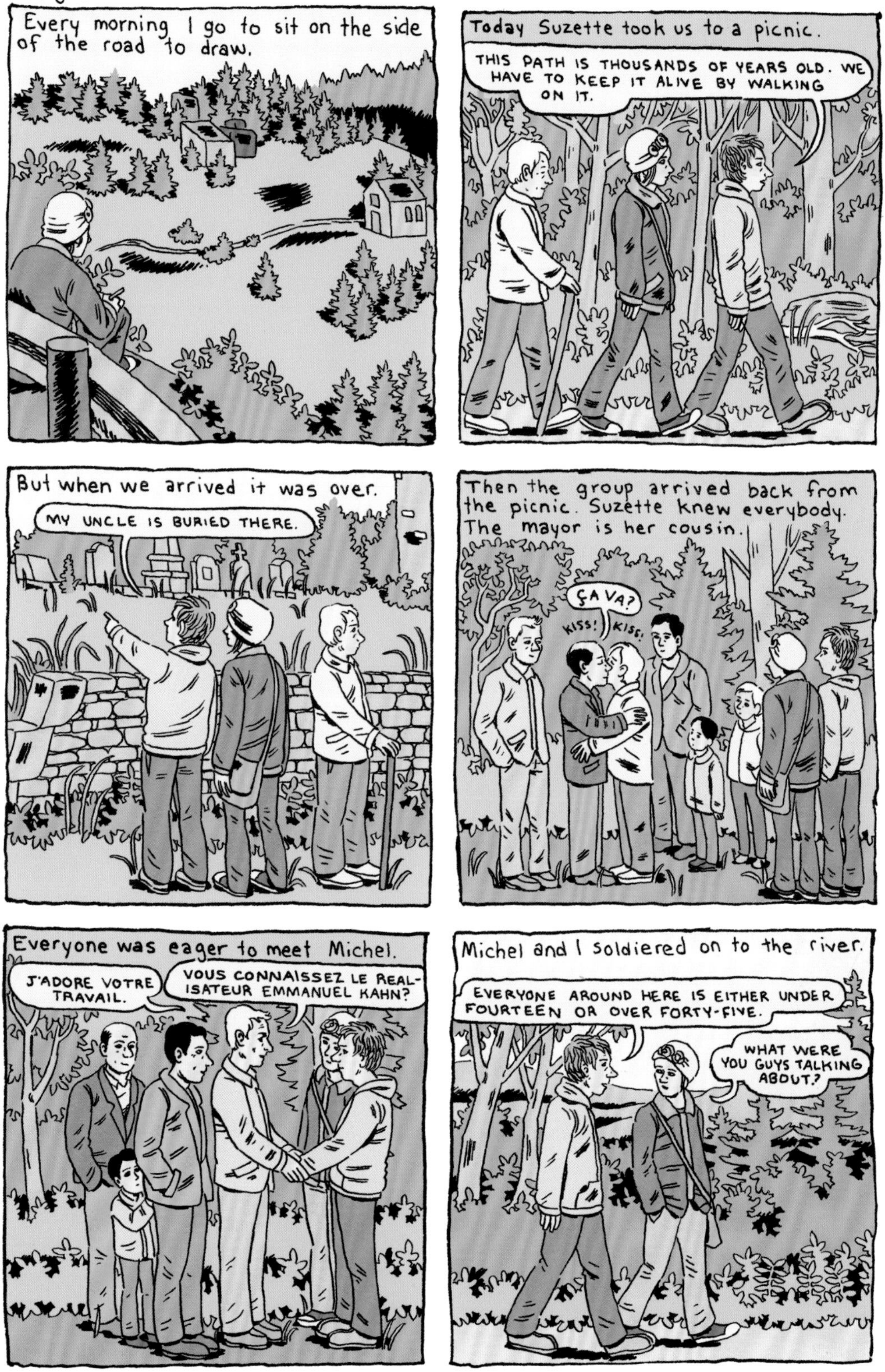

Every morning I go to sit on the side of the road to draw.
Today Suzette took us to a picnic.
THIS PATH IS THOUSANDS OF YEARS OLD. WE HAVE TO KEEP IT ALIVE BY WALKING ON IT.
But when we arrived it was over.
MY UNCLE IS BURIED THERE.
Then the group arrived back from the picnic. Suzette knew everybody. The mayor is her cousin.
ÇA VA?
KISS! KISS!
Everyone was eager to meet Michel.
J'ADORE VOTRE TRAVAIL.
VOUS CONNAISSEZ LE REALISATEUR EMMANUEL KAHN?
Michel and I soldiered on to the river.
EVERYONE AROUND HERE IS EITHER UNDER FOURTEEN OR OVER FORTY-FIVE.
WHAT WERE YOU GUYS TALKING ABOUT?

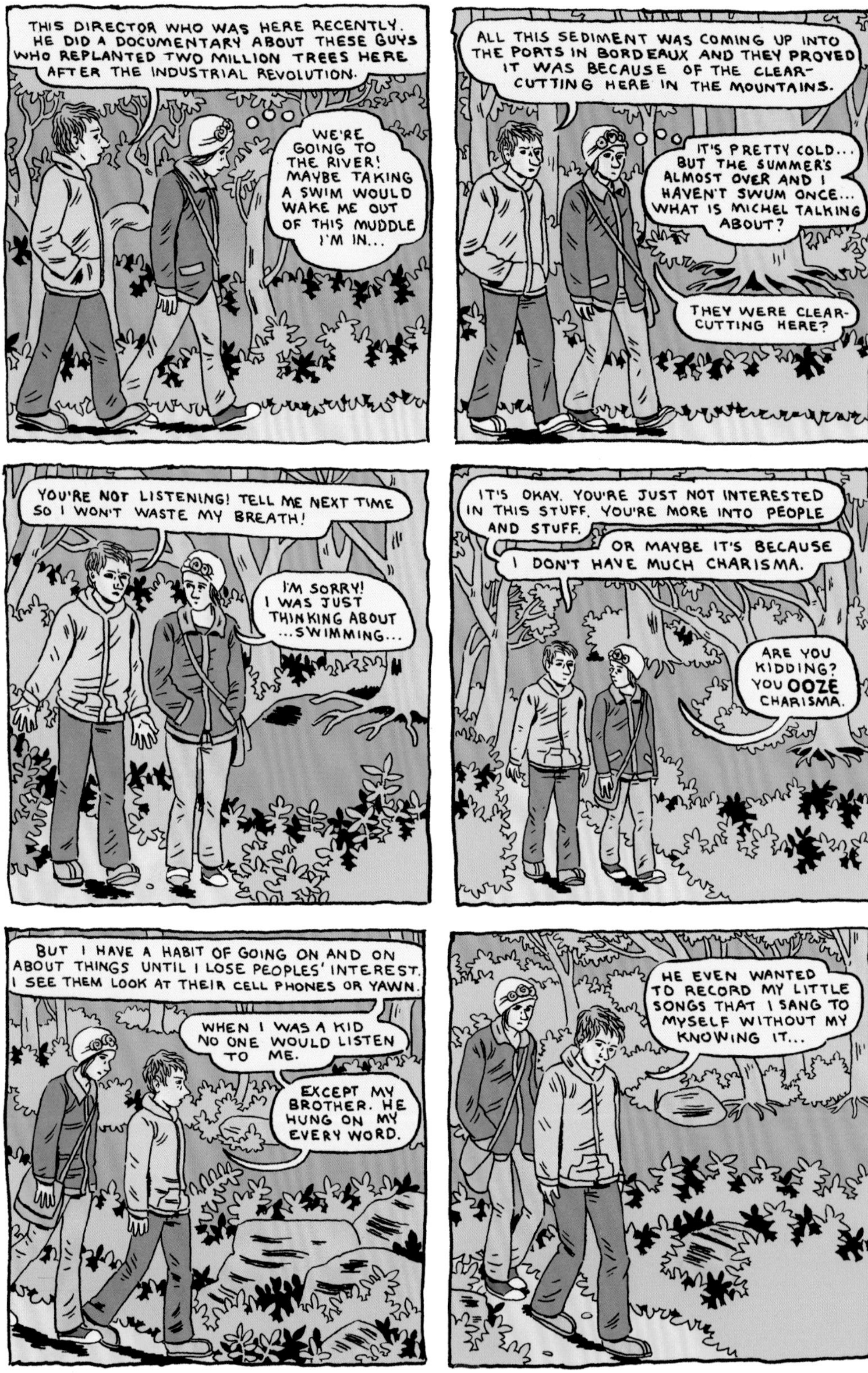
THIS DIRECTOR WHO WAS HERE RECENTLY. HE DID A DOCUMENTARY ABOUT THESE GUYS WHO REPLANTED TWO MILLION TREES HERE AFTER THE INDUSTRIAL REVOLUTION.
WE'RE GOING TO THE RIVER! MAYBE TAKING A SWIM WOULD WAKE ME OUT OF THIS MUDDLE I'M IN...
ALL THIS SEDIMENT WAS COMING UP INTO THE PORTS IN BORDEAUX AND THEY PROVED IT WAS BECAUSE OF THE CLEAR-CUTTING HERE IN THE MOUNTAINS.
IT'S PRETTY COLD... BUT THE SUMMER'S ALMOST OVER AND I HAVEN'T SWUM ONCE... WHAT IS MICHEL TALKING ABOUT?
THEY WERE CLEAR-CUTTING HERE?
YOU'RE NOT LISTENING! TELL ME NEXT TIME SO I WON'T WASTE MY BREATH!
I'M SORRY! I WAS JUST THINKING ABOUT ...SWIMMING...
IT'S OKAY. YOU'RE JUST NOT INTERESTED IN THIS STUFF. YOU'RE MORE INTO PEOPLE AND STUFF.
OR MAYBE IT'S BECAUSE I DON'T HAVE MUCH CHARISMA.
ARE YOU KIDDING? YOU OOZE CHARISMA.
BUT I HAVE A HABIT OF GOING ON AND ON ABOUT THINGS UNTIL I LOSE PEOPLES' INTEREST. I SEE THEM LOOK AT THEIR CELL PHONES OR YAWN.
WHEN I WAS A KID NO ONE WOULD LISTEN TO ME.
EXCEPT MY BROTHER. HE HUNG ON MY EVERY WORD.
HE EVEN WANTED TO RECORD MY LITTLE SONGS THAT I SANG TO MYSELF WITHOUT MY KNOWING IT...

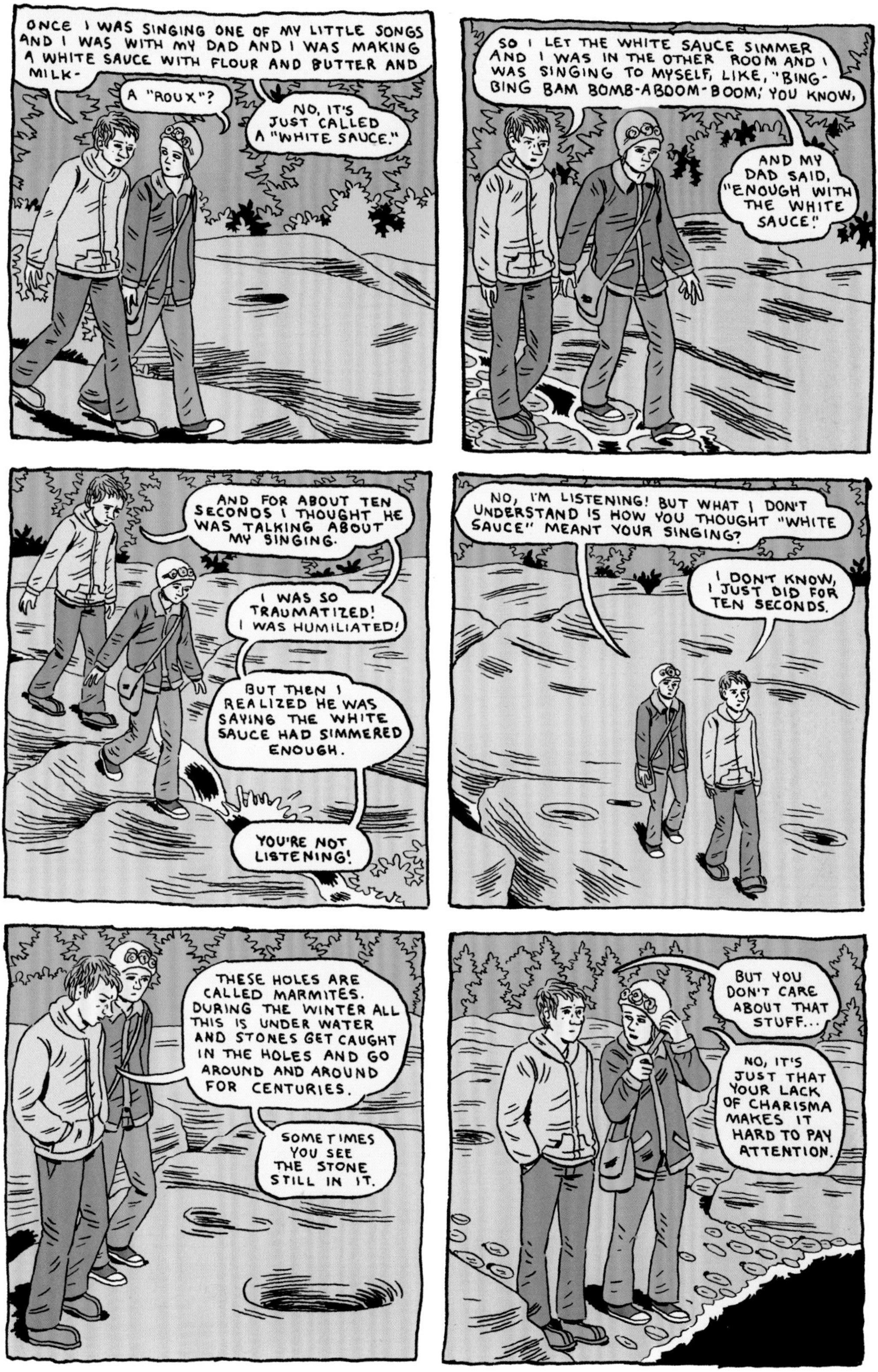
ONCE I WAS SINGING ONE OF MY LITTLE SONGS AND I WAS WITH MY DAD AND I WAS MAKING A WHITE SAUCE WITH FLOUR AND BUTTER AND MILK-
A "ROUX"?
NO, IT'S JUST CALLED A "WHITE SAUCE."
SO I LET THE WHITE SAUCE SIMMER AND I WAS IN THE OTHER ROOM AND I WAS SINGING TO MYSELF, LIKE, "BING-BING BAM BOMB-ABOOM-BOOM," YOU KNOW,
AND MY DAD SAID, "ENOUGH WITH THE WHITE SAUCE!"
AND FOR ABOUT TEN SECONDS I THOUGHT HE WAS TALKING ABOUT MY SINGING.
I WAS SO TRAUMATIZED! I WAS HUMILIATED!
BUT THEN I REALIZED HE WAS SAYING THE WHITE SAUCE HAD SIMMERED ENOUGH.
YOU'RE NOT LISTENING!
NO, I'M LISTENING! BUT WHAT I DON'T UNDERSTAND IS HOW YOU THOUGHT "WHITE SAUCE" MEANT YOUR SINGING?
I DON'T KNOW, I JUST DID FOR TEN SECONDS.
THESE HOLES ARE CALLED MARMITES. DURING THE WINTER ALL THIS IS UNDER WATER AND STONES GET CAUGHT IN THE HOLES AND GO AROUND AND AROUND FOR CENTURIES.
SOMETIMES YOU SEE THE STONE STILL IN IT.
BUT YOU DON'T CARE ABOUT THAT STUFF...
NO, IT'S JUST THAT YOUR LACK OF CHARISMA MAKES IT HARD TO PAY ATTENTION.

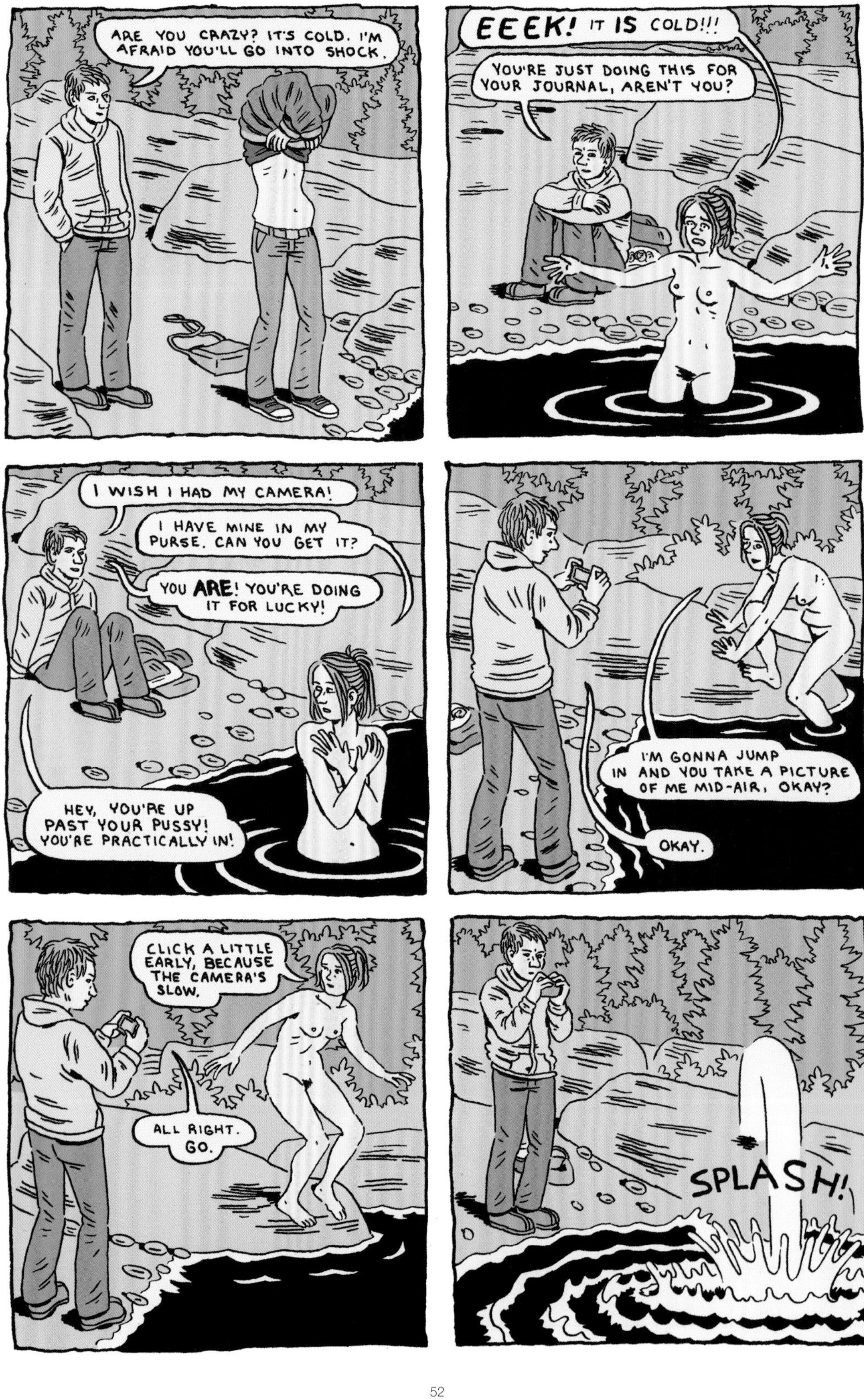
ARE YOU CRAZY? IT'S COLD. I'M AFRAID YOU'LL GO INTO SHOCK.
EEEK! IT IS COLD!!!
YOU'RE JUST DOING THIS FOR YOUR JOURNAL, AREN'T YOU?
I WISH I HAD MY CAMERA!
I HAVE MINE IN MY PURSE. CAN YOU GET IT?
YOU ARE! YOU'RE DOING IT FOR LUCKY!
HEY, YOU'RE UP PAST YOUR PUSSY! YOU'RE PRACTICALLY IN!
I'M GONNA JUMP IN AND YOU TAKE A PICTURE OF ME MID-AIR, OKAY?
OKAY.
CLICK A LITTLE EARLY, BECAUSE THE CAMERA'S SLOW.
ALL RIGHT. GO.
SPLASH!

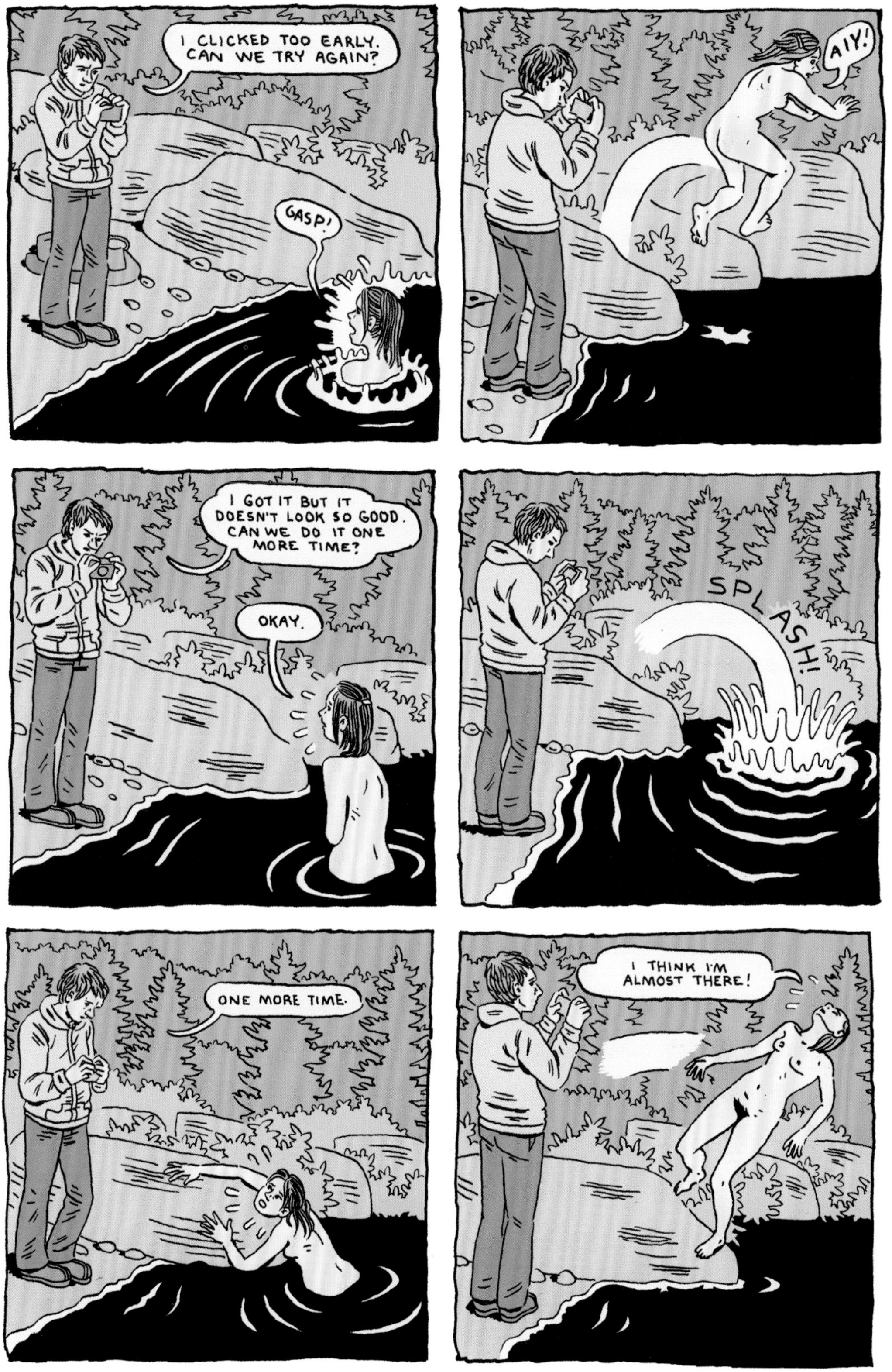
I CLICKED TOO EARLY. CAN WE TRY AGAIN?
GASP!
AIY!
I GOT IT BUT IT DOESN'T LOOK SO GOOD. CAN WE DO IT ONE MORE TIME?
OKAY.
SPLASH!
ONE MORE TIME.
I THINK I'M ALMOST THERE!

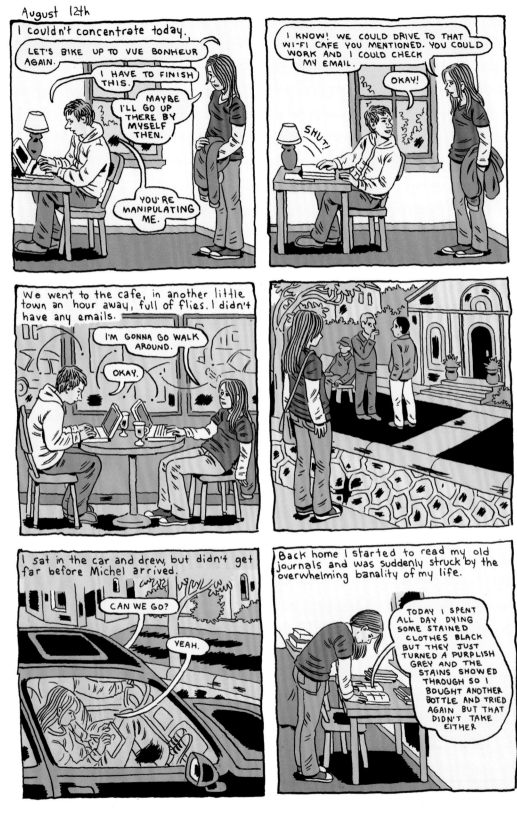

August 12th

I couldn't concentrate today.

LET'S BIKE UP TO VUE BONHEUR AGAIN.

I HAVE TO FINISH THIS.

MAYBE I'LL GO UP THERE BY MYSELF THEN.

YOU'RE MANIPULATING ME.

I KNOW! WE COULD DRIVE TO THAT WI-FI CAFE YOU MENTIONED. YOU COULD WORK AND I COULD CHECK MY EMAIL.

OKAY!

SHUT!

We went to the cafe, in another little town an hour away, full of flies. I didn't have any emails.

I'M GONNA GO WALK AROUND.

OKAY.

I sat in the car and drew, but didn't get far before Michel arrived.

CAN WE GO?

YEAH.

Back home I started to read my old journals and was suddenly struck by the overwhelming banality of my life.

TODAY I SPENT ALL DAY DYING SOME STAINED CLOTHES BLACK BUT THEY JUST TURNED A PURPLISH GREY AND THE STAINS SHOWED THROUGH SO I BOUGHT ANOTHER BOTTLE AND TRIED AGAIN BUT THAT DIDN'T TAKE EITHER

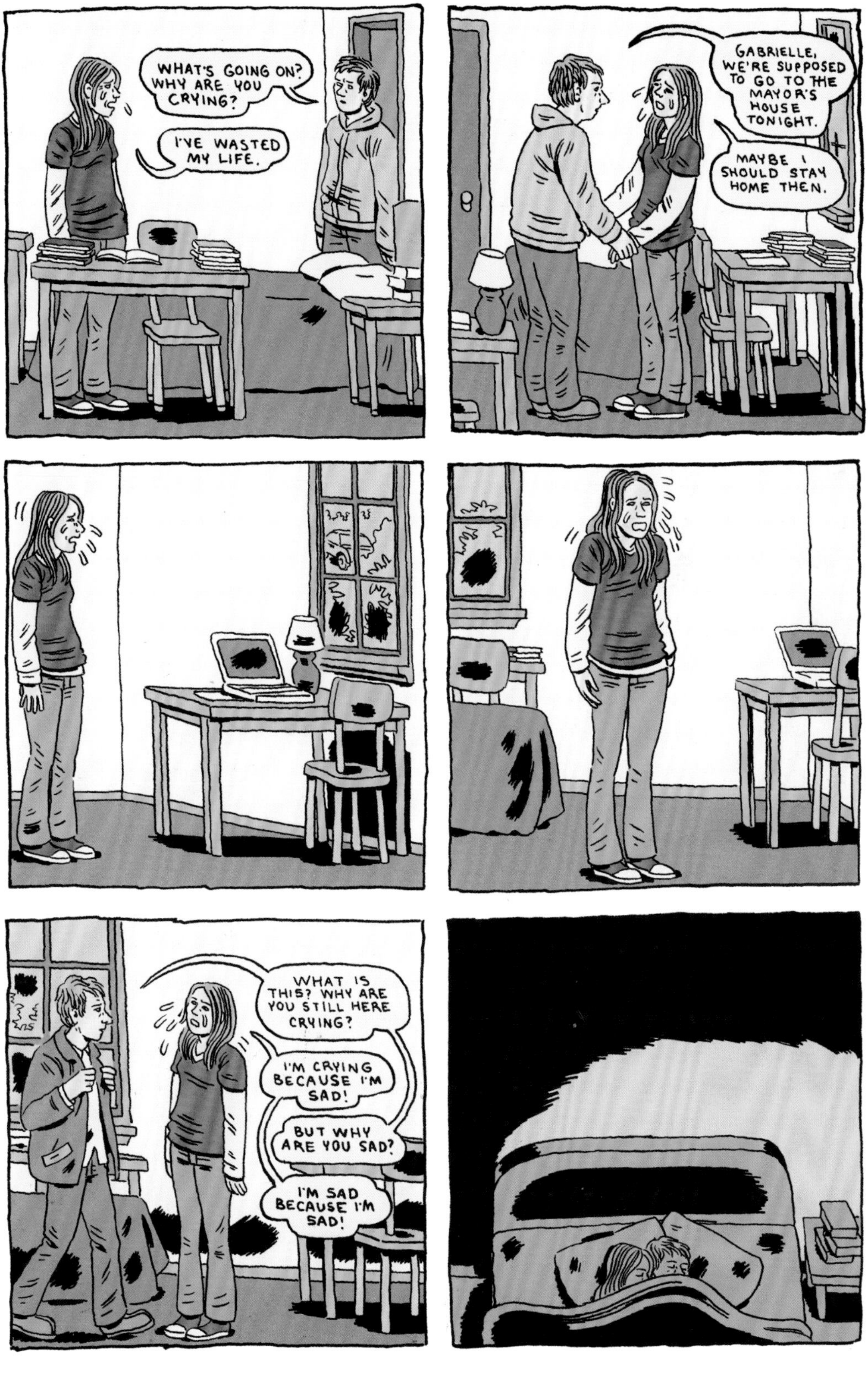
WHAT'S GOING ON? WHY ARE YOU CRYING?
I'VE WASTED MY LIFE.
GABRIELLE, WE'RE SUPPOSED TO GO TO THE MAYOR'S HOUSE TONIGHT.
MAYBE I SHOULD STAY HOME THEN.
WHAT IS THIS? WHY ARE YOU STILL HERE CRYING?
I'M CRYING BECAUSE I'M SAD!
BUT WHY ARE YOU SAD?
I'M SAD BECAUSE I'M SAD!

August 13th

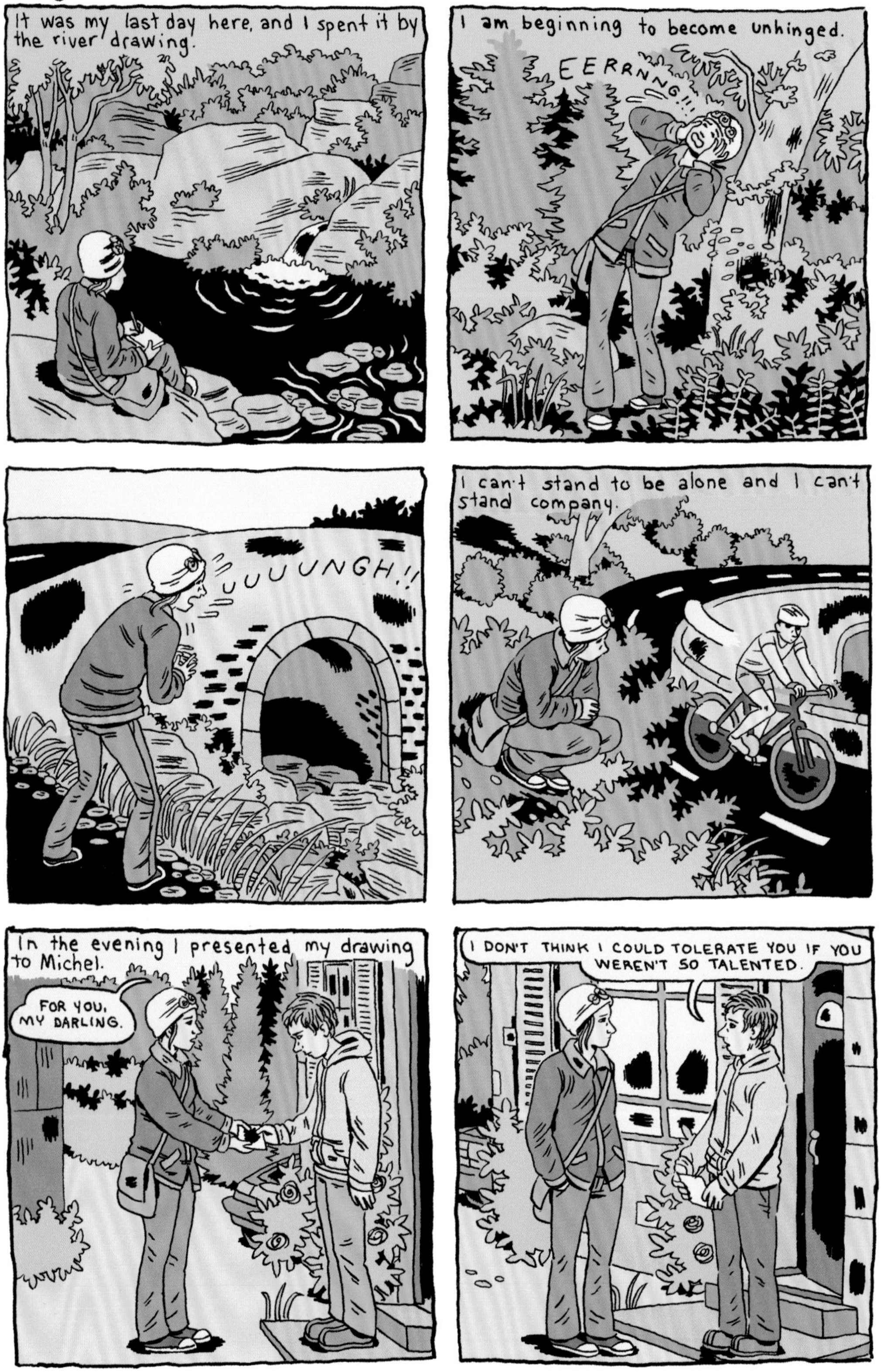

It was my last day here, and I spent it by the river drawing.
I am beginning to become unhinged.
EERRNNG!!!
UUUUNGH!!
I can't stand to be alone and I can't stand company.
In the evening I presented my drawing to Michel.
FOR YOU, MY DARLING.
I DON'T THINK I COULD TOLERATE YOU IF YOU WEREN'T SO TALENTED.

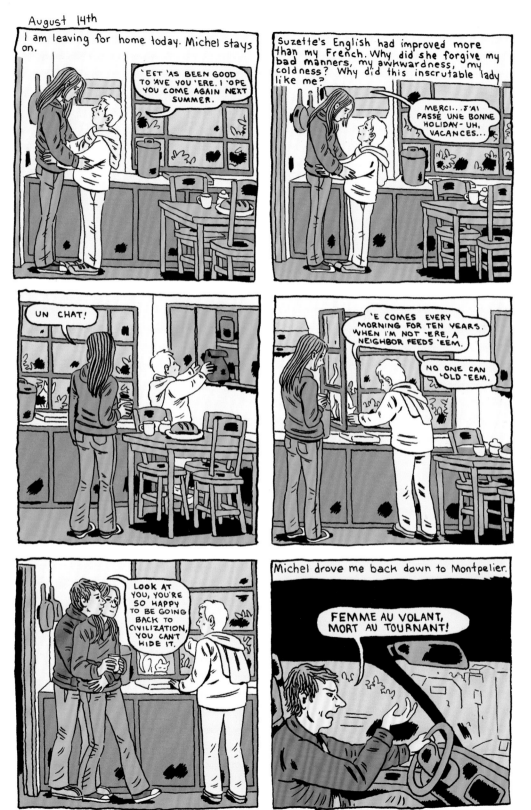

August 14th

I am leaving for home today. Michel stays on.

'EET 'AS BEEN GOOD TO 'AVE YOU 'ERE. I 'OPE YOU COME AGAIN NEXT SUMMER.

Suzette's English had improved more than my French. Why did she forgive my bad manners, my awkwardness, my coldness? Why did this inscrutable lady like me?

MERCI...J'AI PASSÉ UNE BONNE HOLIDAY- UH, VACANCES...

UN CHAT!

'E COMES EVERY MORNING FOR TEN YEARS. WHEN I'M NOT 'ERE, A NEIGHBOR FEEDS 'EEM.

NO ONE CAN 'OLD 'EEM.

LOOK AT YOU, YOU'RE SO HAPPY TO BE GOING BACK TO CIVILIZATION, YOU CAN'T HIDE IT.

Michel drove me back down to Montpelier.

FEMME AU VOLANT, MORT AU TOURNANT!

✳ WOMAN AT THE WHEEL, DEATH AT THE CURB.

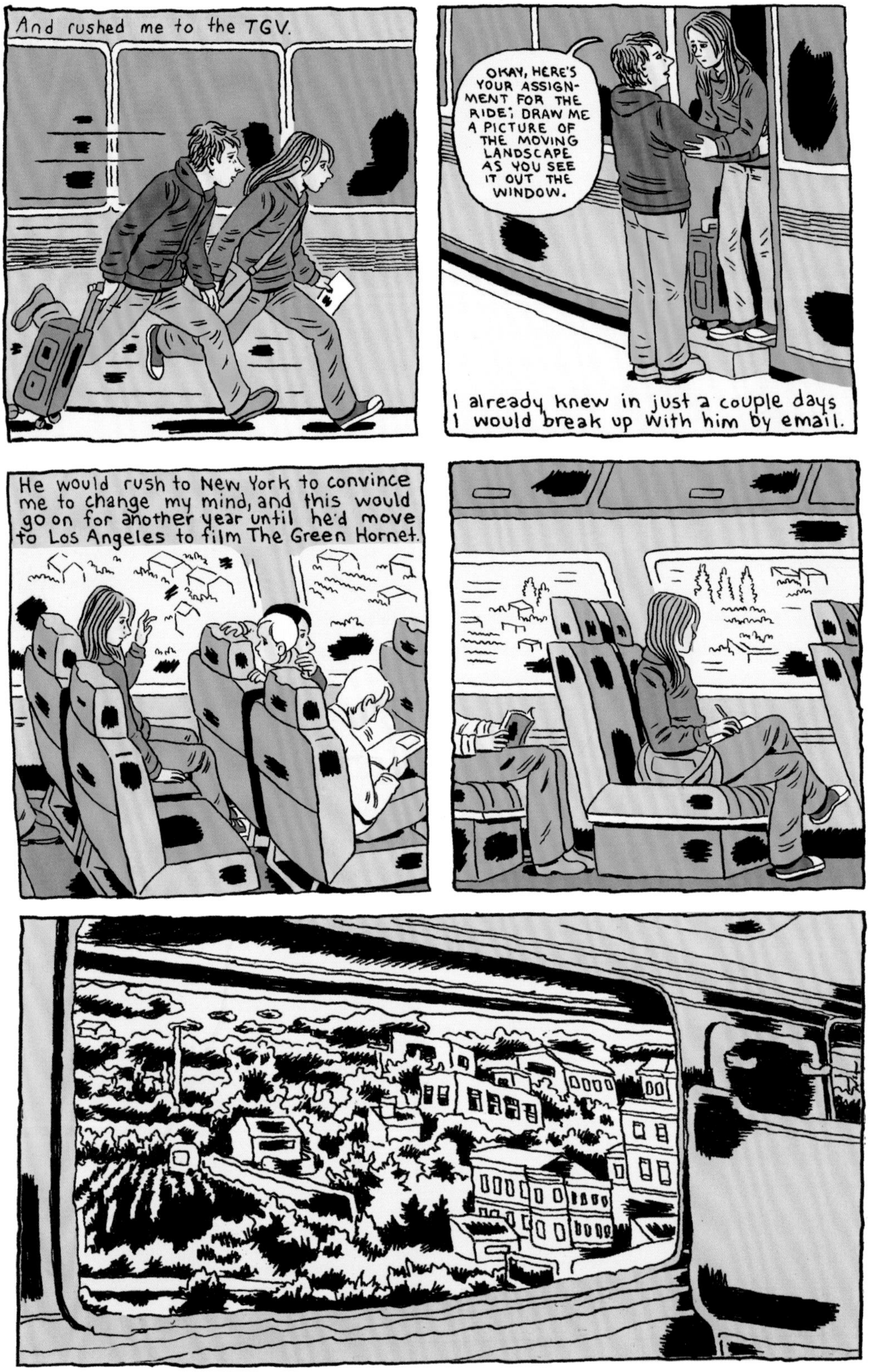
And rushed me to the TGV.
OKAY, HERE'S YOUR ASSIGNMENT FOR THE RIDE: DRAW ME A PICTURE OF THE MOVING LANDSCAPE AS YOU SEE IT OUT THE WINDOW.
I already knew in just a couple days I would break up with him by email.
He would rush to New York to convince me to change my mind, and this would go on for another year until he'd move to Los Angeles to film The Green Hornet.

Carnivore

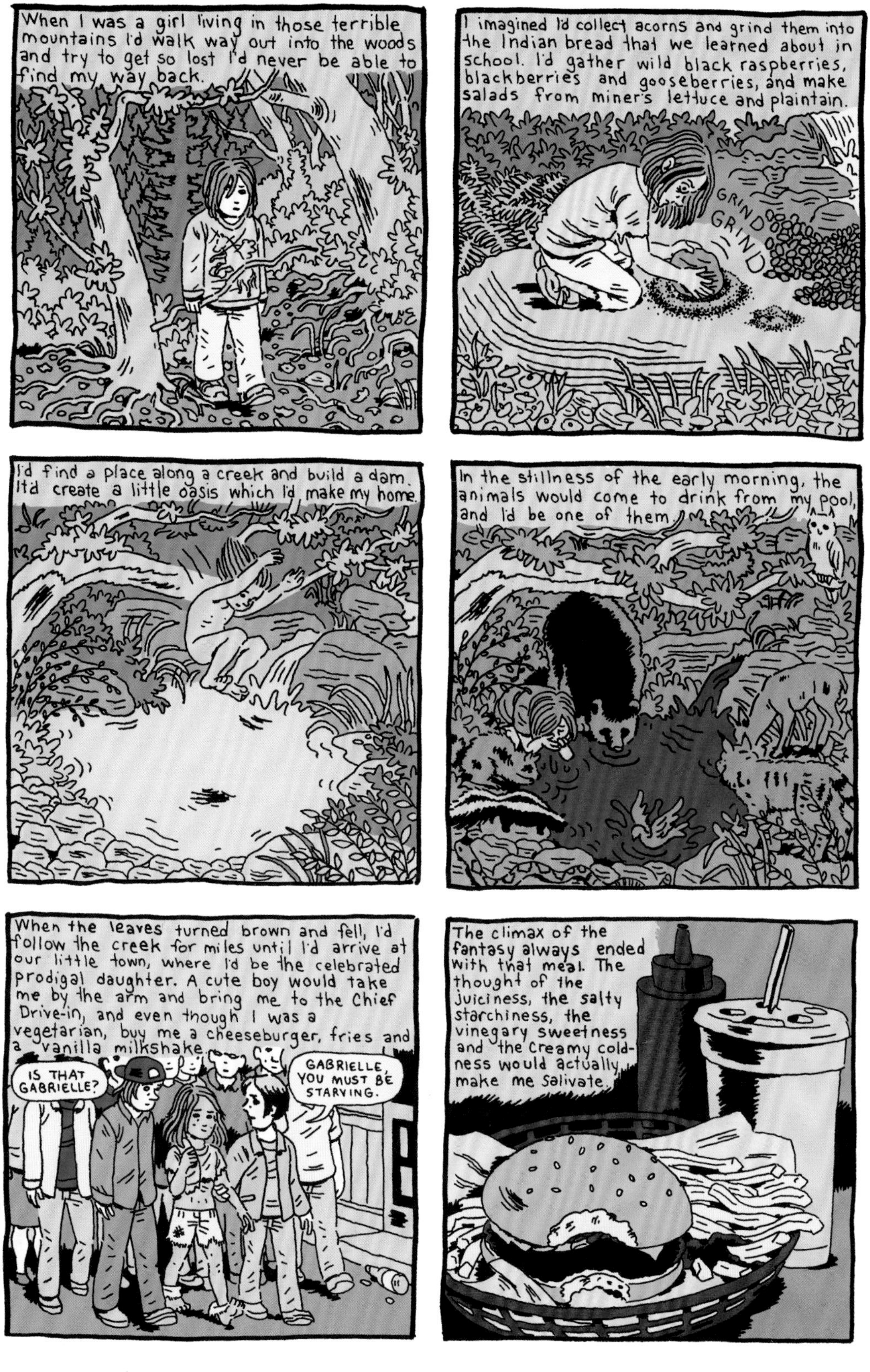
When I was a girl living in those terrible mountains I'd walk way out into the woods and try to get so lost I'd never be able to find my way back.
I imagined I'd collect acorns and grind them into the Indian bread that we learned about in school. I'd gather wild black raspberries, blackberries and gooseberries, and make salads from miner's lettuce and plaintain.
GRIND GRIND GRIND
I'd find a place along a creek and build a dam. It'd create a little oasis which I'd make my home.
In the stillness of the early morning, the animals would come to drink from my pool, and I'd be one of them.
When the leaves turned brown and fell, I'd follow the creek for miles until I'd arrive at our little town, where I'd be the celebrated prodigal daughter. A cute boy would take me by the arm and bring me to the Chief Drive-in, and even though I was a vegetarian, buy me a cheeseburger, fries and a vanilla milkshake.
IS THAT GABRIELLE?
GABRIELLE, YOU MUST BE STARVING.
The climax of the fantasy always ended with that meal. The thought of the juiciness, the salty starchiness, the vinegary sweetness and the creamy coldness would actually make me salivate.

# chapter three
# 2008-2009

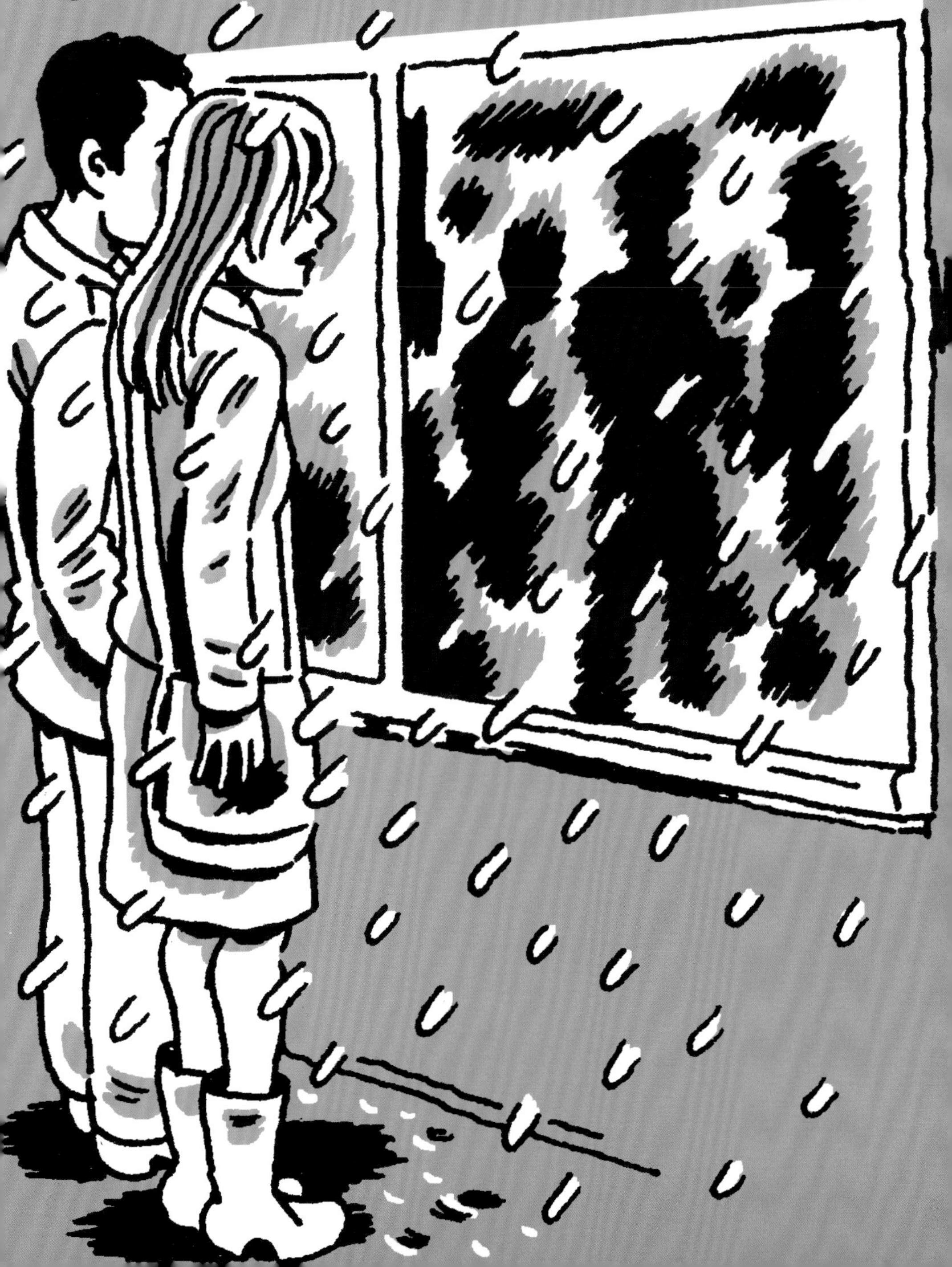

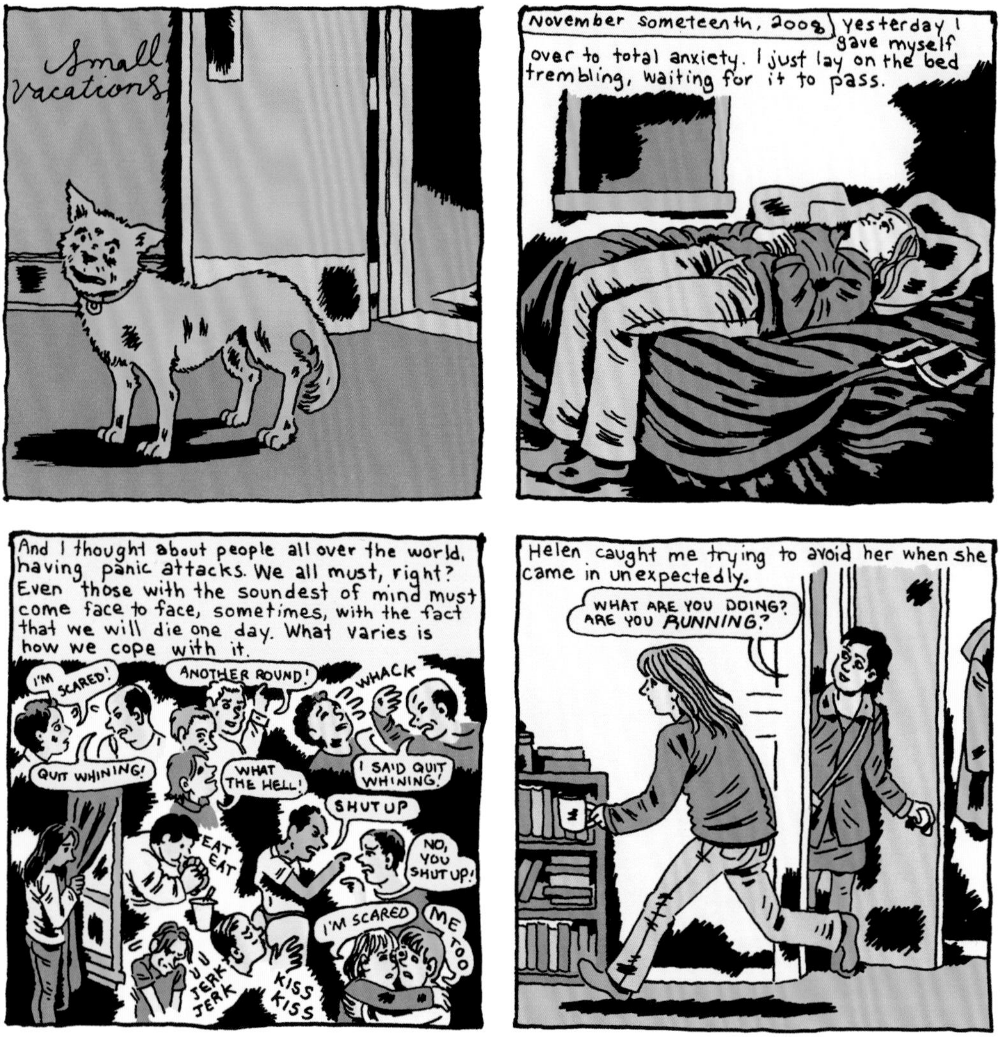
Small vacations
November someteenth, 2008
yesterday I gave myself over to total anxiety. I just lay on the bed trembling, waiting for it to pass.
And I thought about people all over the world, having panic attacks. We all must, right? Even those with the soundest of mind must come face to face, sometimes, with the fact that we will die one day. What varies is how we cope with it.
I'M SCARED!
ANOTHER ROUND!
WHACK
QUIT WHINING!
WHAT THE HELL!
I SAID QUIT WHINING!
SHUT UP
EAT EAT
NO, YOU SHUT UP!
I'M SCARED
ME TOO
JERK JERK
KISS KISS
Helen caught me trying to avoid her when she came in unexpectedly.
WHAT ARE YOU DOING? ARE YOU RUNNING?

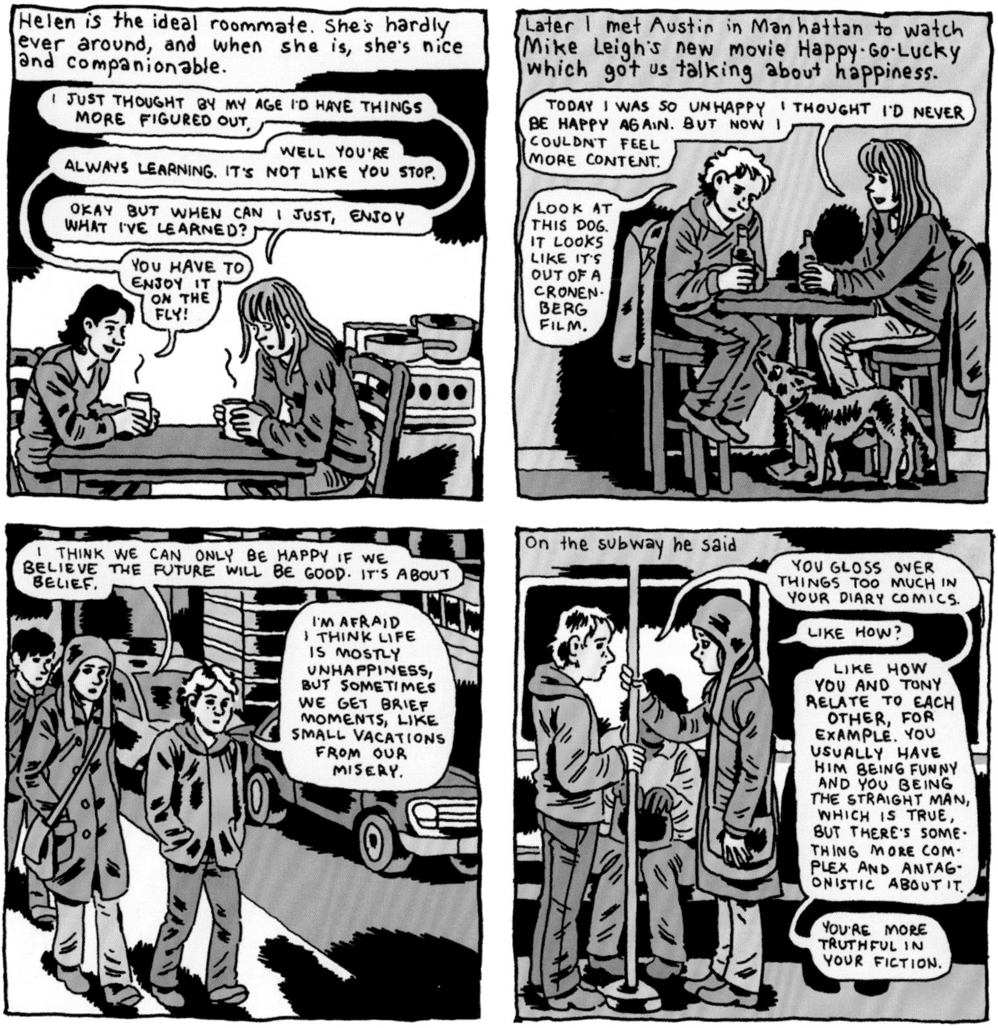
Helen is the ideal roommate. She's hardly ever around, and when she is, she's nice and companionable.
I JUST THOUGHT BY MY AGE I'D HAVE THINGS MORE FIGURED OUT.
WELL YOU'RE ALWAYS LEARNING. IT'S NOT LIKE YOU STOP.
OKAY BUT WHEN CAN I JUST, ENJOY WHAT I'VE LEARNED?
YOU HAVE TO ENJOY IT ON THE FLY!
Later I met Austin in Manhattan to watch Mike Leigh's new movie Happy-Go-Lucky which got us talking about happiness.
TODAY I WAS SO UNHAPPY I THOUGHT I'D NEVER BE HAPPY AGAIN. BUT NOW I COULDN'T FEEL MORE CONTENT.
LOOK AT THIS DOG. IT LOOKS LIKE IT'S OUT OF A CRONENBERG FILM.
I THINK WE CAN ONLY BE HAPPY IF WE BELIEVE THE FUTURE WILL BE GOOD. IT'S ABOUT BELIEF.
I'M AFRAID I THINK LIFE IS MOSTLY UNHAPPINESS, BUT SOMETIMES WE GET BRIEF MOMENTS, LIKE SMALL VACATIONS FROM OUR MISERY.
On the subway he said
YOU GLOSS OVER THINGS TOO MUCH IN YOUR DIARY COMICS.
LIKE HOW?
LIKE HOW YOU AND TONY RELATE TO EACH OTHER, FOR EXAMPLE. YOU USUALLY HAVE HIM BEING FUNNY AND YOU BEING THE STRAIGHT MAN, WHICH IS TRUE, BUT THERE'S SOMETHING MORE COMPLEX AND ANTAGONISTIC ABOUT IT.
YOU'RE MORE TRUTHFUL IN YOUR FICTION.

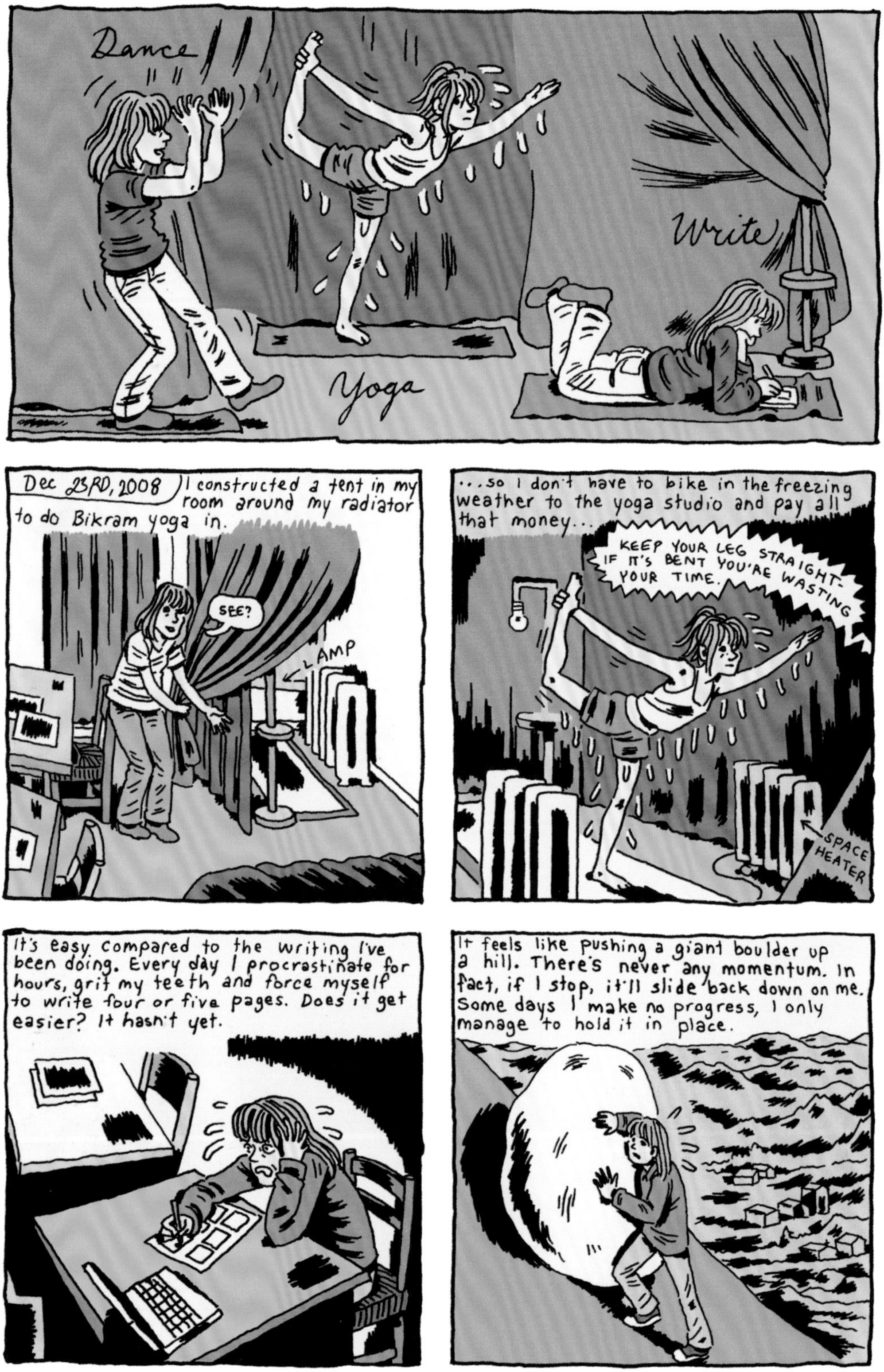

Dance
Yoga
Write
Dec 23RD, 2008
I constructed a tent in my room around my radiator to do Bikram yoga in.
SEE?
LAMP
...so I don't have to bike in the freezing weather to the yoga studio and pay all that money...
KEEP YOUR LEG STRAIGHT- IF IT'S BENT YOU'RE WASTING YOUR TIME.
SPACE HEATER
It's easy compared to the writing I've been doing. Every day I procrastinate for hours, grit my teeth and force myself to write four or five pages. Does it get easier? It hasn't yet.
It feels like pushing a giant boulder up a hill. There's never any momentum. In fact, if I stop, it'll slide back down on me. Some days I make no progress, I only manage to hold it in place.

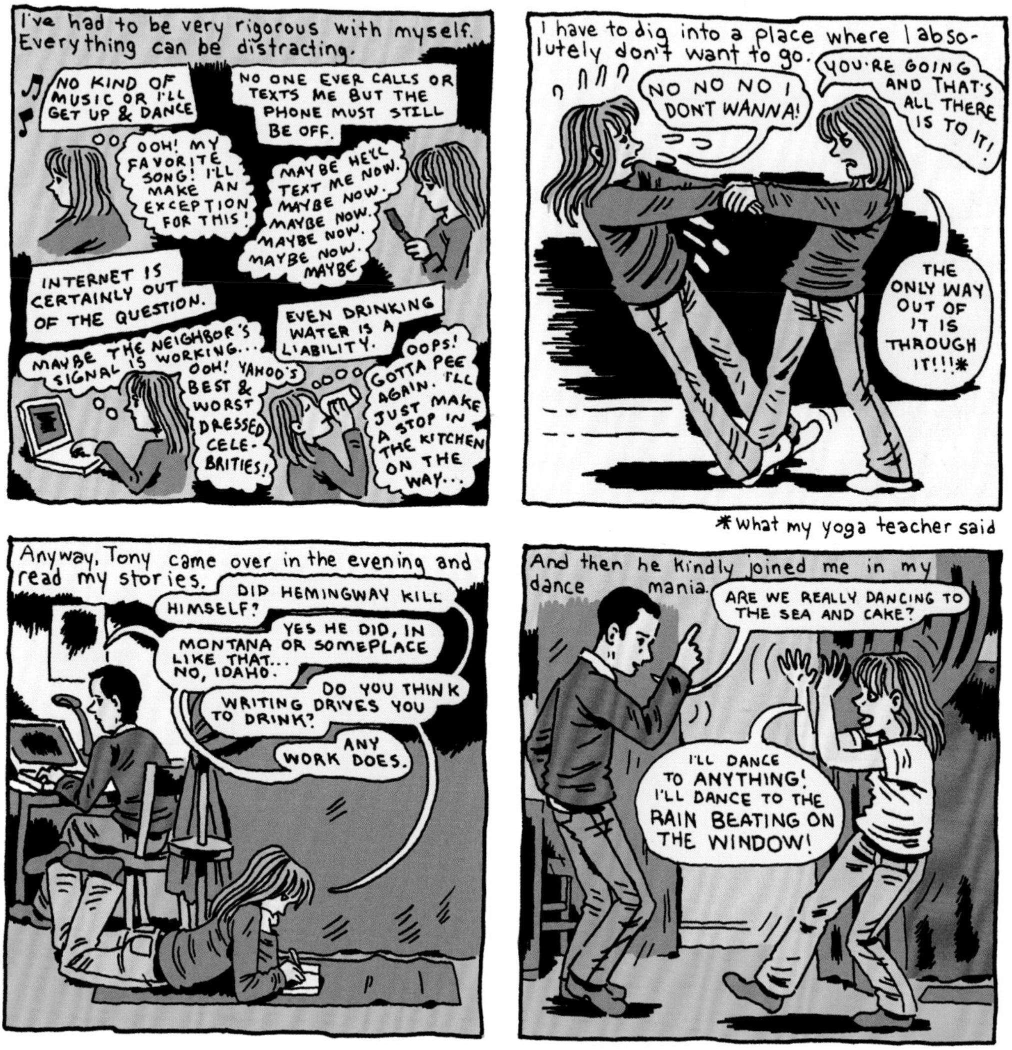
I've had to be very rigorous with myself. Everything can be distracting.
NO KIND OF MUSIC OR I'LL GET UP & DANCE
NO ONE EVER CALLS OR TEXTS ME BUT THE PHONE MUST STILL BE OFF.
OOH! MY FAVORITE SONG! I'LL MAKE AN EXCEPTION FOR THIS!
MAYBE HE'LL TEXT ME NOW. MAYBE NOW. MAYBE NOW. MAYBE NOW. MAYBE NOW. MAYBE
INTERNET IS CERTAINLY OUT OF THE QUESTION.
EVEN DRINKING WATER IS A LIABILITY.
MAYBE THE NEIGHBOR'S SIGNAL IS WORKING...
OOH! YAHOO'S BEST & WORST DRESSED CELE-BRITIES!
OOPS! GOTTA PEE AGAIN. I'LL JUST MAKE A STOP IN THE KITCHEN ON THE WAY...
I have to dig into a place where I abso-lutely don't want to go.
NO NO NO I DON'T WANNA!
YOU'RE GOING AND THAT'S ALL THERE IS TO IT!
THE ONLY WAY OUT OF IT IS THROUGH IT!!!*
*what my yoga teacher said
Anyway, Tony came over in the evening and read my stories.
DID HEMINGWAY KILL HIMSELF?
YES HE DID, IN MONTANA OR SOMEPLACE LIKE THAT... NO, IDAHO.
DO YOU THINK WRITING DRIVES YOU TO DRINK?
ANY WORK DOES.
And then he kindly joined me in my dance mania.
ARE WE REALLY DANCING TO THE SEA AND CAKE?
I'LL DANCE TO ANYTHING! I'LL DANCE TO THE RAIN BEATING ON THE WINDOW!

Late Bloomin'

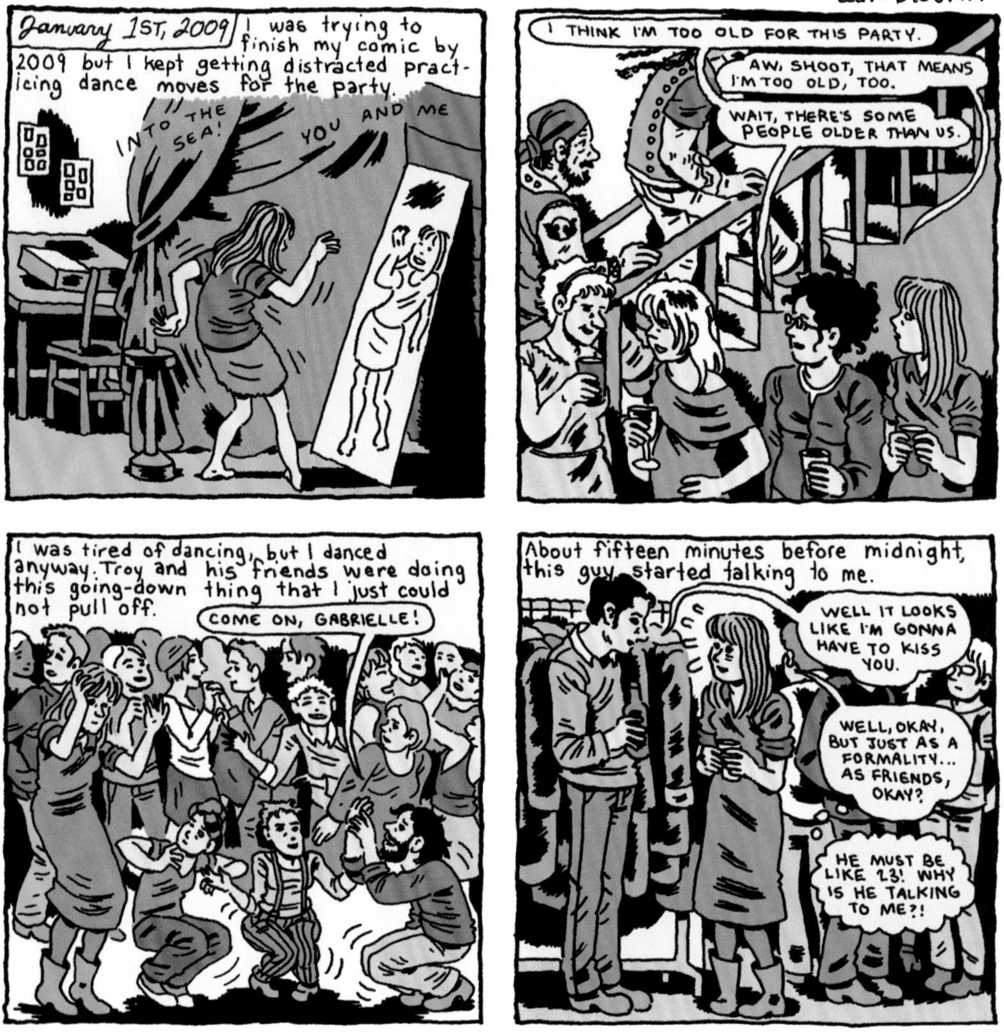
January 1ST, 2009
I was trying to finish my comic by 2009 but I kept getting distracted practicing dance moves for the party.
INTO THE SEA!
YOU AND ME
I THINK I'M TOO OLD FOR THIS PARTY.
AW, SHOOT, THAT MEANS I'M TOO OLD, TOO.
WAIT, THERE'S SOME PEOPLE OLDER THAN US.
I was tired of dancing, but I danced anyway. Troy and his friends were doing this going-down thing that I just could not pull off.
COME ON, GABRIELLE!
About fifteen minutes before midnight, this guy started talking to me.
WELL IT LOOKS LIKE I'M GONNA HAVE TO KISS YOU.
WELL, OKAY, BUT JUST AS A FORMALITY... AS FRIENDS, OKAY?
HE MUST BE LIKE 23! WHY IS HE TALKING TO ME?!

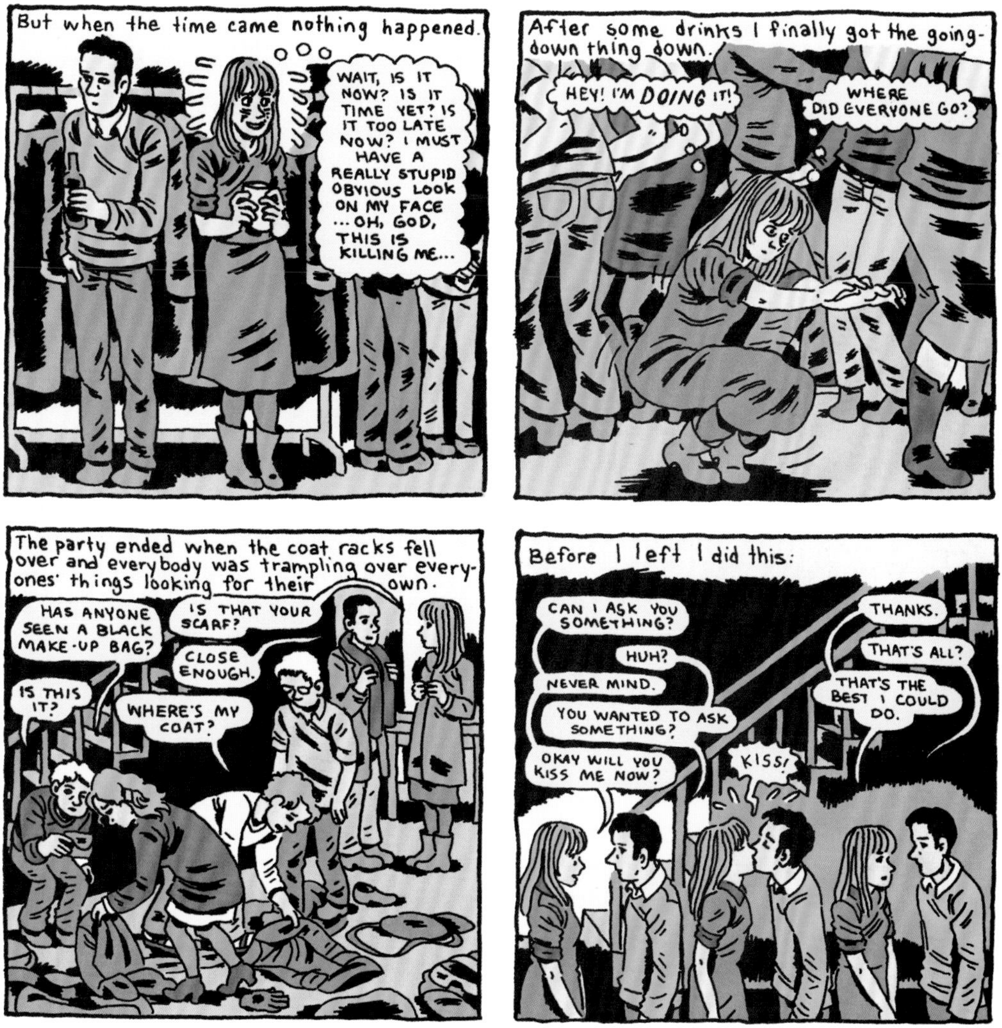
But when the time came nothing happened.
WAIT, IS IT NOW? IS IT TIME YET? IS IT TOO LATE NOW? I MUST HAVE A REALLY STUPID OBVIOUS LOOK ON MY FACE ...OH, GOD, THIS IS KILLING ME...
After some drinks I finally got the going-down thing down.
HEY! I'M DOING IT!
WHERE DID EVERYONE GO?
The party ended when the coat racks fell over and everybody was trampling over everyones' things looking for their own.
HAS ANYONE SEEN A BLACK MAKE-UP BAG?
IS THAT YOUR SCARF?
CLOSE ENOUGH.
IS THIS IT?
WHERE'S MY COAT?
Before I left I did this:
CAN I ASK YOU SOMETHING?
HUH?
NEVER MIND.
YOU WANTED TO ASK SOMETHING?
OKAY WILL YOU KISS ME NOW?
KISS!
THANKS.
THAT'S ALL?
THAT'S THE BEST I COULD DO.

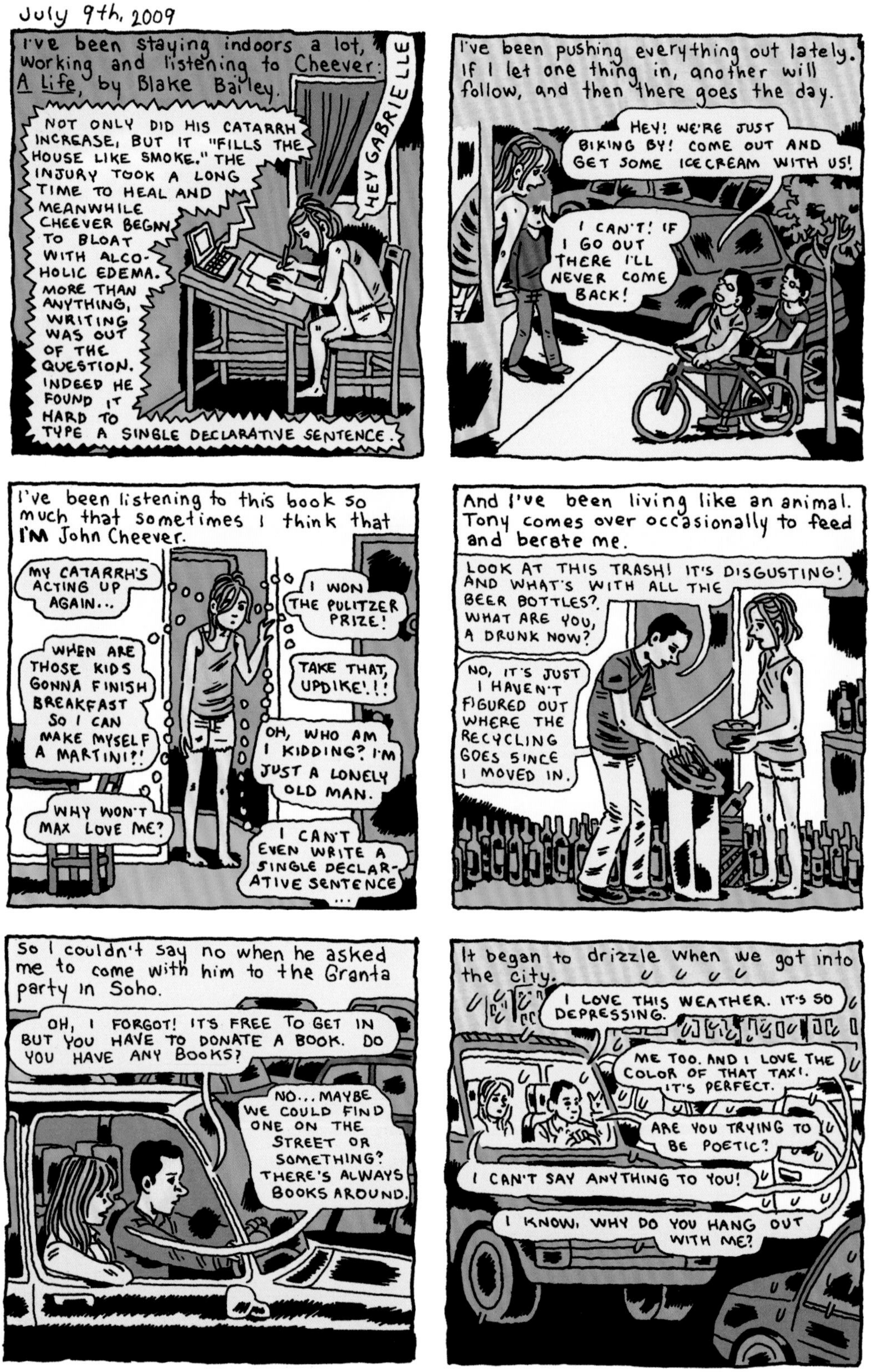
July 9th, 2009
I've been staying indoors a lot, working and listening to Cheever: A Life, by Blake Bailey.
NOT ONLY DID HIS CATARRH INCREASE, BUT IT "FILLS THE HOUSE LIKE SMOKE." THE INJURY TOOK A LONG TIME TO HEAL AND MEANWHILE CHEEVER BEGAN TO BLOAT WITH ALCOHOLIC EDEMA. MORE THAN ANYTHING, WRITING WAS OUT OF THE QUESTION. INDEED HE FOUND IT HARD TO TYPE A SINGLE DECLARATIVE SENTENCE.
HEY GABRIELLE
I've been pushing everything out lately. If I let one thing in, another will follow, and then there goes the day.
HEY! WE'RE JUST BIKING BY! COME OUT AND GET SOME ICECREAM WITH US!
I CAN'T! IF I GO OUT THERE I'LL NEVER COME BACK!
I've been listening to this book so much that sometimes I think that I'M John Cheever.
MY CATARRH'S ACTING UP AGAIN...
WHEN ARE THOSE KIDS GONNA FINISH BREAKFAST SO I CAN MAKE MYSELF A MARTINI?!
WHY WON'T MAX LOVE ME?
I WON THE PULITZER PRIZE!
TAKE THAT, UPDIKE!!!
OH, WHO AM I KIDDING? I'M JUST A LONELY OLD MAN.
I CAN'T EVEN WRITE A SINGLE DECLARATIVE SENTENCE...
And I've been living like an animal. Tony comes over occasionally to feed and berate me.
LOOK AT THIS TRASH! IT'S DISGUSTING! AND WHAT'S WITH ALL THE BEER BOTTLES? WHAT ARE YOU, A DRUNK NOW?
NO, IT'S JUST I HAVEN'T FIGURED OUT WHERE THE RECYCLING GOES SINCE I MOVED IN.
So I couldn't say no when he asked me to come with him to the Granta party in Soho.
OH, I FORGOT! IT'S FREE TO GET IN BUT YOU HAVE TO DONATE A BOOK. DO YOU HAVE ANY BOOKS?
NO... MAYBE WE COULD FIND ONE ON THE STREET OR SOMETHING? THERE'S ALWAYS BOOKS AROUND.
It began to drizzle when we got into the city.
I LOVE THIS WEATHER. IT'S SO DEPRESSING.
ME TOO. AND I LOVE THE COLOR OF THAT TAXI. IT'S PERFECT.
ARE YOU TRYING TO BE POETIC?
I CAN'T SAY ANYTHING TO YOU!
I KNOW. WHY DO YOU HANG OUT WITH ME?

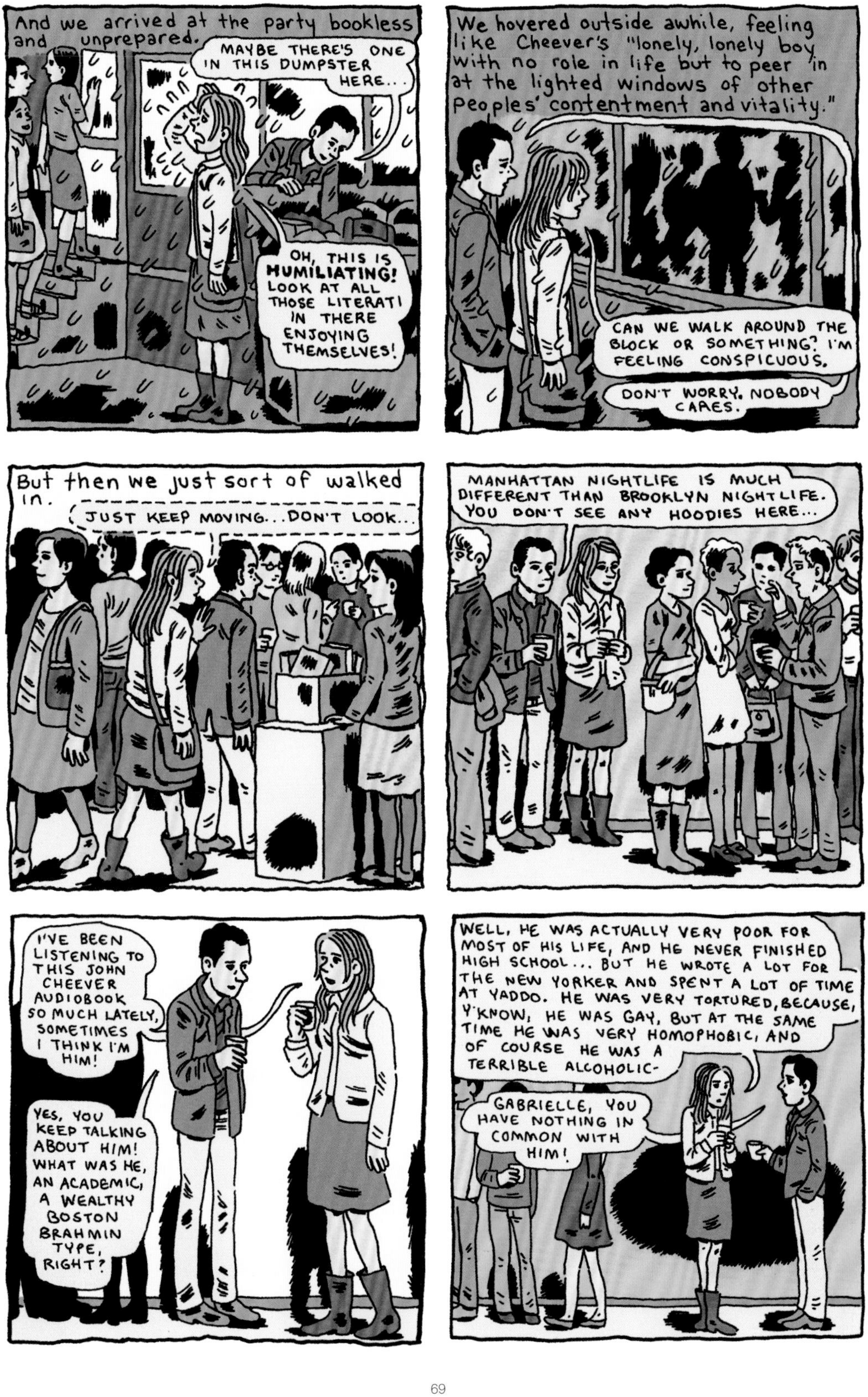
And we arrived at the party bookless and unprepared.
MAYBE THERE'S ONE IN THIS DUMPSTER HERE...
OH, THIS IS HUMILIATING! LOOK AT ALL THOSE LITERATI IN THERE ENJOYING THEMSELVES!
We hovered outside awhile, feeling like Cheever's "lonely, lonely boy with no role in life but to peer in at the lighted windows of other peoples' contentment and vitality."
CAN WE WALK AROUND THE BLOCK OR SOMETHING? I'M FEELING CONSPICUOUS.
DON'T WORRY. NOBODY CARES.
But then we just sort of walked in.
JUST KEEP MOVING...DON'T LOOK...
MANHATTAN NIGHTLIFE IS MUCH DIFFERENT THAN BROOKLYN NIGHTLIFE. YOU DON'T SEE ANY HOODIES HERE...
I'VE BEEN LISTENING TO THIS JOHN CHEEVER AUDIOBOOK SO MUCH LATELY, SOMETIMES I THINK I'M HIM!
YES, YOU KEEP TALKING ABOUT HIM! WHAT WAS HE, AN ACADEMIC, A WEALTHY BOSTON BRAHMIN TYPE, RIGHT?
WELL, HE WAS ACTUALLY VERY POOR FOR MOST OF HIS LIFE, AND HE NEVER FINISHED HIGH SCHOOL... BUT HE WROTE A LOT FOR THE NEW YORKER AND SPENT A LOT OF TIME AT YADDO. HE WAS VERY TORTURED, BECAUSE, Y'KNOW, HE WAS GAY, BUT AT THE SAME TIME HE WAS VERY HOMOPHOBIC, AND OF COURSE HE WAS A TERRIBLE ALCOHOLIC-
GABRIELLE, YOU HAVE NOTHING IN COMMON WITH HIM!

# chapter four
## 2009-2010

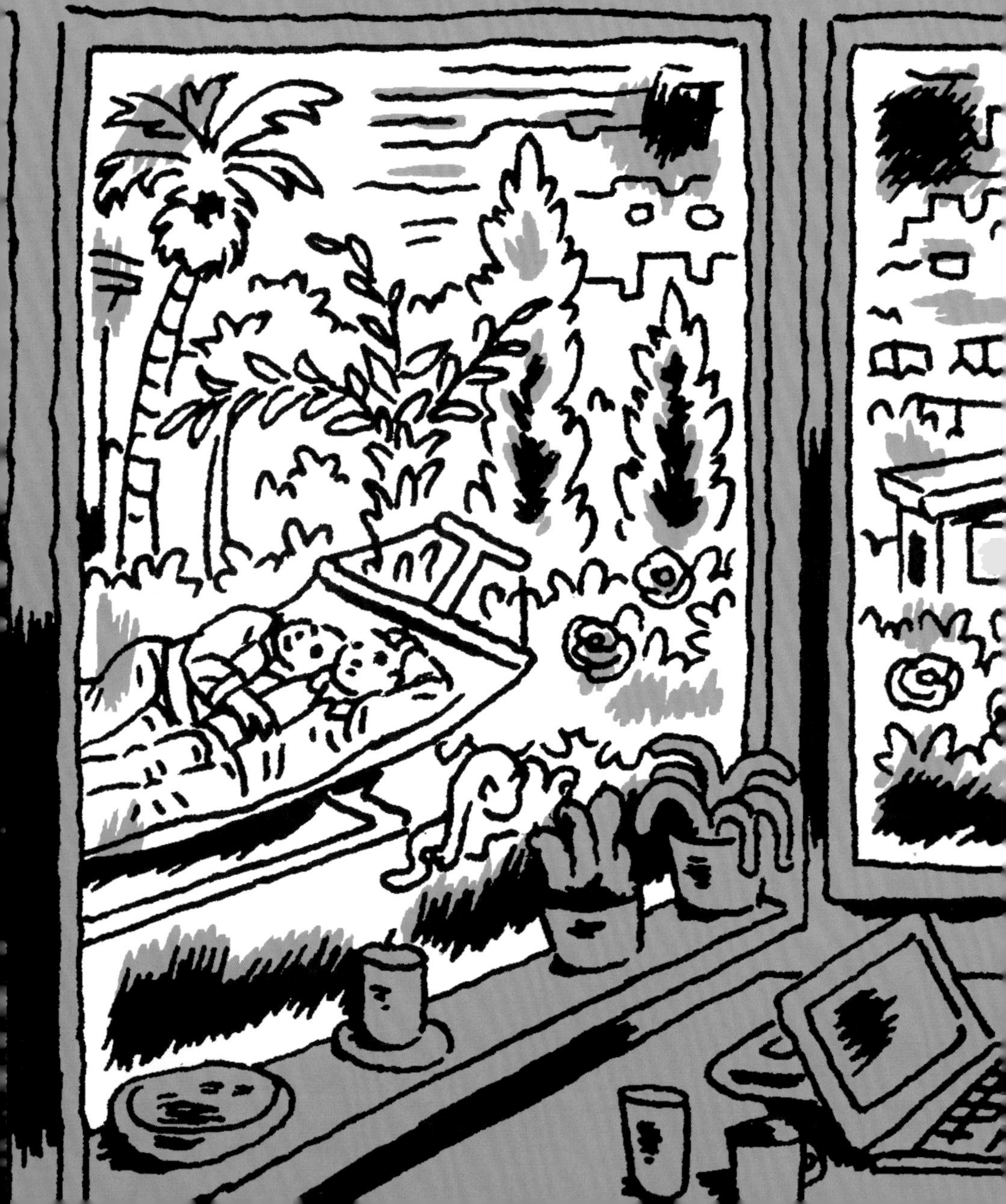

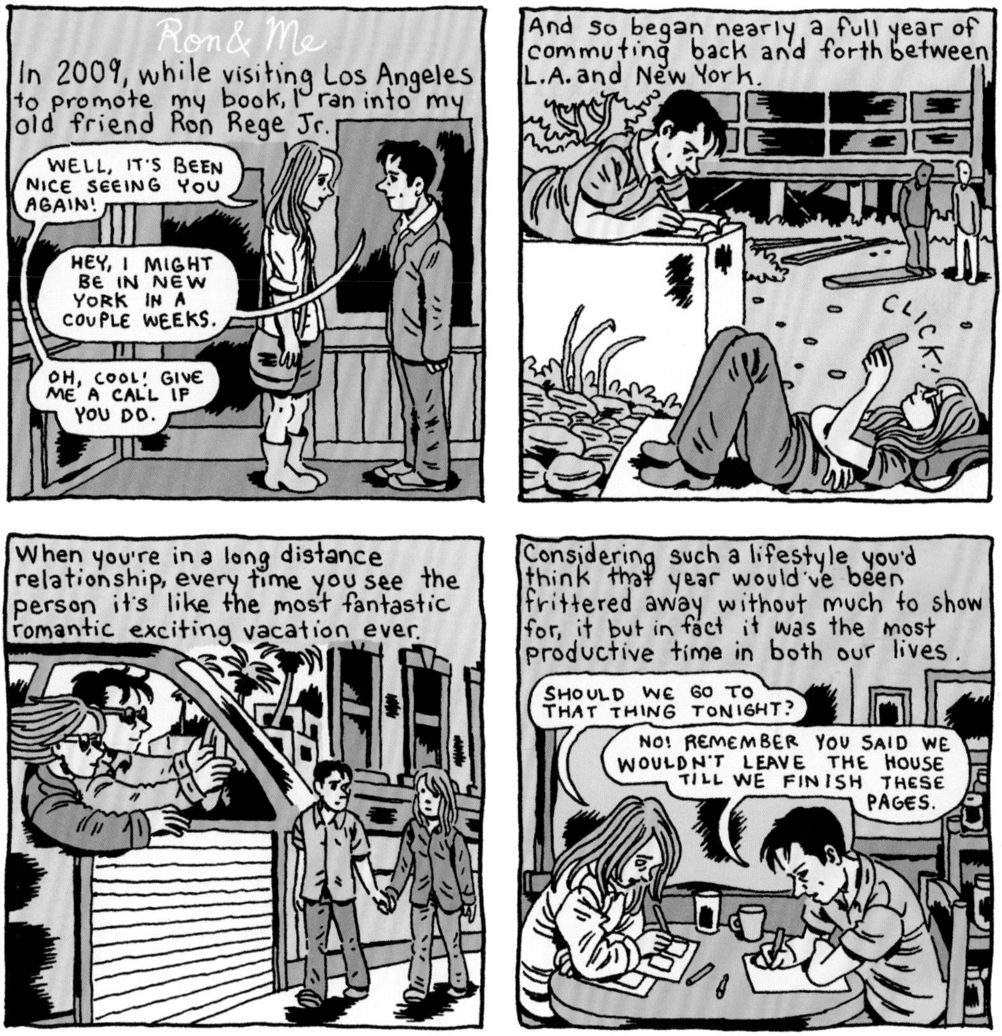
Ron & Me
In 2009, while visiting Los Angeles to promote my book, I ran into my old friend Ron Rege Jr.
WELL, IT'S BEEN NICE SEEING YOU AGAIN!
HEY, I MIGHT BE IN NEW YORK IN A COUPLE WEEKS.
OH, COOL! GIVE ME A CALL IF YOU DO.
And so began nearly a full year of commuting back and forth between L.A. and New York.
CLICK!
When you're in a long distance relationship, every time you see the person it's like the most fantastic romantic exciting vacation ever.
Considering such a lifestyle you'd think that year would've been frittered away without much to show for, it but in fact it was the most productive time in both our lives.
SHOULD WE GO TO THAT THING TONIGHT?
NO! REMEMBER YOU SAID WE WOULDN'T LEAVE THE HOUSE TILL WE FINISH THESE PAGES.

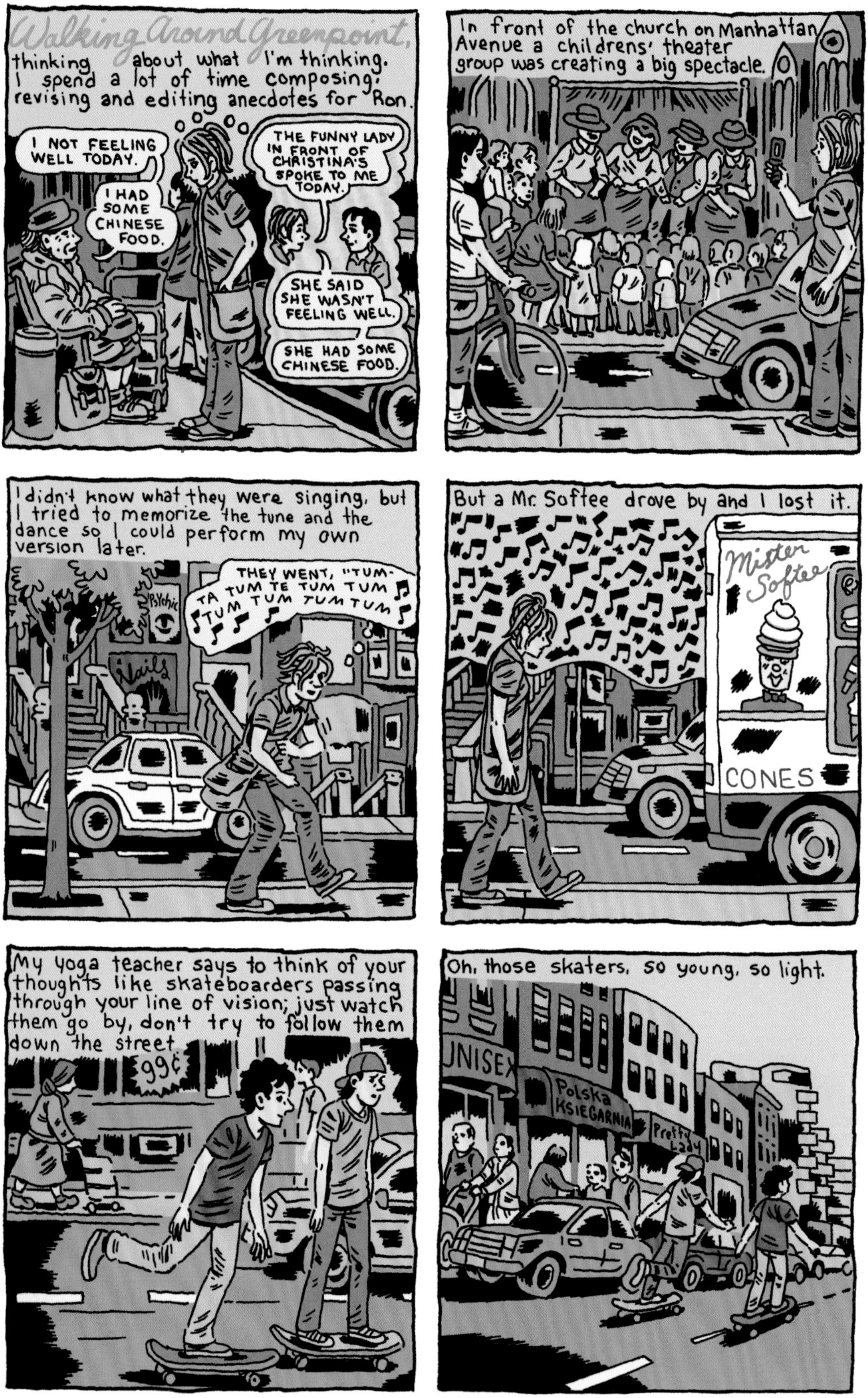
Walking Around Greenpoint, thinking about what I'm thinking. I spend a lot of time composing, revising and editing anecdotes for Ron.
I NOT FEELING WELL TODAY.
I HAD SOME CHINESE FOOD.
THE FUNNY LADY IN FRONT OF CHRISTINA'S SPOKE TO ME TODAY.
SHE SAID SHE WASN'T FEELING WELL.
SHE HAD SOME CHINESE FOOD.
In front of the church on Manhattan Avenue a childrens' theater group was creating a big spectacle.
I didn't know what they were singing, but I tried to memorize the tune and the dance so I could perform my own version later.
Psychic
Nails
THEY WENT, "TUM-TA TUM TE TUM TUM TUM TUM TUM TUM TUM
But a Mr. Softee drove by and I lost it.
Mister Softee
CONES
My yoga teacher says to think of your thoughts like skateboarders passing through your line of vision; just watch them go by, don't try to follow them down the street.
99¢
Oh, those skaters, so young, so light.
UNISEX
Polska KSIEGARNIA
Pretty Lady

# LosAngeles

**August 2nd** Catsitting with Ron in Echo Park. We've been instructed to give Centerfold a lot of love, but the only time she'll have me is before I've had my coffee.

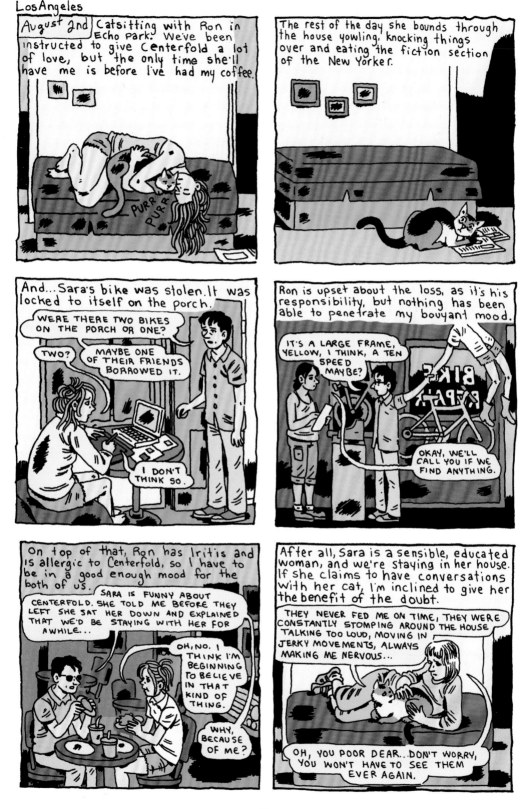

> PURR PURR

The rest of the day she bounds through the house yowling, knocking things over and eating the fiction section of the New Yorker.

And... Sara's bike was stolen. It was locked to itself on the porch.

> WERE THERE TWO BIKES ON THE PORCH OR ONE?

> TWO?

> MAYBE ONE OF THEIR FRIENDS BORROWED IT.

> I DON'T THINK SO.

Ron is upset about the loss, as it's his responsibility, but nothing has been able to penetrate my bouyant mood.

> IT'S A LARGE FRAME, YELLOW, I THINK, A TEN SPEED MAYBE?

> BIKE EXPRESS

> OKAY, WE'LL CALL YOU IF WE FIND ANYTHING.

On top of that, Ron has Iritis and is allergic to Centerfold, so I have to be in a good enough mood for the both of us.

> SARA IS FUNNY ABOUT CENTERFOLD. SHE TOLD ME BEFORE THEY LEFT SHE SAT HER DOWN AND EXPLAINED THAT WE'D BE STAYING WITH HER FOR AWHILE...

> OH, NO. I THINK I'M BEGINNING TO BELIEVE IN THAT KIND OF THING.

> WHY, BECAUSE OF ME?

After all, Sara is a sensible, educated woman, and we're staying in her house. If she claims to have conversations with her cat, I'm inclined to give her the benefit of the doubt.

> THEY NEVER FED ME ON TIME, THEY WERE CONSTANTLY STOMPING AROUND THE HOUSE TALKING TOO LOUD, MOVING IN JERKY MOVEMENTS, ALWAYS MAKING ME NERVOUS...

> OH, YOU POOR DEAR... DON'T WORRY, YOU WON'T HAVE TO SEE THEM EVER AGAIN.

73

August 7th 2009

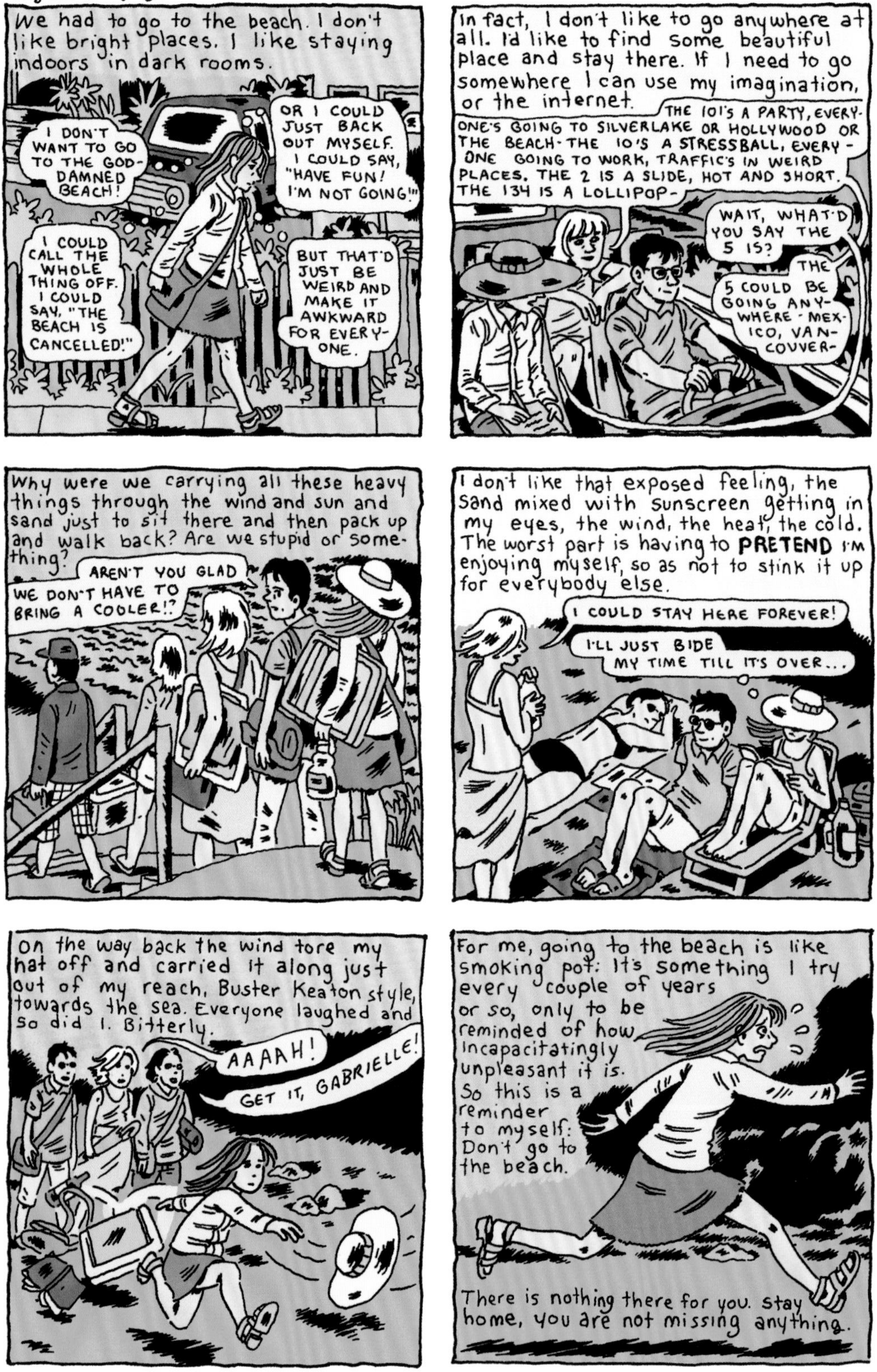
We had to go to the beach. I don't like bright places. I like staying indoors in dark rooms.
I DON'T WANT TO GO TO THE GOD-DAMNED BEACH!
OR I COULD JUST BACK OUT MYSELF. I COULD SAY, "HAVE FUN! I'M NOT GOING!"
I COULD CALL THE WHOLE THING OFF. I COULD SAY, "THE BEACH IS CANCELLED!"
BUT THAT'D JUST BE WEIRD AND MAKE IT AWKWARD FOR EVERYONE.
In fact, I don't like to go anywhere at all. I'd like to find some beautiful place and stay there. If I need to go somewhere I can use my imagination, or the internet.
THE 101'S A PARTY, EVERYONE'S GOING TO SILVERLAKE OR HOLLYWOOD OR THE BEACH - THE 10'S A STRESSBALL, EVERYONE GOING TO WORK, TRAFFIC'S IN WEIRD PLACES. THE 2 IS A SLIDE, HOT AND SHORT. THE 134 IS A LOLLIPOP-
WAIT, WHAT'D YOU SAY THE 5 IS?
THE 5 COULD BE GOING ANYWHERE - MEXICO, VANCOUVER-
Why were we carrying all these heavy things through the wind and sun and sand just to sit there and then pack up and walk back? Are we stupid or something?
AREN'T YOU GLAD WE DON'T HAVE TO BRING A COOLER!?
I don't like that exposed feeling, the sand mixed with sunscreen getting in my eyes, the wind, the heat, the cold. The worst part is having to PRETEND I'm enjoying myself, so as not to stink it up for everybody else.
I COULD STAY HERE FOREVER!
I'LL JUST BIDE MY TIME TILL IT'S OVER...
On the way back the wind tore my hat off and carried it along just out of my reach, Buster Keaton style, towards the sea. Everyone laughed and so did I. Bitterly.
AAAAH!
GET IT, GABRIELLE!
For me, going to the beach is like smoking pot: It's something I try every couple of years or so, only to be reminded of how incapacitatingly unpleasant it is. So this is a reminder to myself: Don't go to the beach.
There is nothing there for you. Stay home, you are not missing anything.

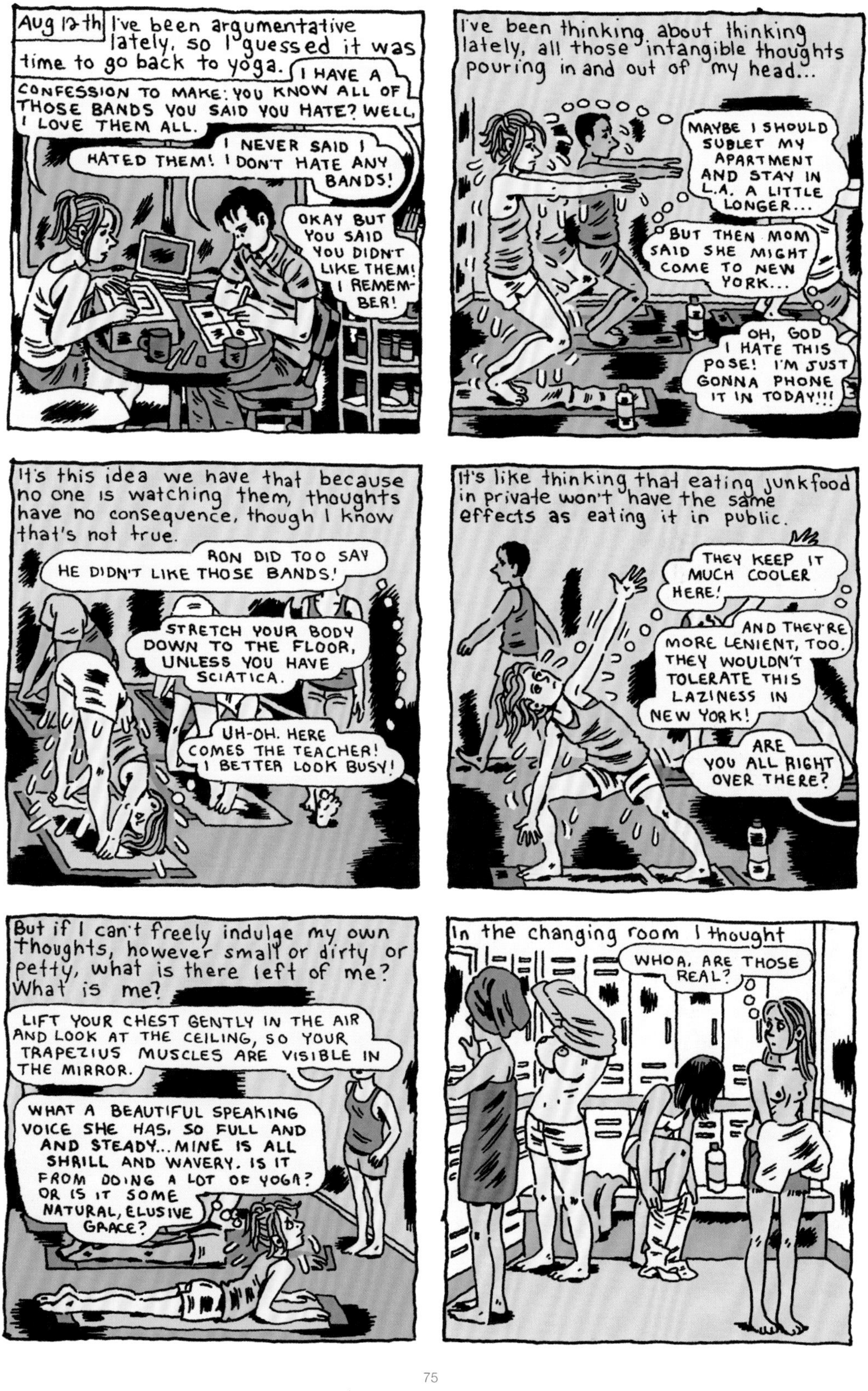
Aug 12th
I've been argumentative lately, so I guessed it was time to go back to yoga.
I HAVE A CONFESSION TO MAKE: YOU KNOW ALL OF THOSE BANDS YOU SAID YOU HATE? WELL, I LOVE THEM ALL.
I NEVER SAID I HATED THEM! I DON'T HATE ANY BANDS!
OKAY BUT YOU SAID YOU DIDN'T LIKE THEM! I REMEMBER!
I've been thinking about thinking lately, all those intangible thoughts pouring in and out of my head...
MAYBE I SHOULD SUBLET MY APARTMENT AND STAY IN L.A. A LITTLE LONGER...
BUT THEN MOM SAID SHE MIGHT COME TO NEW YORK...
OH, GOD I HATE THIS POSE! I'M JUST GONNA PHONE IT IN TODAY!!!
It's this idea we have that because no one is watching them, thoughts have no consequence, though I know that's not true.
RON DID TOO SAY HE DIDN'T LIKE THOSE BANDS!
STRETCH YOUR BODY DOWN TO THE FLOOR, UNLESS YOU HAVE SCIATICA.
UH-OH. HERE COMES THE TEACHER! I BETTER LOOK BUSY!
It's like thinking that eating junkfood in private won't have the same effects as eating it in public.
THEY KEEP IT MUCH COOLER HERE!
AND THEY'RE MORE LENIENT, TOO. THEY WOULDN'T TOLERATE THIS LAZINESS IN NEW YORK!
ARE YOU ALL RIGHT OVER THERE?
But if I can't freely indulge my own thoughts, however small or dirty or petty, what is there left of me? What is me?
LIFT YOUR CHEST GENTLY IN THE AIR AND LOOK AT THE CEILING, SO YOUR TRAPEZIUS MUSCLES ARE VISIBLE IN THE MIRROR.
WHAT A BEAUTIFUL SPEAKING VOICE SHE HAS, SO FULL AND AND STEADY... MINE IS ALL SHRILL AND WAVERY. IS IT FROM DOING A LOT OF YOGA? OR IS IT SOME NATURAL, ELUSIVE GRACE?
In the changing room I thought
WHOA, ARE THOSE REAL?

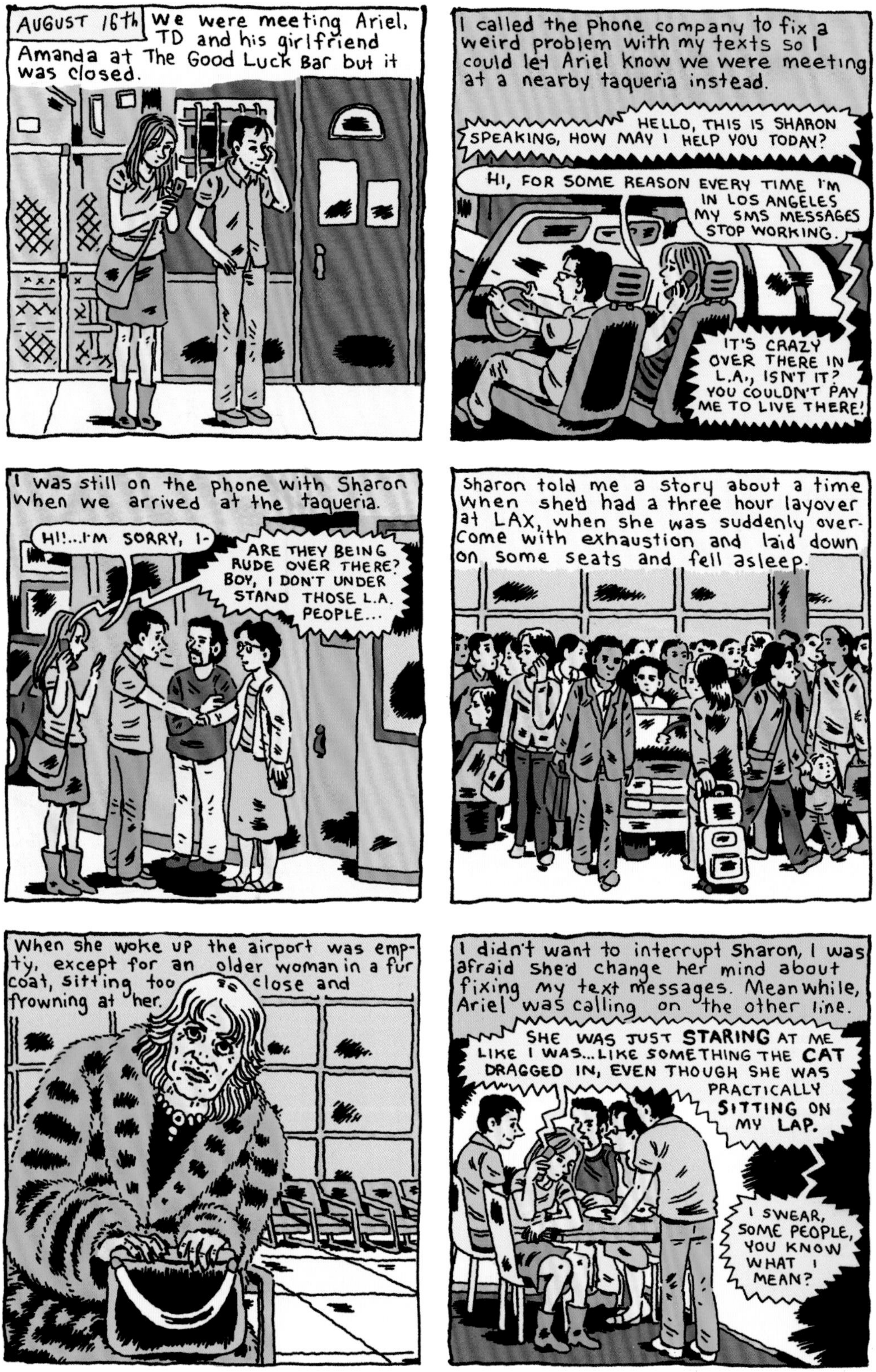
AUGUST 16th We were meeting Ariel, TD and his girlfriend Amanda at The Good Luck Bar but it was closed.
I called the phone company to fix a weird problem with my texts so I could let Ariel know we were meeting at a nearby taqueria instead.
HELLO, THIS IS SHARON SPEAKING, HOW MAY I HELP YOU TODAY?
HI, FOR SOME REASON EVERY TIME I'M IN LOS ANGELES MY SMS MESSAGES STOP WORKING.
IT'S CRAZY OVER THERE IN L.A., ISN'T IT? YOU COULDN'T PAY ME TO LIVE THERE!
I was still on the phone with Sharon when we arrived at the taqueria.
HI!...I'M SORRY, I-
ARE THEY BEING RUDE OVER THERE? BOY, I DON'T UNDER STAND THOSE L.A. PEOPLE...
Sharon told me a story about a time when she'd had a three hour layover at LAX, when she was suddenly over-come with exhaustion and laid down on some seats and fell asleep.
When she woke up the airport was emp-ty, except for an older woman in a fur coat, sitting too close and frowning at her.
I didn't want to interrupt Sharon, I was afraid she'd change her mind about fixing my text messages. Meanwhile, Ariel was calling on the other line.
SHE WAS JUST STARING AT ME LIKE I WAS...LIKE SOMETHING THE CAT DRAGGED IN, EVEN THOUGH SHE WAS PRACTICALLY SITTING ON MY LAP.
I SWEAR, SOME PEOPLE, YOU KNOW WHAT I MEAN?

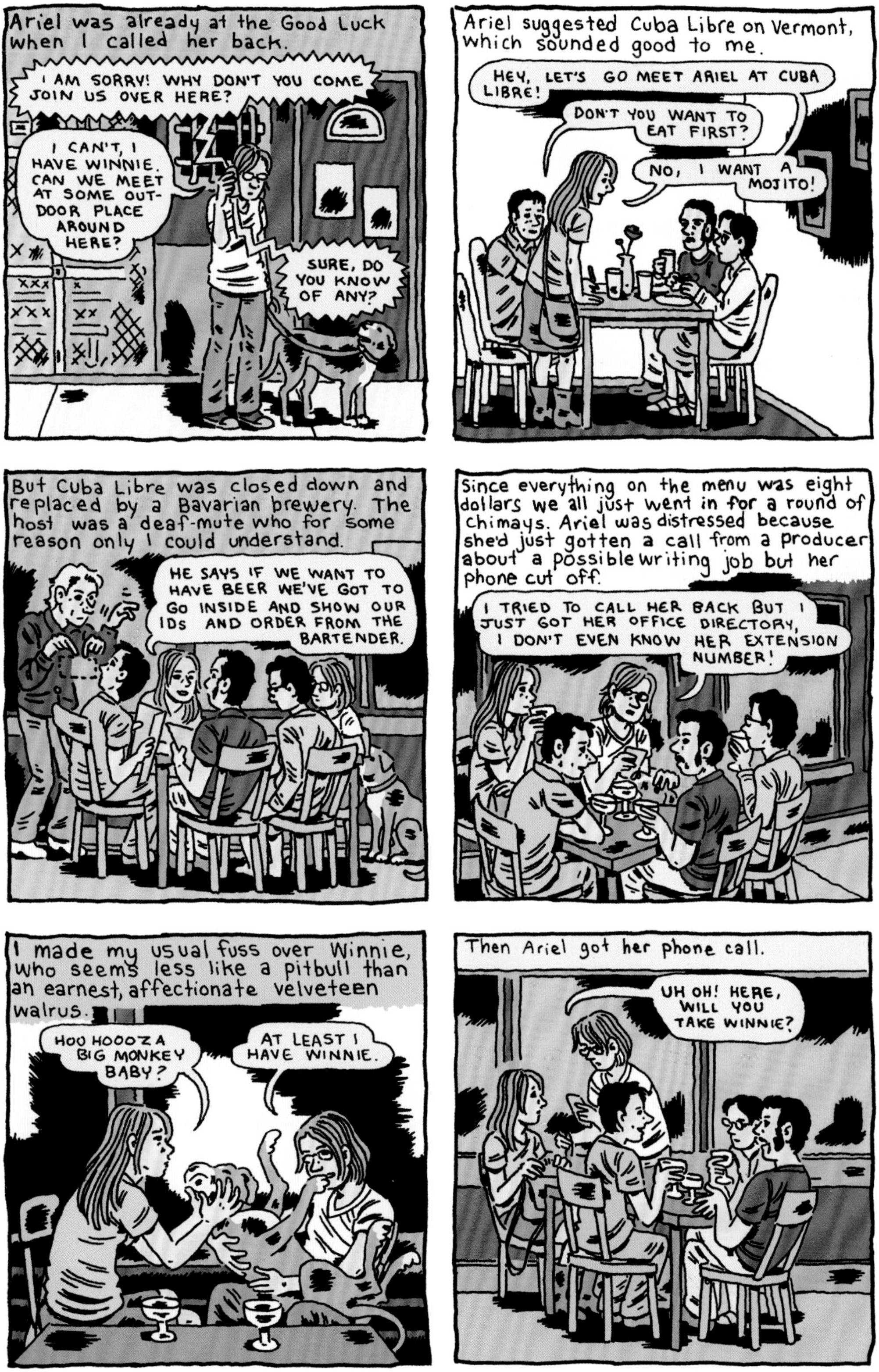
Ariel was already at the Good Luck when I called her back.
I AM SORRY! WHY DON'T YOU COME JOIN US OVER HERE?
I CAN'T, I HAVE WINNIE. CAN WE MEET AT SOME OUT-DOOR PLACE AROUND HERE?
SURE, DO YOU KNOW OF ANY?
Ariel suggested Cuba Libre on Vermont, which sounded good to me.
HEY, LET'S GO MEET ARIEL AT CUBA LIBRE!
DON'T YOU WANT TO EAT FIRST?
NO, I WANT A MOJITO!
But Cuba Libre was closed down and replaced by a Bavarian brewery. The host was a deaf-mute who for some reason only I could understand.
HE SAYS IF WE WANT TO HAVE BEER WE'VE GOT TO GO INSIDE AND SHOW OUR IDS AND ORDER FROM THE BARTENDER.
Since everything on the menu was eight dollars we all just went in for a round of chimays. Ariel was distressed because she'd just gotten a call from a producer about a possible writing job but her phone cut off.
I TRIED TO CALL HER BACK BUT I JUST GOT HER OFFICE DIRECTORY, I DON'T EVEN KNOW HER EXTENSION NUMBER!
I made my usual fuss over Winnie, who seems less like a pitbull than an earnest, affectionate velveteen walrus.
HOO HOOOZ A BIG MONKEY BABY?
AT LEAST I HAVE WINNIE.
Then Ariel got her phone call.
UH OH! HERE, WILL YOU TAKE WINNIE?

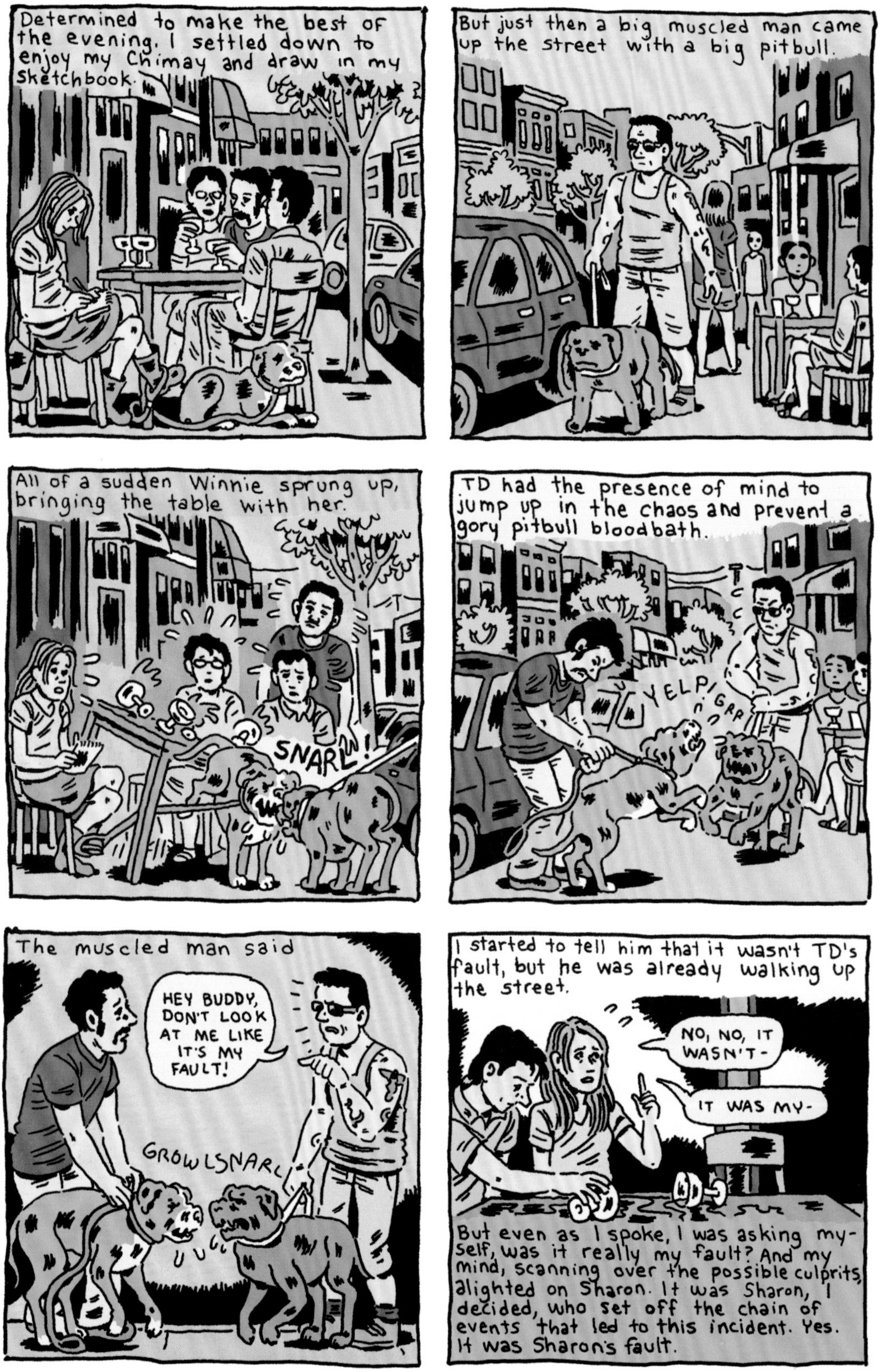
Determined to make the best of the evening, I settled down to enjoy my Chimay and draw in my sketchbook.
But just then a big muscled man came up the street with a big pitbull.
All of a sudden Winnie sprung up, bringing the table with her.
SNARL!
TD had the presence of mind to jump up in the chaos and prevent a gory pitbull bloodbath.
YELP! GRR
The muscled man said
HEY BUDDY, DON'T LOOK AT ME LIKE IT'S MY FAULT!
GROWLSNARL
I started to tell him that it wasn't TD's fault, but he was already walking up the street.
NO, NO, IT WASN'T-
IT WAS MY-
But even as I spoke, I was asking myself, was it really my fault? And my mind, scanning over the possible culprits, alighted on Sharon. It was Sharon, I decided, who set off the chain of events that led to this incident. Yes. It was Sharon's fault.

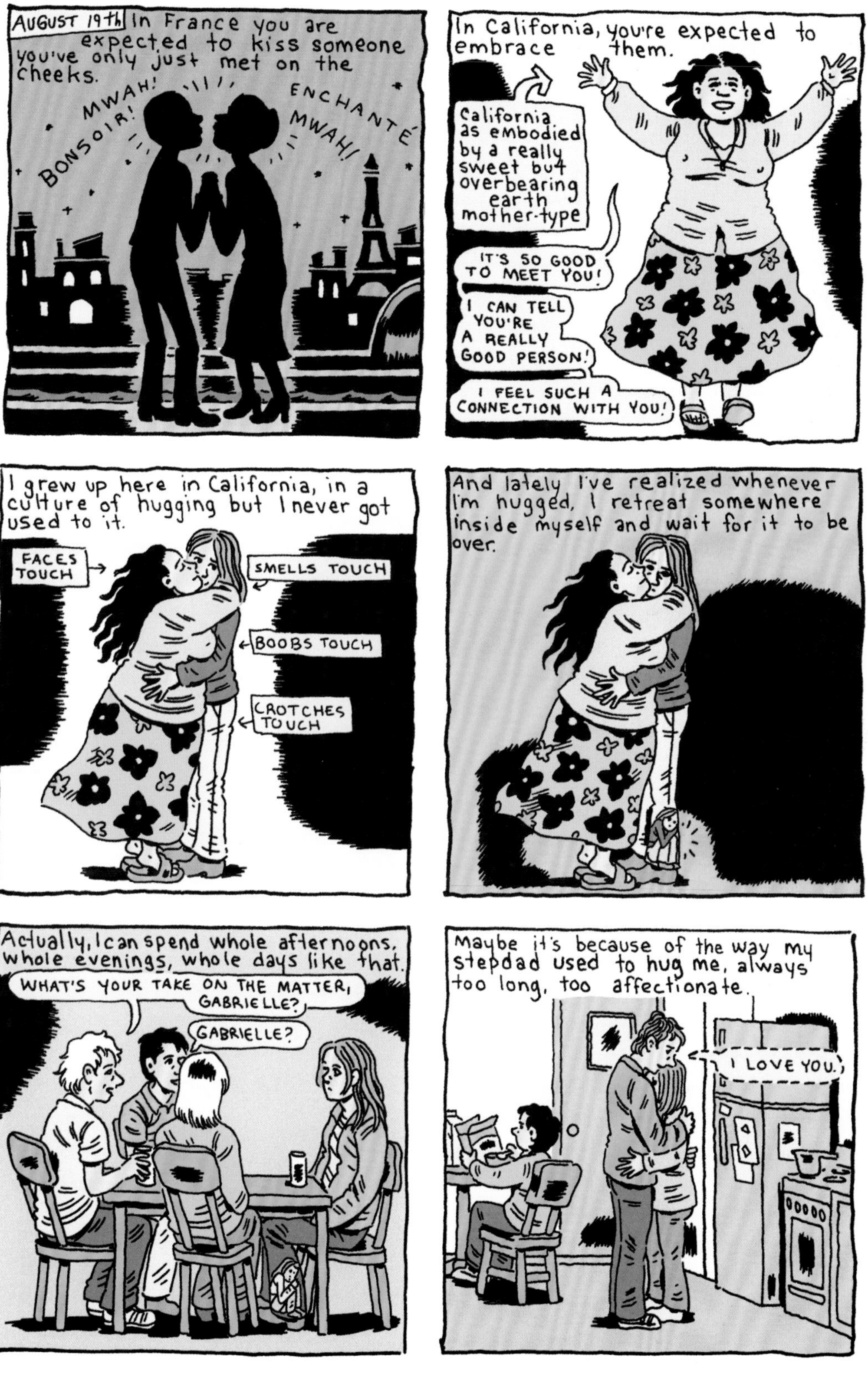
AUGUST 19th In France you are expected to kiss someone you've only just met on the cheeks.
MWAH!
BONSOIR!
ENCHANTÉ
MWAH!
In California, you're expected to embrace them.
California as embodied by a really sweet but overbearing earth mother-type
IT'S SO GOOD TO MEET YOU!
I CAN TELL YOU'RE A REALLY GOOD PERSON!
I FEEL SUCH A CONNECTION WITH YOU!
I grew up here in California, in a culture of hugging but I never got used to it.
FACES TOUCH
SMELLS TOUCH
BOOBS TOUCH
CROTCHES TOUCH
And lately I've realized whenever I'm hugged, I retreat somewhere inside myself and wait for it to be over.
Actually, I can spend whole afternoons, whole evenings, whole days like that.
WHAT'S YOUR TAKE ON THE MATTER, GABRIELLE?
GABRIELLE?
Maybe it's because of the way my stepdad used to hug me, always too long, too affectionate.
I LOVE YOU.

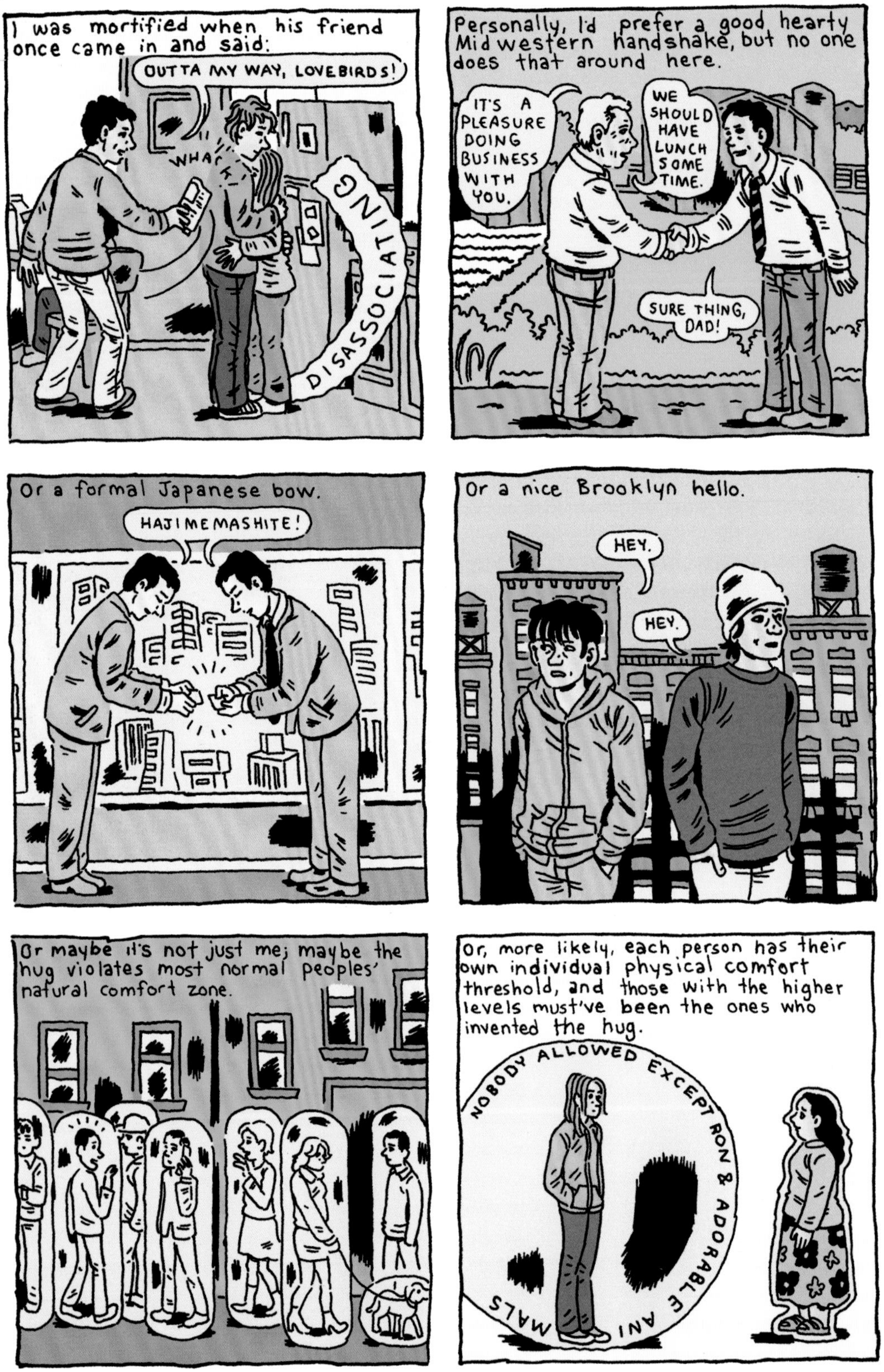
I was mortified when his friend once came in and said:
OUTTA MY WAY, LOVEBIRDS!
WHAC
DISASSOCIATING
Personally, I'd prefer a good hearty Midwestern handshake, but no one does that around here.
IT'S A PLEASURE DOING BUSINESS WITH YOU.
WE SHOULD HAVE LUNCH SOME TIME.
SURE THING, DAD!
Or a formal Japanese bow.
HAJIMEMASHITE!
Or a nice Brooklyn hello.
HEY.
HEY.
Or maybe it's not just me; maybe the hug violates most normal peoples' natural comfort zone.
Or, more likely, each person has their own individual physical comfort threshold, and those with the higher levels must've been the ones who invented the hug.
NOBODY ALLOWED EXCEPT RON & ADORABLE ANIMALS

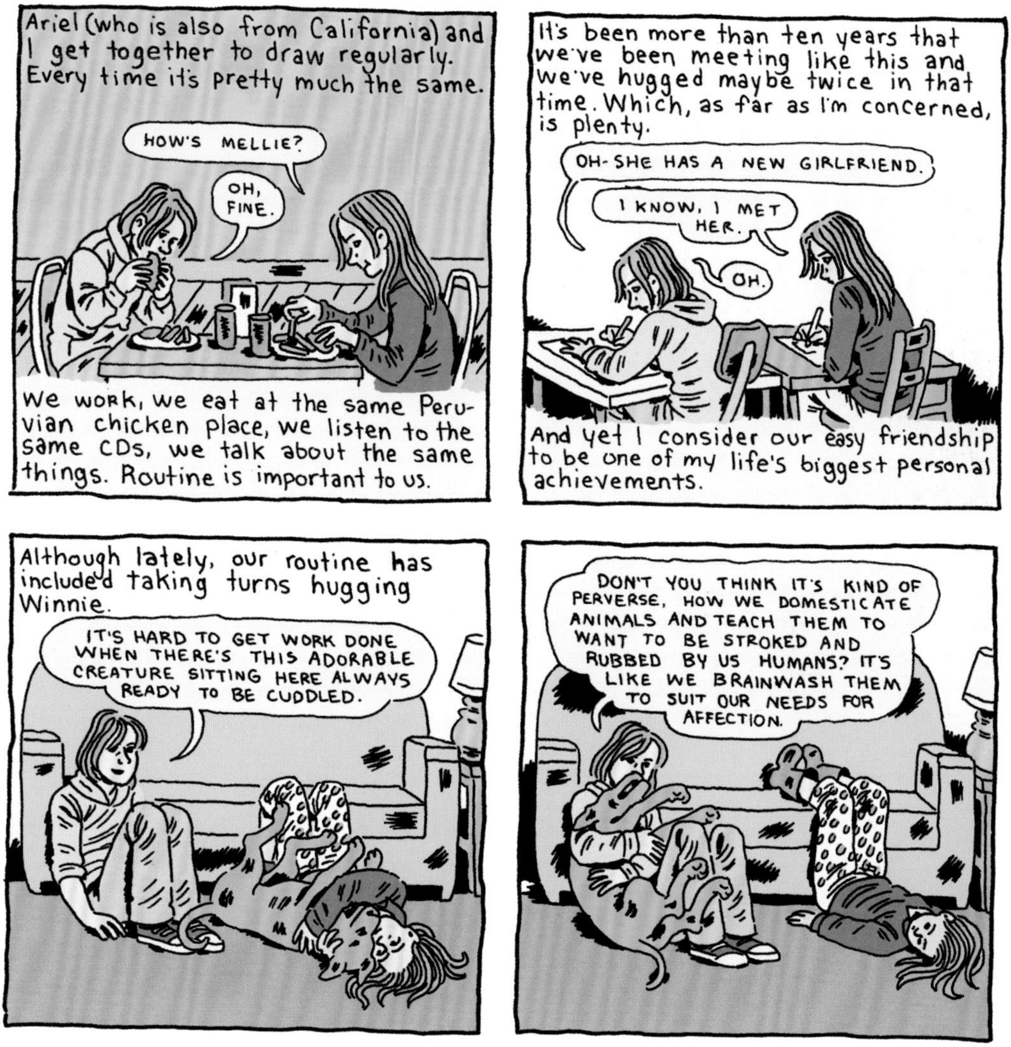

Ariel (who is also from California) and I get together to draw regularly. Every time it's pretty much the same.
HOW'S MELLIE?
OH, FINE.
We work, we eat at the same Peruvian chicken place, we listen to the same CDs, we talk about the same things. Routine is important to us.
It's been more than ten years that we've been meeting like this and we've hugged maybe twice in that time. Which, as far as I'm concerned, is plenty.
OH- SHE HAS A NEW GIRLFRIEND.
I KNOW, I MET HER.
OH.
And yet I consider our easy friendship to be one of my life's biggest personal achievements.
Although lately, our routine has included taking turns hugging Winnie.
IT'S HARD TO GET WORK DONE WHEN THERE'S THIS ADORABLE CREATURE SITTING HERE ALWAYS READY TO BE CUDDLED.
DON'T YOU THINK IT'S KIND OF PERVERSE, HOW WE DOMESTICATE ANIMALS AND TEACH THEM TO WANT TO BE STROKED AND RUBBED BY US HUMANS? IT'S LIKE WE BRAINWASH THEM TO SUIT OUR NEEDS FOR AFFECTION.

From Touching Peace: Practicing the Art of Mindful Living, by Thích Nhất Hạnh

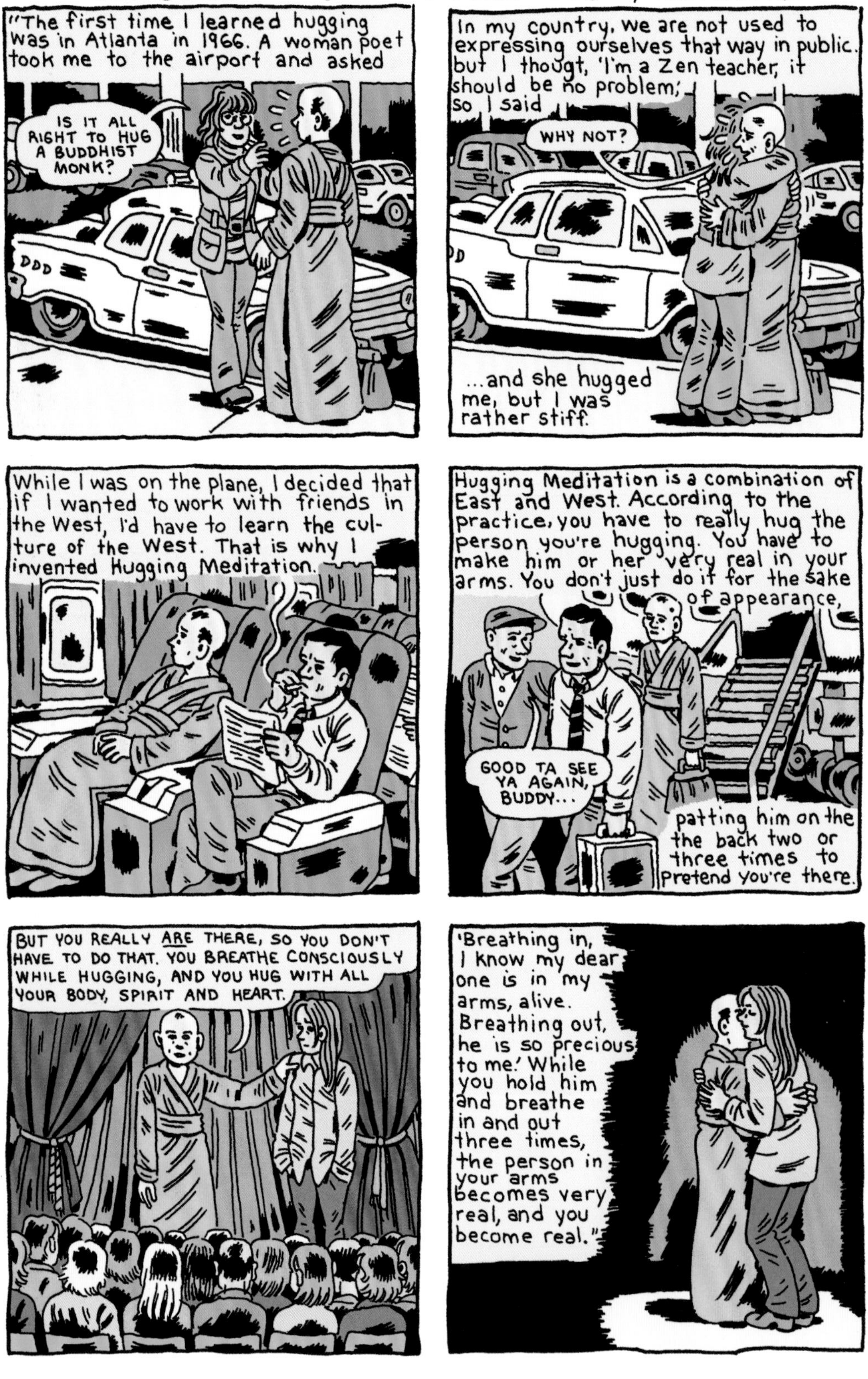
"The first time I learned hugging was in Atlanta in 1966. A woman poet took me to the airport and asked
IS IT ALL RIGHT TO HUG A BUDDHIST MONK?
DDD
In my country, we are not used to expressing ourselves that way in public. but I thougt, 'I'm a Zen teacher, it should be no problem,' so I said
WHY NOT?
...and she hugged me, but I was rather stiff.
While I was on the plane, I decided that if I wanted to work with friends in the West, I'd have to learn the culture of the West. That is why I invented Hugging Meditation.
Hugging Meditation is a combination of East and West. According to the practice, you have to really hug the person you're hugging. You have to make him or her very real in your arms. You don't just do it for the sake of appearance,
GOOD TA SEE YA AGAIN, BUDDY...
patting him on the the back two or three times to pretend you're there.
BUT YOU REALLY ARE THERE, SO YOU DON'T HAVE TO DO THAT. YOU BREATHE CONSCIOUSLY WHILE HUGGING, AND YOU HUG WITH ALL YOUR BODY, SPIRIT AND HEART.
'Breathing in, I know my dear one is in my arms, alive. Breathing out, he is so precious to me.' While you hold him and breathe in and out three times, the person in your arms becomes very real, and you become real."

**Oct 8th** Going to Minneapolis for a presentation at a book festival and a talk at an art school.

I HAVE TO SPEAK FOR AN HOUR! WHAT DO I HAVE TO SAY THAT'LL FILL AN HOUR?

IT'S A COMICS CLASS, RIGHT?

YEAH.

THAT'S EASY. COMICS CLASSES ARE ALWAYS THE SAME.

YOU JUST TALK ABOUT YOUR CAREER FOR AWHILE, AND THEN THERE'S A Q&A, AND THEY REALLY ONLY WANT TO KNOW ONE THING.

WHAT'S THAT?

'DO YOU MAKE A LIVING FROM YOUR COMICS?'

'HOW CAN I MAKE MONEY FROM MY COMICS.'

I feel I need to disclaim this "story." I set myself the task of reporting my trip, though there's not much to it, and I can't back out now. It's my compulsion to do this, it's my way, I suppose, of fighting against the feeling of meaninglessness constantly crowding in.

It was already winter in Minneapolis, and to fortify myself against the cold I bought a package of peanut butter cups. I was just stuffing the first one in my mouth when Tomk and Nikki arrived.

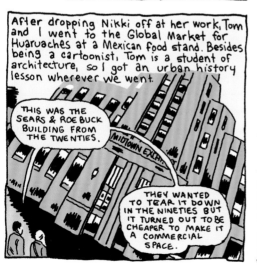

After dropping Nikki off at her work, Tom and I went to the Global Market for Huaruaches at a Mexican food stand. Besides being a cartoonist, Tom is a student of architecture, so I got an urban history lesson wherever we went.

THIS WAS THE SEARS & ROEBUCK BUILDING FROM THE TWENTIES.

THEY WANTED TO TEAR IT DOWN IN THE NINETIES BUT IT TURNED OUT TO BE CHEAPER TO MAKE IT A COMMERCIAL SPACE.

Then we had hamburgers at Grumpy's with Michael Drivas from Big Brain Comics, who taught me a little about football.

SO, HE WAS THE STAR OF THE PACKERS AND NOW HE'S THE STAR OF THE VIKINGS, AND THE TWO TEAMS ARE PLAYING EACH OTHER?

WELL, HE WAS WITH THE JETS IN BE-TWEEN.

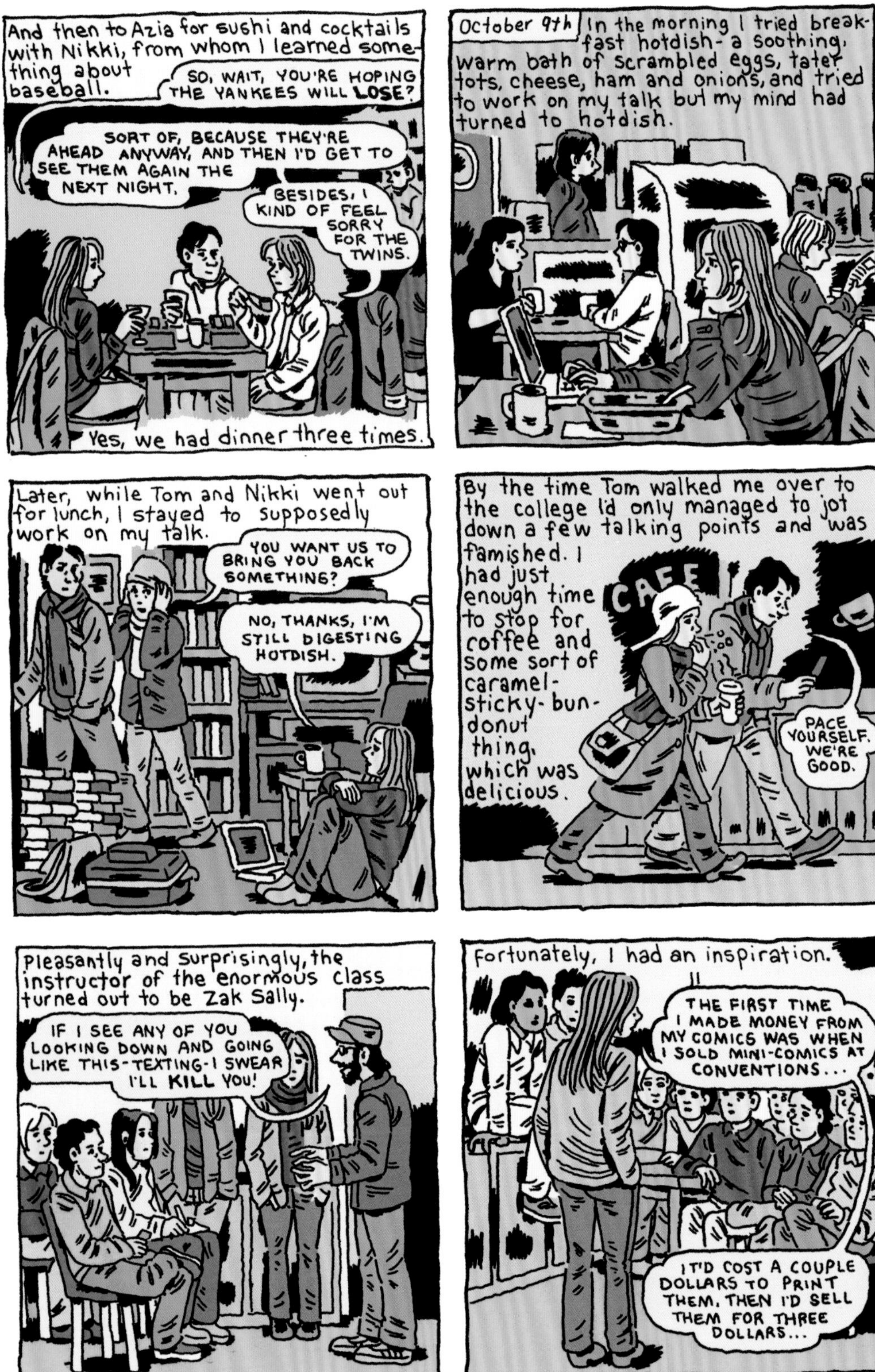
And then to Azia for sushi and cocktails with Nikki, from whom I learned something about baseball.
SO, WAIT, YOU'RE HOPING THE YANKEES WILL **LOSE**?
SORT OF, BECAUSE THEY'RE AHEAD ANYWAY, AND THEN I'D GET TO SEE THEM AGAIN THE NEXT NIGHT.
BESIDES, I KIND OF FEEL SORRY FOR THE TWINS.
Yes, we had dinner three times.
October 9th
In the morning I tried breakfast hotdish- a soothing, warm bath of scrambled eggs, tater tots, cheese, ham and onions, and tried to work on my talk but my mind had turned to hotdish.
Later, while Tom and Nikki went out for lunch, I stayed to supposedly work on my talk.
YOU WANT US TO BRING YOU BACK SOMETHING?
NO, THANKS, I'M STILL DIGESTING HOTDISH.
By the time Tom walked me over to the college I'd only managed to jot down a few talking points and was famished. I had just enough time to stop for coffee and some sort of caramel-sticky-bun-donut thing, which was delicious.
CAFE
PACE YOURSELF. WE'RE GOOD.
Pleasantly and surprisingly, the instructor of the enormous class turned out to be Zak Sally.
IF I SEE ANY OF YOU LOOKING DOWN AND GOING LIKE THIS-TEXTING-I SWEAR I'LL **KILL** YOU!
Fortunately, I had an inspiration.
THE FIRST TIME I MADE MONEY FROM MY COMICS WAS WHEN I SOLD MINI-COMICS AT CONVENTIONS...
IT'D COST A COUPLE DOLLARS TO PRINT THEM, THEN I'D SELL THEM FOR THREE DOLLARS...

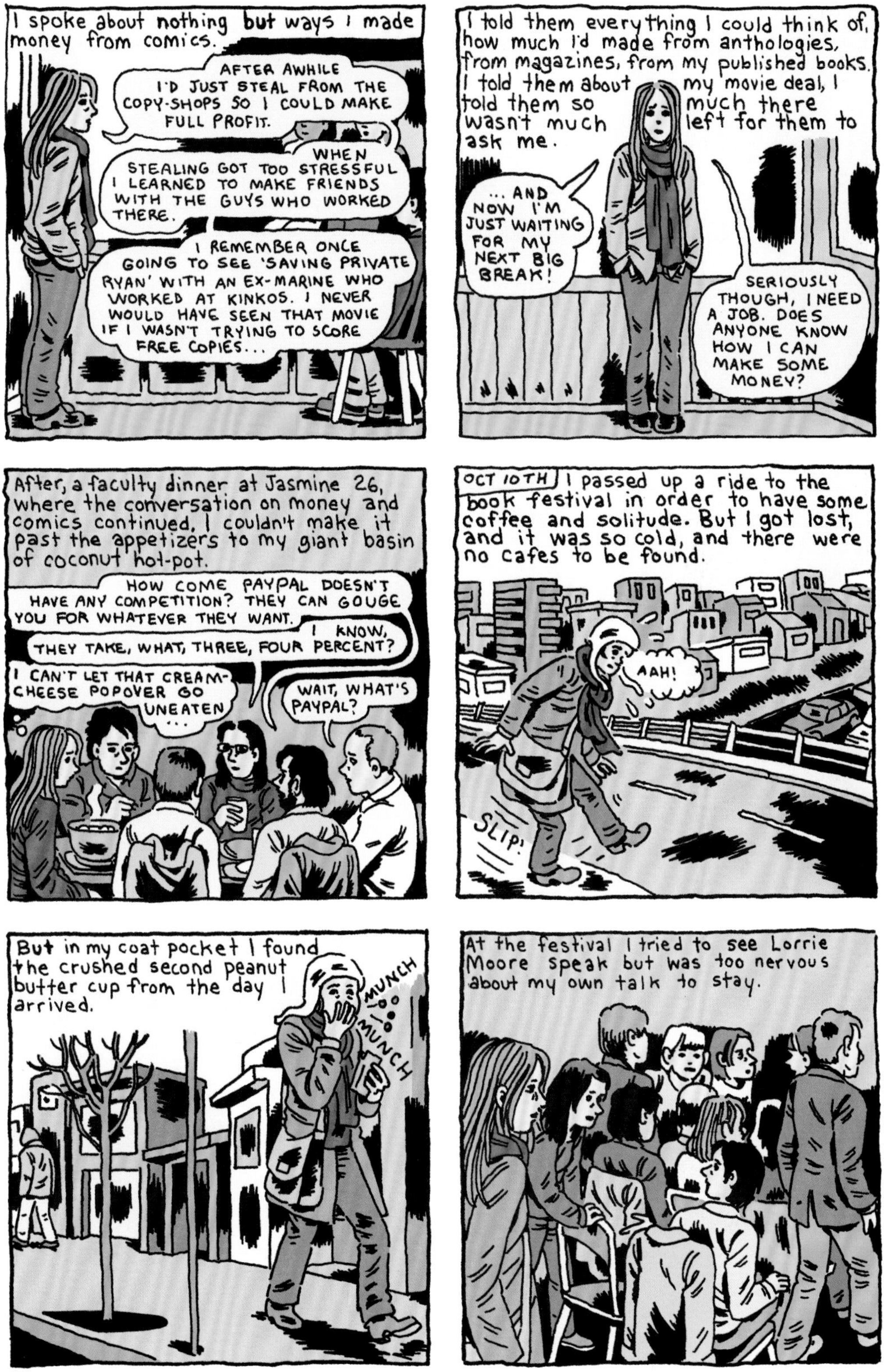
I spoke about nothing but ways I made money from comics.
AFTER AWHILE I'D JUST STEAL FROM THE COPY-SHOPS SO I COULD MAKE FULL PROFIT.
WHEN STEALING GOT TOO STRESSFUL I LEARNED TO MAKE FRIENDS WITH THE GUYS WHO WORKED THERE.
I REMEMBER ONCE GOING TO SEE 'SAVING PRIVATE RYAN' WITH AN EX-MARINE WHO WORKED AT KINKOS. I NEVER WOULD HAVE SEEN THAT MOVIE IF I WASN'T TRYING TO SCORE FREE COPIES...
I told them everything I could think of, how much I'd made from anthologies, from magazines, from my published books. I told them about my movie deal, I told them so much there wasn't much left for them to ask me.
... AND NOW I'M JUST WAITING FOR MY NEXT BIG BREAK!
SERIOUSLY THOUGH, I NEED A JOB. DOES ANYONE KNOW HOW I CAN MAKE SOME MONEY?
After, a faculty dinner at Jasmine 26, where the conversation on money and comics continued, I couldn't make it past the appetizers to my giant basin of coconut hot-pot.
HOW COME PAYPAL DOESN'T HAVE ANY COMPETITION? THEY CAN GOUGE YOU FOR WHATEVER THEY WANT.
I KNOW, THEY TAKE, WHAT, THREE, FOUR PERCENT?
I CAN'T LET THAT CREAM-CHEESE POPOVER GO UNEATEN ...
WAIT, WHAT'S PAYPAL?
OCT 10TH I passed up a ride to the book festival in order to have some coffee and solitude. But I got lost, and it was so cold, and there were no cafes to be found.
AAH!
SLIP!
But in my coat pocket I found the crushed second peanut butter cup from the day I arrived.
MUNCH
MUNCH
At the festival I tried to see Lorrie Moore speak but was too nervous about my own talk to stay.

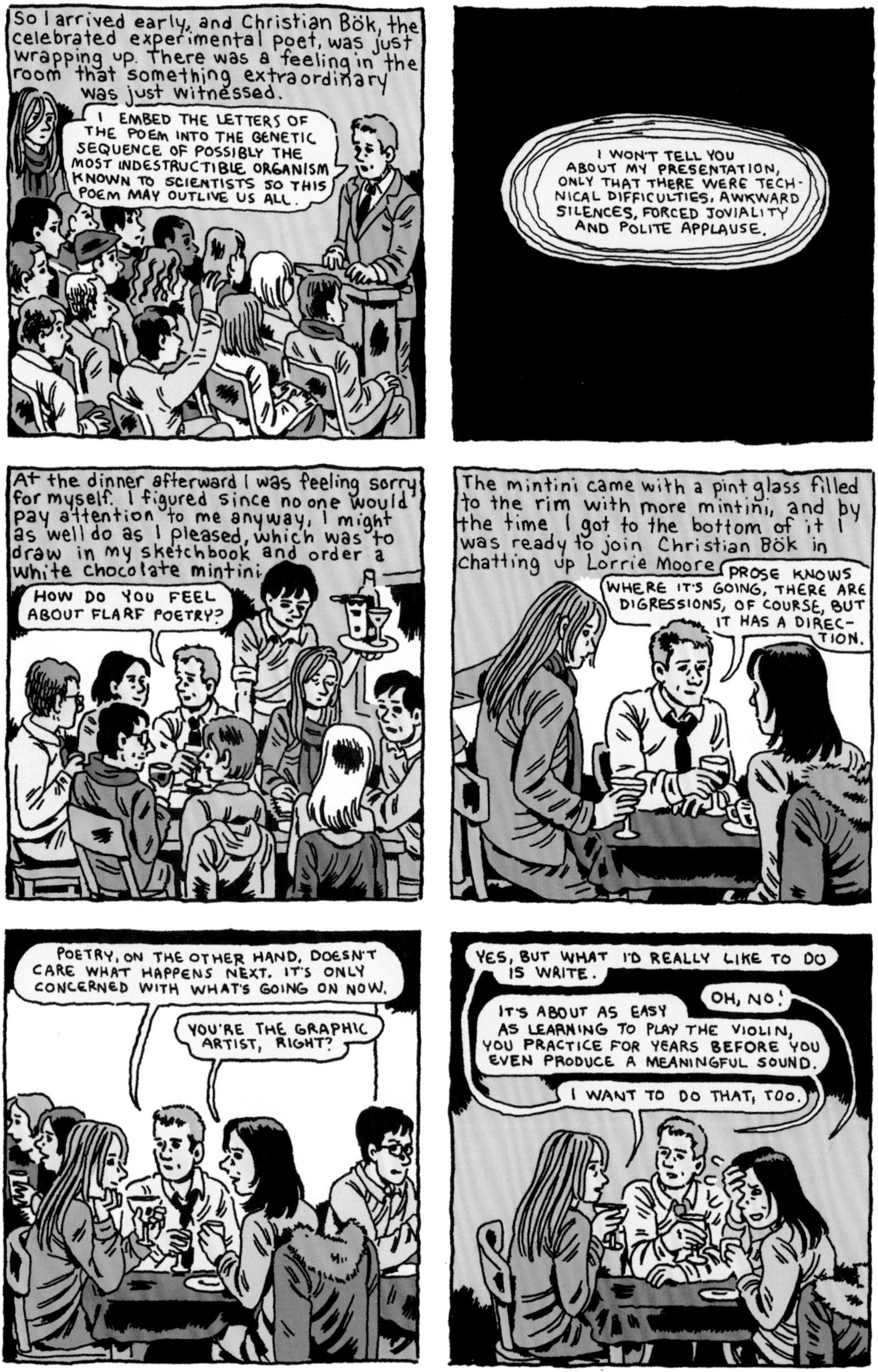
So I arrived early, and Christian Bök, the celebrated experimental poet, was just wrapping up. There was a feeling in the room that something extraordinary was just witnessed.
I EMBED THE LETTERS OF THE POEM INTO THE GENETIC SEQUENCE OF POSSIBLY THE MOST INDESTRUCTIBLE ORGANISM KNOWN TO SCIENTISTS SO THIS POEM MAY OUTLIVE US ALL.
I WON'T TELL YOU ABOUT MY PRESENTATION, ONLY THAT THERE WERE TECHNICAL DIFFICULTIES, AWKWARD SILENCES, FORCED JOVIALITY AND POLITE APPLAUSE.
At the dinner afterward I was feeling sorry for myself. I figured since no one would pay attention to me anyway, I might as well do as I pleased, which was to draw in my sketchbook and order a white chocolate mintini.
HOW DO YOU FEEL ABOUT FLARF POETRY?
The mintini came with a pint glass filled to the rim with more mintini, and by the time I got to the bottom of it I was ready to join Christian Bök in chatting up Lorrie Moore.
PROSE KNOWS WHERE IT'S GOING, THERE ARE DIGRESSIONS, OF COURSE, BUT IT HAS A DIRECTION.
POETRY, ON THE OTHER HAND, DOESN'T CARE WHAT HAPPENS NEXT. IT'S ONLY CONCERNED WITH WHAT'S GOING ON NOW.
YOU'RE THE GRAPHIC ARTIST, RIGHT?
YES, BUT WHAT I'D REALLY LIKE TO DO IS WRITE.
OH, NO!
IT'S ABOUT AS EASY AS LEARNING TO PLAY THE VIOLIN, YOU PRACTICE FOR YEARS BEFORE YOU EVEN PRODUCE A MEANINGFUL SOUND.
I WANT TO DO THAT, TOO.

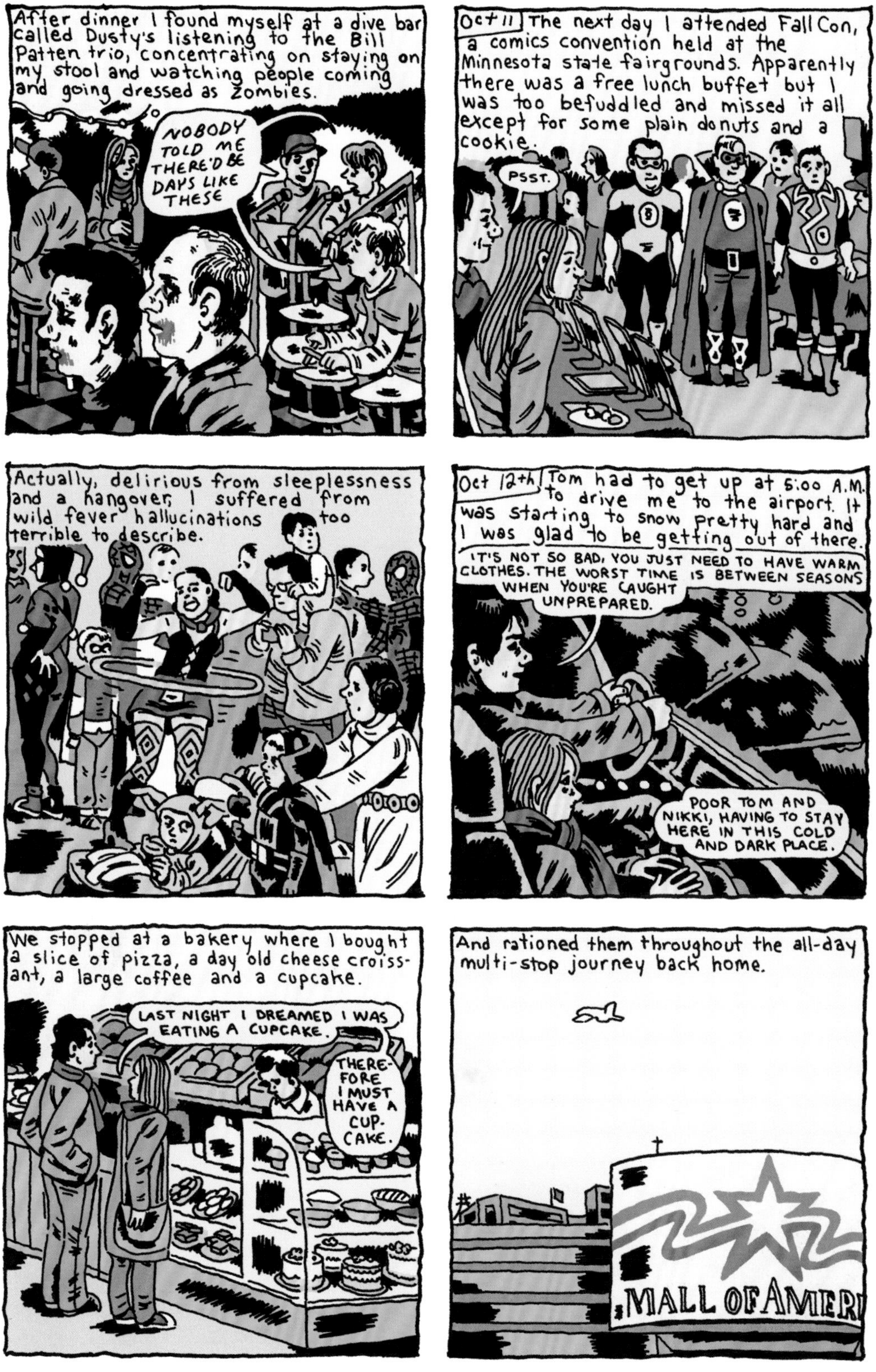
After dinner I found myself at a dive bar called Dusty's listening to the Bill Patten trio, concentrating on staying on my stool and watching people coming and going dressed as zombies.
NOBODY TOLD ME THERE'D BE DAYS LIKE THESE
Oct 11
The next day I attended Fall Con, a comics convention held at the Minnesota state fairgrounds. Apparently there was a free lunch buffet but I was too befuddled and missed it all except for some plain donuts and a cookie.
PSST.
Actually, delirious from sleeplessness and a hangover, I suffered from wild fever hallucinations too terrible to describe.
Oct 12th
Tom had to get up at 5:00 A.M. to drive me to the airport. It was starting to snow pretty hard and I was glad to be getting out of there.
IT'S NOT SO BAD, YOU JUST NEED TO HAVE WARM CLOTHES. THE WORST TIME IS BETWEEN SEASONS WHEN YOU'RE CAUGHT UNPREPARED.
POOR TOM AND NIKKI, HAVING TO STAY HERE IN THIS COLD AND DARK PLACE.
We stopped at a bakery where I bought a slice of pizza, a day old cheese croissant, a large coffee and a cupcake.
LAST NIGHT I DREAMED I WAS EATING A CUPCAKE.
THEREFORE I MUST HAVE A CUPCAKE.
And rationed them throughout the all-day multi-stop journey back home.
MALL OF AMERI

Oct 23, 2009 Straggly

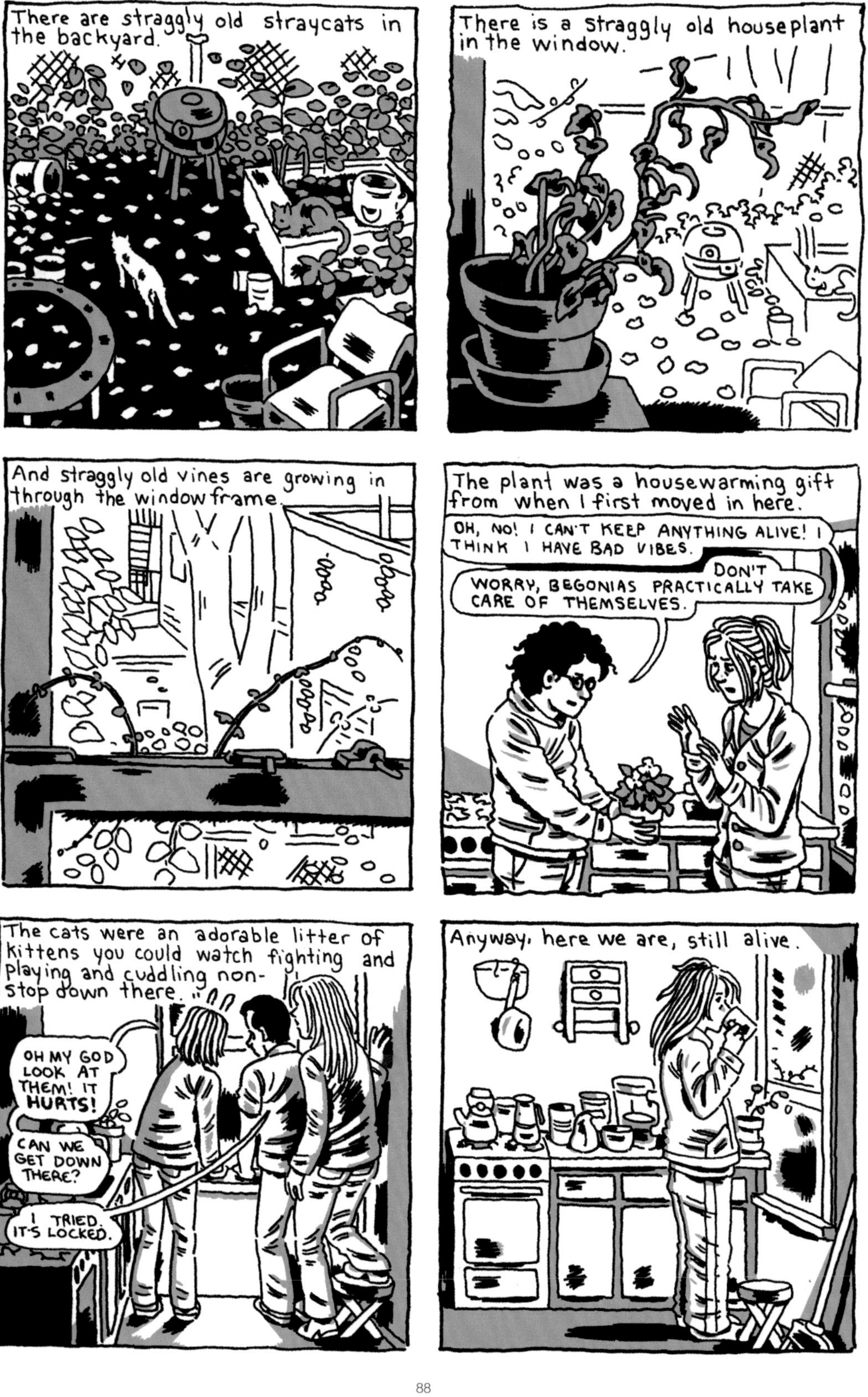

There are straggly old straycats in the backyard.
There is a straggly old houseplant in the window.
And straggly old vines are growing in through the window frame.
The plant was a housewarming gift from when I first moved in here.
OH, NO! I CAN'T KEEP ANYTHING ALIVE! I THINK I HAVE BAD VIBES.
DON'T WORRY, BEGONIAS PRACTICALLY TAKE CARE OF THEMSELVES.
The cats were an adorable litter of kittens you could watch fighting and playing and cuddling non-stop down there.
OH MY GOD LOOK AT THEM! IT HURTS!
CAN WE GET DOWN THERE?
I TRIED. IT'S LOCKED.
Anyway, here we are, still alive.

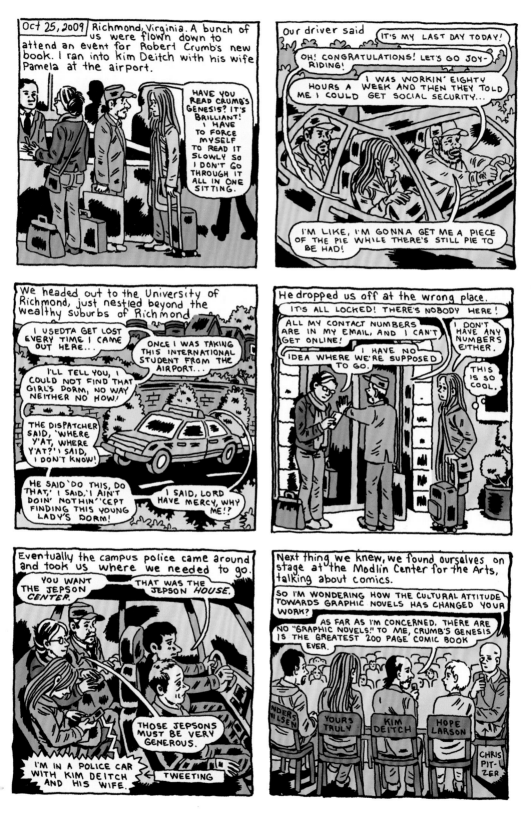

Oct 25, 2009 | Richmond, Virginia. A bunch of us were flown down to attend an event for Robert Crumb's new book. I ran into Kim Deitch with his wife Pamela at the airport.

HAVE YOU READ CRUMB'S GENESIS? IT'S BRILLIANT! I HAVE TO FORCE MYSELF TO READ IT SLOWLY SO I DON'T GO THROUGH IT ALL IN ONE SITTING.

Our driver said

IT'S MY LAST DAY TODAY!

OH! CONGRATULATIONS! LET'S GO JOY-RIDING!

I WAS WORKIN' EIGHTY HOURS A WEEK AND THEN THEY TOLD ME I COULD GET SOCIAL SECURITY...

I'M LIKE, I'M GONNA GET ME A PIECE OF THE PIE WHILE THERE'S STILL PIE TO BE HAD!

We headed out to the University of Richmond, just nestled beyond the wealthy suburbs of Richmond

I USEDTA GET LOST EVERY TIME I CAME OUT HERE...

ONCE I WAS TAKING THIS INTERNATIONAL STUDENT FROM THE AIRPORT...

I'LL TELL YOU, I COULD NOT FIND THAT GIRL'S DORM, NO WAY NEITHER NO HOW!

THE DISPATCHER SAID, 'WHERE Y'AT, WHERE Y'AT?' I SAID, I DON'T KNOW!

HE SAID 'DO THIS, DO THAT,' I SAID, 'I AIN'T DOIN' NOTHIN''CEPT FINDING THIS YOUNG LADY'S DORM!

I SAID, LORD HAVE MERCY, WHY ME!?

He dropped us off at the wrong place.

IT'S ALL LOCKED! THERE'S NOBODY HERE!

ALL MY CONTACT NUMBERS ARE IN MY EMAIL, AND I CAN'T GET ONLINE!

I DON'T HAVE ANY NUMBERS EITHER.

I HAVE NO IDEA WHERE WE'RE SUPPOSED TO GO.

THIS IS SO COOL.

Eventually the campus police came around and took us where we needed to go.

YOU WANT THE JEPSON CENTER.

THAT WAS THE JEPSON HOUSE.

THOSE JEPSONS MUST BE VERY GENEROUS.

I'M IN A POLICE CAR WITH KIM DEITCH AND HIS WIFE.

← TWEETING

Next thing we knew, we found ourselves on stage at the Modlin Center for the Arts, talking about comics.

SO I'M WONDERING HOW THE CULTURAL ATTITUDE TOWARDS GRAPHIC NOVELS HAS CHANGED YOUR WORK?

AS FAR AS I'M CONCERNED, THERE ARE NO "GRAPHIC NOVELS." TO ME, CRUMB'S GENESIS IS THE GREATEST 200 PAGE COMIC BOOK EVER.

ANDERS NILSEN

YOURS TRULY

KIM DEITCH

HOPE LARSON

CHRIS PITZER

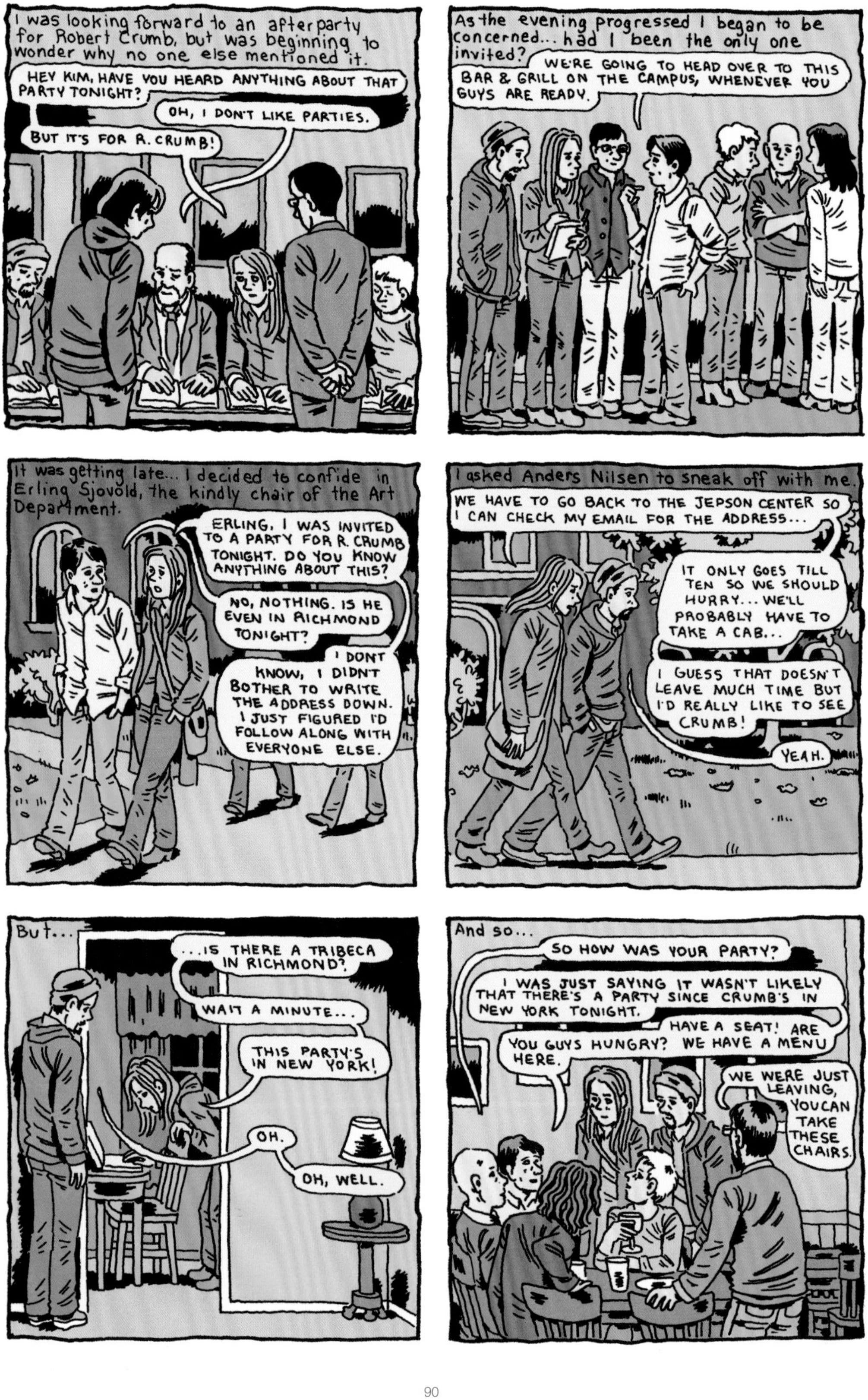
I was looking forward to an afterparty for Robert Crumb, but was beginning to wonder why no one else mentioned it.
HEY KIM, HAVE YOU HEARD ANYTHING ABOUT THAT PARTY TONIGHT?
OH, I DON'T LIKE PARTIES.
BUT IT'S FOR R. CRUMB!
As the evening progressed I began to be concerned... had I been the only one invited?
WE'RE GOING TO HEAD OVER TO THIS BAR & GRILL ON THE CAMPUS, WHENEVER YOU GUYS ARE READY.
It was getting late... I decided to confide in Erling Sjovold, the kindly chair of the Art Department.
ERLING, I WAS INVITED TO A PARTY FOR R. CRUMB TONIGHT. DO YOU KNOW ANYTHING ABOUT THIS?
NO, NOTHING. IS HE EVEN IN RICHMOND TONIGHT?
I DONT KNOW, I DIDN'T BOTHER TO WRITE THE ADDRESS DOWN. I JUST FIGURED I'D FOLLOW ALONG WITH EVERYONE ELSE.
I asked Anders Nilsen to sneak off with me.
WE HAVE TO GO BACK TO THE JEPSON CENTER SO I CAN CHECK MY EMAIL FOR THE ADDRESS...
IT ONLY GOES TILL TEN SO WE SHOULD HURRY... WE'LL PROBABLY HAVE TO TAKE A CAB...
I GUESS THAT DOESN'T LEAVE MUCH TIME BUT I'D REALLY LIKE TO SEE CRUMB!
YEAH.
But...
...IS THERE A TRIBECA IN RICHMOND?
WAIT A MINUTE...
THIS PARTY'S IN NEW YORK!
OH.
OH, WELL.
And so...
SO HOW WAS YOUR PARTY?
I WAS JUST SAYING IT WASN'T LIKELY THAT THERE'S A PARTY SINCE CRUMB'S IN NEW YORK TONIGHT.
HAVE A SEAT! ARE YOU GUYS HUNGRY? WE HAVE A MENU HERE.
WE WERE JUST LEAVING, YOU CAN TAKE THESE CHAIRS.

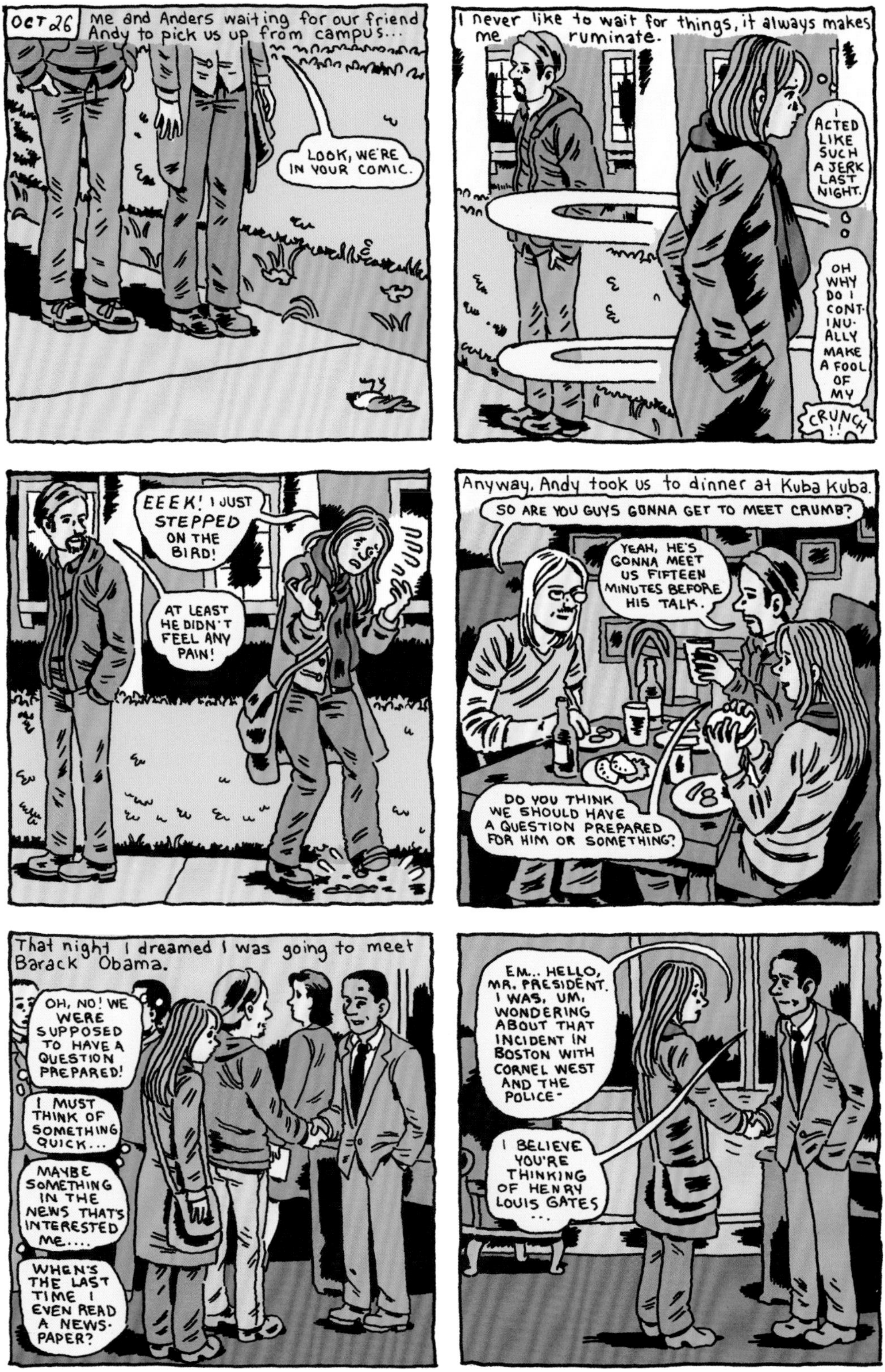
OCT 26
Me and Anders waiting for our friend Andy to pick us up from campus...
LOOK, WE'RE IN YOUR COMIC.
I never like to wait for things, it always makes me ruminate.
I ACTED LIKE SUCH A JERK LAST NIGHT.
OH WHY DO I CONTINUALLY MAKE A FOOL OF MY
CRUNCH!!
EEEK! I JUST STEPPED ON THE BIRD!
AT LEAST HE DIDN'T FEEL ANY PAIN!
Anyway, Andy took us to dinner at Kuba Kuba.
SO ARE YOU GUYS GONNA GET TO MEET CRUMB?
YEAH, HE'S GONNA MEET US FIFTEEN MINUTES BEFORE HIS TALK.
DO YOU THINK WE SHOULD HAVE A QUESTION PREPARED FOR HIM OR SOMETHING?
That night I dreamed I was going to meet Barack Obama.
OH, NO! WE WERE SUPPOSED TO HAVE A QUESTION PREPARED!
I MUST THINK OF SOMETHING QUICK...
MAYBE SOMETHING IN THE NEWS THAT'S INTERESTED ME....
WHEN'S THE LAST TIME I EVEN READ A NEWSPAPER?
EM.. HELLO, MR. PRESIDENT. I WAS, UM, WONDERING ABOUT THAT INCIDENT IN BOSTON WITH CORNEL WEST AND THE POLICE-
I BELIEVE YOU'RE THINKING OF HENRY LOUIS GATES...

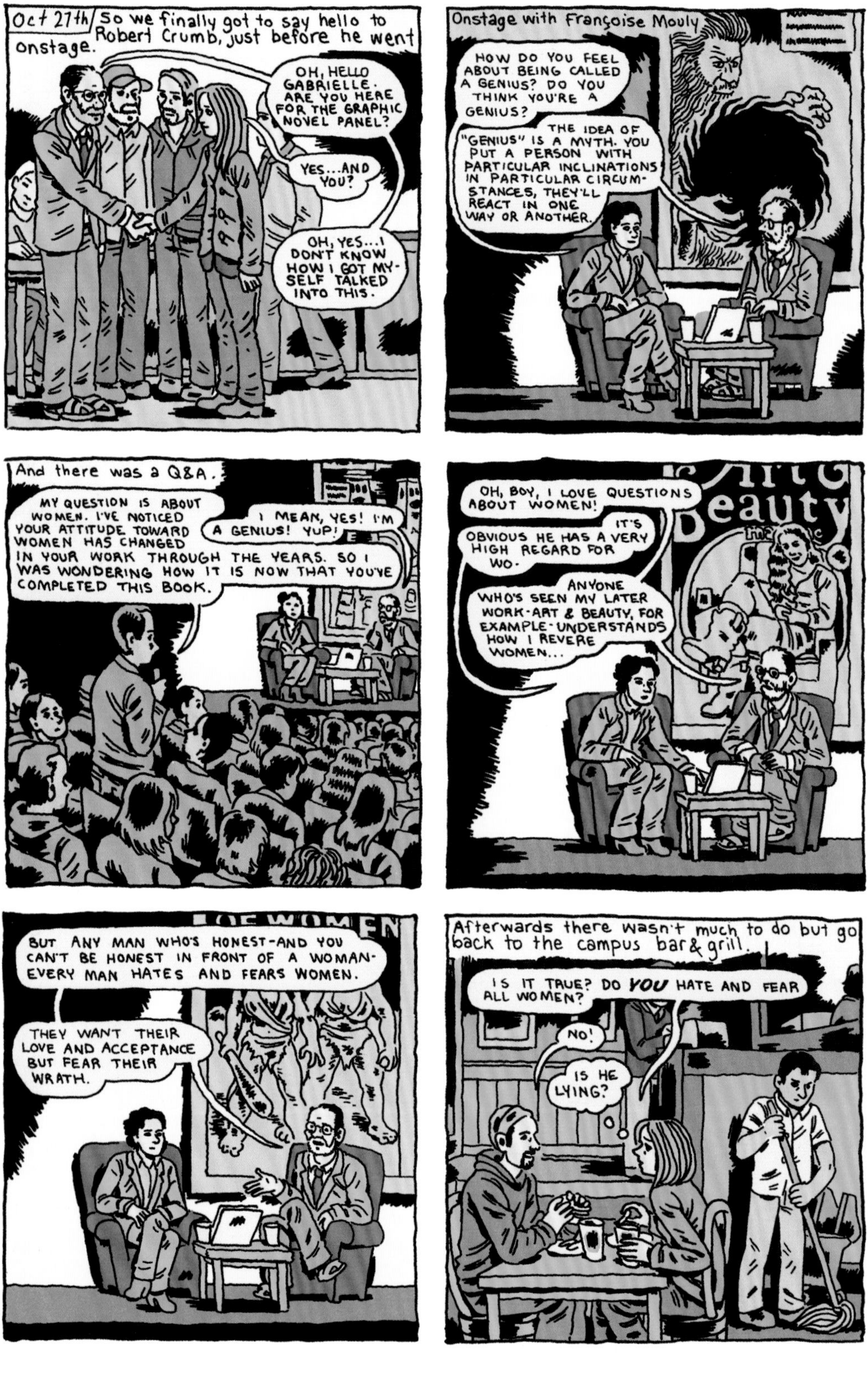
Oct 27th So we finally got to say hello to Robert Crumb, just before he went onstage.
OH, HELLO GABRIELLE. ARE YOU HERE FOR THE GRAPHIC NOVEL PANEL?
YES...AND YOU?
OH, YES...I DON'T KNOW HOW I GOT MYSELF TALKED INTO THIS.
Onstage with Françoise Mouly
HOW DO YOU FEEL ABOUT BEING CALLED A GENIUS? DO YOU THINK YOU'RE A GENIUS?
THE IDEA OF "GENIUS" IS A MYTH. YOU PUT A PERSON WITH PARTICULAR INCLINATIONS IN PARTICULAR CIRCUMSTANCES, THEY'LL REACT IN ONE WAY OR ANOTHER.
And there was a Q&A.
I MEAN, YES! I'M A GENIUS! YUP!
MY QUESTION IS ABOUT WOMEN. I'VE NOTICED YOUR ATTITUDE TOWARD WOMEN HAS CHANGED IN YOUR WORK THROUGH THE YEARS. SO I WAS WONDERING HOW IT IS NOW THAT YOU'VE COMPLETED THIS BOOK.
OH, BOY, I LOVE QUESTIONS ABOUT WOMEN!
IT'S OBVIOUS HE HAS A VERY HIGH REGARD FOR WO-
ANYONE WHO'S SEEN MY LATER WORK-ART & BEAUTY, FOR EXAMPLE-UNDERSTANDS HOW I REVERE WOMEN...
BUT ANY MAN WHO'S HONEST-AND YOU CAN'T BE HONEST IN FRONT OF A WOMAN-EVERY MAN HATES AND FEARS WOMEN.
THEY WANT THEIR LOVE AND ACCEPTANCE BUT FEAR THEIR WRATH.
Afterwards there wasn't much to do but go back to the campus bar & grill.
IS IT TRUE? DO YOU HATE AND FEAR ALL WOMEN?
NO!
IS HE LYING?

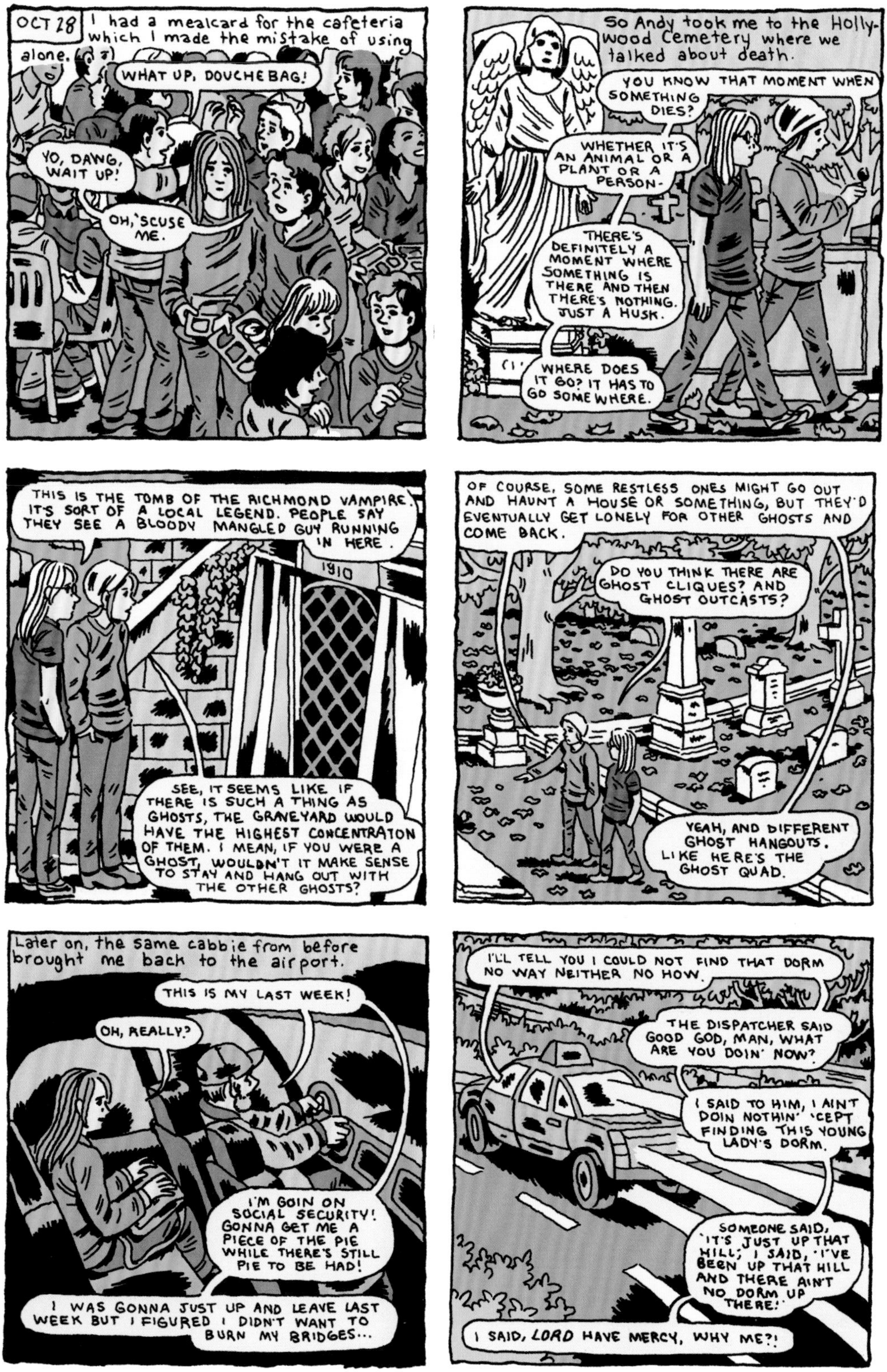
OCT 28 I had a mealcard for the cafeteria which I made the mistake of using alone.
WHAT UP, DOUCHEBAG!
YO, DAWG, WAIT UP!
OH, 'SCUSE ME.
So Andy took me to the Hollywood Cemetery where we talked about death.
YOU KNOW THAT MOMENT WHEN SOMETHING DIES?
WHETHER IT'S AN ANIMAL OR A PLANT OR A PERSON-
THERE'S DEFINITELY A MOMENT WHERE SOMETHING IS THERE AND THEN THERE'S NOTHING. JUST A HUSK.
WHERE DOES IT GO? IT HAS TO GO SOMEWHERE.
THIS IS THE TOMB OF THE RICHMOND VAMPIRE. IT'S SORT OF A LOCAL LEGEND. PEOPLE SAY THEY SEE A BLOODY MANGLED GUY RUNNING IN HERE.
1910
SEE, IT SEEMS LIKE IF THERE IS SUCH A THING AS GHOSTS, THE GRAVEYARD WOULD HAVE THE HIGHEST CONCENTRATON OF THEM. I MEAN, IF YOU WERE A GHOST, WOULDN'T IT MAKE SENSE TO STAY AND HANG OUT WITH THE OTHER GHOSTS?
OF COURSE, SOME RESTLESS ONES MIGHT GO OUT AND HAUNT A HOUSE OR SOMETHING, BUT THEY'D EVENTUALLY GET LONELY FOR OTHER GHOSTS AND COME BACK.
DO YOU THINK THERE ARE GHOST CLIQUES? AND GHOST OUTCASTS?
YEAH, AND DIFFERENT GHOST HANGOUTS. LIKE HERE'S THE GHOST QUAD.
Later on, the same cabbie from before brought me back to the airport.
THIS IS MY LAST WEEK!
OH, REALLY?
I'M GOIN ON SOCIAL SECURITY! GONNA GET ME A PIECE OF THE PIE WHILE THERE'S STILL PIE TO BE HAD!
I WAS GONNA JUST UP AND LEAVE LAST WEEK BUT I FIGURED I DIDN'T WANT TO BURN MY BRIDGES...
I'LL TELL YOU I COULD NOT FIND THAT DORM NO WAY NEITHER NO HOW.
THE DISPATCHER SAID GOOD GOD, MAN, WHAT ARE YOU DOIN' NOW?
I SAID TO HIM, I AIN'T DOIN NOTHIN' 'CEPT FINDING THIS YOUNG LADY'S DORM.
SOMEONE SAID, 'IT'S JUST UP THAT HILL'; I SAID, 'I'VE BEEN UP THAT HILL AND THERE AIN'T NO DORM UP THERE!'
I SAID, LORD HAVE MERCY, WHY ME?!

Thanksgiving with Uncle Larry

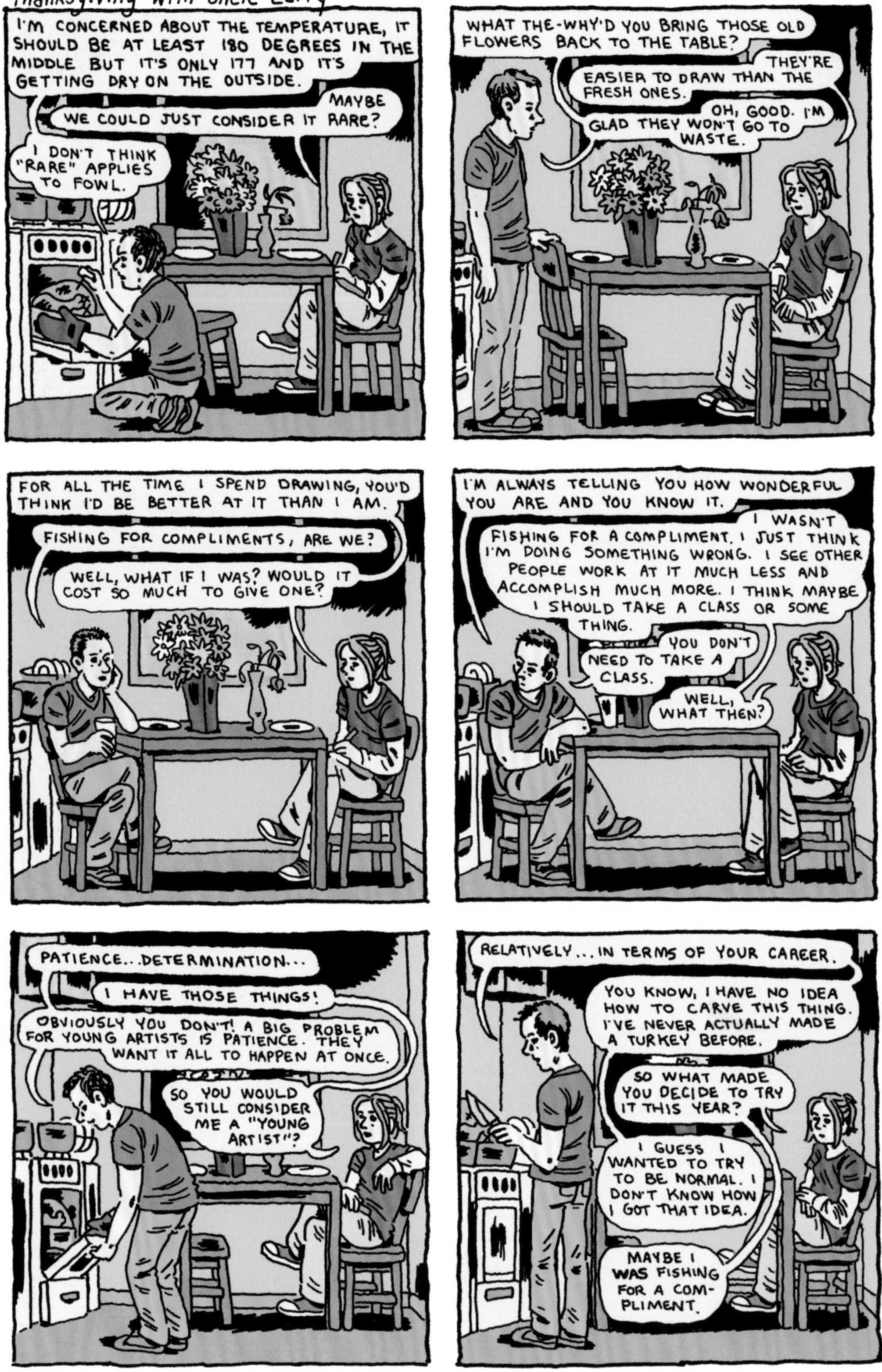

I'M CONCERNED ABOUT THE TEMPERATURE, IT SHOULD BE AT LEAST 180 DEGREES IN THE MIDDLE BUT IT'S ONLY 177 AND IT'S GETTING DRY ON THE OUTSIDE.
MAYBE WE COULD JUST CONSIDER IT RARE?
I DON'T THINK "RARE" APPLIES TO FOWL.
WHAT THE-WHY'D YOU BRING THOSE OLD FLOWERS BACK TO THE TABLE?
THEY'RE EASIER TO DRAW THAN THE FRESH ONES.
OH, GOOD. I'M GLAD THEY WON'T GO TO WASTE.
FOR ALL THE TIME I SPEND DRAWING, YOU'D THINK I'D BE BETTER AT IT THAN I AM.
FISHING FOR COMPLIMENTS, ARE WE?
WELL, WHAT IF I WAS? WOULD IT COST SO MUCH TO GIVE ONE?
I'M ALWAYS TELLING YOU HOW WONDERFUL YOU ARE AND YOU KNOW IT.
I WASN'T FISHING FOR A COMPLIMENT. I JUST THINK I'M DOING SOMETHING WRONG. I SEE OTHER PEOPLE WORK AT IT MUCH LESS AND ACCOMPLISH MUCH MORE. I THINK MAYBE I SHOULD TAKE A CLASS OR SOME THING.
YOU DON'T NEED TO TAKE A CLASS.
WELL, WHAT THEN?
PATIENCE...DETERMINATION...
I HAVE THOSE THINGS!
OBVIOUSLY YOU DON'T! A BIG PROBLEM FOR YOUNG ARTISTS IS PATIENCE. THEY WANT IT ALL TO HAPPEN AT ONCE.
SO YOU WOULD STILL CONSIDER ME A "YOUNG ARTIST"?
RELATIVELY... IN TERMS OF YOUR CAREER.
YOU KNOW, I HAVE NO IDEA HOW TO CARVE THIS THING. I'VE NEVER ACTUALLY MADE A TURKEY BEFORE.
SO WHAT MADE YOU DECIDE TO TRY IT THIS YEAR?
I GUESS I WANTED TO TRY TO BE NORMAL. I DON'T KNOW HOW I GOT THAT IDEA.
MAYBE I WAS FISHING FOR A COM-PLIMENT.

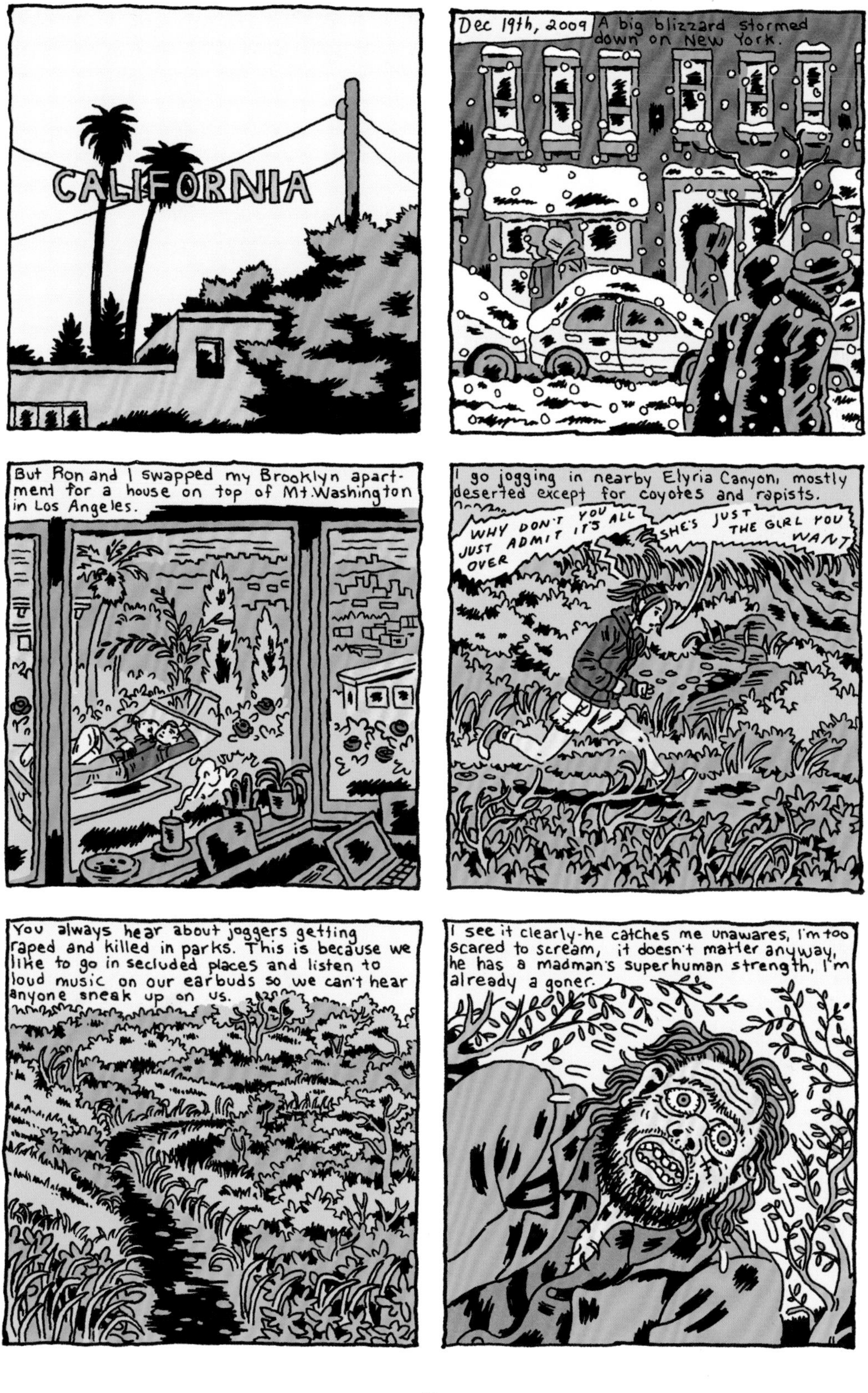
CALIFORNIA
Dec 19th, 2009
A big blizzard stormed down on New York.
But Ron and I swapped my Brooklyn apartment for a house on top of Mt. Washington in Los Angeles.
I go jogging in nearby Elyria Canyon, mostly deserted except for coyotes and rapists.
WHY DON'T YOU JUST ADMIT IT'S ALL OVER
SHE'S JUST THE GIRL YOU WANT
You always hear about joggers getting raped and killed in parks. This is because we like to go in secluded places and listen to loud music on our earbuds so we can't hear anyone sneak up on us.
I see it clearly-he catches me unawares, I'm too scared to scream, it doesn't matter anyway, he has a madman's superhuman strength, I'm already a goner.

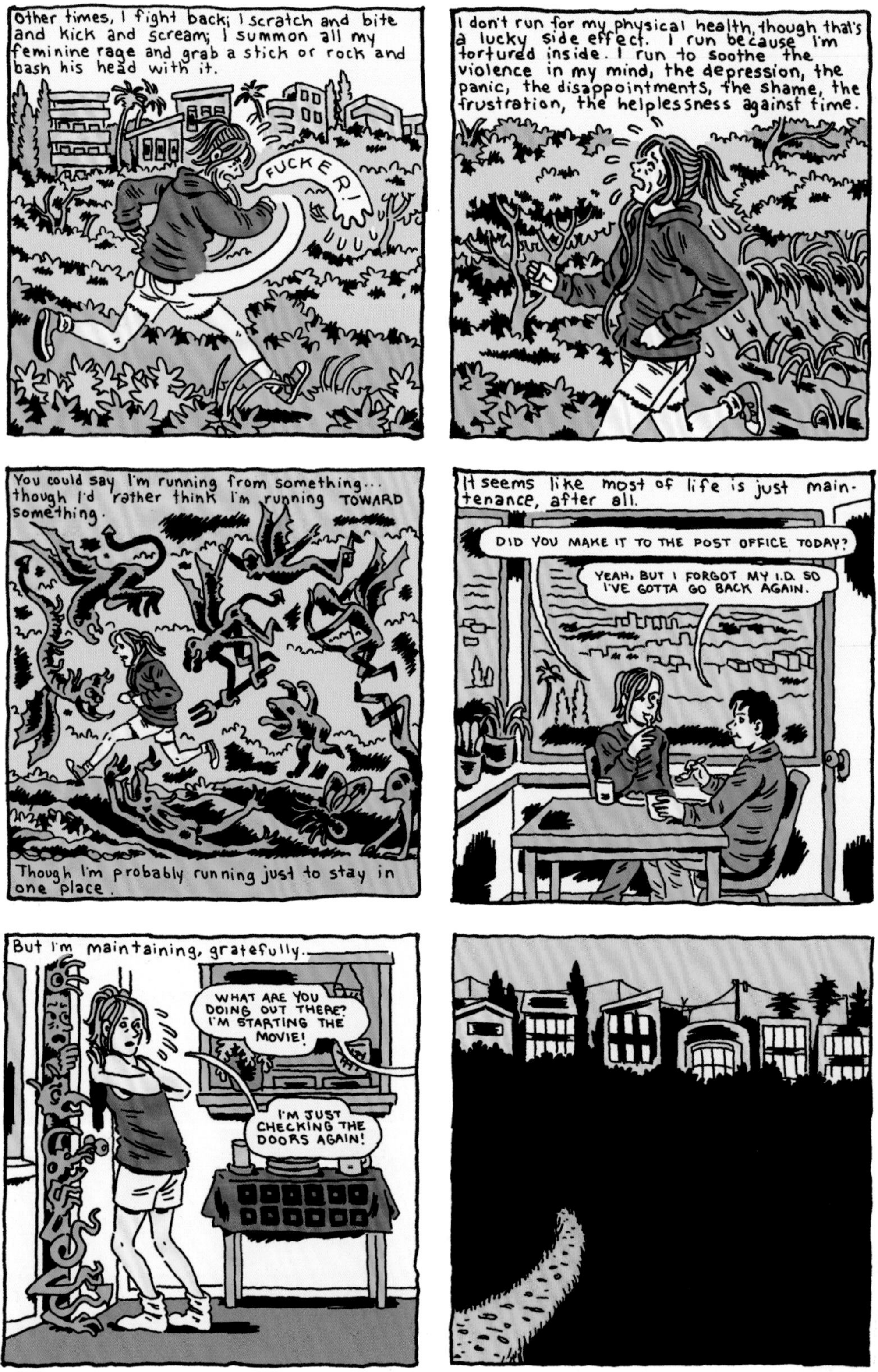

Other times, I fight back; I scratch and bite and kick and scream; I summon all my feminine rage and grab a stick or rock and bash his head with it.
FUCKER!
I don't run for my physical health, though that's a lucky side effect. I run because I'm tortured inside. I run to soothe the violence in my mind, the depression, the panic, the disappointments, the shame, the frustration, the helplessness against time.
You could say I'm running from something... though I'd rather think I'm running TOWARD something.
Though I'm probably running just to stay in one place.
It seems like most of life is just maintenance, after all.
DID YOU MAKE IT TO THE POST OFFICE TODAY?
YEAH, BUT I FORGOT MY I.D. SO I'VE GOTTA GO BACK AGAIN.
But I'm maintaining, gratefully.
WHAT ARE YOU DOING OUT THERE? I'M STARTING THE MOVIE!
I'M JUST CHECKING THE DOORS AGAIN!

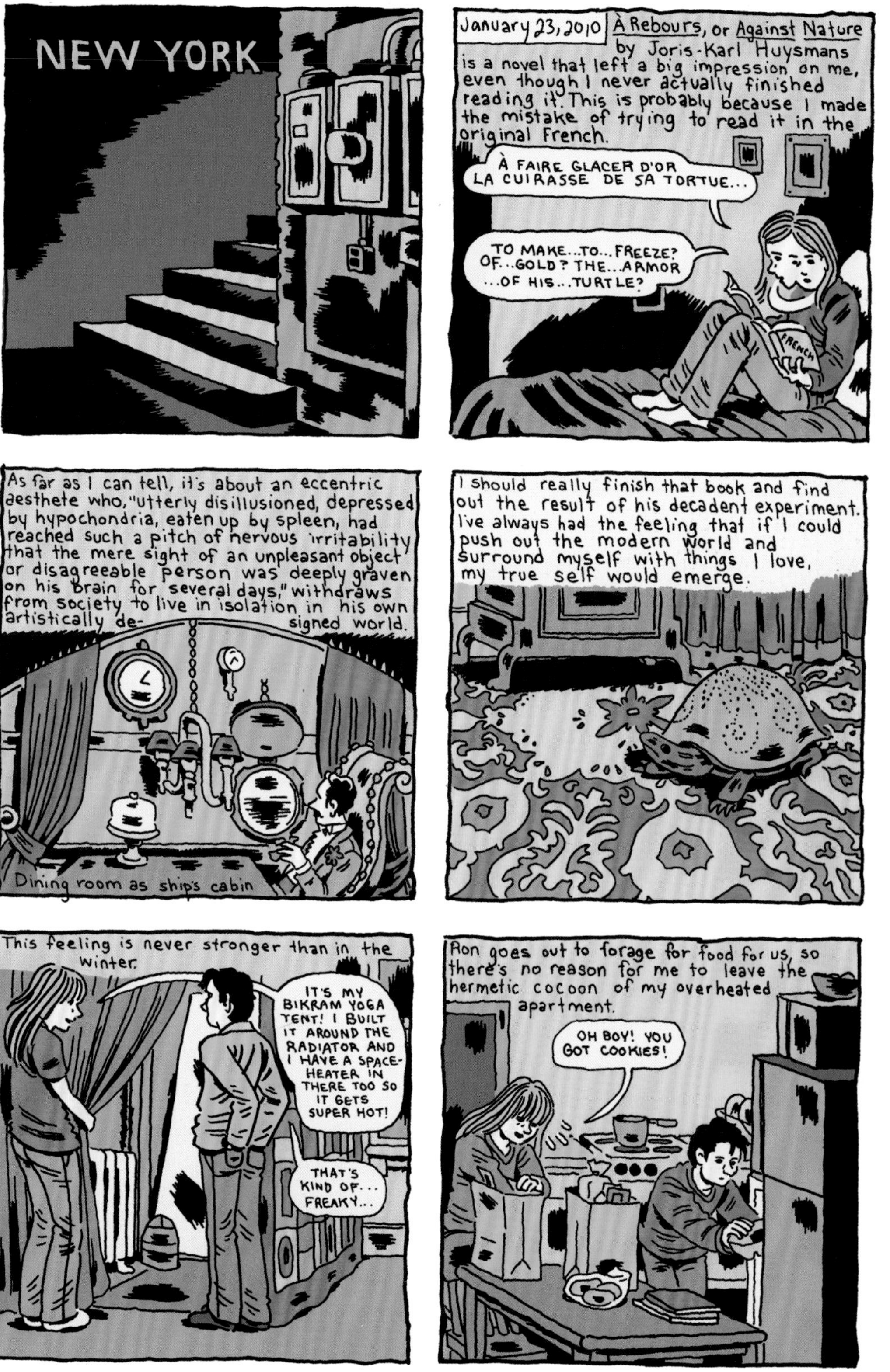
NEW YORK
January 23, 2010
À Rebours, or Against Nature by Joris-Karl Huysmans is a novel that left a big impression on me, even though I never actually finished reading it. This is probably because I made the mistake of trying to read it in the original French.
À FAIRE GLACER D'OR LA CUIRASSE DE SA TORTUE...
TO MAKE...TO...FREEZE? OF...GOLD? THE...ARMOR ...OF HIS...TURTLE?
FRENCH
As far as I can tell, it's about an eccentric aesthete who, "utterly disillusioned, depressed by hypochondria, eaten up by spleen, had reached such a pitch of nervous irritability that the mere sight of an unpleasant object or disagreeable person was deeply graven on his brain for several days," withdraws from society to live in isolation in his own artistically designed world.
Dining room as ship's cabin
I should really finish that book and find out the result of his decadent experiment. I've always had the feeling that if I could push out the modern world and surround myself with things I love, my true self would emerge.
This feeling is never stronger than in the winter.
IT'S MY BIKRAM YOGA TENT! I BUILT IT AROUND THE RADIATOR AND I HAVE A SPACE-HEATER IN THERE TOO SO IT GETS SUPER HOT!
THAT'S KIND OF... FREAKY...
Ron goes out to forage for food for us, so there's no reason for me to leave the hermetic cocoon of my overheated apartment.
OH BOY! YOU GOT COOKIES!

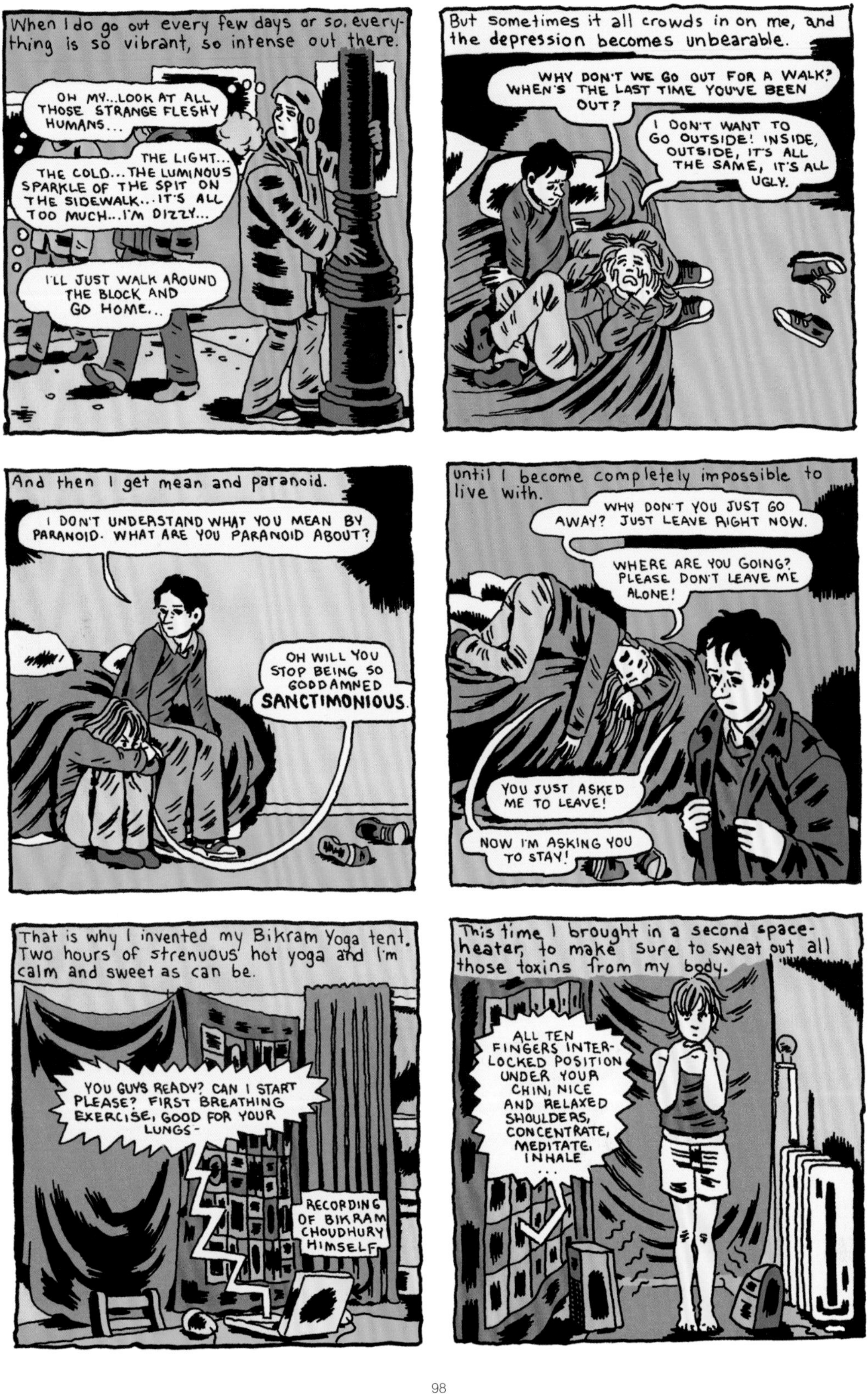
When I do go out every few days or so, everything is so vibrant, so intense out there.
OH MY...LOOK AT ALL THOSE STRANGE FLESHY HUMANS...
THE LIGHT... THE COLD... THE LUMINOUS SPARKLE OF THE SPIT ON THE SIDEWALK... IT'S ALL TOO MUCH...I'M DIZZY...
I'LL JUST WALK AROUND THE BLOCK AND GO HOME...
But sometimes it all crowds in on me, and the depression becomes unbearable.
WHY DON'T WE GO OUT FOR A WALK? WHEN'S THE LAST TIME YOU'VE BEEN OUT?
I DON'T WANT TO GO OUTSIDE! INSIDE, OUTSIDE, IT'S ALL THE SAME, IT'S ALL UGLY.
And then I get mean and paranoid.
I DON'T UNDERSTAND WHAT YOU MEAN BY PARANOID. WHAT ARE YOU PARANOID ABOUT?
OH WILL YOU STOP BEING SO GODDAMNED SANCTIMONIOUS.
until I become completely impossible to live with.
WHY DON'T YOU JUST GO AWAY? JUST LEAVE RIGHT NOW.
WHERE ARE YOU GOING? PLEASE DON'T LEAVE ME ALONE!
YOU JUST ASKED ME TO LEAVE!
NOW I'M ASKING YOU TO STAY!
That is why I invented my Bikram Yoga tent. Two hours of strenuous hot yoga and I'm calm and sweet as can be.
YOU GUYS READY? CAN I START PLEASE? FIRST BREATHING EXERCISE, GOOD FOR YOUR LUNGS-
RECORDING OF BIKRAM CHOUDHURY HIMSELF
This time I brought in a second space-heater, to make sure to sweat out all those toxins from my body.
ALL TEN FINGERS INTER-LOCKED POSITION UNDER YOUR CHIN, NICE AND RELAXED SHOULDERS, CONCENTRATE, MEDITATE, INHALE ...

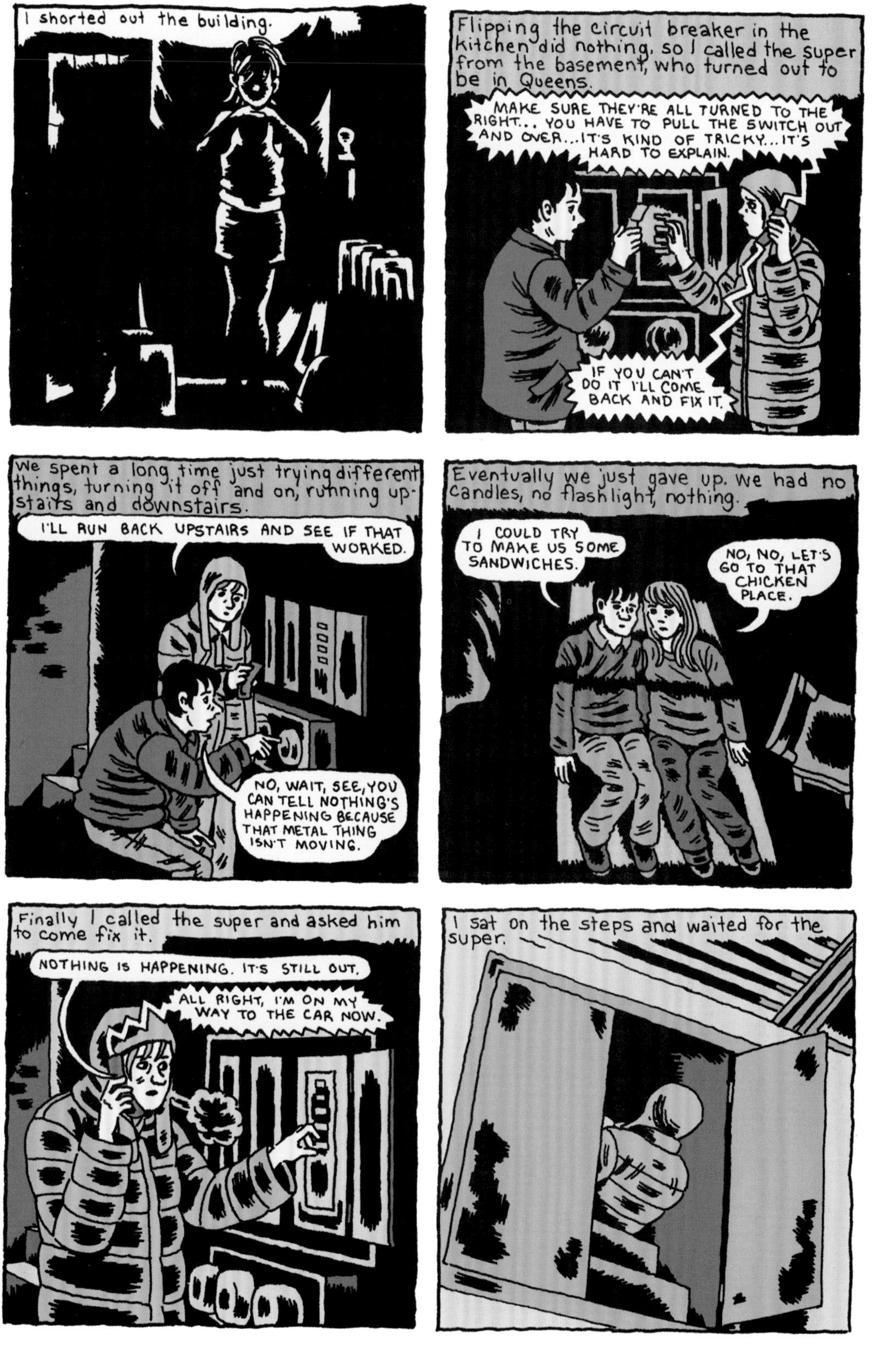
I shorted out the building.
Flipping the circuit breaker in the kitchen did nothing, so I called the super from the basement, who turned out to be in Queens.
MAKE SURE THEY'RE ALL TURNED TO THE RIGHT... YOU HAVE TO PULL THE SWITCH OUT AND OVER...IT'S KIND OF TRICKY...IT'S HARD TO EXPLAIN.
IF YOU CAN'T DO IT I'LL COME BACK AND FIX IT.
We spent a long time just trying different things, turning it off and on, running upstairs and downstairs.
I'LL RUN BACK UPSTAIRS AND SEE IF THAT WORKED.
NO, WAIT, SEE, YOU CAN TELL NOTHING'S HAPPENING BECAUSE THAT METAL THING ISN'T MOVING.
Eventually we just gave up. We had no candles, no flashlight, nothing.
I COULD TRY TO MAKE US SOME SANDWICHES.
NO, NO, LET'S GO TO THAT CHICKEN PLACE.
Finally I called the super and asked him to come fix it.
NOTHING IS HAPPENING. IT'S STILL OUT.
ALL RIGHT, I'M ON MY WAY TO THE CAR NOW.
I sat on the steps and waited for the super.

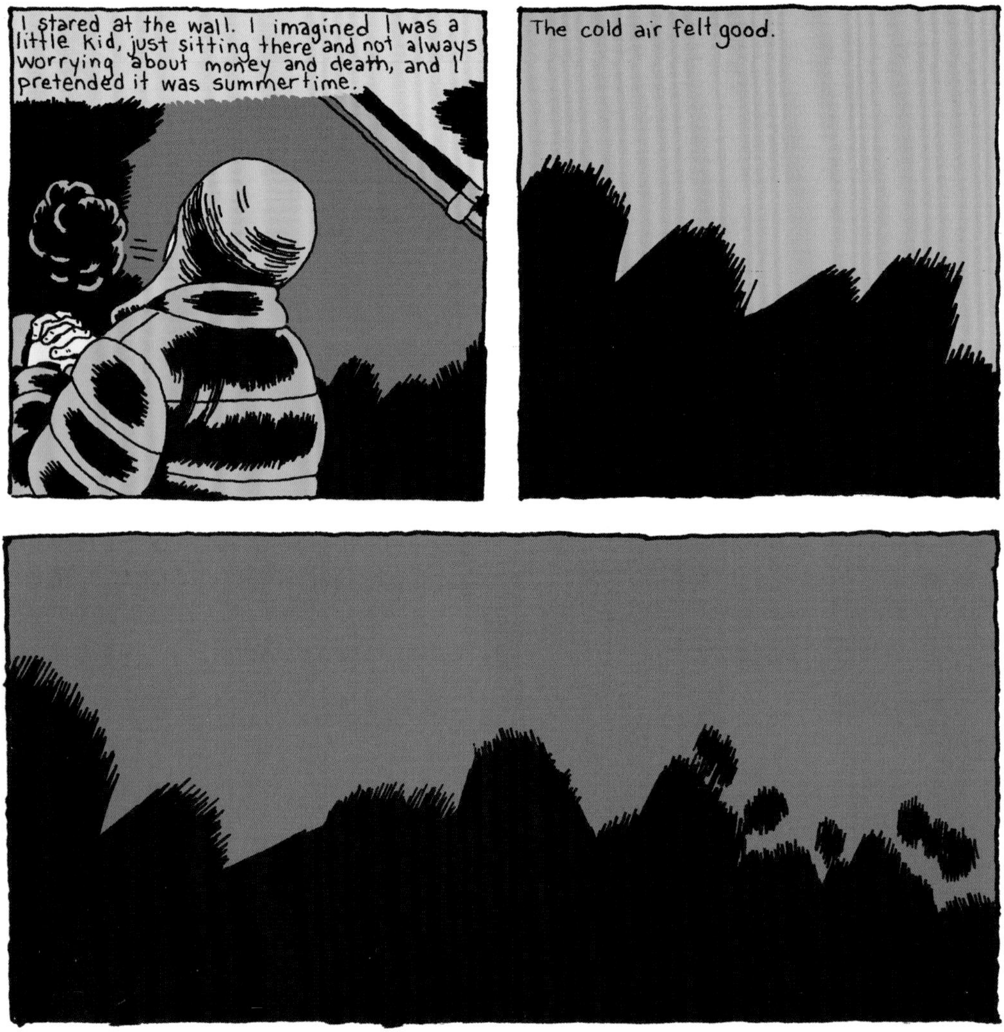
I stared at the wall. I imagined I was a little kid, just sitting there and not always worrying about money and death, and I pretended it was summertime.
The cold air felt good.

# chapter five
## 2010

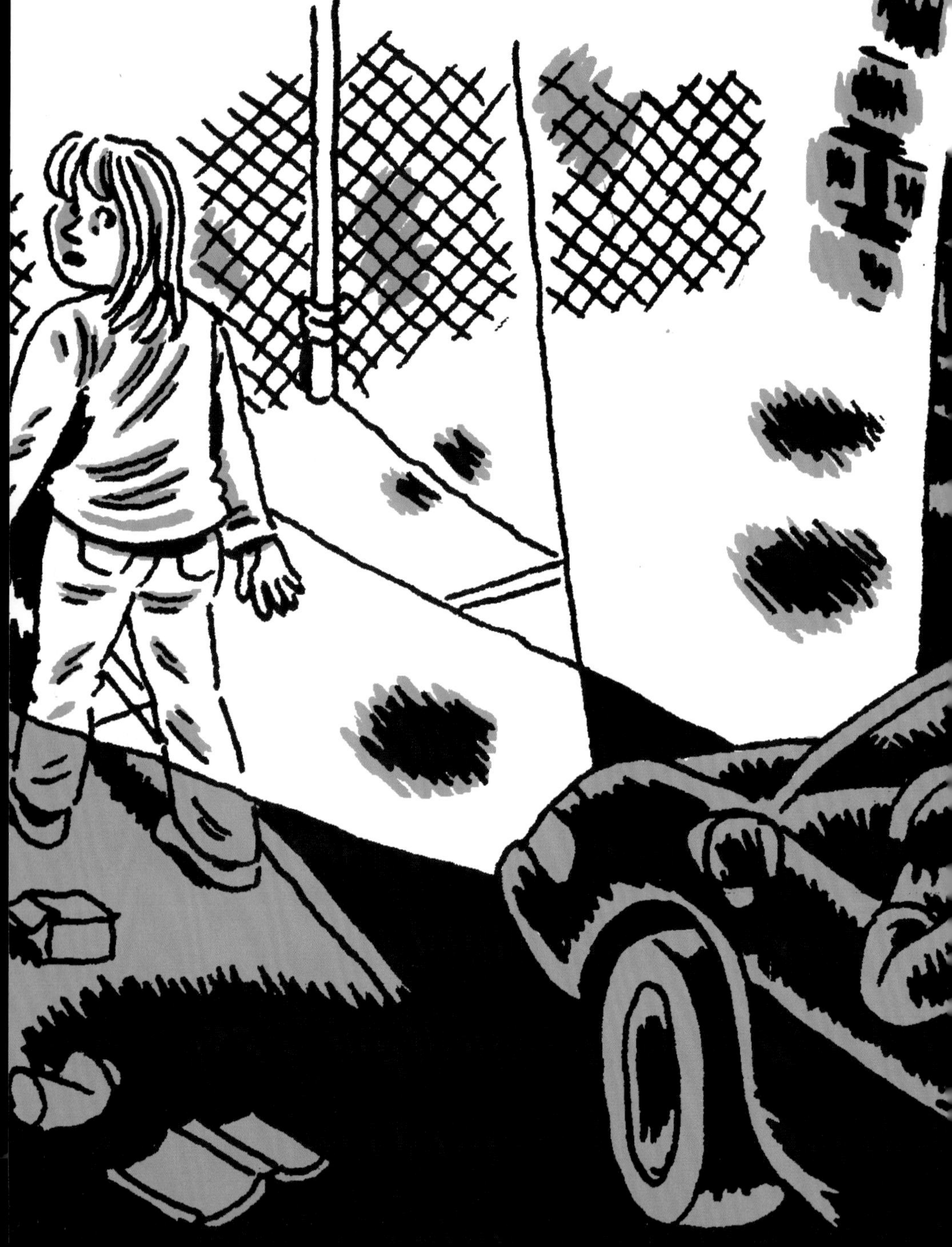

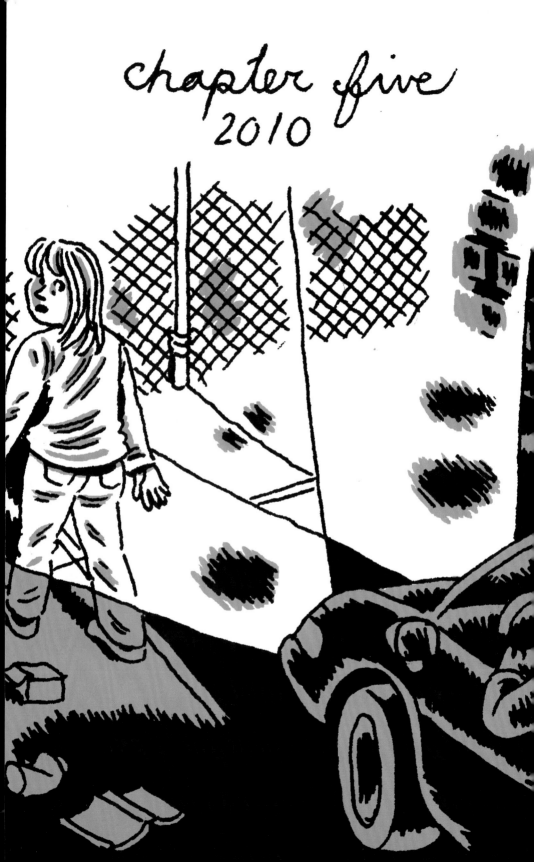

March 10th, 2010 It's not so cold anymore and women are wearing skirts and taking their dogs to the park, but I've been so sad and lonely it may as well go on being winter forever.

Ron has gone back to L.A. again, and that's about it. It seems we are each permanently fixed on opposite sides of the country, and we've run out of steam or money to go on.

I've pretty much spent my life trying to be a cartoonist, and what have I got to show for it? A wikipedia page and arrested development. I

please note: I don't actually smoke. I just drew myself like this to dramatize how pathetic I am. Don't smoke, kids! It's a deadly habit.

But I can't afford to mope, so I decided to pull myself out of my rut and get a haircut.

YOU MUST BE GETTING A LOT OF PEOPLE COMING IN FOR SPRING HAIRCUTS.

OH, YES.

WHAT'S THE POPULAR STYLE THESE DAYS?

SHAGGY.

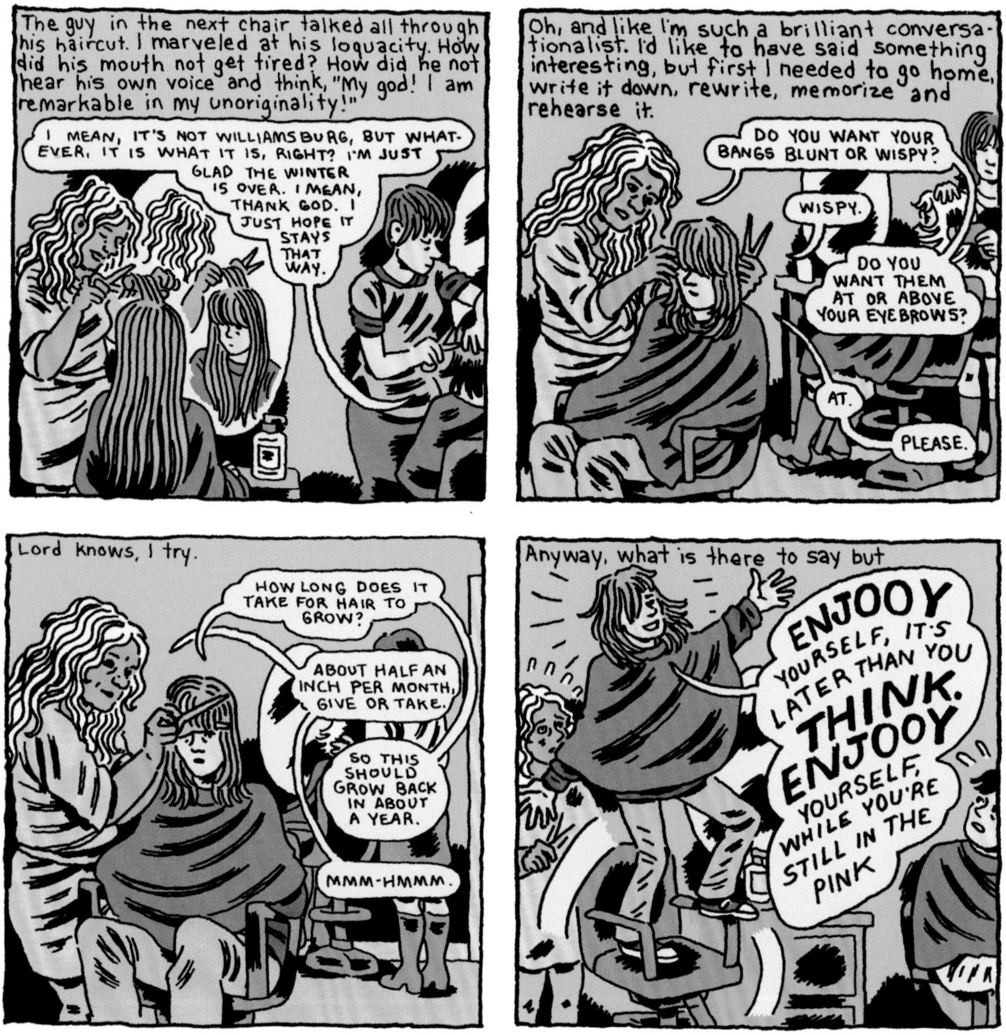
The guy in the next chair talked all through his haircut. I marveled at his loquacity. How did his mouth not get tired? How did he not hear his own voice and think, "My god! I am remarkable in my unoriginality!"
I MEAN, IT'S NOT WILLIAMSBURG, BUT WHATEVER, IT IS WHAT IT IS, RIGHT? I'M JUST GLAD THE WINTER IS OVER. I MEAN, THANK GOD. I JUST HOPE IT STAYS THAT WAY.
Oh, and like I'm such a brilliant conversationalist. I'd like to have said something interesting, but first I needed to go home, write it down, rewrite, memorize and rehearse it.
DO YOU WANT YOUR BANGS BLUNT OR WISPY?
WISPY.
DO YOU WANT THEM AT OR ABOVE YOUR EYEBROWS?
AT.
PLEASE.
Lord knows, I try.
HOW LONG DOES IT TAKE FOR HAIR TO GROW?
ABOUT HALF AN INCH PER MONTH, GIVE OR TAKE.
SO THIS SHOULD GROW BACK IN ABOUT A YEAR.
MMM-HMMM.
Anyway, what is there to say but
ENJOOY YOURSELF, IT'S LATER THAN YOU THINK. ENJOOY YOURSELF, WHILE YOU'RE STILL IN THE PINK

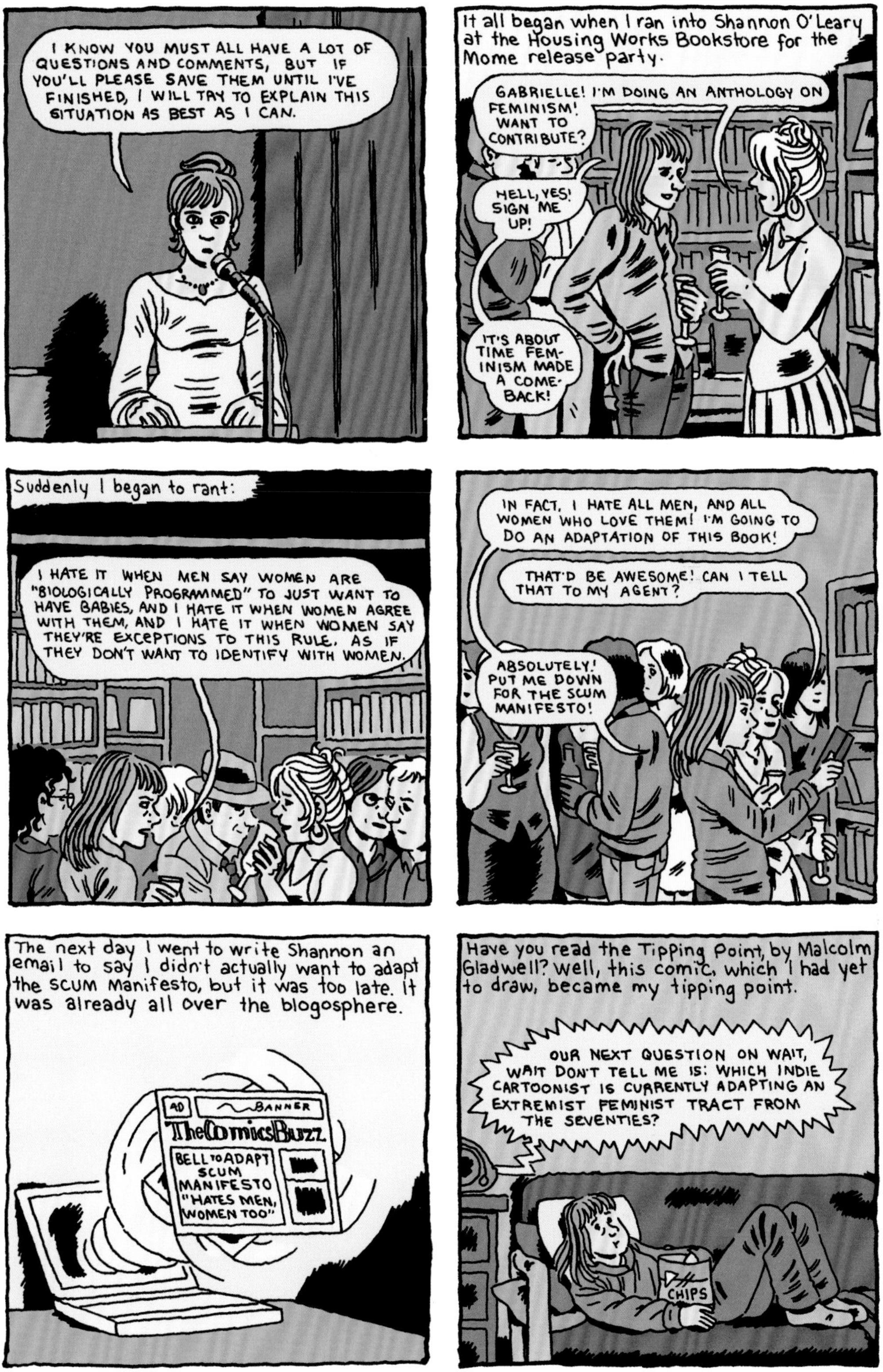
I KNOW YOU MUST ALL HAVE A LOT OF QUESTIONS AND COMMENTS, BUT IF YOU'LL PLEASE SAVE THEM UNTIL I'VE FINISHED, I WILL TRY TO EXPLAIN THIS SITUATION AS BEST AS I CAN.
It all began when I ran into Shannon O'Leary at the Housing Works Bookstore for the Mome release party.
GABRIELLE! I'M DOING AN ANTHOLOGY ON FEMINISM! WANT TO CONTRIBUTE?
HELL, YES! SIGN ME UP!
IT'S ABOUT TIME FEMINISM MADE A COMEBACK!
Suddenly I began to rant:
I HATE IT WHEN MEN SAY WOMEN ARE "BIOLOGICALLY PROGRAMMED" TO JUST WANT TO HAVE BABIES, AND I HATE IT WHEN WOMEN AGREE WITH THEM, AND I HATE IT WHEN WOMEN SAY THEY'RE EXCEPTIONS TO THIS RULE, AS IF THEY DON'T WANT TO IDENTIFY WITH WOMEN.
IN FACT, I HATE ALL MEN, AND ALL WOMEN WHO LOVE THEM! I'M GOING TO DO AN ADAPTATION OF THIS BOOK!
THAT'D BE AWESOME! CAN I TELL THAT TO MY AGENT?
ABSOLUTELY! PUT ME DOWN FOR THE SCUM MANIFESTO!
The next day I went to write Shannon an email to say I didn't actually want to adapt the SCUM Manifesto, but it was too late. It was already all over the blogosphere.
AD
BANNER
The Comics Buzz
BELL TO ADAPT SCUM MANIFESTO "HATES MEN, WOMEN TOO"
Have you read the Tipping Point, by Malcolm Gladwell? Well, this comic, which I had yet to draw, became my tipping point.
OUR NEXT QUESTION ON WAIT, WAIT DON'T TELL ME IS: WHICH INDIE CARTOONIST IS CURRENTLY ADAPTING AN EXTREMIST FEMINIST TRACT FROM THE SEVENTIES?
CHIPS

As a matter of fact, in an interview with Leonard Lopate, Malcolm Gladwell referenced me.

THE SCUM MANIFESTO WAS THE TIPPING POINT FOR GABRIELLE BELL...

Someone told me Stephen Colbert made a joke about it...

APPARENTLY THE TERRORISTS HAVE WON.

And Michelle Obama mentioned it in a commencement address to the graduating class at Sarah Lawrence.

I'M PARTICULARLY INTERESTED TO SEE HOW GABRIELLE BELL HANDLES THE SCUM MANIFESTO.

I was even invited to Stockholm by the Ministry of Culture to present my SCUM comic for the King of Sweden. Apparently Valerie Solanas is a big deal there. So now I've gotta finish this thing by Solanas Dag, March 29th.

AH, SHIT.

Problem is, I can't even get through this stupid book. Every time I pick it up it puts me right to sleep.

SNORE

When I'm stuck on a comic, I have a secret resource. My mother lives alone on the top of a mountain without electricity or a phone. If I want to talk to her, there's nothing to do but wait until she calls me from the pay-phone in town, which she hitchhikes to every few weeks or so for supplies.

Now there's something uncanny about my mother: Whenever I put her in a comic, it's invariably a success. For example: every time my work is chosen for Houghton-Mifflin Harcourt's Best American Comics, it's always about her.

 B.A.C. 2007: Gabrielle the Third: My mother, a lifelong vegetarian, cooks and serves our beloved pet chicken to fend off starvation.

 B.A.C. 2008: my mother's urging me to "read a book" sends me on a "novel" experience.

 B.A.C. 2009: A school bully torments me me until I'm forced to stand up to her. My mother only appears in one panel, and I only got an honorable mention for this one.

And, of course, there's my graphic memoir <u>What My Mother Taught Me</u>, which garnered the National Book Award, enjoyed eleven weeks on the NYT best seller list and has the honor of being the only book to have been chosen twice for Oprah's Book Club.

THIS BOOK IS SO COMPLEX, SO DEEP AND RESONANT, ONLY A SECOND READING WILL DO IT JUSTICE.

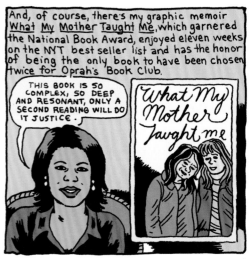

What My Mother Taught me

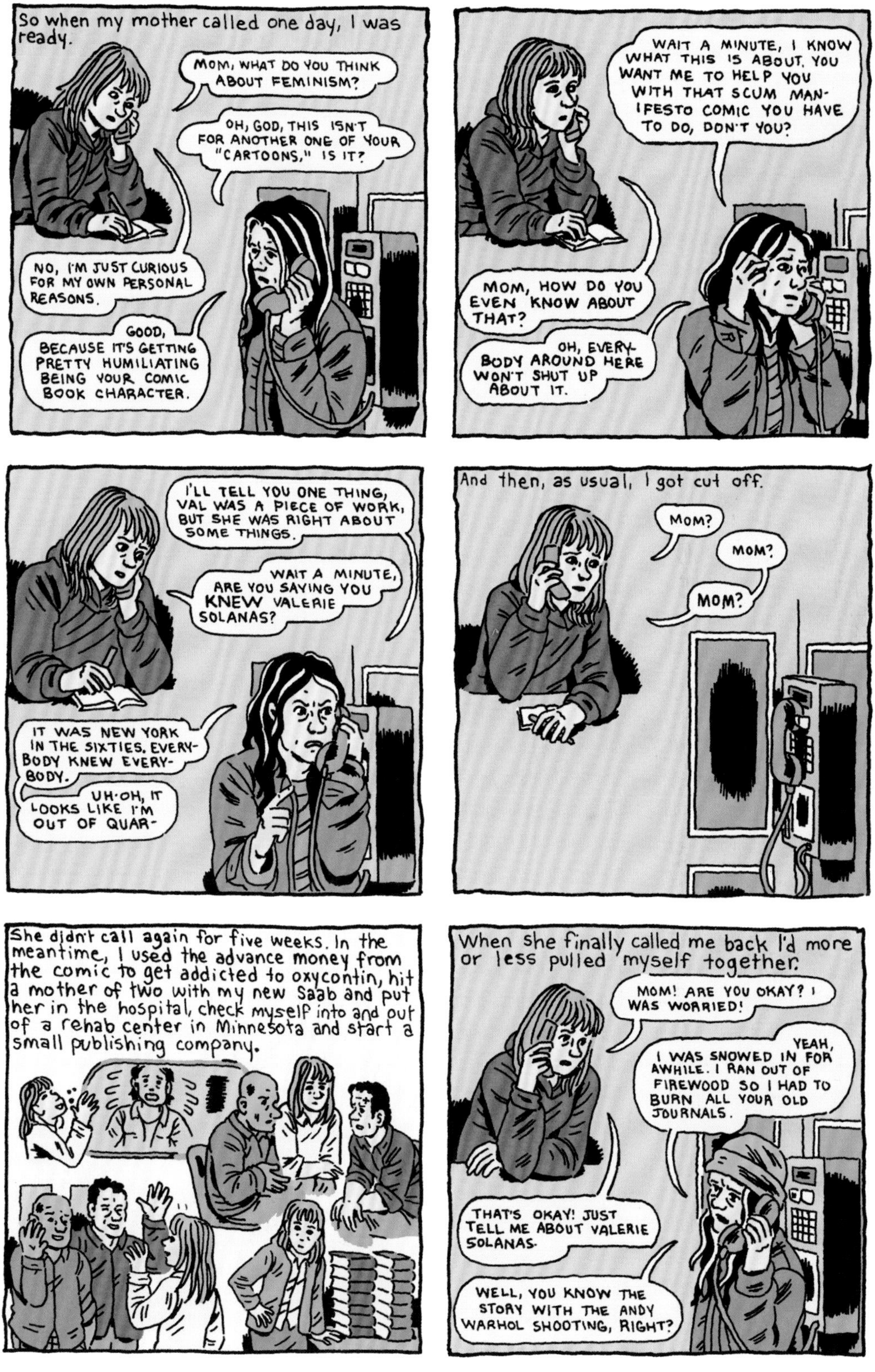
So when my mother called one day, I was ready.
MOM, WHAT DO YOU THINK ABOUT FEMINISM?
OH, GOD, THIS ISN'T FOR ANOTHER ONE OF YOUR "CARTOONS," IS IT?
NO, I'M JUST CURIOUS FOR MY OWN PERSONAL REASONS.
GOOD, BECAUSE IT'S GETTING PRETTY HUMILIATING BEING YOUR COMIC BOOK CHARACTER.
WAIT A MINUTE, I KNOW WHAT THIS IS ABOUT. YOU WANT ME TO HELP YOU WITH THAT SCUM MANIFESTO COMIC YOU HAVE TO DO, DON'T YOU?
MOM, HOW DO YOU EVEN KNOW ABOUT THAT?
OH, EVERYBODY AROUND HERE WON'T SHUT UP ABOUT IT.
I'LL TELL YOU ONE THING, VAL WAS A PIECE OF WORK, BUT SHE WAS RIGHT ABOUT SOME THINGS.
WAIT A MINUTE, ARE YOU SAYING YOU KNEW VALERIE SOLANAS?
IT WAS NEW YORK IN THE SIXTIES. EVERYBODY KNEW EVERYBODY.
UH-OH, IT LOOKS LIKE I'M OUT OF QUAR-
And then, as usual, I got cut off.
MOM?
MOM?
MOM?
She didn't call again for five weeks. In the meantime, I used the advance money from the comic to get addicted to oxycontin, hit a mother of two with my new Saab and put her in the hospital, check myself into and out of a rehab center in Minnesota and start a small publishing company.
When she finally called me back I'd more or less pulled myself together.
MOM! ARE YOU OKAY? I WAS WORRIED!
YEAH, I WAS SNOWED IN FOR AWHILE. I RAN OUT OF FIREWOOD SO I HAD TO BURN ALL YOUR OLD JOURNALS.
THAT'S OKAY! JUST TELL ME ABOUT VALERIE SOLANAS.
WELL, YOU KNOW THE STORY WITH THE ANDY WARHOL SHOOTING, RIGHT?

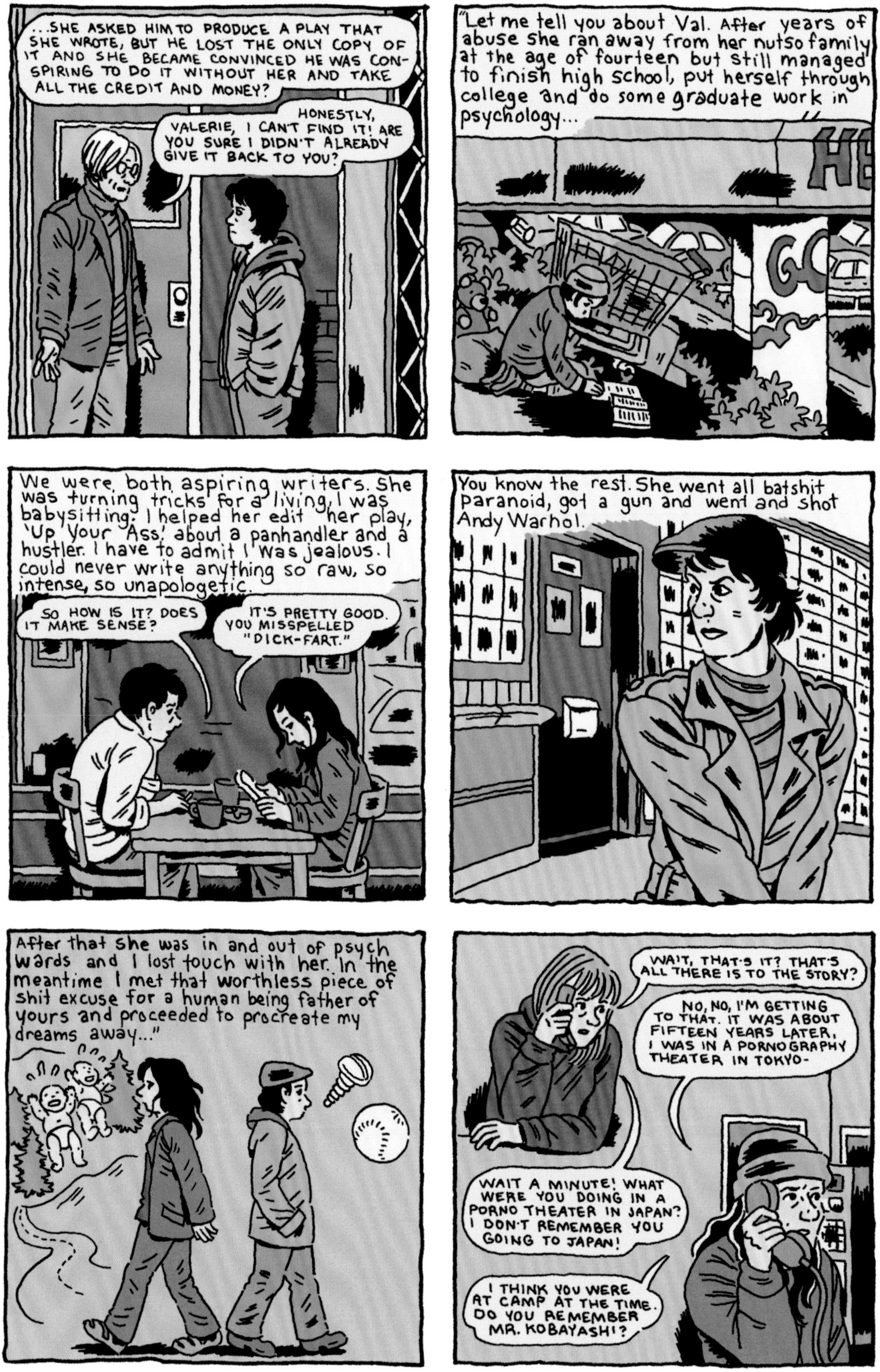
...SHE ASKED HIM TO PRODUCE A PLAY THAT SHE WROTE, BUT HE LOST THE ONLY COPY OF IT AND SHE BECAME CONVINCED HE WAS CONSPIRING TO DO IT WITHOUT HER AND TAKE ALL THE CREDIT AND MONEY?
HONESTLY, VALERIE, I CAN'T FIND IT! ARE YOU SURE I DIDN'T ALREADY GIVE IT BACK TO YOU?
"Let me tell you about Val. After years of abuse she ran away from her nutso family at the age of fourteen but still managed to finish high school, put herself through college and do some graduate work in psychology...
We were both aspiring writers. She was turning tricks for a living, I was babysitting. I helped her edit her play, 'Up Your Ass,' about a panhandler and a hustler. I have to admit I was jealous. I could never write anything so raw, so intense, so unapologetic.
SO HOW IS IT? DOES IT MAKE SENSE?
IT'S PRETTY GOOD. YOU MISSPELLED "DICK-FART."
You know the rest. She went all batshit paranoid, got a gun and went and shot Andy Warhol.
After that she was in and out of psych wards and I lost touch with her. In the meantime I met that worthless piece of shit excuse for a human being father of yours and proceeded to procreate my dreams away..."
WAIT, THAT'S IT? THAT'S ALL THERE IS TO THE STORY?
NO, NO, I'M GETTING TO THAT. IT WAS ABOUT FIFTEEN YEARS LATER, I WAS IN A PORNOGRAPHY THEATER IN TOKYO-
WAIT A MINUTE! WHAT WERE YOU DOING IN A PORNO THEATER IN JAPAN? I DON'T REMEMBER YOU GOING TO JAPAN!
I THINK YOU WERE AT CAMP AT THE TIME. DO YOU REMEMBER MR. KOBAYASHI?

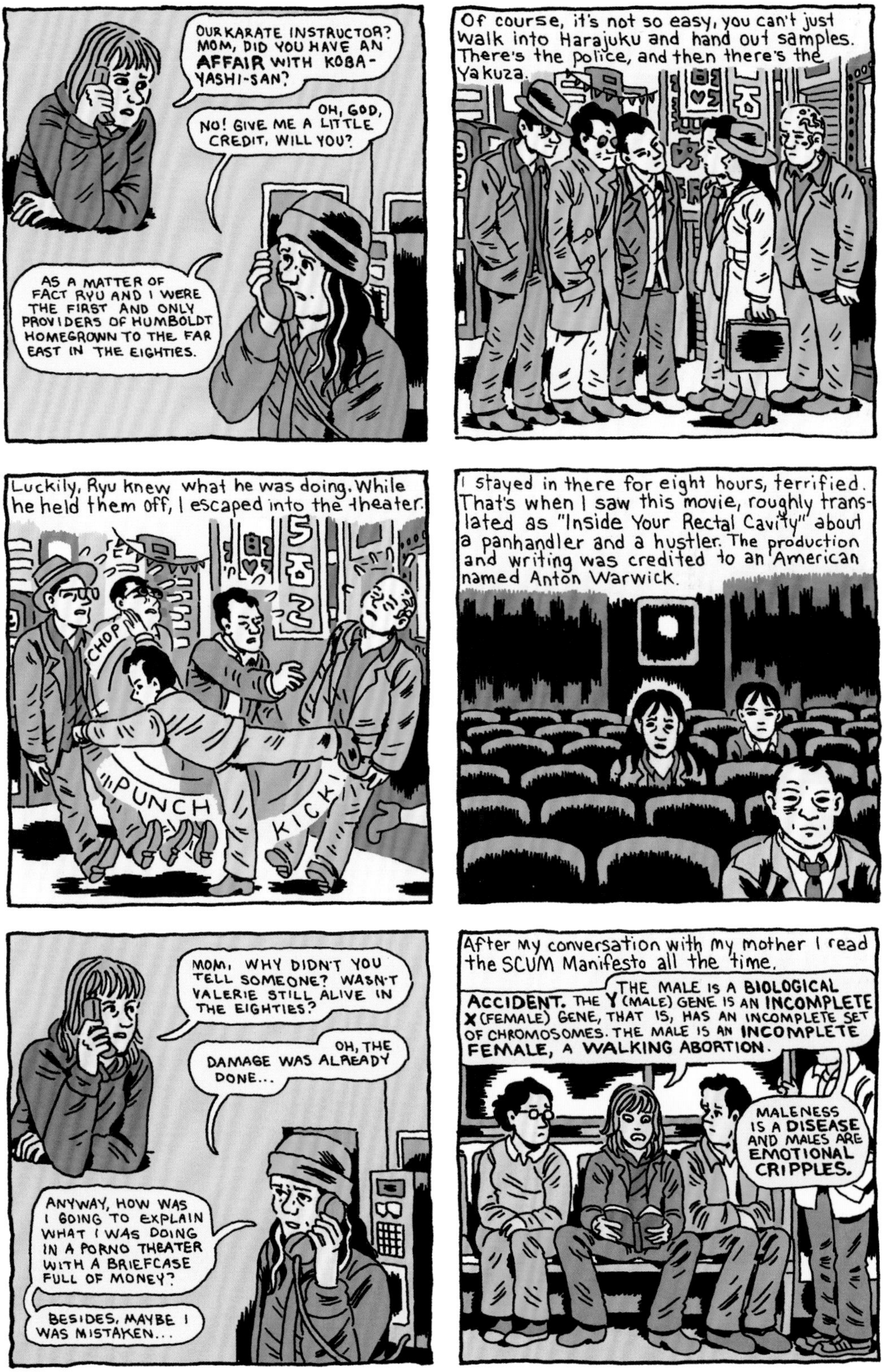
OUR KARATE INSTRUCTOR? MOM, DID YOU HAVE AN AFFAIR WITH KOBA-YASHI-SAN?
OH, GOD, NO! GIVE ME A LITTLE CREDIT, WILL YOU?
AS A MATTER OF FACT RYU AND I WERE THE FIRST AND ONLY PROVIDERS OF HUMBOLDT HOMEGROWN TO THE FAR EAST IN THE EIGHTIES.
Of course, it's not so easy, you can't just walk into Harajuku and hand out samples. There's the police, and then there's the Yakuza.
Luckily, Ryu knew what he was doing. While he held them off, I escaped into the theater.
CHOP
PUNCH
KICK
I stayed in there for eight hours, terrified. That's when I saw this movie, roughly translated as "Inside Your Rectal Cavity" about a panhandler and a hustler. The production and writing was credited to an American named Anton Warwick.
MOM, WHY DIDN'T YOU TELL SOMEONE? WASN'T VALERIE STILL ALIVE IN THE EIGHTIES?
OH, THE DAMAGE WAS ALREADY DONE...
ANYWAY, HOW WAS I GOING TO EXPLAIN WHAT I WAS DOING IN A PORNO THEATER WITH A BRIEFCASE FULL OF MONEY?
BESIDES, MAYBE I WAS MISTAKEN...
After my conversation with my mother I read the SCUM Manifesto all the time.
THE MALE IS A BIOLOGICAL ACCIDENT. THE Y (MALE) GENE IS AN INCOMPLETE X (FEMALE) GENE, THAT IS, HAS AN INCOMPLETE SET OF CHROMOSOMES. THE MALE IS AN INCOMPLETE FEMALE, A WALKING ABORTION.
MALENESS IS A DISEASE AND MALES ARE EMOTIONAL CRIPPLES.

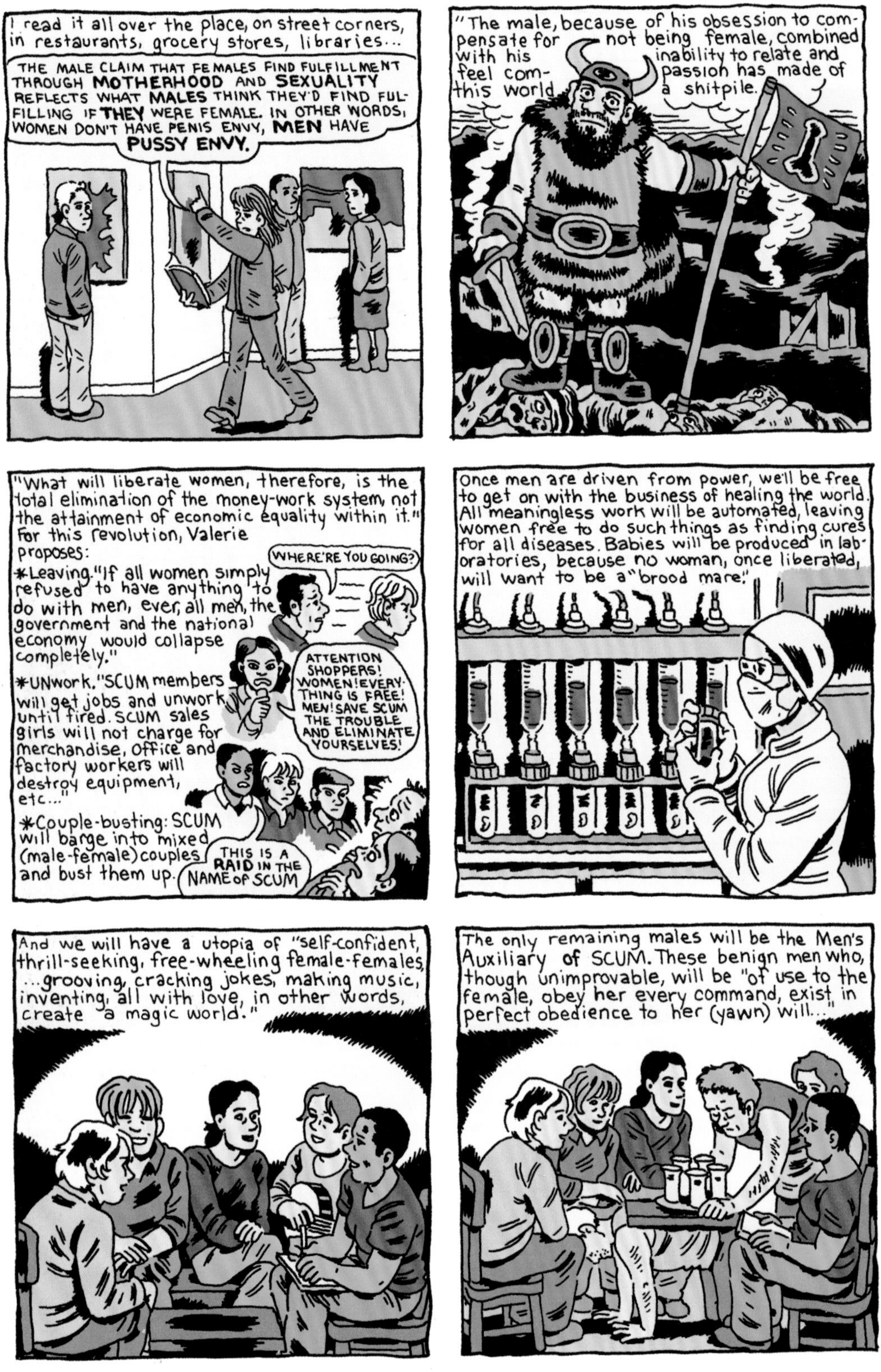
I read it all over the place, on street corners, in restaurants, grocery stores, libraries...
THE MALE CLAIM THAT FEMALES FIND FULFILLMENT THROUGH MOTHERHOOD AND SEXUALITY REFLECTS WHAT MALES THINK THEY'D FIND FULFILLING IF THEY WERE FEMALE. IN OTHER WORDS, WOMEN DON'T HAVE PENIS ENVY, MEN HAVE PUSSY ENVY.
"The male, because of his obsession to compensate for not being female, combined with his inability to relate and feel compassion has made of this world a shitpile.
"What will liberate women, therefore, is the total elimination of the money-work system, not the attainment of economic equality within it." For this revolution, Valerie proposes:
*Leaving. "If all women simply refused to have anything to do with men, ever, all men, the government and the national economy would collapse completely."
WHERE'RE YOU GOING?
*Unwork. "SCUM members will get jobs and unwork until fired. SCUM sales girls will not charge for merchandise, office and factory workers will destroy equipment, etc..."
ATTENTION SHOPPERS! WOMEN! EVERYTHING IS FREE! MEN! SAVE SCUM THE TROUBLE AND ELIMINATE YOURSELVES!
*Couple-busting: SCUM will barge into mixed (male-female) couples and bust them up.
THIS IS A RAID IN THE NAME OF SCUM
Once men are driven from power, we'll be free to get on with the business of healing the world. All meaningless work will be automated, leaving women free to do such things as finding cures for all diseases. Babies will be produced in laboratories, because no woman, once liberated, will want to be a "brood mare."
And we will have a utopia of "self-confident, thrill-seeking, free-wheeling female-females, ...grooving, cracking jokes, making music, inventing, all with love, in other words, create a magic world."
The only remaining males will be the Men's Auxiliary of SCUM. These benign men who, though unimprovable, will be "of use to the female, obey her every command, exist in perfect obedience to her (yawn) will..."

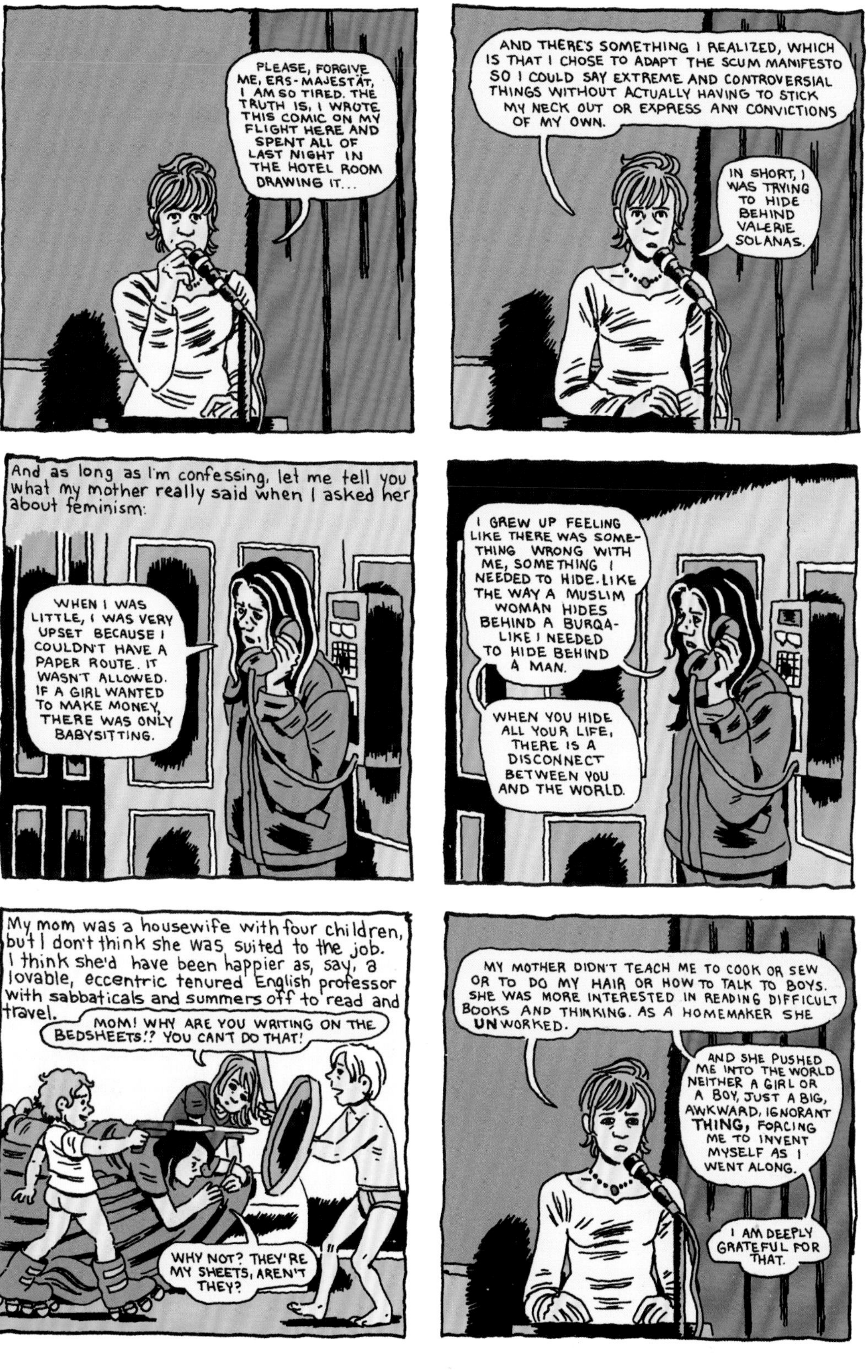
PLEASE, FORGIVE ME, ERS-MAJESTÄT, I AM SO TIRED. THE TRUTH IS, I WROTE THIS COMIC ON MY FLIGHT HERE AND SPENT ALL OF LAST NIGHT IN THE HOTEL ROOM DRAWING IT...
AND THERE'S SOMETHING I REALIZED, WHICH IS THAT I CHOSE TO ADAPT THE SCUM MANIFESTO SO I COULD SAY EXTREME AND CONTROVERSIAL THINGS WITHOUT ACTUALLY HAVING TO STICK MY NECK OUT OR EXPRESS ANY CONVICTIONS OF MY OWN.
IN SHORT, I WAS TRYING TO HIDE BEHIND VALERIE SOLANAS.
And as long as I'm confessing, let me tell you what my mother really said when I asked her about feminism:
WHEN I WAS LITTLE, I WAS VERY UPSET BECAUSE I COULDN'T HAVE A PAPER ROUTE. IT WASN'T ALLOWED. IF A GIRL WANTED TO MAKE MONEY, THERE WAS ONLY BABYSITTING.
I GREW UP FEELING LIKE THERE WAS SOMETHING WRONG WITH ME, SOMETHING I NEEDED TO HIDE. LIKE THE WAY A MUSLIM WOMAN HIDES BEHIND A BURQA- LIKE I NEEDED TO HIDE BEHIND A MAN.
WHEN YOU HIDE ALL YOUR LIFE, THERE IS A DISCONNECT BETWEEN YOU AND THE WORLD.
My mom was a housewife with four children, but I don't think she was suited to the job. I think she'd have been happier as, say, a lovable, eccentric tenured English professor with sabbaticals and summers off to read and travel.
MOM! WHY ARE YOU WRITING ON THE BEDSHEETS!? YOU CAN'T DO THAT!
WHY NOT? THEY'RE MY SHEETS, AREN'T THEY?
MY MOTHER DIDN'T TEACH ME TO COOK OR SEW OR TO DO MY HAIR OR HOW TO TALK TO BOYS. SHE WAS MORE INTERESTED IN READING DIFFICULT BOOKS AND THINKING. AS A HOMEMAKER SHE UNWORKED.
AND SHE PUSHED ME INTO THE WORLD NEITHER A GIRL OR A BOY, JUST A BIG, AWKWARD, IGNORANT THING, FORCING ME TO INVENT MYSELF AS I WENT ALONG.
I AM DEEPLY GRATEFUL FOR THAT.

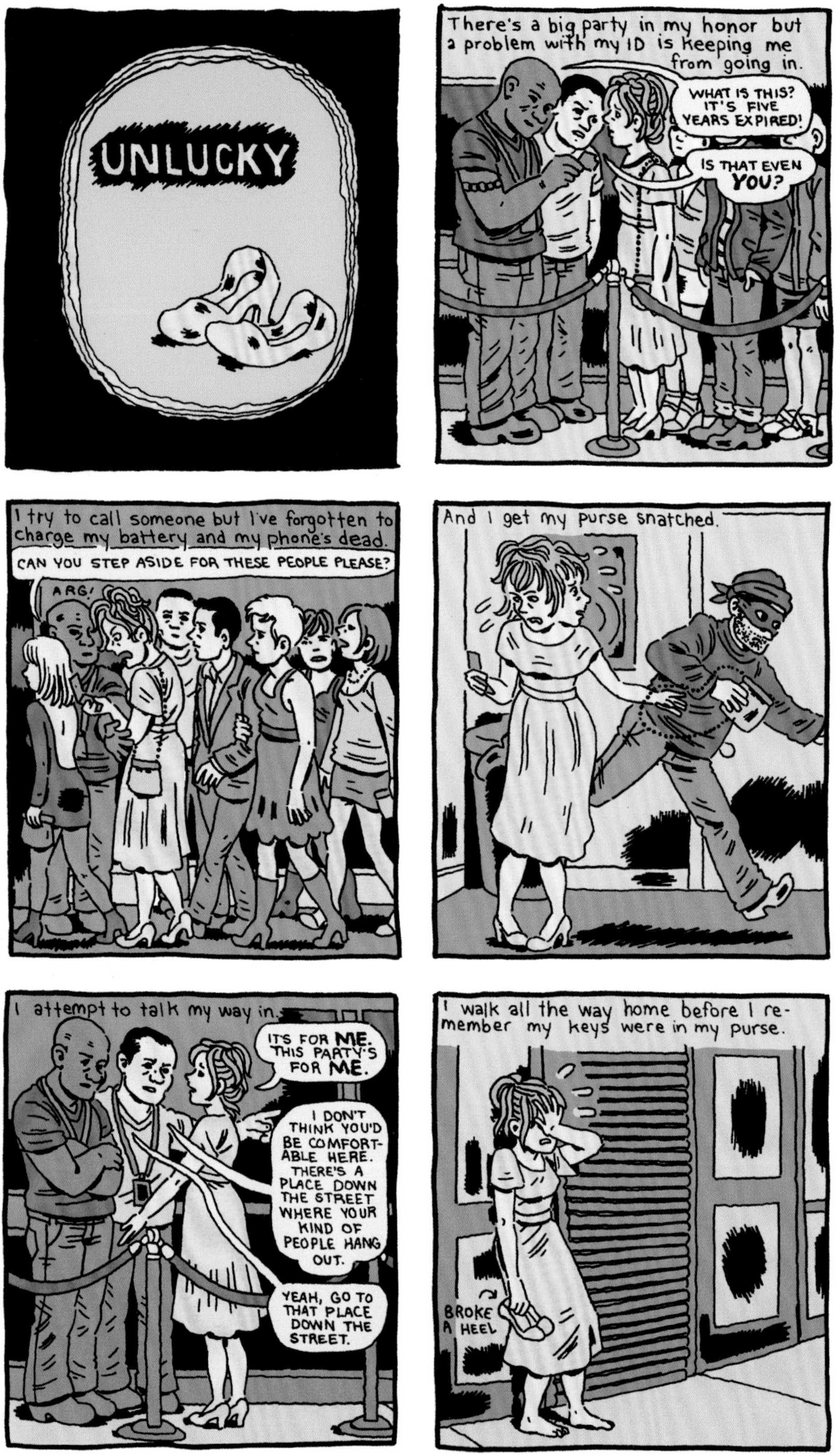
UNLUCKY
There's a big party in my honor but a problem with my ID is keeping me from going in.
WHAT IS THIS? IT'S FIVE YEARS EXPIRED!
IS THAT EVEN YOU?
I try to call someone but I've forgotten to charge my battery and my phone's dead.
CAN YOU STEP ASIDE FOR THESE PEOPLE PLEASE?
ARG!
And I get my purse snatched.
I attempt to talk my way in.
IT'S FOR ME. THIS PARTY'S FOR ME.
I DON'T THINK YOU'D BE COMFORTABLE HERE. THERE'S A PLACE DOWN THE STREET WHERE YOUR KIND OF PEOPLE HANG OUT.
YEAH, GO TO THAT PLACE DOWN THE STREET.
I walk all the way home before I remember my keys were in my purse.
BROKE A HEEL

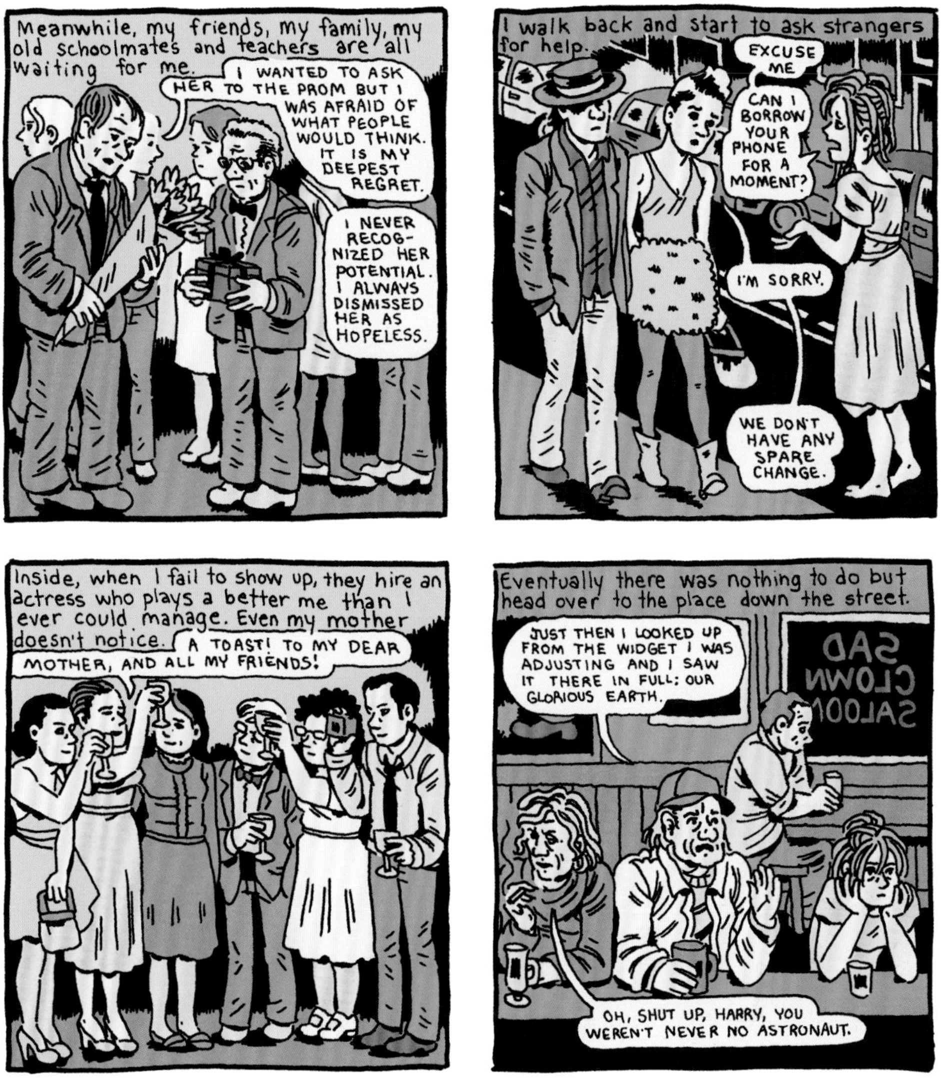
Meanwhile, my friends, my family, my old schoolmates and teachers are all waiting for me.
I WANTED TO ASK HER TO THE PROM BUT I WAS AFRAID OF WHAT PEOPLE WOULD THINK. IT IS MY DEEPEST REGRET.
I NEVER RECOG-NIZED HER POTENTIAL. I ALWAYS DISMISSED HER AS HOPELESS.
I walk back and start to ask strangers for help.
EXCUSE ME
CAN I BORROW YOUR PHONE FOR A MOMENT?
I'M SORRY.
WE DON'T HAVE ANY SPARE CHANGE.
Inside, when I fail to show up, they hire an actress who plays a better me than I ever could manage. Even my mother doesn't notice.
A TOAST! TO MY DEAR MOTHER, AND ALL MY FRIENDS!
Eventually there was nothing to do but head over to the place down the street.
JUST THEN I LOOKED UP FROM THE WIDGET I WAS ADJUSTING AND I SAW IT THERE IN FULL: OUR GLORIOUS EARTH.
OH, SHUT UP, HARRY, YOU WEREN'T NEVER NO ASTRONAUT.

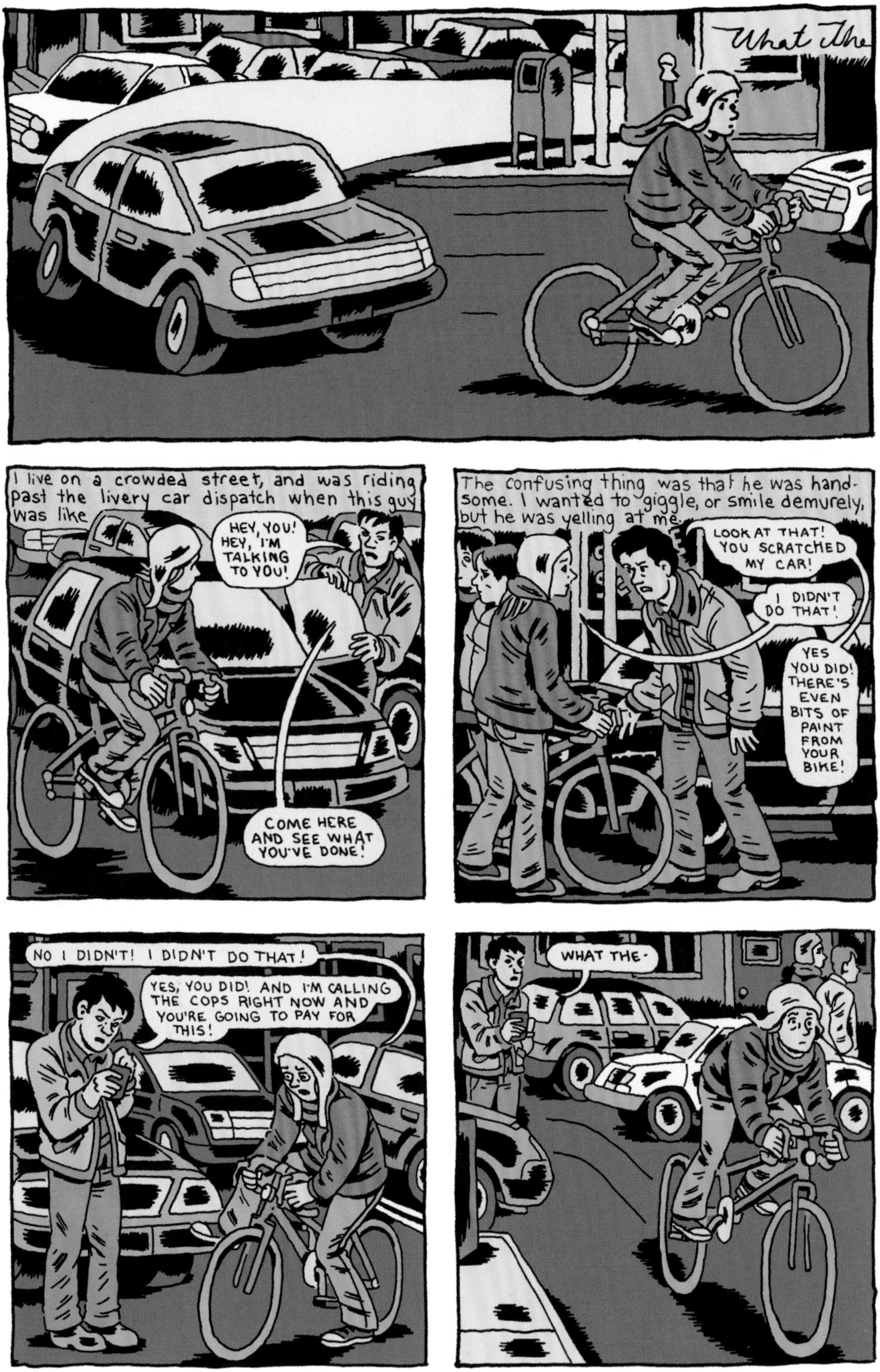
What the
I live on a crowded street, and was riding past the livery car dispatch when this guy was like
HEY, YOU! HEY, I'M TALKING TO YOU!
COME HERE AND SEE WHAT YOU'VE DONE!
The confusing thing was that he was handsome. I wanted to giggle, or smile demurely, but he was yelling at me.
LOOK AT THAT! YOU SCRATCHED MY CAR!
I DIDN'T DO THAT!
YES YOU DID! THERE'S EVEN BITS OF PAINT FROM YOUR BIKE!
NO I DIDN'T! I DIDN'T DO THAT!
YES, YOU DID! AND I'M CALLING THE COPS RIGHT NOW AND YOU'RE GOING TO PAY FOR THIS!
WHAT THE-

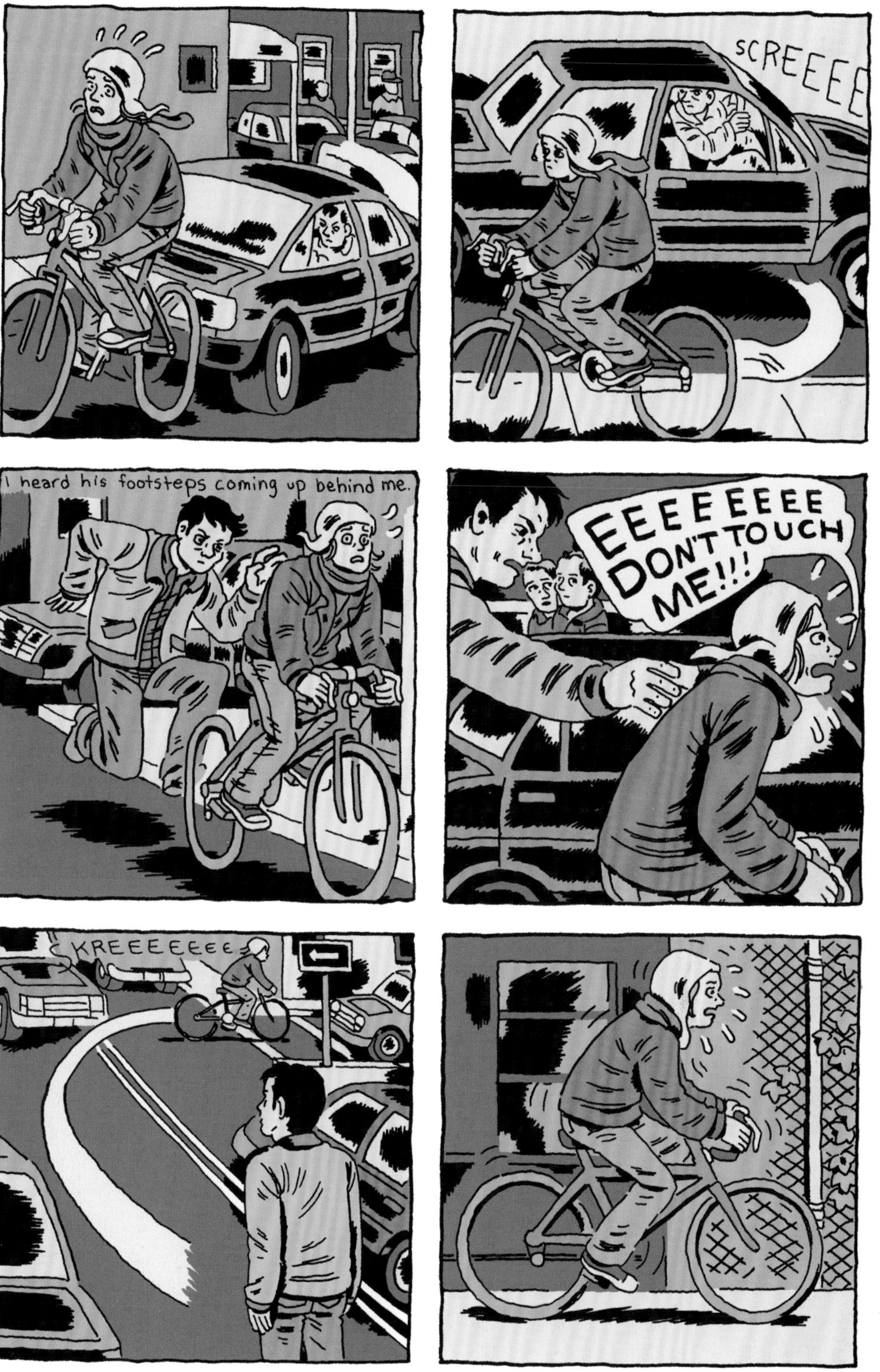
SCREEEEE
I heard his footsteps coming up behind me.
EEEEEEEE DON'T TOUCH ME!!!
KREEEEEEEE

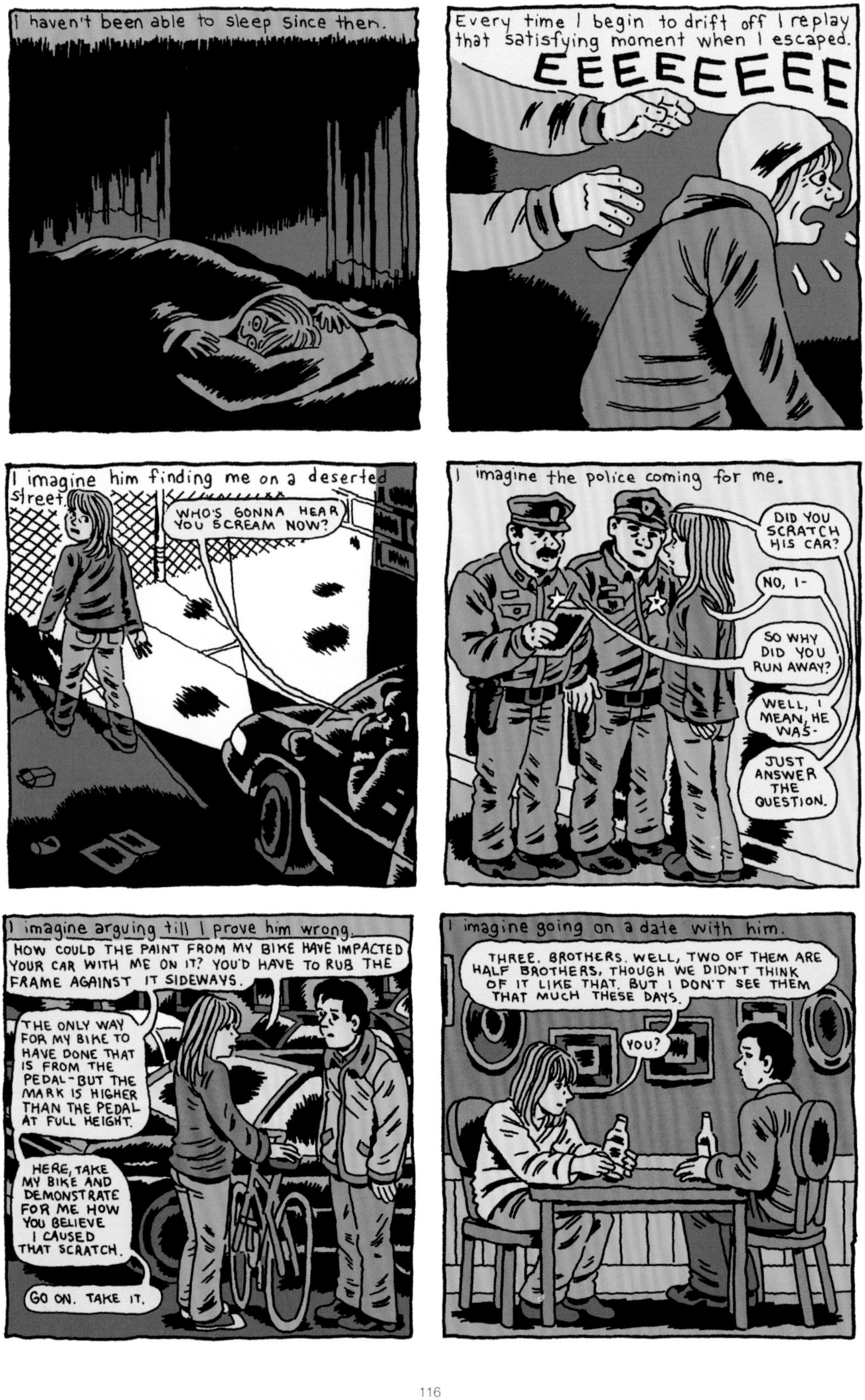

I haven't been able to sleep since then.
Every time I begin to drift off I replay that satisfying moment when I escaped.
EEEEEEEE
I imagine him finding me on a deserted street.
WHO'S GONNA HEAR YOU SCREAM NOW?
I imagine the police coming for me.
DID YOU SCRATCH HIS CAR?
NO, I-
SO WHY DID YOU RUN AWAY?
WELL, I MEAN, HE WAS-
JUST ANSWER THE QUESTION.
I imagine arguing till I prove him wrong.
HOW COULD THE PAINT FROM MY BIKE HAVE IMPACTED YOUR CAR WITH ME ON IT? YOU'D HAVE TO RUB THE FRAME AGAINST IT SIDEWAYS.
THE ONLY WAY FOR MY BIKE TO HAVE DONE THAT IS FROM THE PEDAL-BUT THE MARK IS HIGHER THAN THE PEDAL AT FULL HEIGHT.
HERE, TAKE MY BIKE AND DEMONSTRATE FOR ME HOW YOU BELIEVE I CAUSED THAT SCRATCH.
GO ON. TAKE IT.
I imagine going on a date with him.
THREE. BROTHERS. WELL, TWO OF THEM ARE HALF BROTHERS, THOUGH WE DIDN'T THINK OF IT LIKE THAT. BUT I DON'T SEE THEM THAT MUCH THESE DAYS.
YOU?

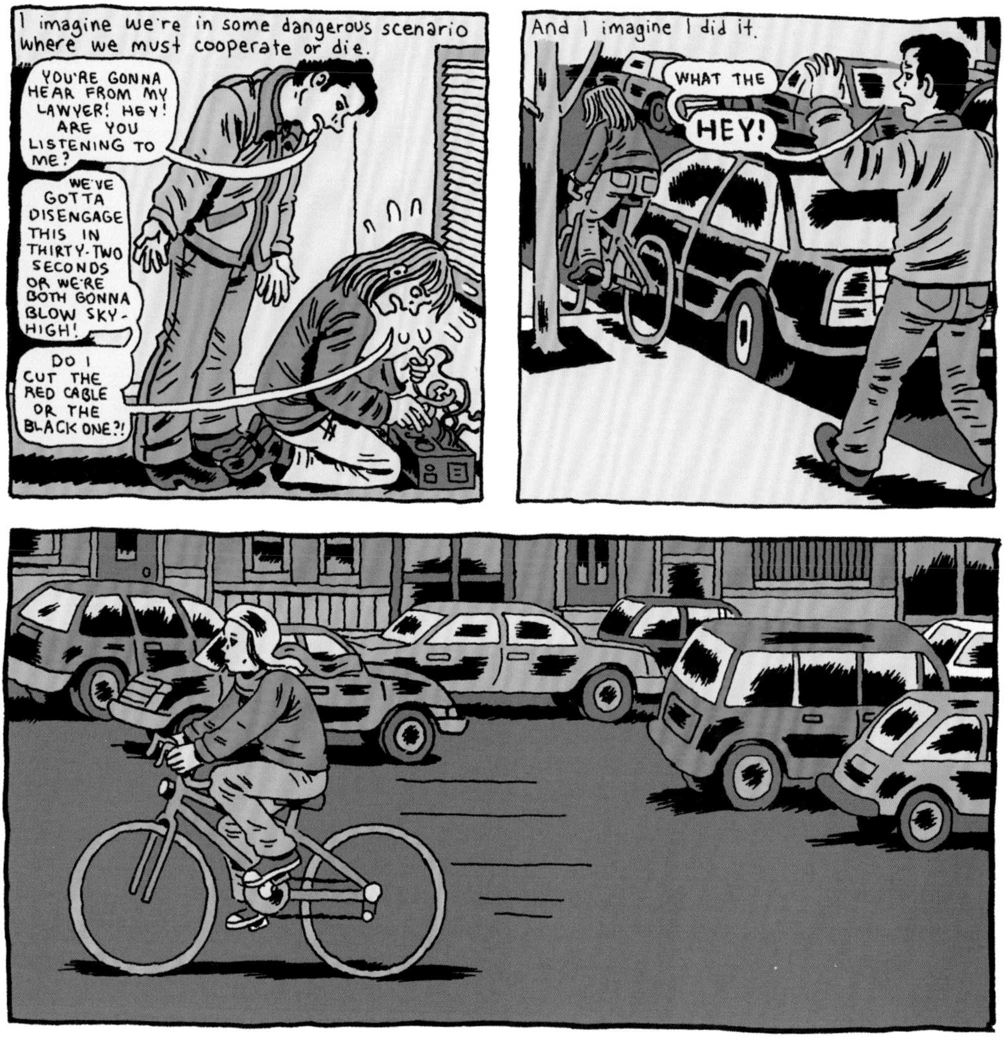
I imagine we're in some dangerous scenario where we must cooperate or die.
YOU'RE GONNA HEAR FROM MY LAWYER! HEY! ARE YOU LISTENING TO ME?
WE'VE GOTTA DISENGAGE THIS IN THIRTY-TWO SECONDS OR WE'RE BOTH GONNA BLOW SKY-HIGH!
DO I CUT THE RED CABLE OR THE BLACK ONE?!
And I imagine I did it.
WHAT THE
HEY!

# Chapter six
## 2010

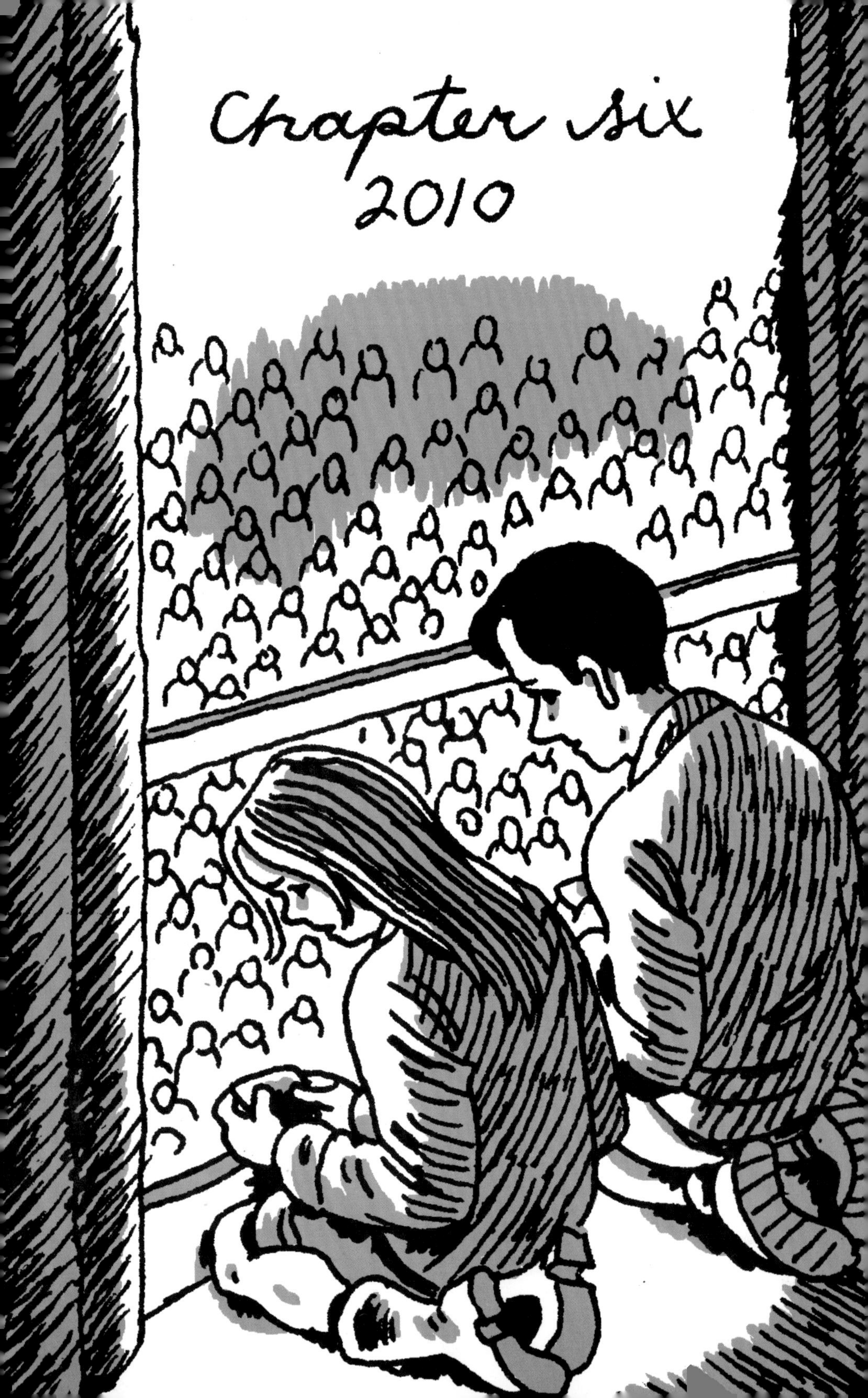

# San Diego Comic-Con Comicumentary

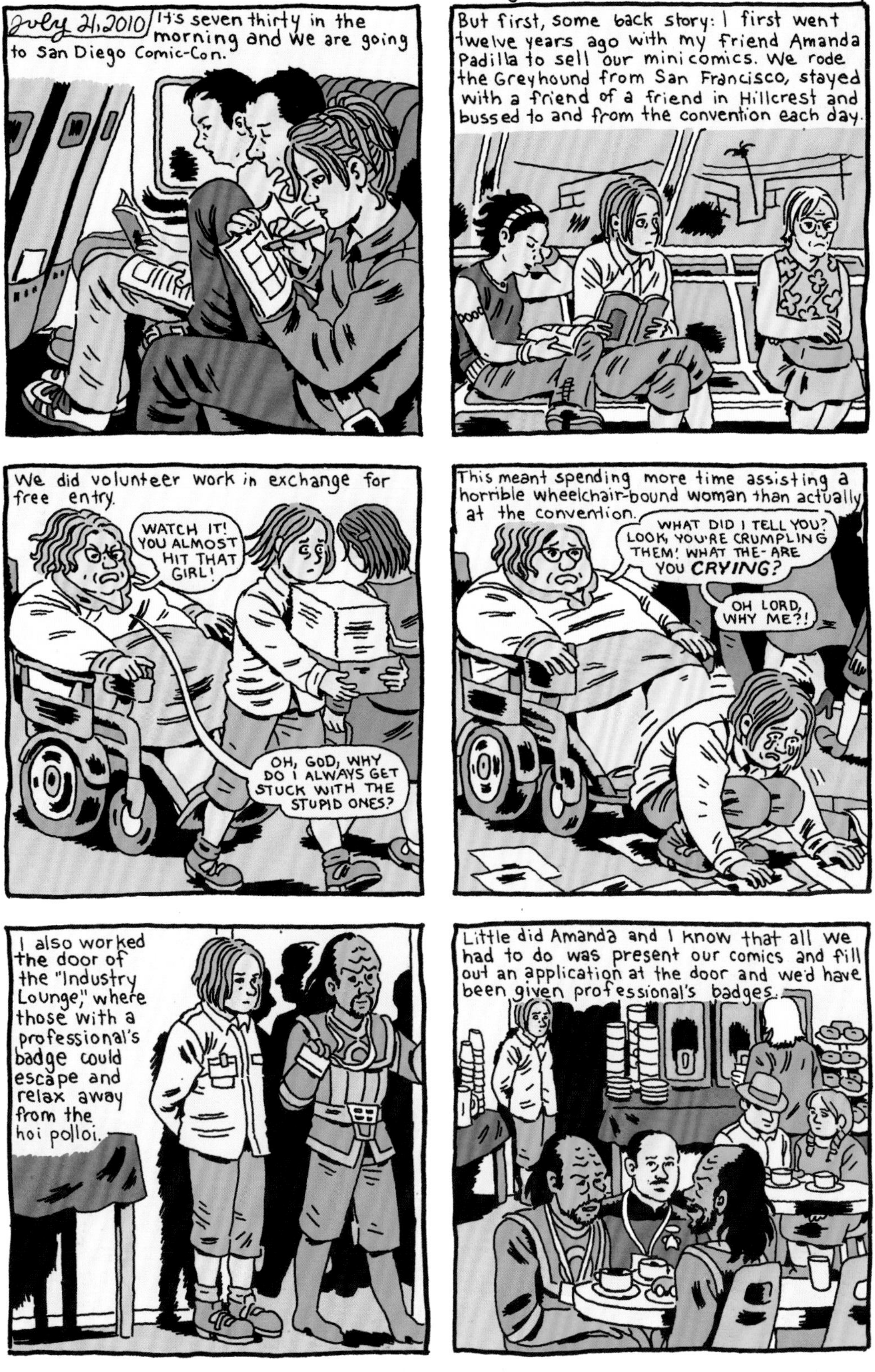

July 21, 2010 It's seven thirty in the morning and we are going to San Diego Comic-Con.
But first, some back story: I first went twelve years ago with my friend Amanda Padilla to sell our mini comics. We rode the Greyhound from San Francisco, stayed with a friend of a friend in Hillcrest and bussed to and from the convention each day.
We did volunteer work in exchange for free entry.
WATCH IT! YOU ALMOST HIT THAT GIRL!
OH, GOD, WHY DO I ALWAYS GET STUCK WITH THE STUPID ONES?
This meant spending more time assisting a horrible wheelchair-bound woman than actually at the convention.
WHAT DID I TELL YOU? LOOK, YOU'RE CRUMPLING THEM! WHAT THE- ARE YOU CRYING?
OH LORD, WHY ME?!
I also worked the door of the "Industry Lounge," where those with a professional's badge could escape and relax away from the hoi polloi.
Little did Amanda and I know that all we had to do was present our comics and fill out an application at the door and we'd have been given professional's badges.

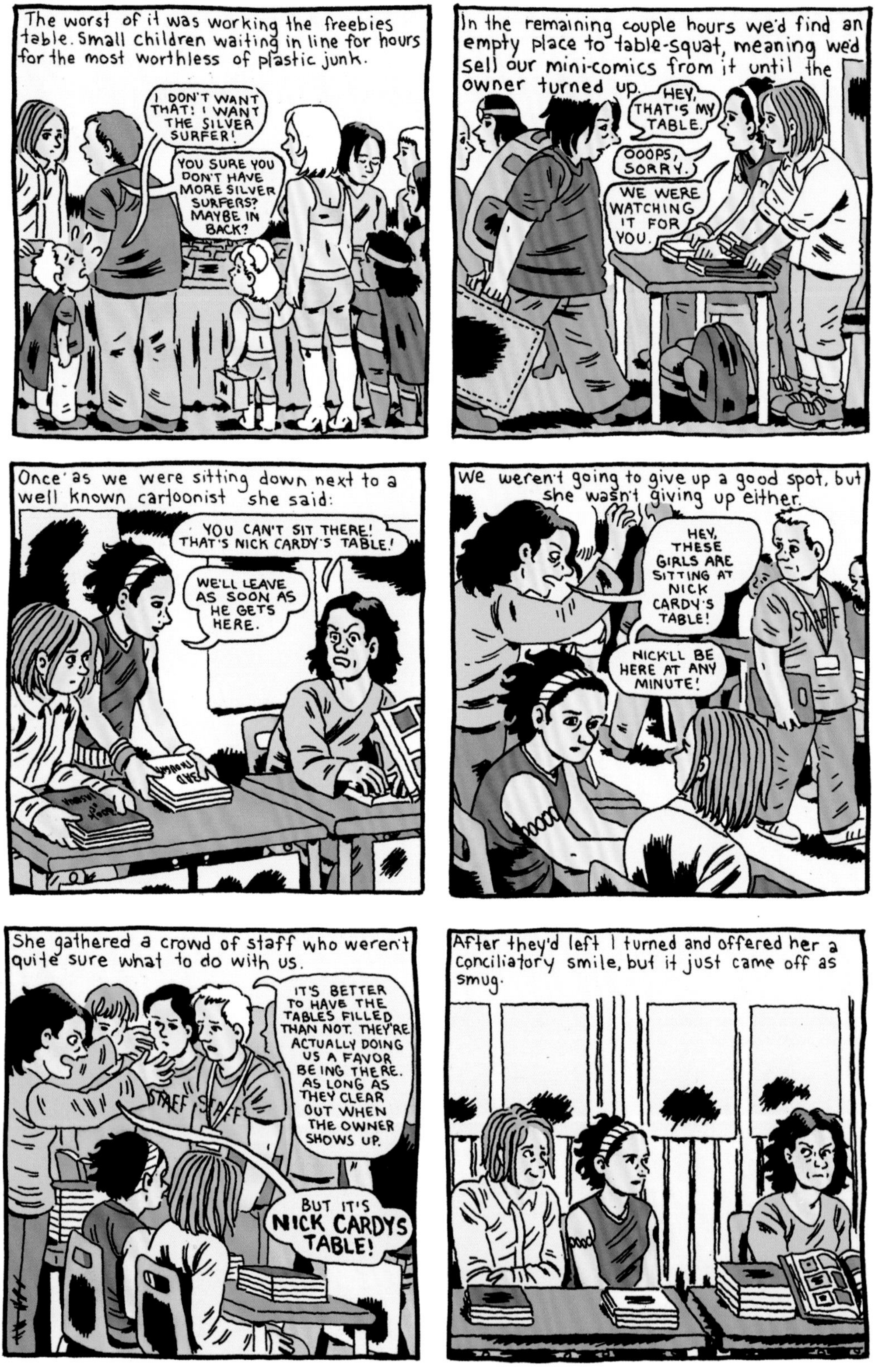
The worst of it was working the freebies table. Small children waiting in line for hours for the most worthless of plastic junk.
I DON'T WANT THAT! I WANT THE SILVER SURFER!
YOU SURE YOU DON'T HAVE MORE SILVER SURFERS? MAYBE IN BACK?
In the remaining couple hours we'd find an empty place to table-squat, meaning we'd sell our mini-comics from it until the owner turned up.
HEY, THAT'S MY TABLE.
OOOPS, SORRY.
WE WERE WATCHING IT FOR YOU.
Once as we were sitting down next to a well known cartoonist she said:
YOU CAN'T SIT THERE! THAT'S NICK CARDY'S TABLE!
WE'LL LEAVE AS SOON AS HE GETS HERE.
We weren't going to give up a good spot, but she wasn't giving up either.
HEY, THESE GIRLS ARE SITTING AT NICK CARDY'S TABLE!
NICK'LL BE HERE AT ANY MINUTE!
STAFF
She gathered a crowd of staff who weren't quite sure what to do with us.
IT'S BETTER TO HAVE THE TABLES FILLED THAN NOT. THEY'RE ACTUALLY DOING US A FAVOR BEING THERE. AS LONG AS THEY CLEAR OUT WHEN THE OWNER SHOWS UP.
BUT IT'S NICK CARDYS TABLE!
STAFF STAFF
After they'd left I turned and offered her a conciliatory smile, but it just came off as smug.

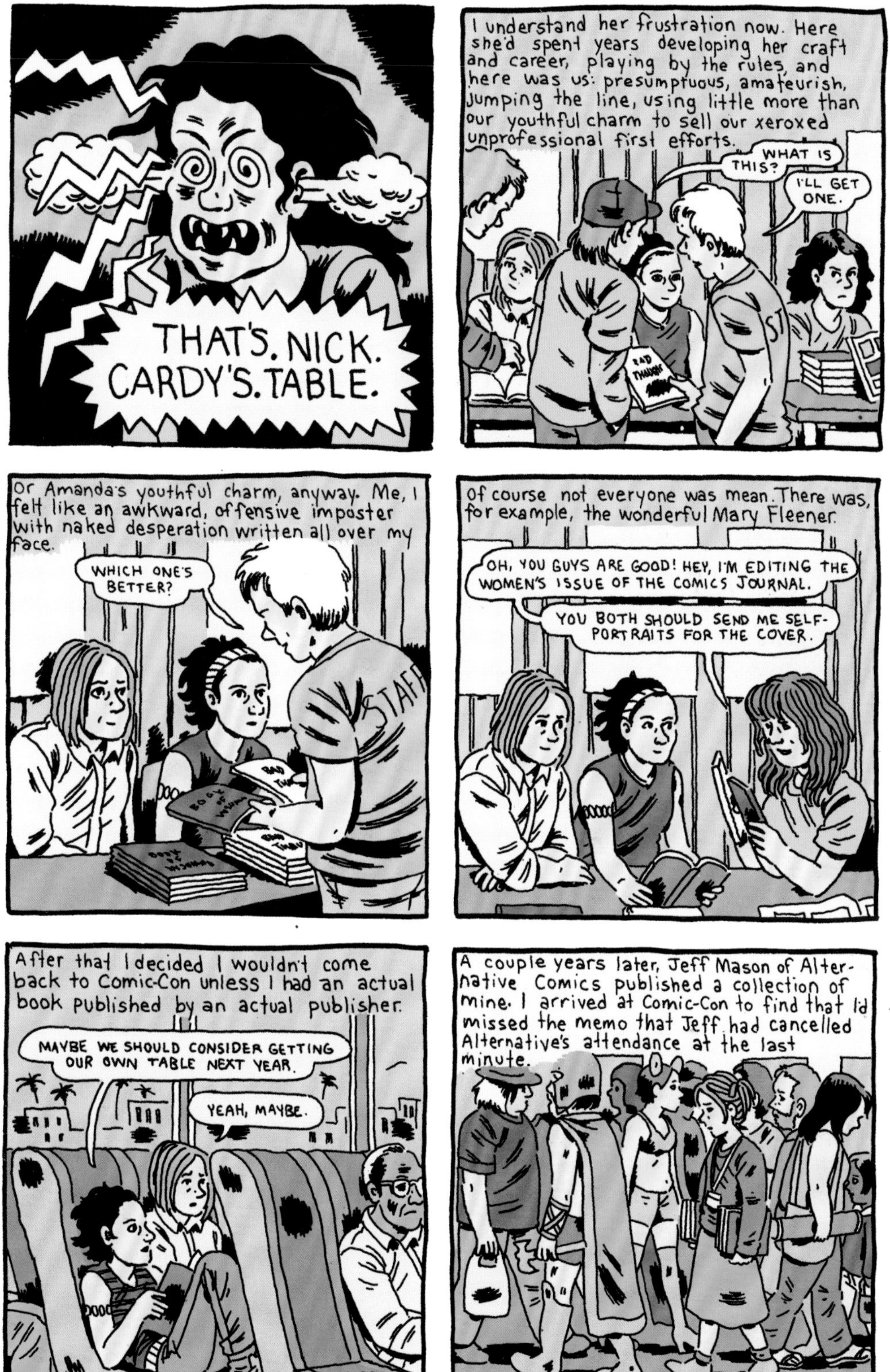
THAT'S. NICK. CARDY'S. TABLE.
I understand her frustration now. Here she'd spent years developing her craft and career, playing by the rules, and here was us: presumptuous, amateurish, jumping the line, using little more than our youthful charm to sell our xeroxed unprofessional first efforts.
WHAT IS THIS?
I'LL GET ONE.
Or Amanda's youthful charm, anyway. Me, I felt like an awkward, offensive imposter with naked desperation written all over my face.
WHICH ONE'S BETTER?
STAFF
Of course not everyone was mean. There was, for example, the wonderful Mary Fleener.
OH, YOU GUYS ARE GOOD! HEY, I'M EDITING THE WOMEN'S ISSUE OF THE COMICS JOURNAL.
YOU BOTH SHOULD SEND ME SELF-PORTRAITS FOR THE COVER.
After that I decided I wouldn't come back to Comic-Con unless I had an actual book published by an actual publisher.
MAYBE WE SHOULD CONSIDER GETTING OUR OWN TABLE NEXT YEAR.
YEAH, MAYBE.
A couple years later, Jeff Mason of Alternative Comics published a collection of mine. I arrived at Comic-Con to find that I'd missed the memo that Jeff had cancelled Alternative's attendance at the last minute.

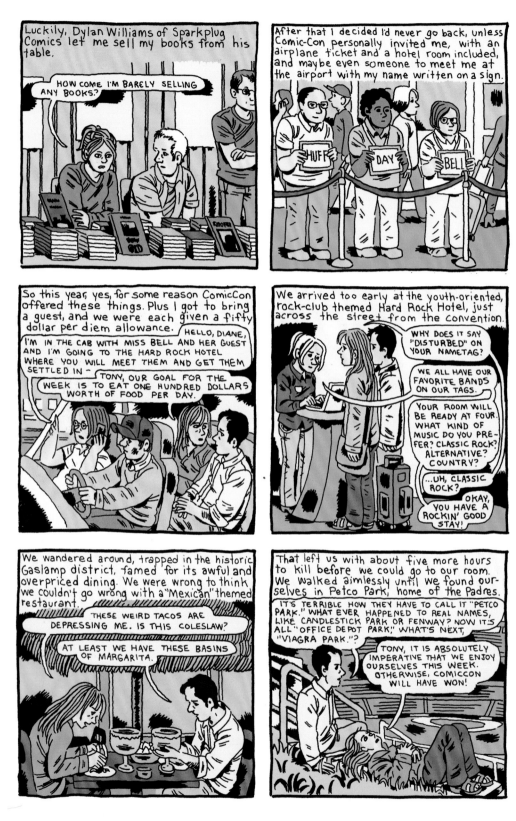

Luckily, Dylan Williams of Sparkplug Comics let me sell my books from his table.

HOW COME I'M BARELY SELLING ANY BOOKS?

After that I decided I'd never go back, unless Comic-Con personally invited me, with an airplane ticket and a hotel room included, and maybe even someone to meet me at the airport with my name written on a sign.

HUFF

DAY

BELL

So this year, yes, for some reason ComicCon offered these things. Plus I got to bring a guest, and we were each given a fifty dollar per diem allowance.

HELLO, DIANE, I'M IN THE CAB WITH MISS BELL AND HER GUEST AND I'M GOING TO THE HARD ROCK HOTEL WHERE YOU WILL MEET THEM AND GET THEM SETTLED IN—

TONY, OUR GOAL FOR THE WEEK IS TO EAT ONE HUNDRED DOLLARS WORTH OF FOOD PER DAY.

We arrived too early at the youth-oriented, rock-club themed Hard Rock Hotel, just across the street from the convention.

WHY DOES IT SAY "DISTURBED" ON YOUR NAMETAG?

WE ALL HAVE OUR FAVORITE BANDS ON OUR TAGS.

YOUR ROOM WILL BE READY AT FOUR. WHAT KIND OF MUSIC DO YOU PRE-FER? CLASSIC ROCK? ALTERNATIVE? COUNTRY?

...UH, CLASSIC ROCK?

OKAY, YOU HAVE A ROCKIN' GOOD STAY!

We wandered around, trapped in the historic Gaslamp district, famed for its awful and overpriced dining. We were wrong to think we couldn't go wrong with a "Mexican" themed restaurant.

THESE WEIRD TACOS ARE DEPRESSING ME. IS THIS COLESLAW?

AT LEAST WE HAVE THESE BASINS OF MARGARITA.

That left us with about five more hours to kill before we could go to our room. We walked aimlessly until we found our-selves in Petco Park, home of the Padres.

IT'S TERRIBLE HOW THEY HAVE TO CALL IT "PETCO PARK." WHAT EVER HAPPENED TO REAL NAMES, LIKE CANDLESTICK PARK OR FENWAY? NOW IT'S ALL "OFFICE DEPOT PARK." WHAT'S NEXT, "VIAGRA PARK."?

TONY, IT IS ABSOLUTELY IMPERATIVE THAT WE ENJOY OURSELVES THIS WEEK. OTHERWISE, COMICCON WILL HAVE WON!

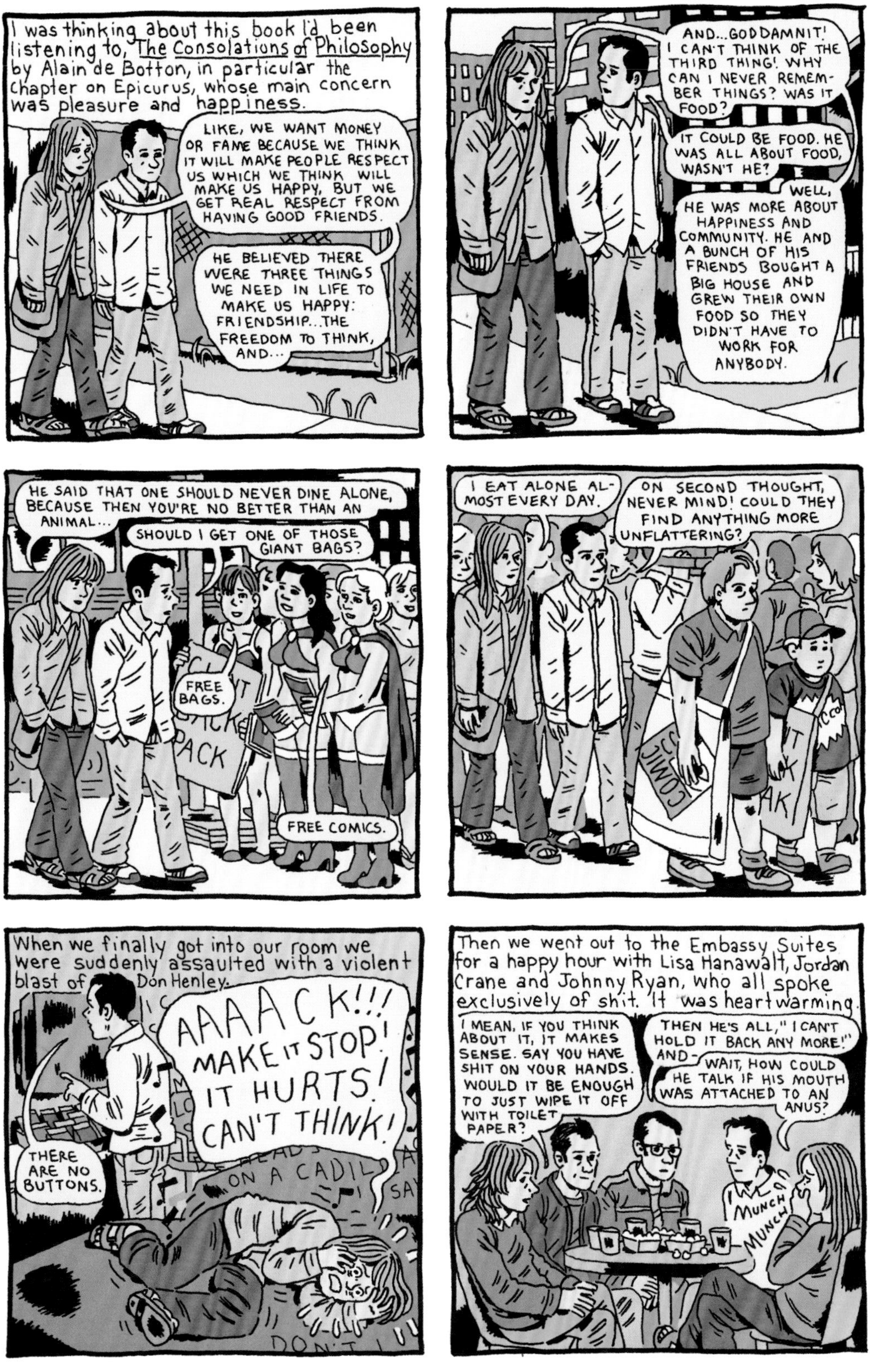
I was thinking about this book I'd been listening to, The Consolations of Philosophy by Alain de Botton, in particular the chapter on Epicurus, whose main concern was pleasure and happiness.
LIKE, WE WANT MONEY OR FAME BECAUSE WE THINK IT WILL MAKE PEOPLE RESPECT US WHICH WE THINK WILL MAKE US HAPPY, BUT WE GET REAL RESPECT FROM HAVING GOOD FRIENDS.
HE BELIEVED THERE WERE THREE THINGS WE NEED IN LIFE TO MAKE US HAPPY: FRIENDSHIP...THE FREEDOM TO THINK, AND...
AND...GODDAMNIT! I CAN'T THINK OF THE THIRD THING! WHY CAN I NEVER REMEMBER THINGS? WAS IT FOOD?
IT COULD BE FOOD. HE WAS ALL ABOUT FOOD, WASN'T HE?
WELL, HE WAS MORE ABOUT HAPPINESS AND COMMUNITY. HE AND A BUNCH OF HIS FRIENDS BOUGHT A BIG HOUSE AND GREW THEIR OWN FOOD SO THEY DIDN'T HAVE TO WORK FOR ANYBODY.
HE SAID THAT ONE SHOULD NEVER DINE ALONE, BECAUSE THEN YOU'RE NO BETTER THAN AN ANIMAL...
SHOULD I GET ONE OF THOSE GIANT BAGS?
FREE BAGS.
FREE COMICS.
I EAT ALONE ALMOST EVERY DAY.
ON SECOND THOUGHT, NEVER MIND! COULD THEY FIND ANYTHING MORE UNFLATTERING?
When we finally got into our room we were suddenly assaulted with a violent blast of Don Henley.
AAAACK!!! MAKE IT STOP! IT HURTS! CAN'T THINK!
THERE ARE NO BUTTONS.
ON A CADIL
Then we went out to the Embassy Suites for a happy hour with Lisa Hanawalt, Jordan Crane and Johnny Ryan, who all spoke exclusively of shit. It was heartwarming.
I MEAN, IF YOU THINK ABOUT IT, IT MAKES SENSE. SAY YOU HAVE SHIT ON YOUR HANDS. WOULD IT BE ENOUGH TO JUST WIPE IT OFF WITH TOILET PAPER?
THEN HE'S ALL, "I CAN'T HOLD IT BACK ANY MORE!" AND-
WAIT, HOW COULD HE TALK IF HIS MOUTH WAS ATTACHED TO AN ANUS?
MUNCH
MUNCH

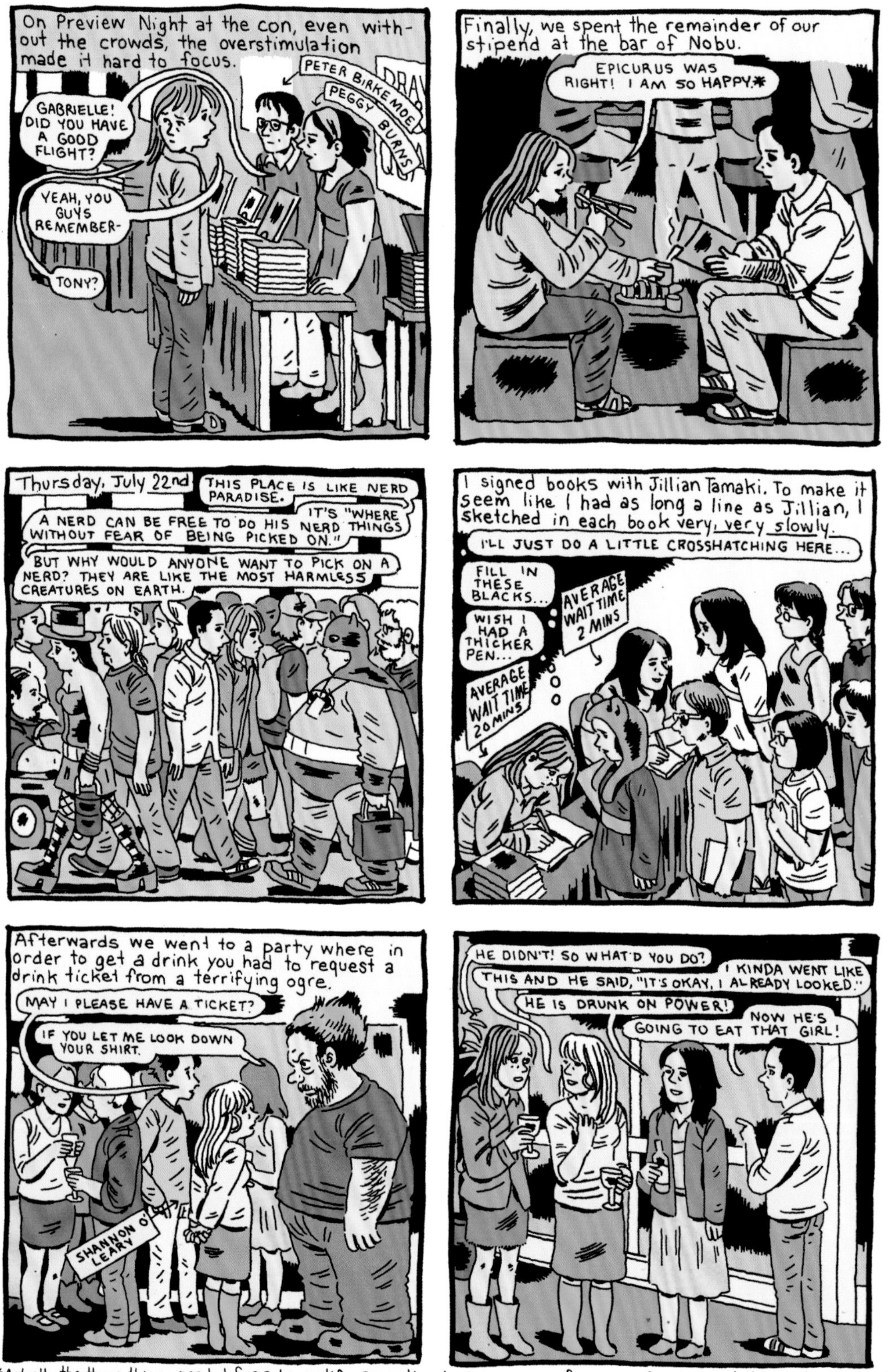
On Preview Night at the con, even without the crowds, the overstimulation made it hard to focus.
PETER BIRKEMOE
PEGGY BURNS
GABRIELLE! DID YOU HAVE A GOOD FLIGHT?
YEAH, YOU GUYS REMEMBER-
TONY?
Finally, we spent the remainder of our stipend at the bar of Nobu.
EPICURUS WAS RIGHT! I AM SO HAPPY.*
Thursday, July 22nd
THIS PLACE IS LIKE NERD PARADISE.
IT'S "WHERE A NERD CAN BE FREE TO DO HIS NERD THINGS WITHOUT FEAR OF BEING PICKED ON."
BUT WHY WOULD ANYONE WANT TO PICK ON A NERD? THEY ARE LIKE THE MOST HARMLESS CREATURES ON EARTH.
I signed books with Jillian Tamaki. To make it seem like I had as long a line as Jillian, I sketched in each book very, very slowly.
I'LL JUST DO A LITTLE CROSSHATCHING HERE...
FILL IN THESE BLACKS...
WISH I HAD A THICKER PEN...
AVERAGE WAIT TIME 2 MINS
AVERAGE WAIT TIME 20 MINS
Afterwards we went to a party where in order to get a drink you had to request a drink ticket from a terrifying ogre.
MAY I PLEASE HAVE A TICKET?
IF YOU LET ME LOOK DOWN YOUR SHIRT.
SHANNON O'LEARY
HE DIDN'T! SO WHAT'D YOU DO?
I KINDA WENT LIKE THIS AND HE SAID, "IT'S OKAY, I ALREADY LOOKED."
HE IS DRUNK ON POWER!
NOW HE'S GOING TO EAT THAT GIRL!

*Actually the three things needed for a happy life, according to Epicurus are friendship, freedom and the ability to think

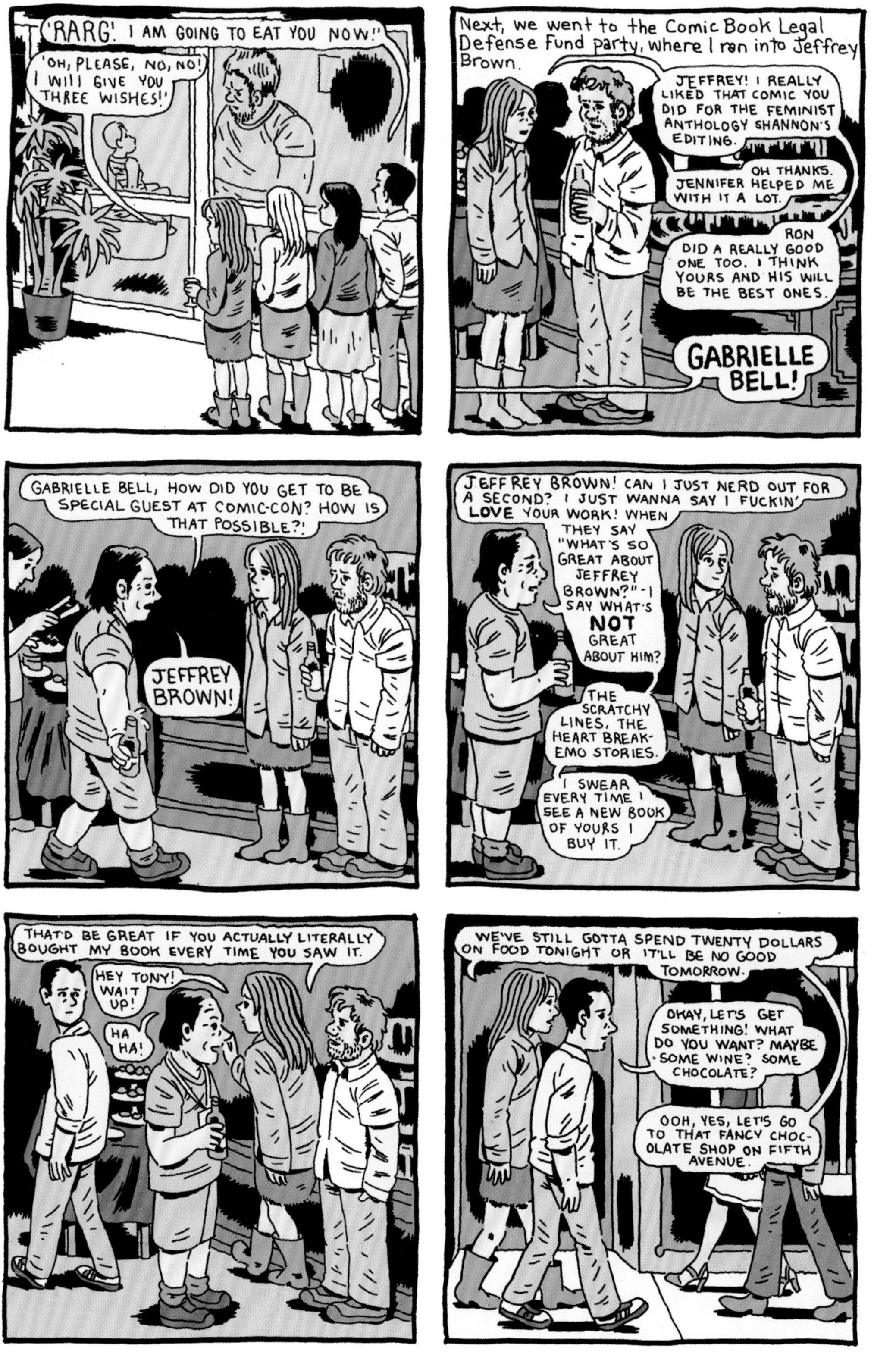
'RARG! I AM GOING TO EAT YOU NOW!'
'OH, PLEASE, NO, NO! I WILL GIVE YOU THREE WISHES!'
Next, we went to the Comic Book Legal Defense Fund party, where I ran into Jeffrey Brown.
JEFFREY! I REALLY LIKED THAT COMIC YOU DID FOR THE FEMINIST ANTHOLOGY SHANNON'S EDITING.
OH THANKS. JENNIFER HELPED ME WITH IT A LOT.
RON DID A REALLY GOOD ONE TOO. I THINK YOURS AND HIS WILL BE THE BEST ONES.
GABRIELLE BELL!
GABRIELLE BELL, HOW DID YOU GET TO BE SPECIAL GUEST AT COMIC-CON? HOW IS THAT POSSIBLE?!
JEFFREY BROWN!
JEFFREY BROWN! CAN I JUST NERD OUT FOR A SECOND? I JUST WANNA SAY I FUCKIN' LOVE YOUR WORK! WHEN THEY SAY "WHAT'S SO GREAT ABOUT JEFFREY BROWN?" - I SAY WHAT'S NOT GREAT ABOUT HIM?
THE SCRATCHY LINES, THE HEART BREAK-EMO STORIES.
I SWEAR EVERY TIME I SEE A NEW BOOK OF YOURS I BUY IT.
THAT'D BE GREAT IF YOU ACTUALLY LITERALLY BOUGHT MY BOOK EVERY TIME YOU SAW IT.
HEY TONY! WAIT UP!
HA HA!
WE'VE STILL GOTTA SPEND TWENTY DOLLARS ON FOOD TONIGHT OR IT'LL BE NO GOOD TOMORROW.
OKAY, LET'S GET SOMETHING! WHAT DO YOU WANT? MAYBE SOME WINE? SOME CHOCOLATE?
OOH, YES, LET'S GO TO THAT FANCY CHOCOLATE SHOP ON FIFTH AVENUE.

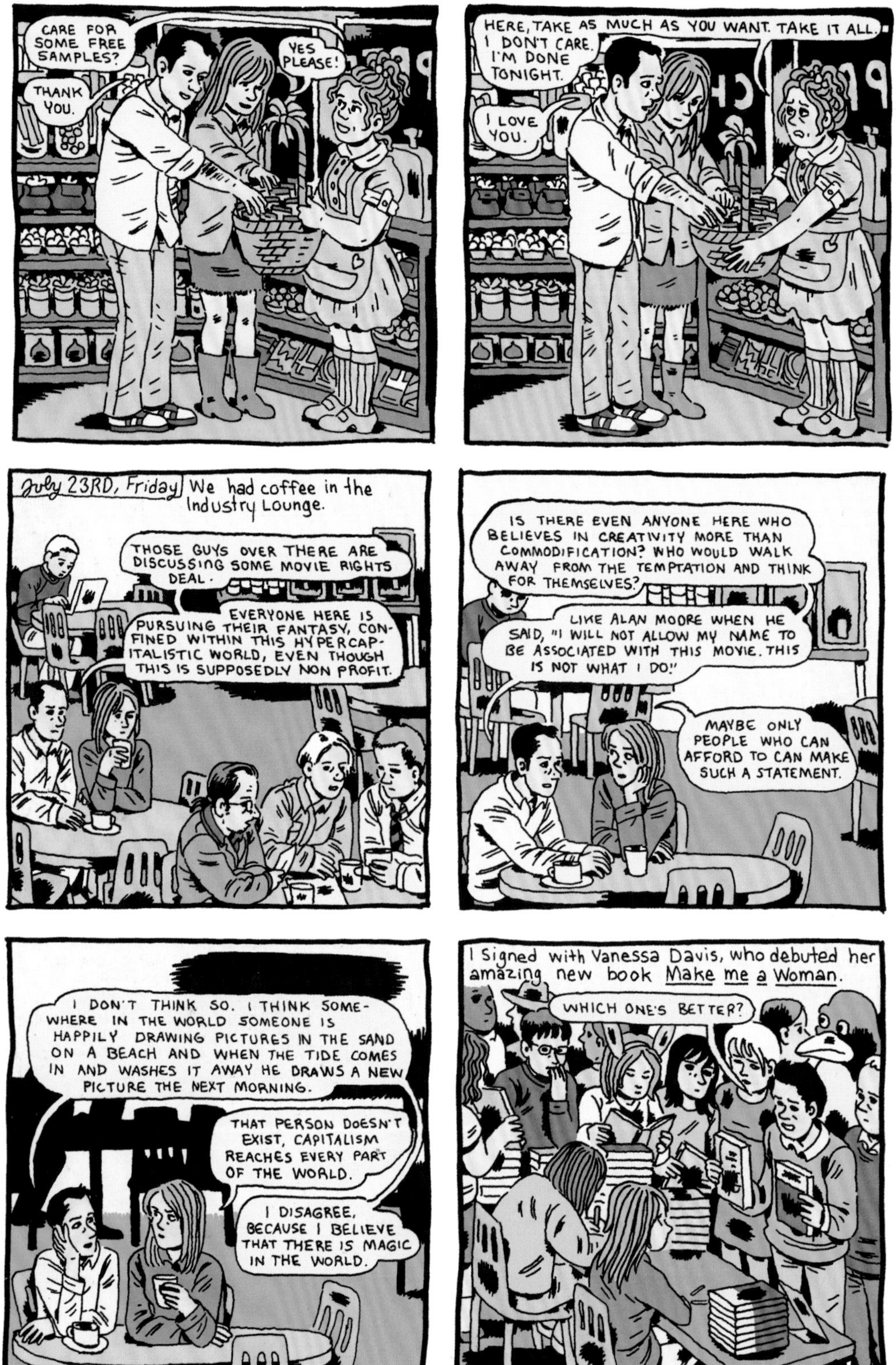

CARE FOR SOME FREE SAMPLES?
THANK YOU.
YES PLEASE!
HERE, TAKE AS MUCH AS YOU WANT. TAKE IT ALL. I DON'T CARE. I'M DONE TONIGHT.
I LOVE YOU.
July 23RD, Friday
We had coffee in the Industry Lounge.
THOSE GUYS OVER THERE ARE DISCUSSING SOME MOVIE RIGHTS DEAL.
EVERYONE HERE IS PURSUING THEIR FANTASY, CONFINED WITHIN THIS HYPERCAPITALISTIC WORLD, EVEN THOUGH THIS IS SUPPOSEDLY NON PROFIT.
IS THERE EVEN ANYONE HERE WHO BELIEVES IN CREATIVITY MORE THAN COMMODIFICATION? WHO WOULD WALK AWAY FROM THE TEMPTATION AND THINK FOR THEMSELVES?
LIKE ALAN MOORE WHEN HE SAID, "I WILL NOT ALLOW MY NAME TO BE ASSOCIATED WITH THIS MOVIE. THIS IS NOT WHAT I DO."
MAYBE ONLY PEOPLE WHO CAN AFFORD TO CAN MAKE SUCH A STATEMENT.
I DON'T THINK SO. I THINK SOMEWHERE IN THE WORLD SOMEONE IS HAPPILY DRAWING PICTURES IN THE SAND ON A BEACH AND WHEN THE TIDE COMES IN AND WASHES IT AWAY HE DRAWS A NEW PICTURE THE NEXT MORNING.
THAT PERSON DOESN'T EXIST, CAPITALISM REACHES EVERY PART OF THE WORLD.
I DISAGREE, BECAUSE I BELIEVE THAT THERE IS MAGIC IN THE WORLD.
I Signed with Vanessa Davis, who debuted her amazing new book Make me a Woman.
WHICH ONE'S BETTER?

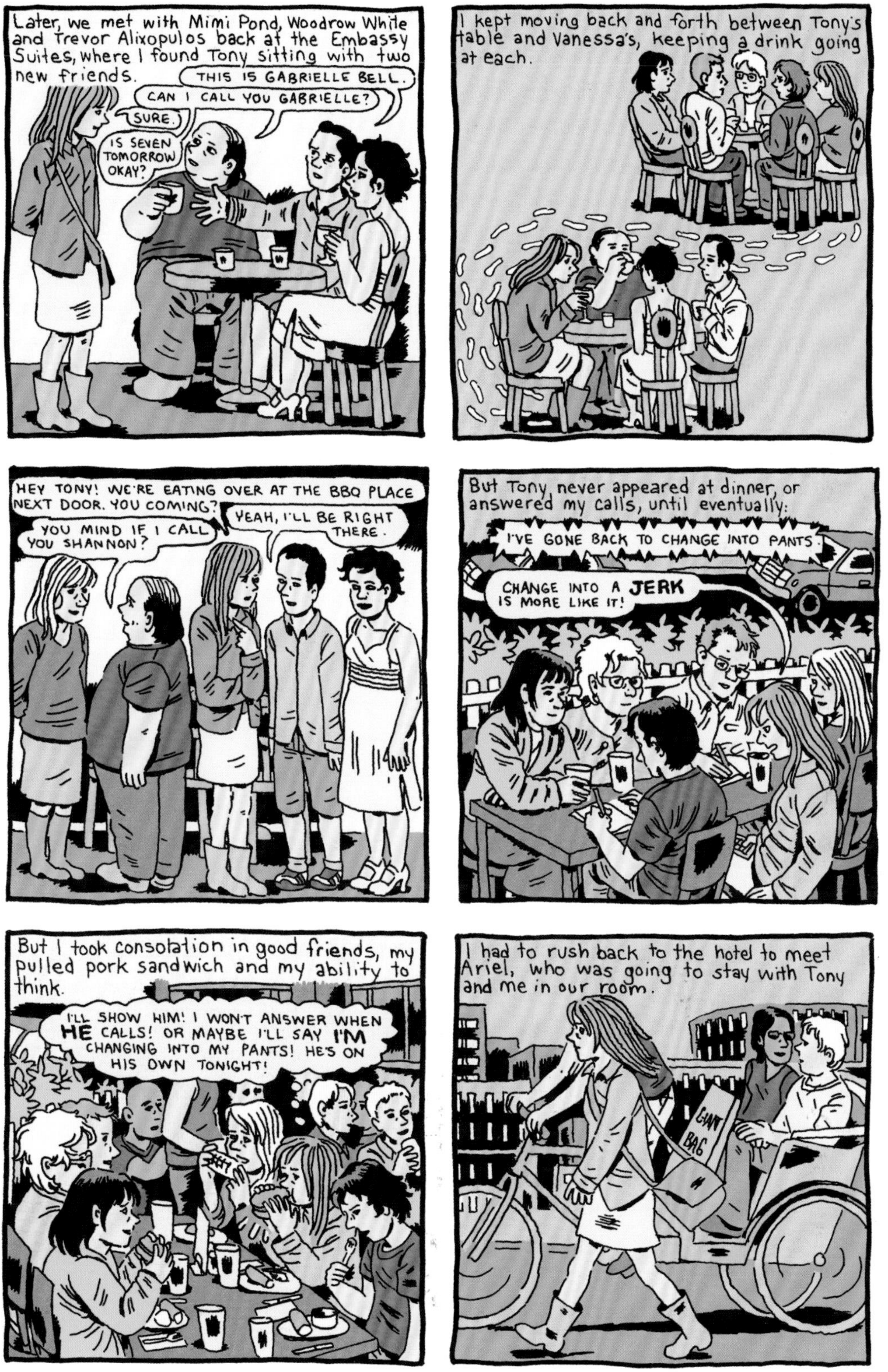
Later, we met with Mimi Pond, Woodrow White and Trevor Alixopulos back at the Embassy Suites, where I found Tony sitting with two new friends.
THIS IS GABRIELLE BELL.
CAN I CALL YOU GABRIELLE?
SURE.
IS SEVEN TOMORROW OKAY?
I kept moving back and forth between Tony's table and Vanessa's, keeping a drink going at each.
HEY TONY! WE'RE EATING OVER AT THE BBQ PLACE NEXT DOOR. YOU COMING?
YEAH, I'LL BE RIGHT THERE.
YOU MIND IF I CALL YOU SHANNON?
But Tony never appeared at dinner, or answered my calls, until eventually:
I'VE GONE BACK TO CHANGE INTO PANTS.
CHANGE INTO A JERK IS MORE LIKE IT!
But I took consolation in good friends, my pulled pork sandwich and my ability to think.
I'LL SHOW HIM! I WON'T ANSWER WHEN HE CALLS! OR MAYBE I'LL SAY I'M CHANGING INTO MY PANTS! HE'S ON HIS OWN TONIGHT!
I had to rush back to the hotel to meet Ariel, who was going to stay with Tony and me in our room.
GIANT BAG

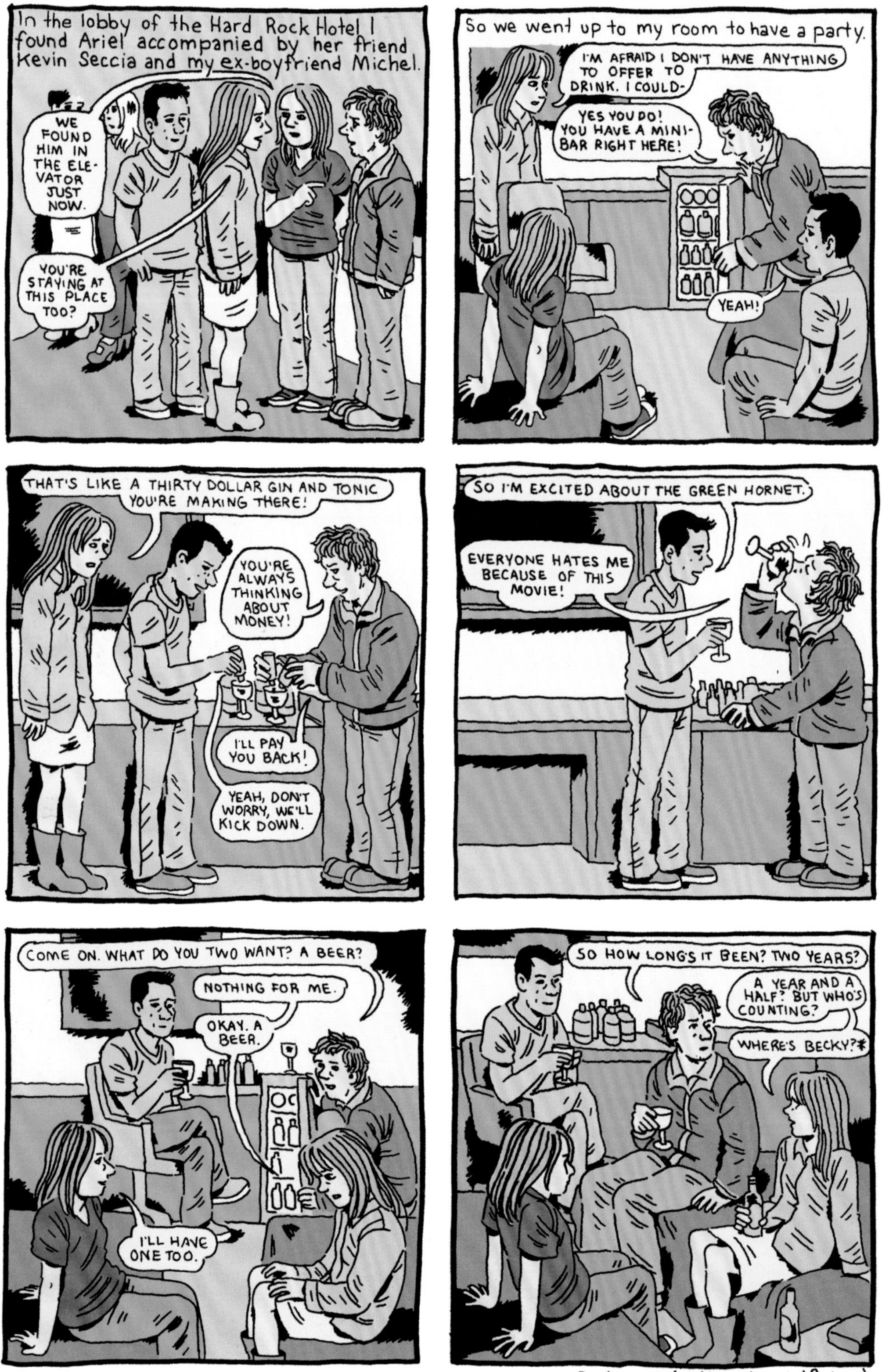
In the lobby of the Hard Rock Hotel I found Ariel accompanied by her friend Kevin Seccia and my ex-boyfriend Michel.
WE FOUND HIM IN THE ELEVATOR JUST NOW.
YOU'RE STAYING AT THIS PLACE TOO?
So we went up to my room to have a party.
I'M AFRAID I DON'T HAVE ANYTHING TO OFFER TO DRINK. I COULD-
YES YOU DO! YOU HAVE A MINI-BAR RIGHT HERE!
YEAH!
THAT'S LIKE A THIRTY DOLLAR GIN AND TONIC YOU'RE MAKING THERE!
YOU'RE ALWAYS THINKING ABOUT MONEY!
I'LL PAY YOU BACK!
YEAH, DON'T WORRY, WE'LL KICK DOWN.
SO I'M EXCITED ABOUT THE GREEN HORNET.
EVERYONE HATES ME BECAUSE OF THIS MOVIE!
COME ON. WHAT DO YOU TWO WANT? A BEER?
NOTHING FOR ME.
OKAY. A BEER.
I'LL HAVE ONE TOO.
SO HOW LONG'S IT BEEN? TWO YEARS?
A YEAR AND A HALF? BUT WHO'S COUNTING?
WHERE'S BECKY?*

* Becky Stark, Michel's girlfriend

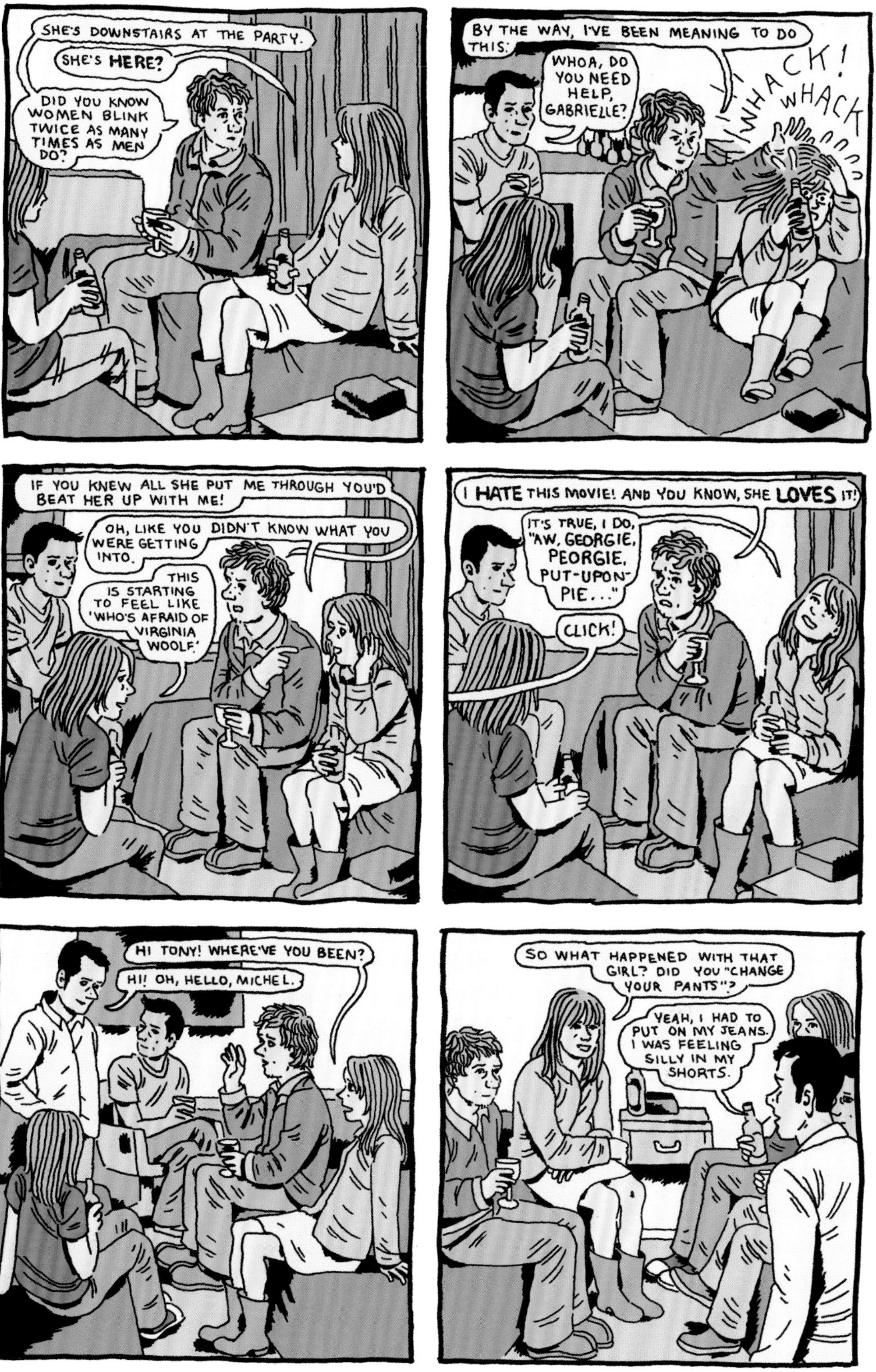
SHE'S DOWNSTAIRS AT THE PARTY.
SHE'S HERE?
DID YOU KNOW WOMEN BLINK TWICE AS MANY TIMES AS MEN DO?
BY THE WAY, I'VE BEEN MEANING TO DO THIS:
WHOA, DO YOU NEED HELP, GABRIELLE?
WHACK! WHACK
IF YOU KNEW ALL SHE PUT ME THROUGH YOU'D BEAT HER UP WITH ME!
OH, LIKE YOU DIDN'T KNOW WHAT YOU WERE GETTING INTO.
THIS IS STARTING TO FEEL LIKE 'WHO'S AFRAID OF VIRGINIA WOOLF'
I HATE THIS MOVIE! AND YOU KNOW, SHE LOVES IT!
IT'S TRUE, I DO, "AW, GEORGIE, PEORGIE, PUT-UPON-PIE..."
CLICK!
HI TONY! WHERE'VE YOU BEEN?
HI! OH, HELLO, MICHEL.
SO WHAT HAPPENED WITH THAT GIRL? DID YOU "CHANGE YOUR PANTS"?
YEAH, I HAD TO PUT ON MY JEANS. I WAS FEELING SILLY IN MY SHORTS.

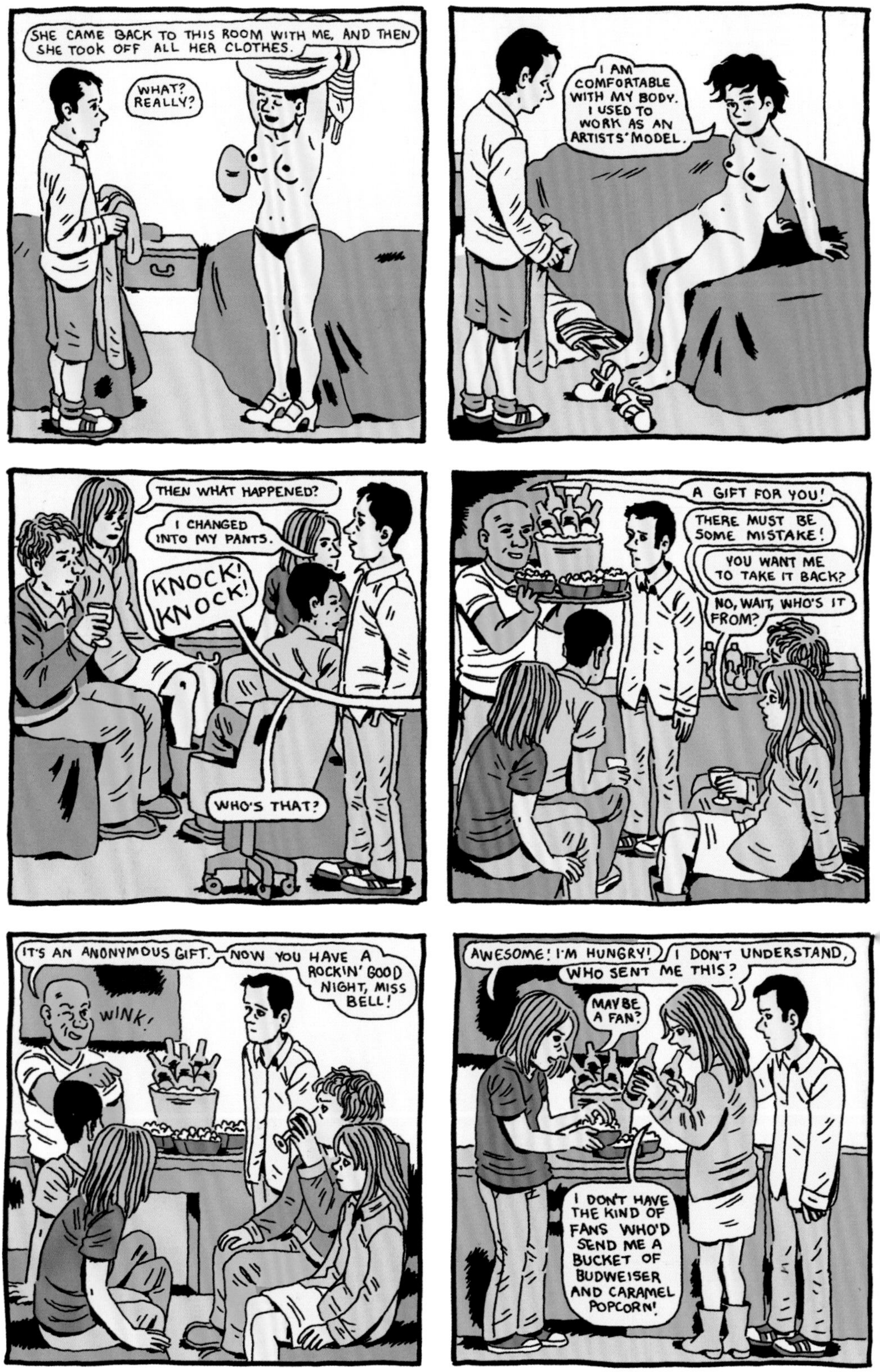
SHE CAME BACK TO THIS ROOM WITH ME, AND THEN SHE TOOK OFF ALL HER CLOTHES.
WHAT? REALLY?
I AM COMFORTABLE WITH MY BODY. I USED TO WORK AS AN ARTISTS' MODEL.
THEN WHAT HAPPENED?
I CHANGED INTO MY PANTS.
KNOCK! KNOCK!
WHO'S THAT?
A GIFT FOR YOU!
THERE MUST BE SOME MISTAKE!
YOU WANT ME TO TAKE IT BACK?
NO, WAIT, WHO'S IT FROM?
IT'S AN ANONYMOUS GIFT.
NOW YOU HAVE A ROCKIN' GOOD NIGHT, MISS BELL!
WINK!
AWESOME! I'M HUNGRY!
I DON'T UNDERSTAND, WHO SENT ME THIS?
MAYBE A FAN?
I DON'T HAVE THE KIND OF FANS WHO'D SEND ME A BUCKET OF BUDWEISER AND CARAMEL POPCORN!

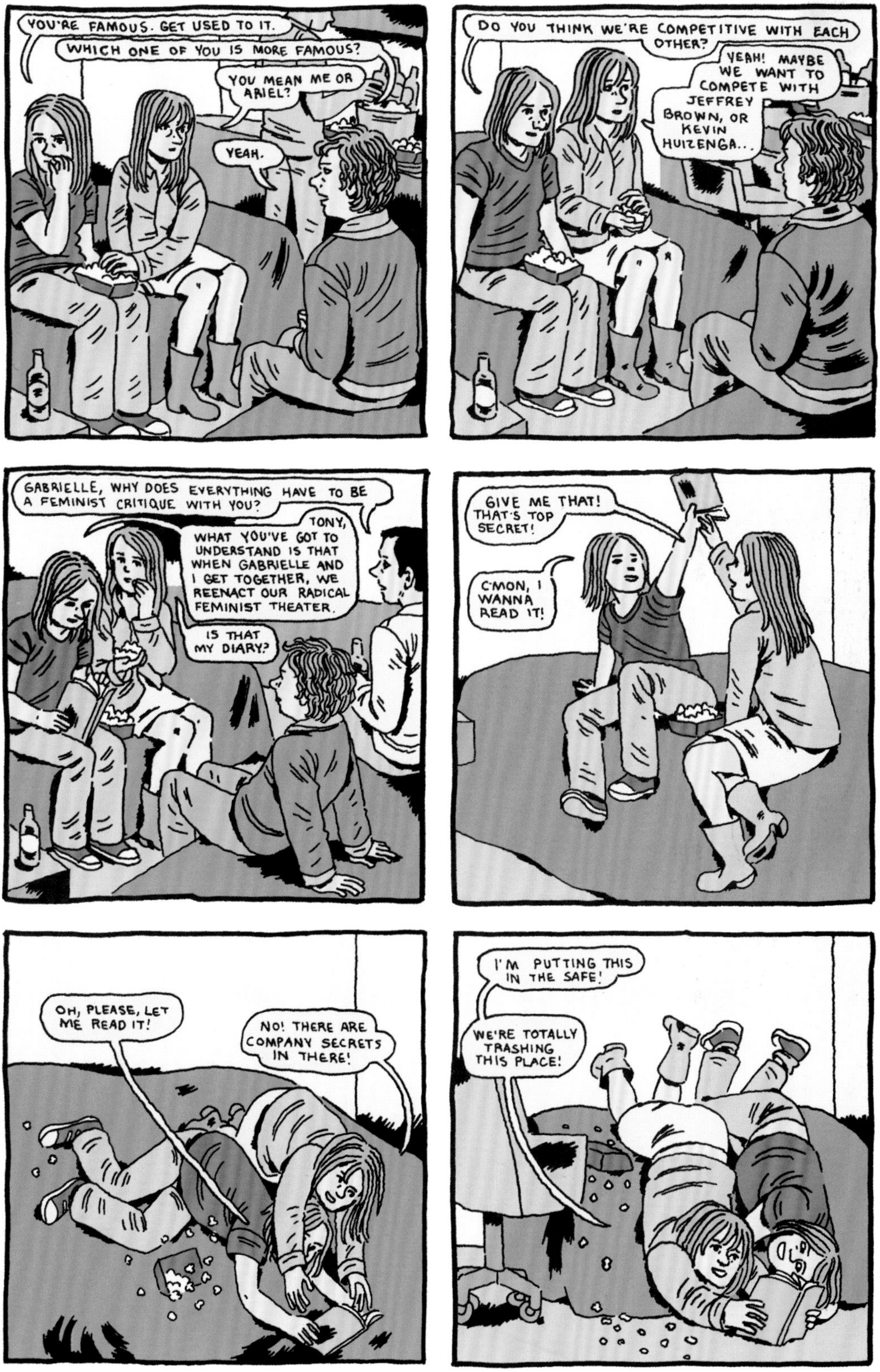
YOU'RE FAMOUS. GET USED TO IT.
WHICH ONE OF YOU IS MORE FAMOUS?
YOU MEAN ME OR ARIEL?
YEAH.
DO YOU THINK WE'RE COMPETITIVE WITH EACH OTHER?
YEAH! MAYBE WE WANT TO COMPETE WITH JEFFREY BROWN, OR KEVIN HUIZENGA...
GABRIELLE, WHY DOES EVERYTHING HAVE TO BE A FEMINIST CRITIQUE WITH YOU?
TONY, WHAT YOU'VE GOT TO UNDERSTAND IS THAT WHEN GABRIELLE AND I GET TOGETHER, WE REENACT OUR RADICAL FEMINIST THEATER.
IS THAT MY DIARY?
GIVE ME THAT! THAT'S TOP SECRET!
C'MON, I WANNA READ IT!
OH, PLEASE, LET ME READ IT!
NO! THERE ARE COMPANY SECRETS IN THERE!
I'M PUTTING THIS IN THE SAFE!
WE'RE TOTALLY TRASHING THIS PLACE!

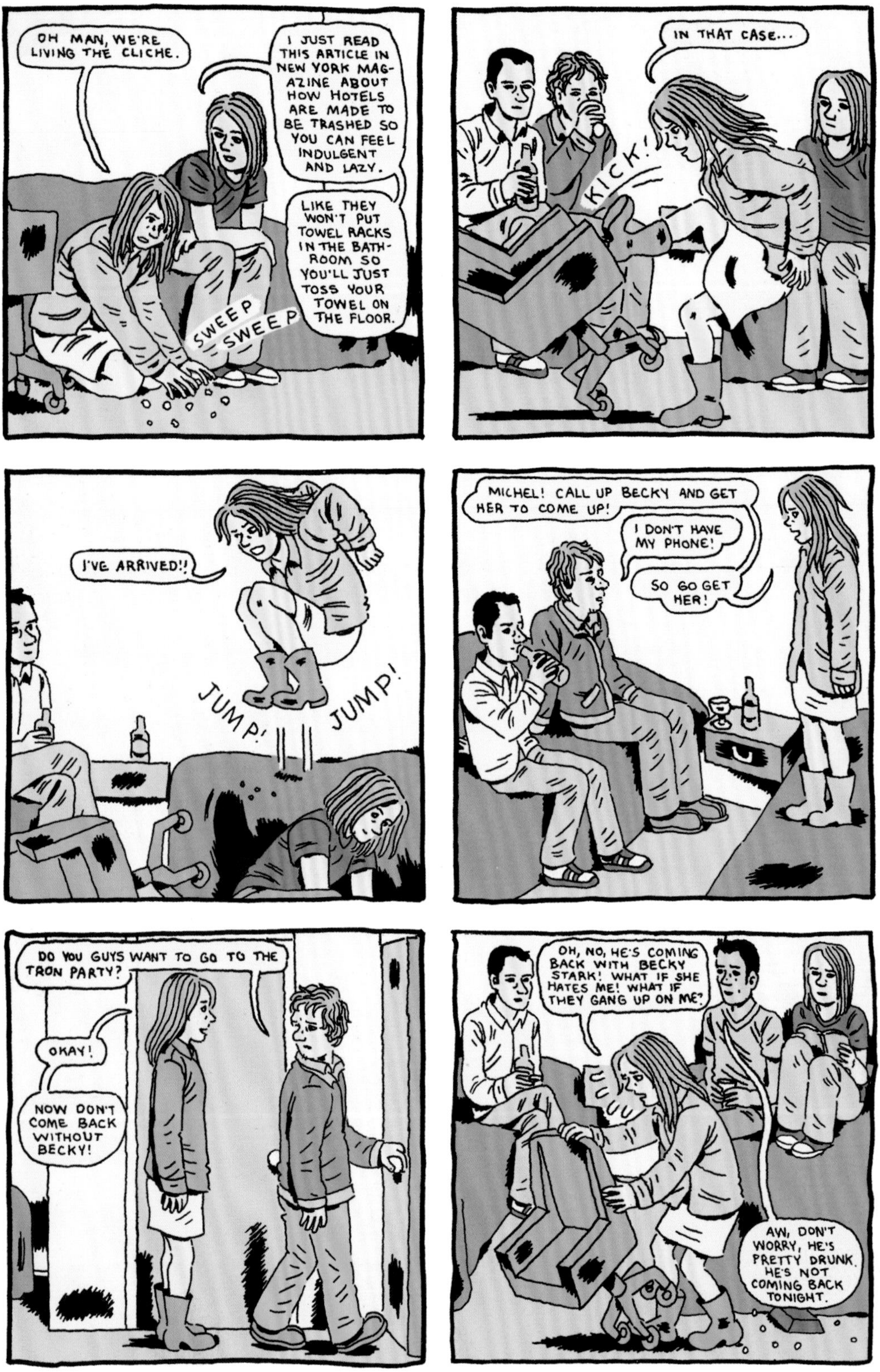
OH MAN, WE'RE LIVING THE CLICHE.
I JUST READ THIS ARTICLE IN NEW YORK MAGAZINE ABOUT HOW HOTELS ARE MADE TO BE TRASHED SO YOU CAN FEEL INDULGENT AND LAZY.
LIKE THEY WON'T PUT TOWEL RACKS IN THE BATHROOM SO YOU'LL JUST TOSS YOUR TOWEL ON THE FLOOR.
SWEEP
SWEEP
IN THAT CASE...
KICK!
I'VE ARRIVED!!
JUMP!
JUMP!
MICHEL! CALL UP BECKY AND GET HER TO COME UP!
I DON'T HAVE MY PHONE!
SO GO GET HER!
DO YOU GUYS WANT TO GO TO THE TRON PARTY?
OKAY!
NOW DON'T COME BACK WITHOUT BECKY!
OH, NO, HE'S COMING BACK WITH BECKY STARK! WHAT IF SHE HATES ME! WHAT IF THEY GANG UP ON ME?
AW, DON'T WORRY, HE'S PRETTY DRUNK. HE'S NOT COMING BACK TONIGHT.

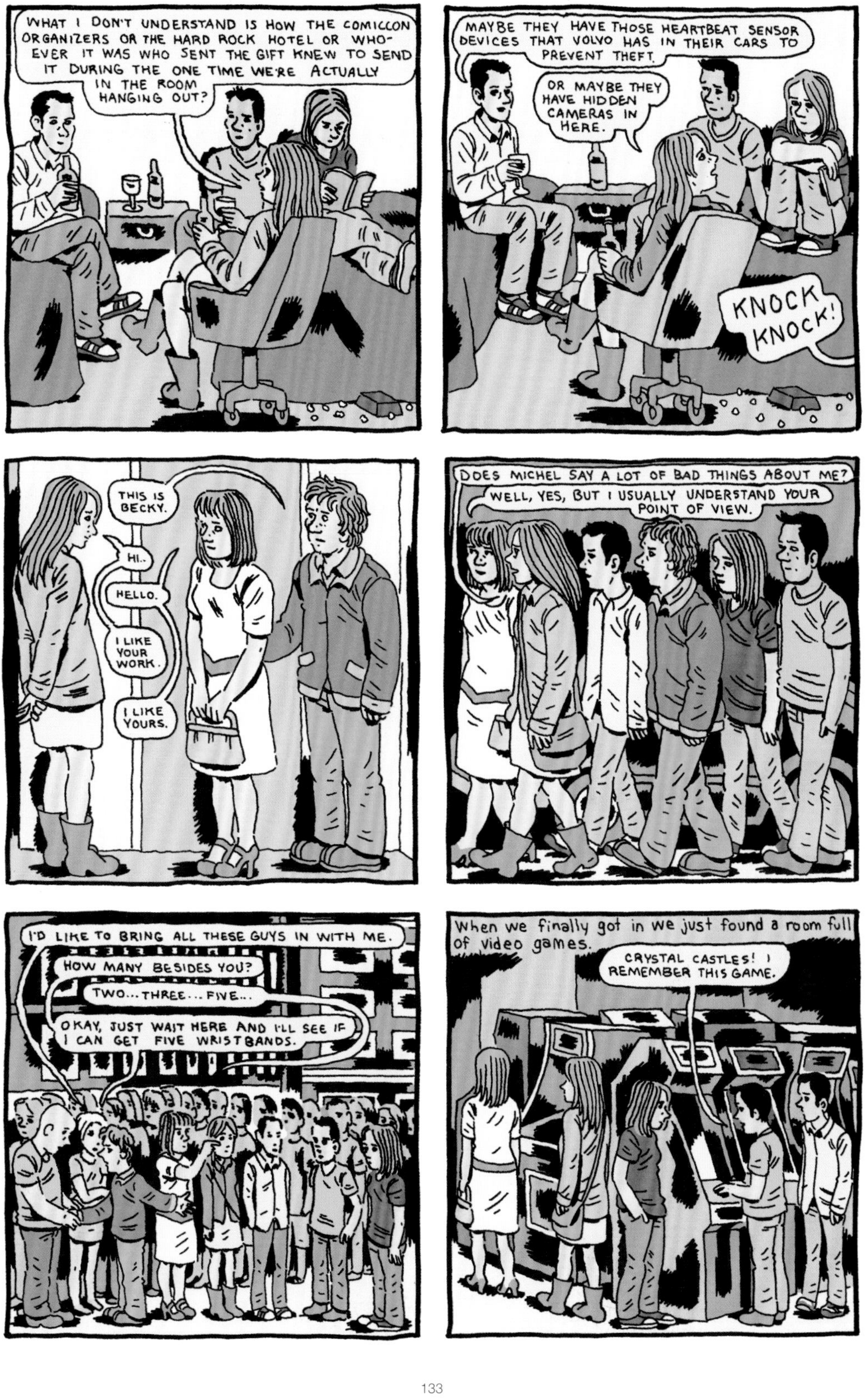
WHAT I DON'T UNDERSTAND IS HOW THE COMICCON ORGANIZERS OR THE HARD ROCK HOTEL OR WHO-EVER IT WAS WHO SENT THE GIFT KNEW TO SEND IT DURING THE ONE TIME WE'RE ACTUALLY IN THE ROOM HANGING OUT?
MAYBE THEY HAVE THOSE HEARTBEAT SENSOR DEVICES THAT VOLVO HAS IN THEIR CARS TO PREVENT THEFT.
OR MAYBE THEY HAVE HIDDEN CAMERAS IN HERE.
KNOCK KNOCK!
THIS IS BECKY.
HI..
HELLO.
I LIKE YOUR WORK.
I LIKE YOURS.
DOES MICHEL SAY A LOT OF BAD THINGS ABOUT ME?
WELL, YES, BUT I USUALLY UNDERSTAND YOUR POINT OF VIEW.
I'D LIKE TO BRING ALL THESE GUYS IN WITH ME.
HOW MANY BESIDES YOU?
TWO... THREE... FIVE...
OKAY, JUST WAIT HERE AND I'LL SEE IF I CAN GET FIVE WRISTBANDS.
When we finally got in we just found a room full of video games.
CRYSTAL CASTLES! I REMEMBER THIS GAME.

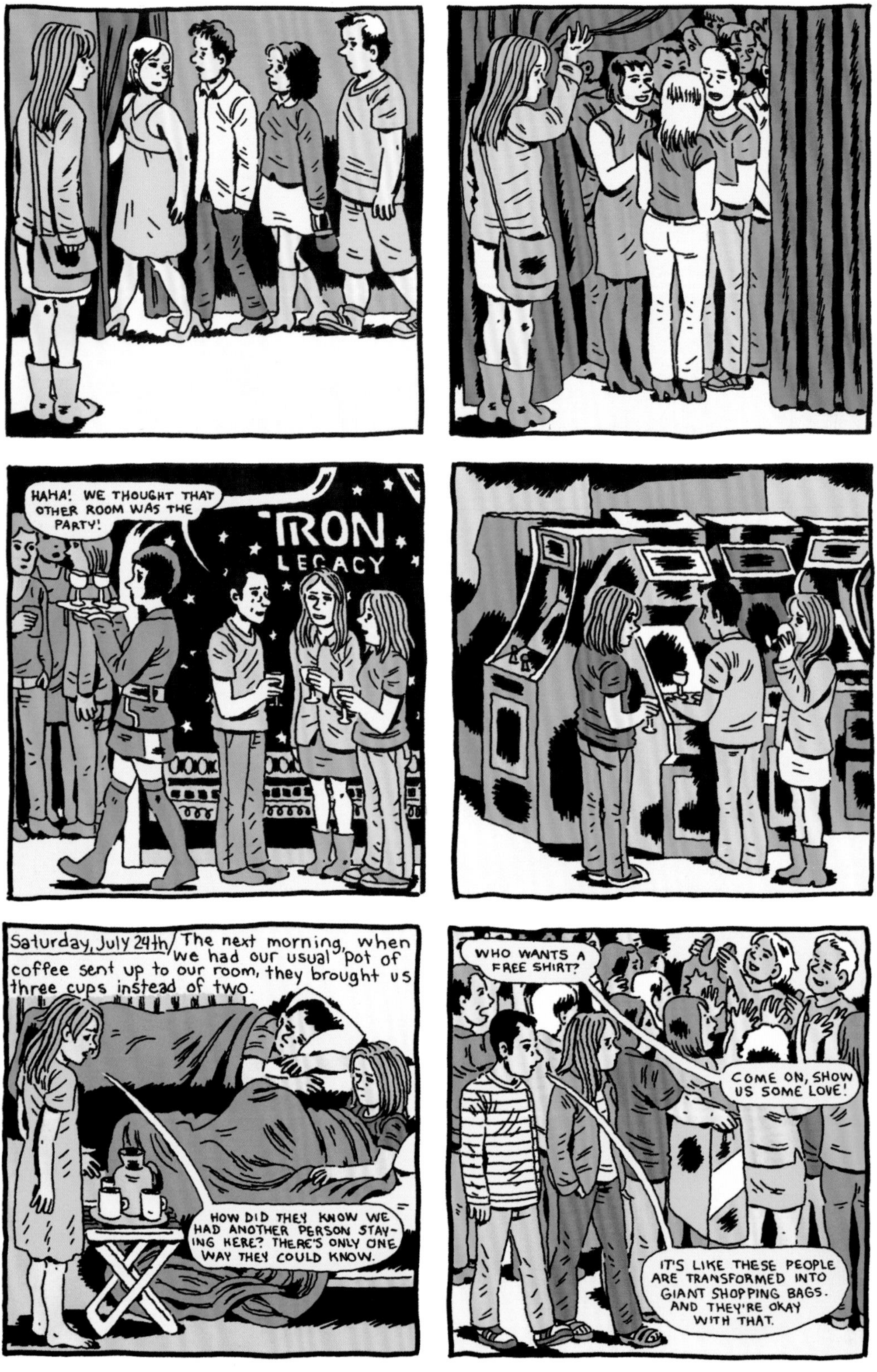
HAHA! WE THOUGHT THAT OTHER ROOM WAS THE PARTY!
TRON LEGACY
Saturday, July 24th/ The next morning, when we had our usual pot of coffee sent up to our room, they brought us three cups instead of two.
HOW DID THEY KNOW WE HAD ANOTHER PERSON STAYING HERE? THERE'S ONLY ONE WAY THEY COULD KNOW.
WHO WANTS A FREE SHIRT?
COME ON, SHOW US SOME LOVE!
IT'S LIKE THESE PEOPLE ARE TRANSFORMED INTO GIANT SHOPPING BAGS. AND THEY'RE OKAY WITH THAT.

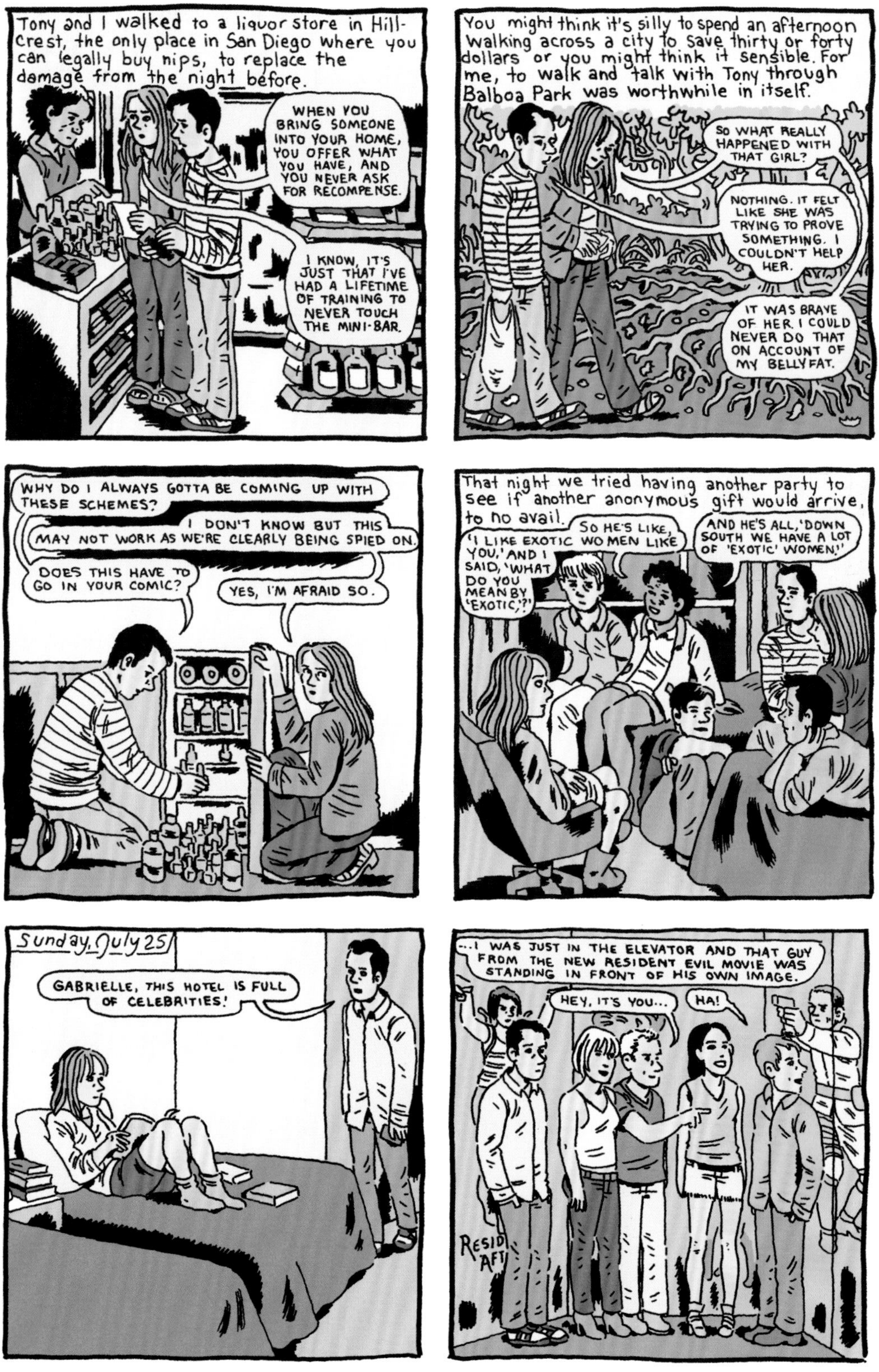
Tony and I walked to a liquor store in Hill-Crest, the only place in San Diego where you can legally buy nips, to replace the damage from the night before.
WHEN YOU BRING SOMEONE INTO YOUR HOME, YOU OFFER WHAT YOU HAVE, AND YOU NEVER ASK FOR RECOMPENSE.
I KNOW, IT'S JUST THAT I'VE HAD A LIFETIME OF TRAINING TO NEVER TOUCH THE MINI-BAR.
You might think it's silly to spend an afternoon walking across a city to save thirty or forty dollars or you might think it sensible. For me, to walk and talk with Tony through Balboa Park was worthwhile in itself.
SO WHAT REALLY HAPPENED WITH THAT GIRL?
NOTHING. IT FELT LIKE SHE WAS TRYING TO PROVE SOMETHING. I COULDN'T HELP HER.
IT WAS BRAVE OF HER. I COULD NEVER DO THAT ON ACCOUNT OF MY BELLYFAT.
WHY DO I ALWAYS GOTTA BE COMING UP WITH THESE SCHEMES?
I DON'T KNOW BUT THIS MAY NOT WORK AS WE'RE CLEARLY BEING SPIED ON.
DOES THIS HAVE TO GO IN YOUR COMIC?
YES, I'M AFRAID SO.
That night we tried having another party to see if another anonymous gift would arrive, to no avail.
SO HE'S LIKE, 'I LIKE EXOTIC WOMEN LIKE YOU,' AND I SAID, 'WHAT DO YOU MEAN BY 'EXOTIC'?'
AND HE'S ALL, 'DOWN SOUTH WE HAVE A LOT OF 'EXOTIC' WOMEN!'
Sunday, July 25
GABRIELLE, THIS HOTEL IS FULL OF CELEBRITIES!
...I WAS JUST IN THE ELEVATOR AND THAT GUY FROM THE NEW RESIDENT EVIL MOVIE WAS STANDING IN FRONT OF HIS OWN IMAGE.
HEY, IT'S YOU...
HA!
RESID
AFT

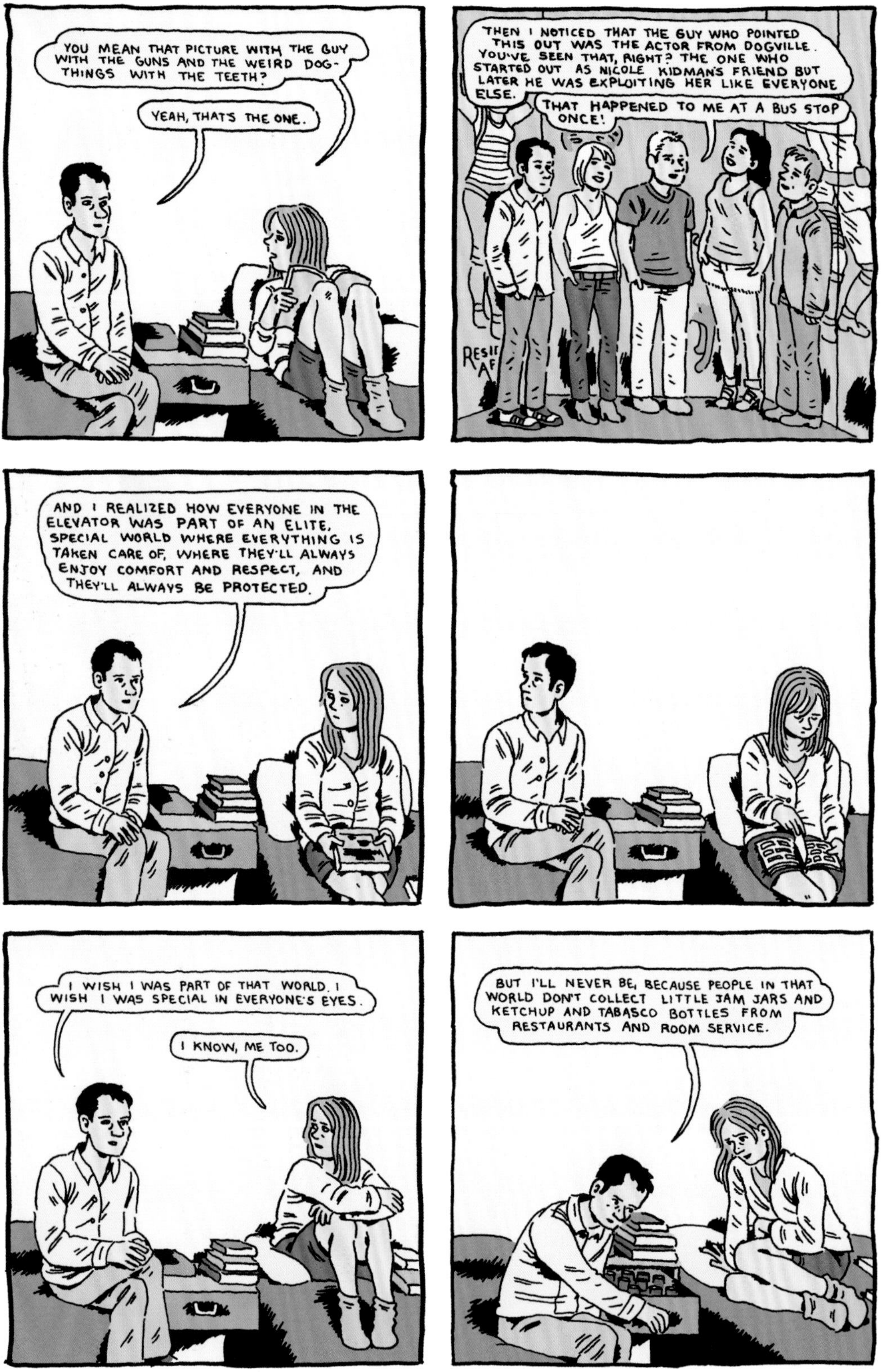

YOU MEAN THAT PICTURE WITH THE GUY WITH THE GUNS AND THE WEIRD DOG-THINGS WITH THE TEETH?
YEAH, THAT'S THE ONE.
THEN I NOTICED THAT THE GUY WHO POINTED THIS OUT WAS THE ACTOR FROM DOGVILLE. YOU'VE SEEN THAT, RIGHT? THE ONE WHO STARTED OUT AS NICOLE KIDMAN'S FRIEND BUT LATER HE WAS EXPLOITING HER LIKE EVERYONE ELSE.
THAT HAPPENED TO ME AT A BUS STOP ONCE!
AND I REALIZED HOW EVERYONE IN THE ELEVATOR WAS PART OF AN ELITE, SPECIAL WORLD WHERE EVERYTHING IS TAKEN CARE OF, WHERE THEY'LL ALWAYS ENJOY COMFORT AND RESPECT, AND THEY'LL ALWAYS BE PROTECTED.
I WISH I WAS PART OF THAT WORLD. I WISH I WAS SPECIAL IN EVERYONE'S EYES.
I KNOW, ME TOO.
BUT I'LL NEVER BE, BECAUSE PEOPLE IN THAT WORLD DON'T COLLECT LITTLE JAM JARS AND KETCHUP AND TABASCO BOTTLES FROM RESTAURANTS AND ROOM SERVICE.

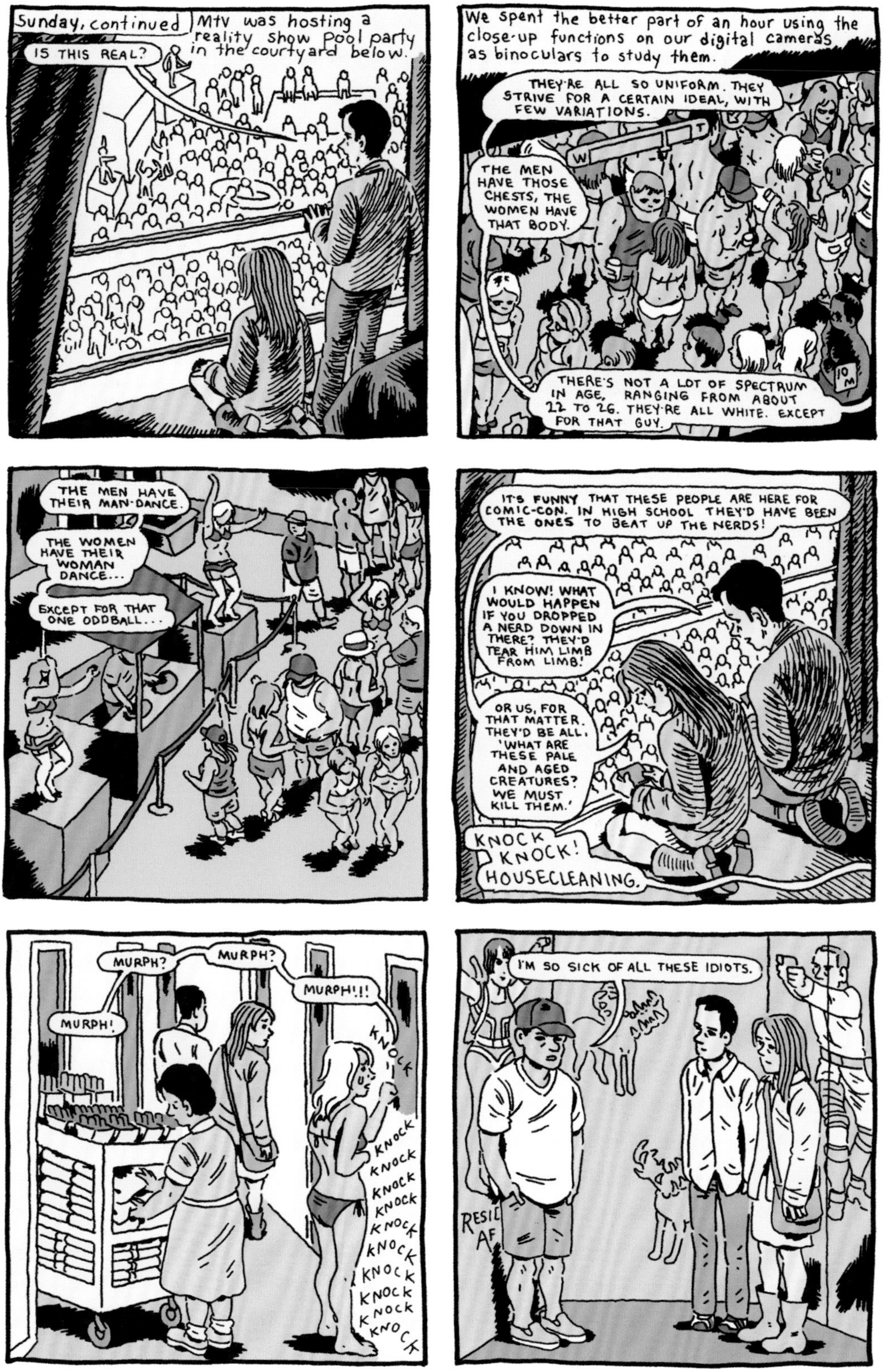

Sunday, continued
Mtv was hosting a reality show pool party in the courtyard below.
IS THIS REAL?
We spent the better part of an hour using the close-up functions on our digital cameras as binoculars to study them.
THEY'RE ALL SO UNIFORM. THEY STRIVE FOR A CERTAIN IDEAL, WITH FEW VARIATIONS.
THE MEN HAVE THOSE CHESTS, THE WOMEN HAVE THAT BODY.
THERE'S NOT A LOT OF SPECTRUM IN AGE, RANGING FROM ABOUT 22 TO 26. THEY'RE ALL WHITE. EXCEPT FOR THAT GUY.
THE MEN HAVE THEIR MAN-DANCE.
THE WOMEN HAVE THEIR WOMAN DANCE...
EXCEPT FOR THAT ONE ODDBALL...
IT'S FUNNY THAT THESE PEOPLE ARE HERE FOR COMIC-CON. IN HIGH SCHOOL THEY'D HAVE BEEN THE ONES TO BEAT UP THE NERDS!
I KNOW! WHAT WOULD HAPPEN IF YOU DROPPED A NERD DOWN IN THERE? THEY'D TEAR HIM LIMB FROM LIMB!
OR US, FOR THAT MATTER. THEY'D BE ALL, 'WHAT ARE THESE PALE AND AGED CREATURES? WE MUST KILL THEM.'
KNOCK KNOCK!
HOUSECLEANING.
MURPH?
MURPH?
MURPH!!!
MURPH!
KNOCK KNOCK KNOCK KNOCK KNOCK KNOCK KNOCK KNOCK KNOCK KNOCK KNOCK
I'M SO SICK OF ALL THESE IDIOTS.

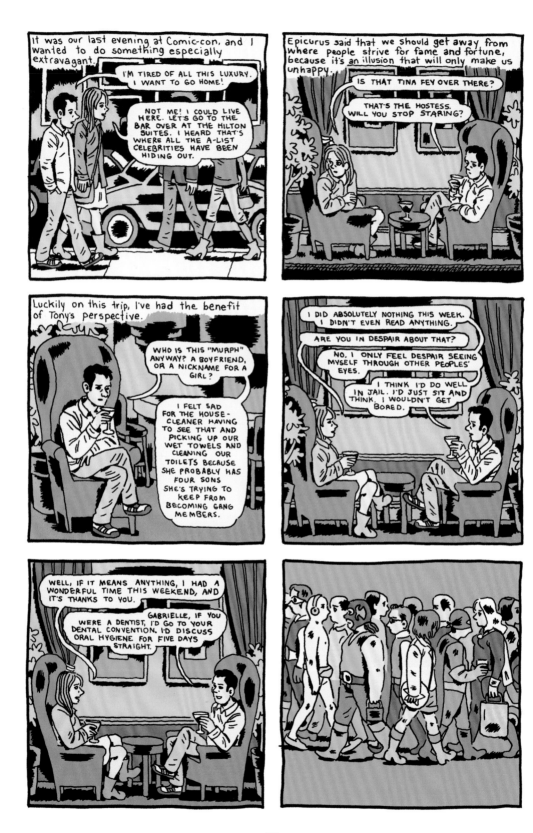

It was our last evening at Comic-con, and I wanted to do something especially extravagant.

I'M TIRED OF ALL THIS LUXURY, I WANT TO GO HOME!

NOT ME! I COULD LIVE HERE. LET'S GO TO THE BAR OVER AT THE HILTON SUITES. I HEARD THAT'S WHERE ALL THE A-LIST CELEBRITIES HAVE BEEN HIDING OUT.

Epicurus said that we should get away from where people strive for fame and fortune, because it's an illusion that will only make us unhappy.

IS THAT TINA FEY OVER THERE?

THAT'S THE HOSTESS. WILL YOU STOP STARING?

Luckily on this trip, I've had the benefit of Tony's perspective.

WHO IS THIS "MURPH" ANYWAY? A BOYFRIEND, OR A NICKNAME FOR A GIRL?

I FELT SAD FOR THE HOUSE-CLEANER HAVING TO SEE THAT AND PICKING UP OUR WET TOWELS AND CLEANING OUR TOILETS BECAUSE SHE PROBABLY HAS FOUR SONS SHE'S TRYING TO KEEP FROM BECOMING GANG MEMBERS.

I DID ABSOLUTELY NOTHING THIS WEEK. I DIDN'T EVEN READ ANYTHING.

ARE YOU IN DESPAIR ABOUT THAT?

NO, I ONLY FEEL DESPAIR SEEING MYSELF THROUGH OTHER PEOPLES' EYES.

I THINK I'D DO WELL IN JAIL. I'D JUST SIT AND THINK. I WOULDN'T GET BORED.

WELL, IF IT MEANS ANYTHING, I HAD A WONDERFUL TIME THIS WEEKEND, AND IT'S THANKS TO YOU.

GABRIELLE, IF YOU WERE A DENTIST, I'D GO TO YOUR DENTAL CONVENTION, I'D DISCUSS ORAL HYGIENE FOR FIVE DAYS STRAIGHT.

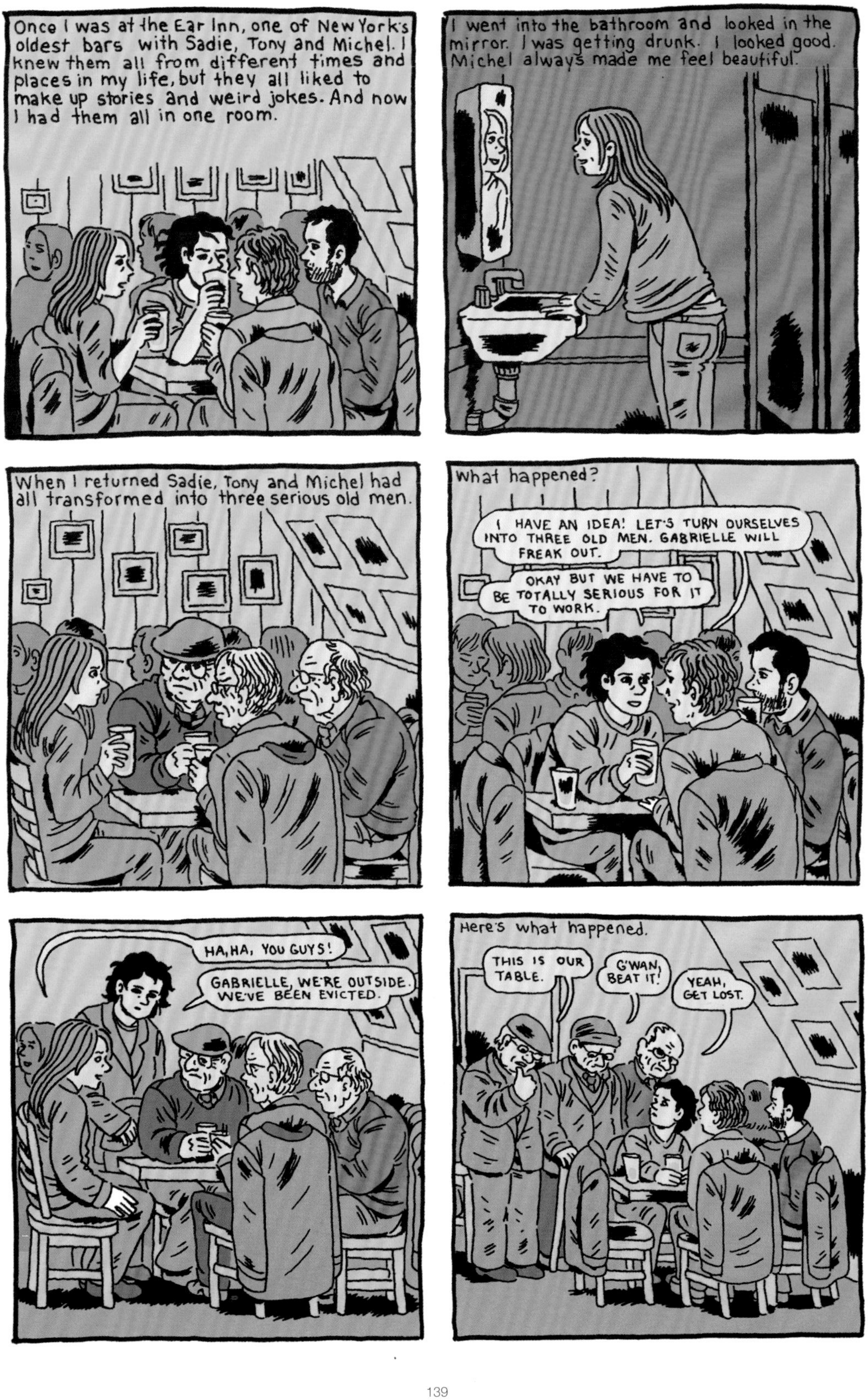
Once I was at the Ear Inn, one of New York's oldest bars with Sadie, Tony and Michel. I knew them all from different times and places in my life, but they all liked to make up stories and weird jokes. And now I had them all in one room.
I went into the bathroom and looked in the mirror. I was getting drunk. I looked good. Michel always made me feel beautiful.
When I returned Sadie, Tony and Michel had all transformed into three serious old men.
What happened?
I HAVE AN IDEA! LET'S TURN OURSELVES INTO THREE OLD MEN. GABRIELLE WILL FREAK OUT.
OKAY BUT WE HAVE TO BE TOTALLY SERIOUS FOR IT TO WORK.
HA, HA, YOU GUYS!
GABRIELLE, WE'RE OUTSIDE. WE'VE BEEN EVICTED.
Here's what happened.
THIS IS OUR TABLE.
G'WAN, BEAT IT!
YEAH, GET LOST.

# chapter seven
## 2010

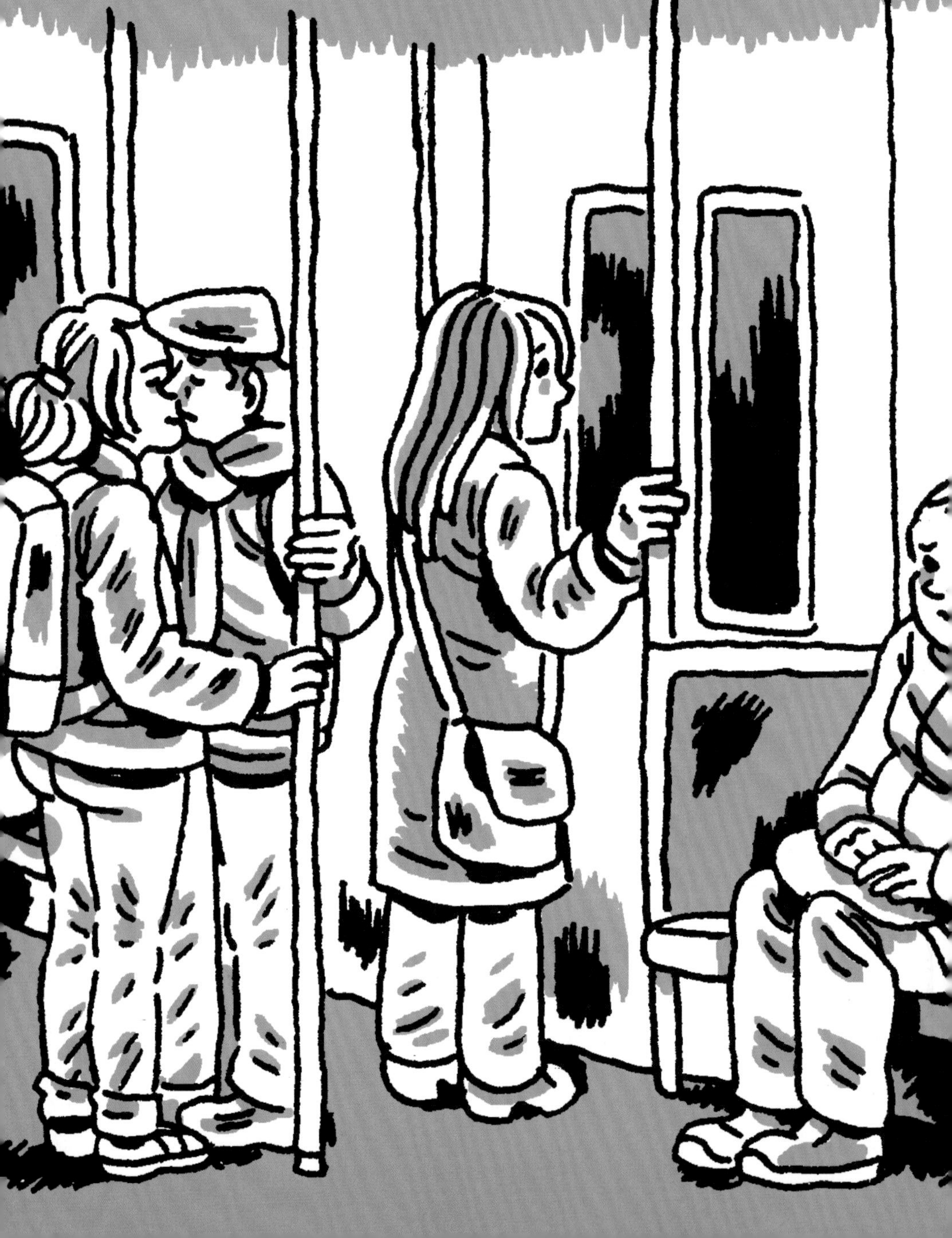

# The Comics of Business

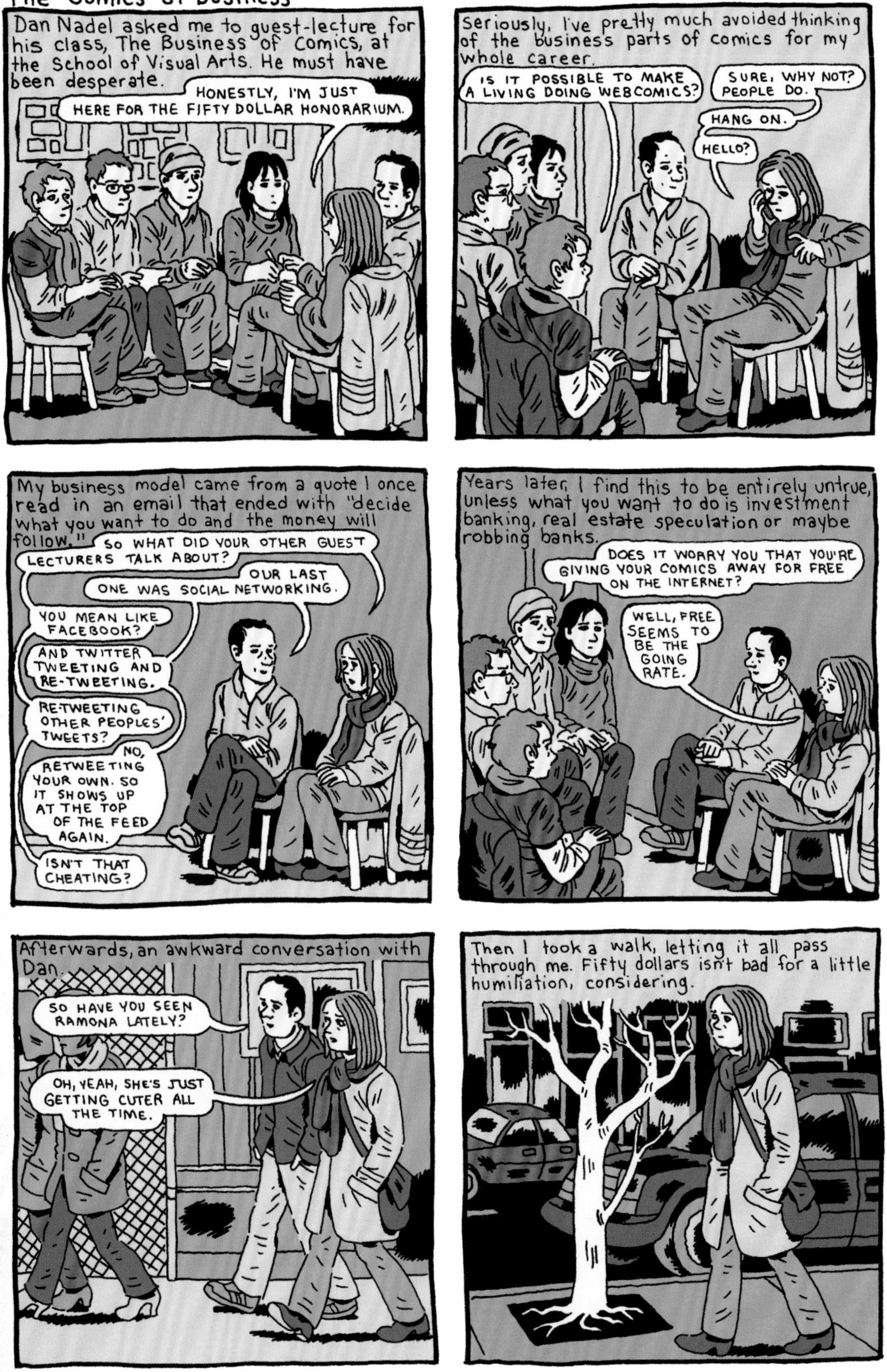
Dan Nadel asked me to guest-lecture for his class, The Business of Comics, at the School of Visual Arts. He must have been desperate.
HONESTLY, I'M JUST HERE FOR THE FIFTY DOLLAR HONORARIUM.
Seriously, I've pretty much avoided thinking of the business parts of comics for my whole career.
IS IT POSSIBLE TO MAKE A LIVING DOING WEBCOMICS?
SURE, WHY NOT? PEOPLE DO.
HANG ON.
HELLO?
My business model came from a quote I once read in an email that ended with "decide what you want to do and the money will follow."
SO WHAT DID YOUR OTHER GUEST LECTURERS TALK ABOUT?
OUR LAST ONE WAS SOCIAL NETWORKING.
YOU MEAN LIKE FACEBOOK?
AND TWITTER TWEETING AND RE-TWEETING.
RE-TWEETING OTHER PEOPLES' TWEETS?
NO, RETWEETING YOUR OWN. SO IT SHOWS UP AT THE TOP OF THE FEED AGAIN.
ISN'T THAT CHEATING?
Years later, I find this to be entirely untrue, unless what you want to do is investment banking, real estate speculation or maybe robbing banks.
DOES IT WORRY YOU THAT YOU'RE GIVING YOUR COMICS AWAY FOR FREE ON THE INTERNET?
WELL, FREE SEEMS TO BE THE GOING RATE.
Afterwards, an awkward conversation with Dan.
SO HAVE YOU SEEN RAMONA LATELY?
OH, YEAH, SHE'S JUST GETTING CUTER ALL THE TIME.
Then I took a walk, letting it all pass through me. Fifty dollars isn't bad for a little humiliation, considering.

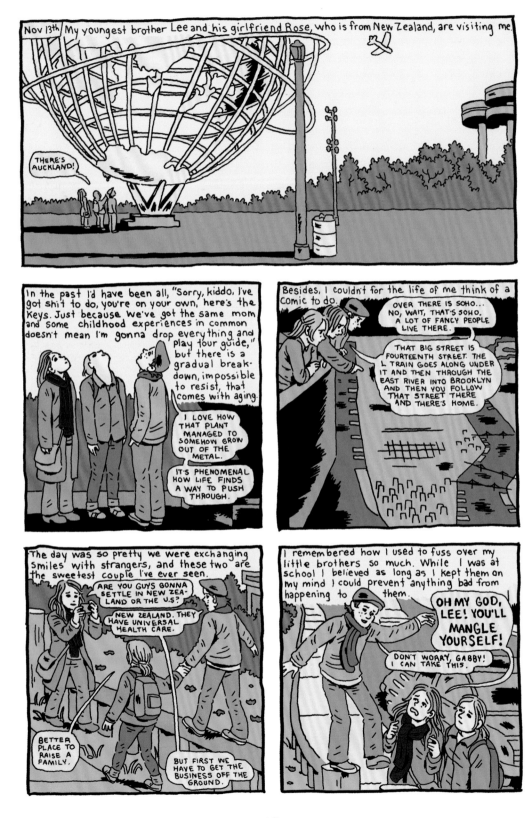

Nov 13th My youngest brother Lee and his girlfriend Rose, who is from New Zealand, are visiting me.

THERE'S AUCKLAND!

In the past I'd have been all, "Sorry, kiddo, I've got shit to do, you're on your own, here's the Keys. Just because we've got the same mom and some childhood experiences in common doesn't mean I'm gonna drop everything and play tour guide," but there is a gradual break-down, impossible to resist, that comes with aging.

I LOVE HOW THAT PLANT MANAGED TO SOMEHOW GROW OUT OF THE METAL.

IT'S PHENOMENAL HOW LIFE FINDS A WAY TO PUSH THROUGH.

Besides, I couldn't for the life of me think of a comic to do.

OVER THERE IS SOHO... NO, WAIT, THAT'S SOHO. A LOT OF FANCY PEOPLE LIVE THERE.

THAT BIG STREET IS FOURTEENTH STREET. THE L TRAIN GOES ALONG UNDER IT AND THEN THROUGH THE EAST RIVER INTO BROOKLYN AND THEN YOU FOLLOW THAT STREET THERE AND THERE'S HOME.

The day was so pretty we were exchanging smiles with strangers, and these two are the sweetest couple I've ever seen.

ARE YOU GUYS GONNA SETTLE IN NEW ZEALAND OR THE U.S?

NEW ZEALAND. THEY HAVE UNIVERSAL HEALTH CARE.

BETTER PLACE TO RAISE A FAMILY.

BUT FIRST WE HAVE TO GET THE BUSINESS OFF THE GROUND.

I remembered how I used to fuss over my little brothers so much. While I was at school I believed as long as I kept them on my mind I could prevent anything bad from happening to them.

OH MY GOD, LEE! YOU'LL MANGLE YOURSELF!

DON'T WORRY, GABBY! I CAN TAKE THIS.

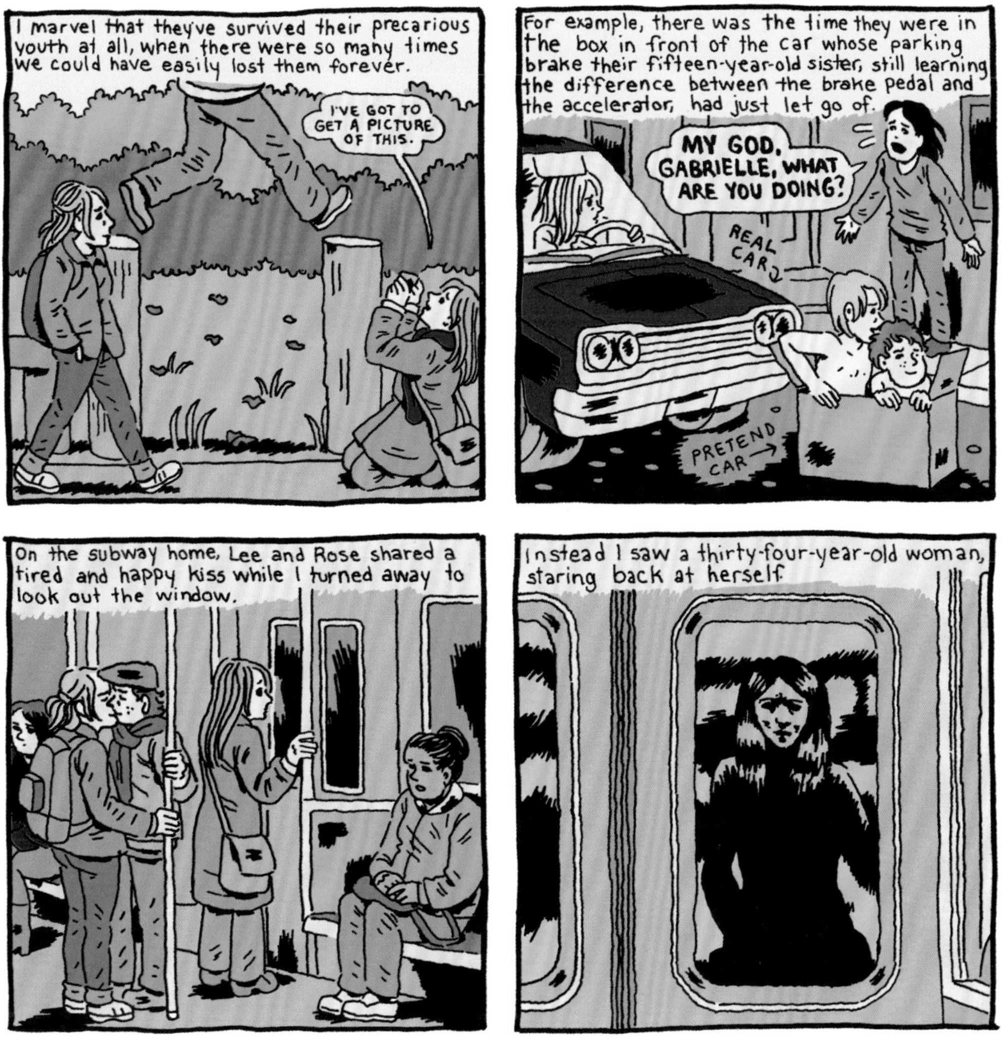
I marvel that they've survived their precarious youth at all, when there were so many times we could have easily lost them forever.
I'VE GOT TO GET A PICTURE OF THIS.
For example, there was the time they were in the box in front of the car whose parking brake their fifteen-year-old sister, still learning the difference between the brake pedal and the accelerator, had just let go of.
MY GOD, GABRIELLE, WHAT ARE YOU DOING?
REAL CAR
PRETEND CAR
On the subway home, Lee and Rose shared a tired and happy kiss while I turned away to look out the window.
Instead I saw a thirty-four-year-old woman, staring back at herself.

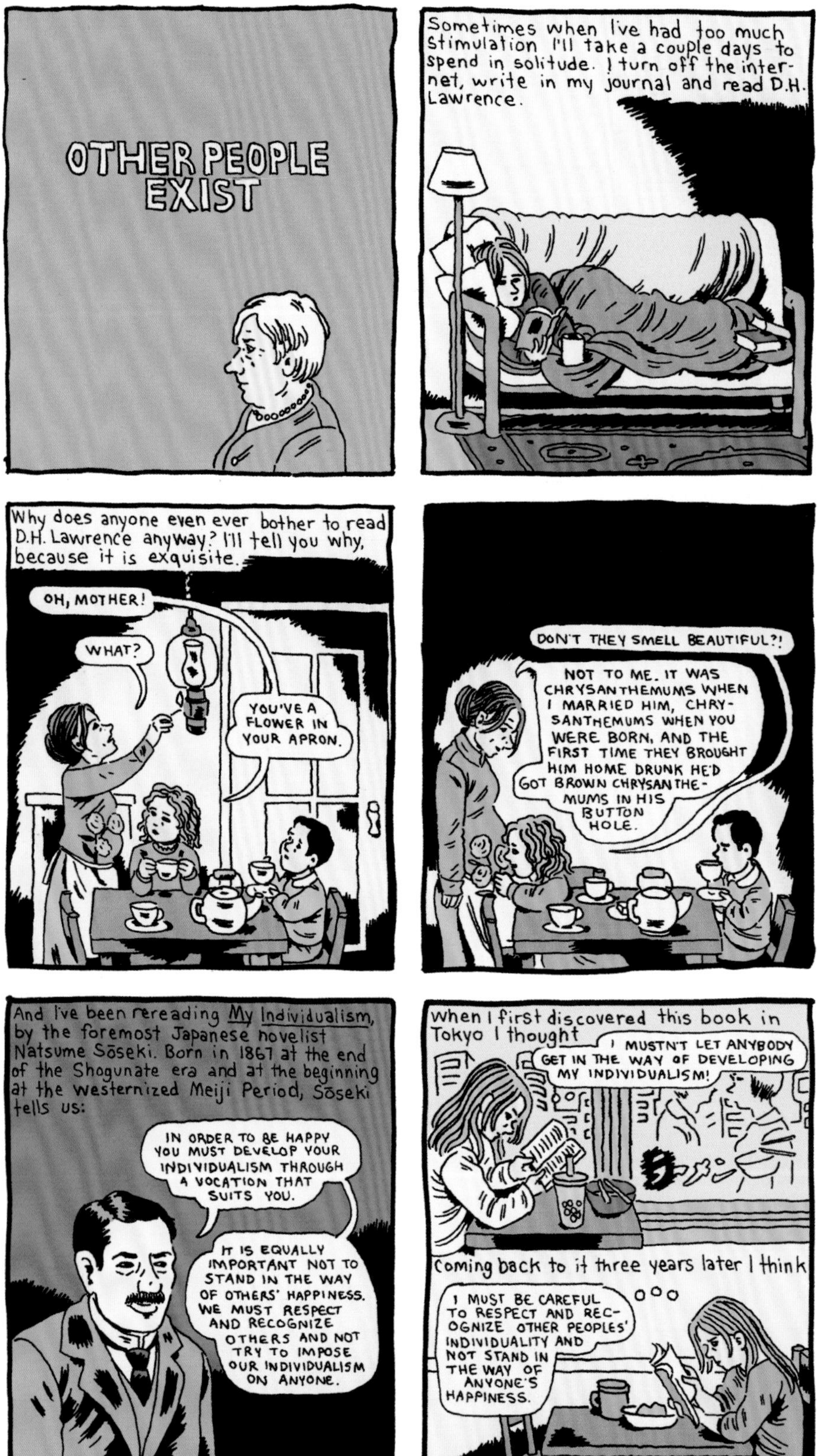
OTHER PEOPLE EXIST
Sometimes when I've had too much stimulation I'll take a couple days to spend in solitude. I turn off the internet, write in my journal and read D.H. Lawrence.
Why does anyone even ever bother to read D.H. Lawrence anyway? I'll tell you why, because it is exquisite.
OH, MOTHER!
WHAT?
YOU'VE A FLOWER IN YOUR APRON.
DON'T THEY SMELL BEAUTIFUL?!
NOT TO ME. IT WAS CHRYSANTHEMUMS WHEN I MARRIED HIM, CHRYSANTHEMUMS WHEN YOU WERE BORN, AND THE FIRST TIME THEY BROUGHT HIM HOME DRUNK HE'D GOT BROWN CHRYSANTHEMUMS IN HIS BUTTON HOLE.
And I've been rereading My Individualism, by the foremost Japanese novelist Natsume Sōseki. Born in 1867 at the end of the Shogunate era and at the beginning at the westernized Meiji Period, Sōseki tells us:
IN ORDER TO BE HAPPY YOU MUST DEVELOP YOUR INDIVIDUALISM THROUGH A VOCATION THAT SUITS YOU.
IT IS EQUALLY IMPORTANT NOT TO STAND IN THE WAY OF OTHERS' HAPPINESS. WE MUST RESPECT AND RECOGNIZE OTHERS AND NOT TRY TO IMPOSE OUR INDIVIDUALISM ON ANYONE.
When I first discovered this book in Tokyo I thought
I MUSTN'T LET ANYBODY GET IN THE WAY OF DEVELOPING MY INDIVIDUALISM!
Coming back to it three years later I think
I MUST BE CAREFUL TO RESPECT AND RECOGNIZE OTHER PEOPLES' INDIVIDUALITY AND NOT STAND IN THE WAY OF ANYONE'S HAPPINESS.

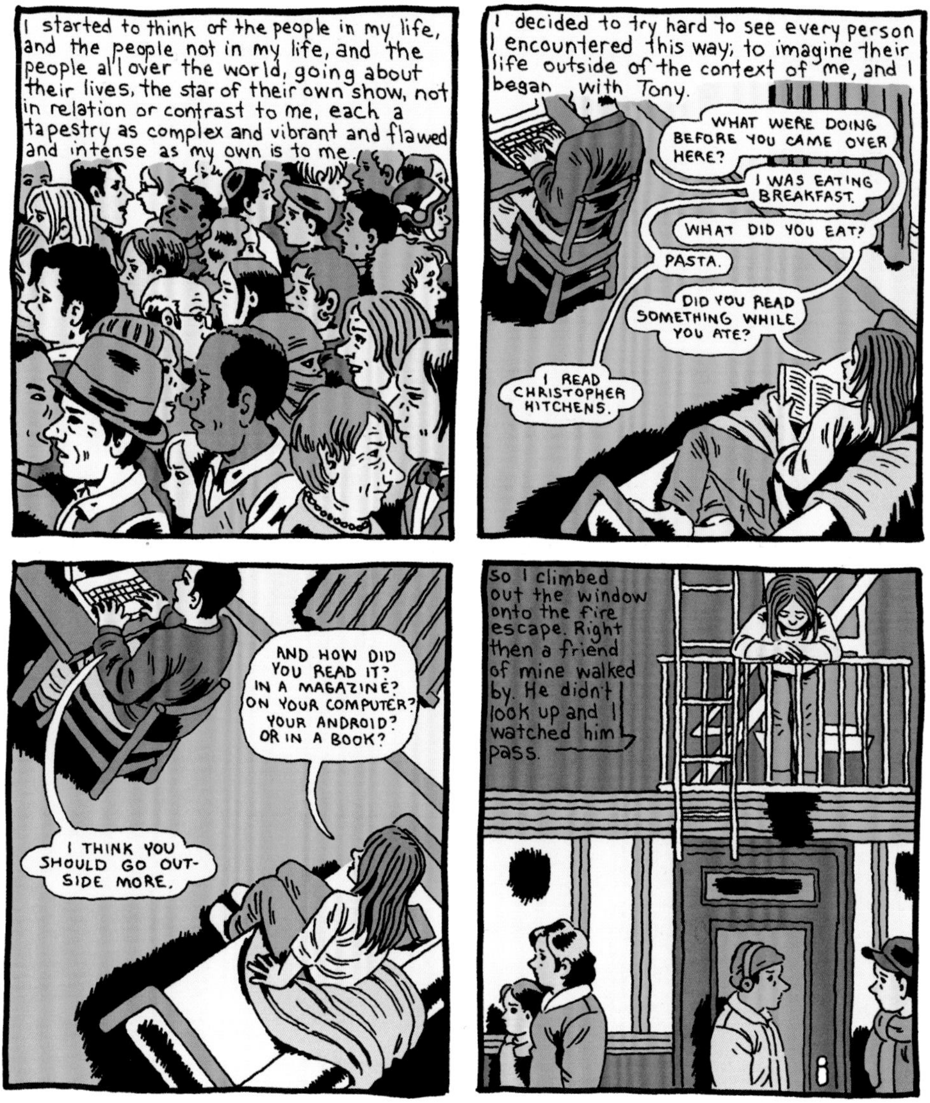
I started to think of the people in my life, and the people not in my life, and the people all over the world, going about their lives, the star of their own show, not in relation or contrast to me, each a tapestry as complex and vibrant and flawed and intense as my own is to me.
I decided to try hard to see every person I encountered this way; to imagine their life outside of the context of me, and I began with Tony.
WHAT WERE DOING BEFORE YOU CAME OVER HERE?
I WAS EATING BREAKFAST.
WHAT DID YOU EAT?
PASTA.
DID YOU READ SOMETHING WHILE YOU ATE?
I READ CHRISTOPHER HITCHENS.
AND HOW DID YOU READ IT? IN A MAGAZINE? ON YOUR COMPUTER? YOUR ANDROID? OR IN A BOOK?
I THINK YOU SHOULD GO OUTSIDE MORE.
So I climbed out the window onto the fire escape. Right then a friend of mine walked by. He didn't look up and I watched him pass.

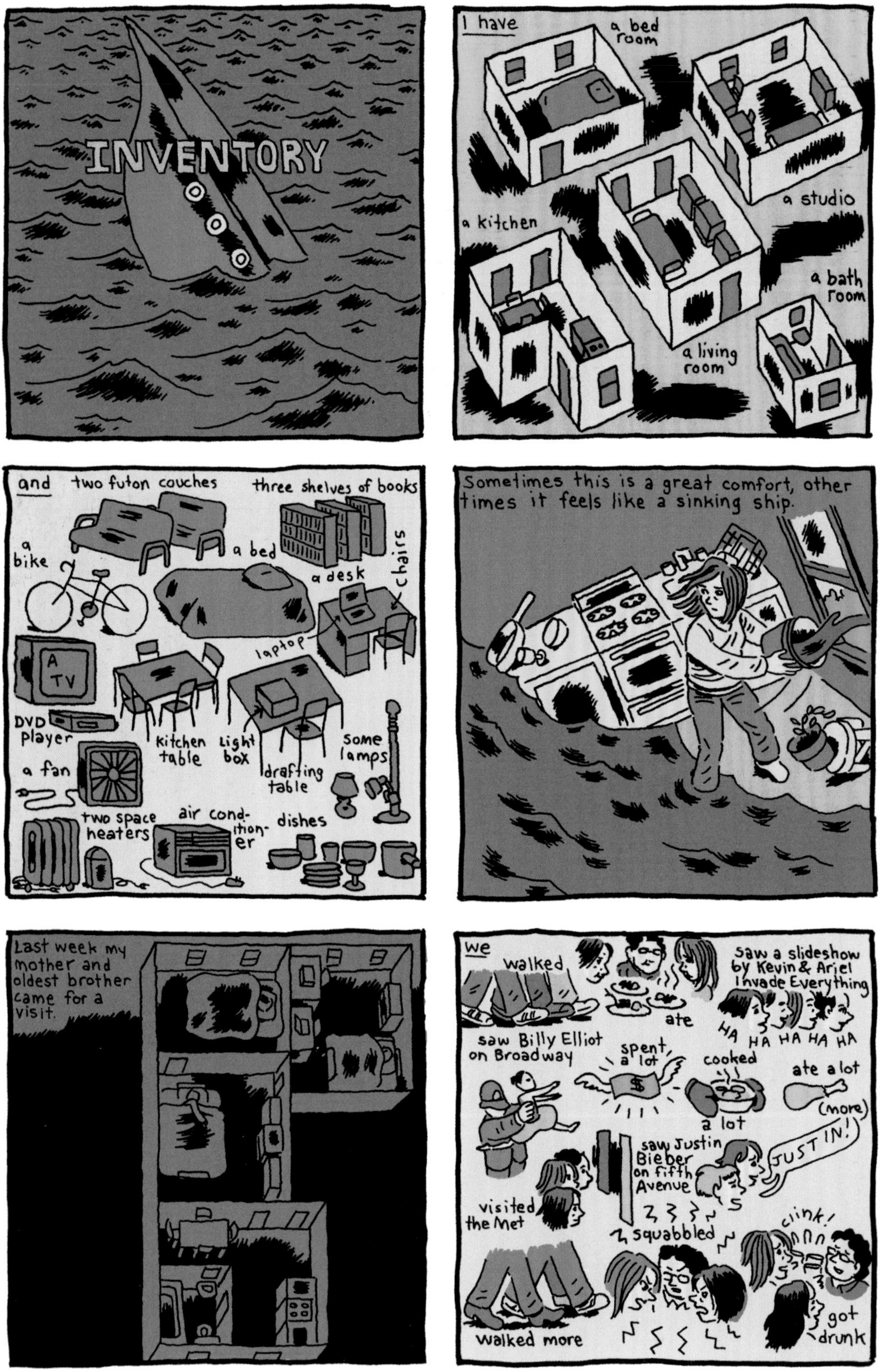

INVENTORY
I have
a bed room
a studio
a kitchen
a bath room
a living room
and
two futon couches
three shelves of books
a bike
a bed
a desk
chairs
laptop
A TV
DVD player
kitchen table
light box
drafting table
some lamps
a fan
two space heaters
air cond-ition-er
dishes
Sometimes this is a great comfort, other times it feels like a sinking ship.
Last week my mother and oldest brother came for a visit.
we
walked
ate
saw a slideshow by Kevin & Ariel Invade Everything
HA HA HA HA HA
saw Billy Elliot on Broadway
spent a lot
cooked a lot
ate a lot
(more)
saw Justin Bieber on fifth Avenue
JUST IN!
visited the Met
squabbled
clink!
walked more
got drunk

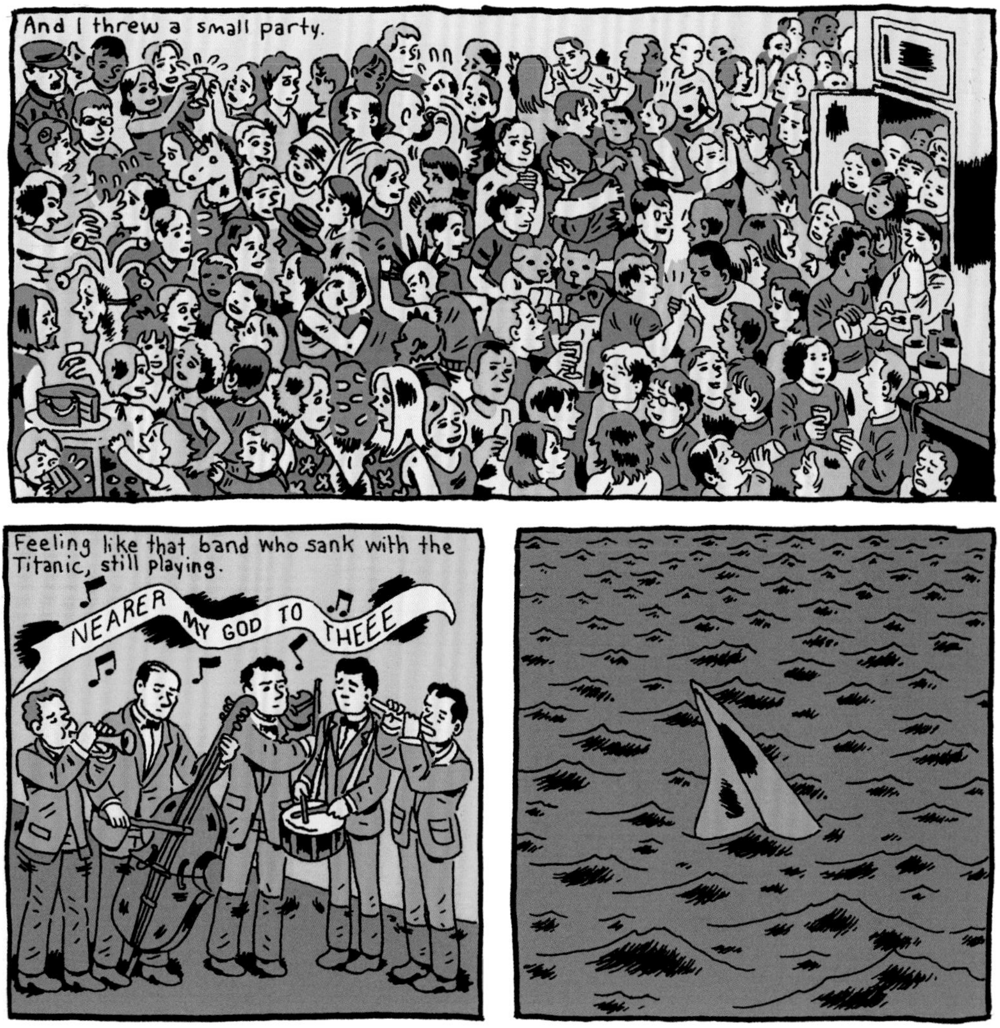
And I threw a small party.
Feeling like that band who sank with the Titanic, still playing.
NEARER MY GOD TO THEEE

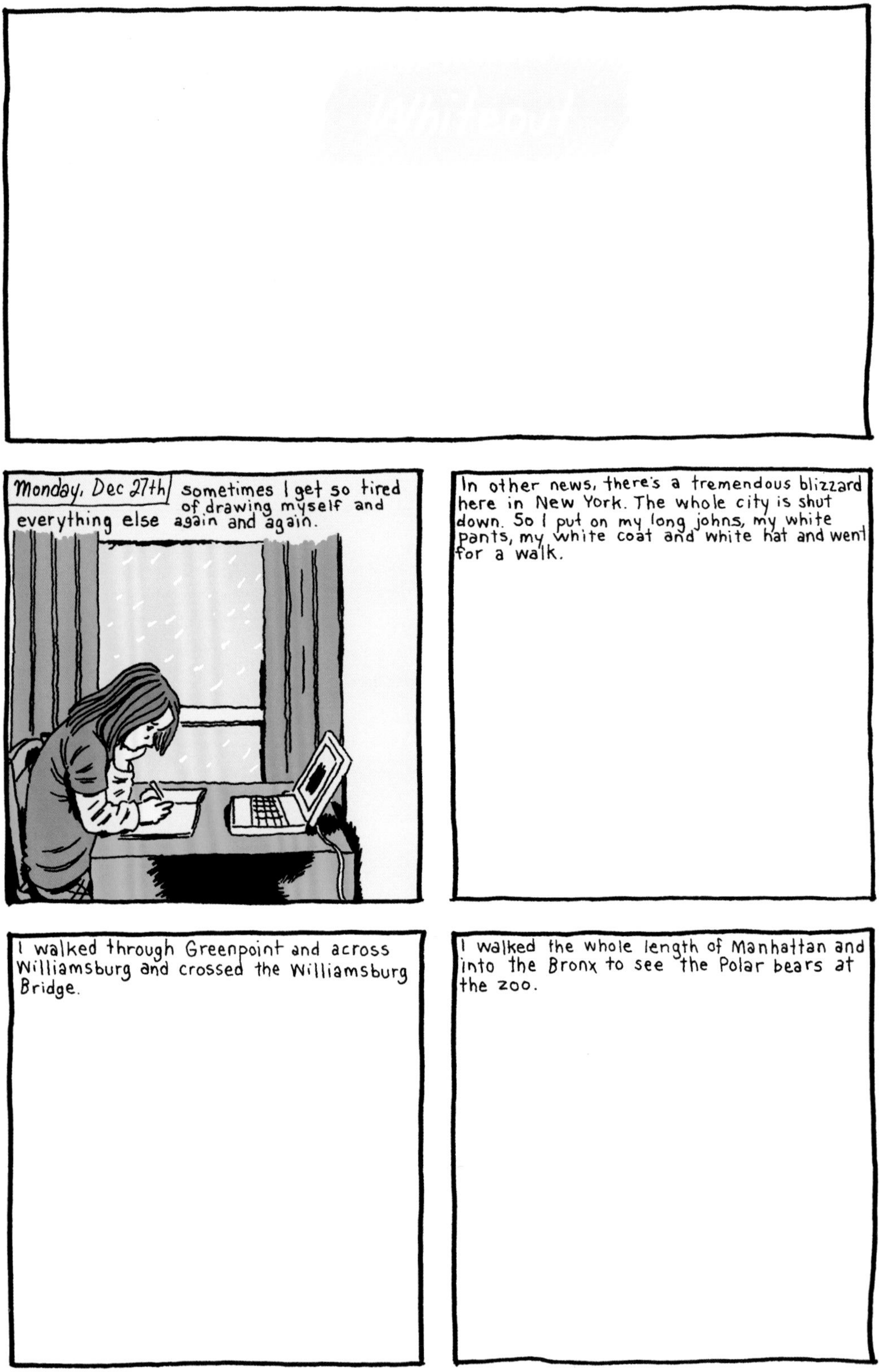
Monday, Dec 27th
sometimes I get so tired of drawing myself and everything else again and again.
In other news, there's a tremendous blizzard here in New York. The whole city is shut down. So I put on my long johns, my white pants, my white coat and white hat and went for a walk.
I walked through Greenpoint and across Williamsburg and crossed the Williamsburg Bridge.
I walked the whole length of Manhattan and into the Bronx to see the Polar bears at the zoo.

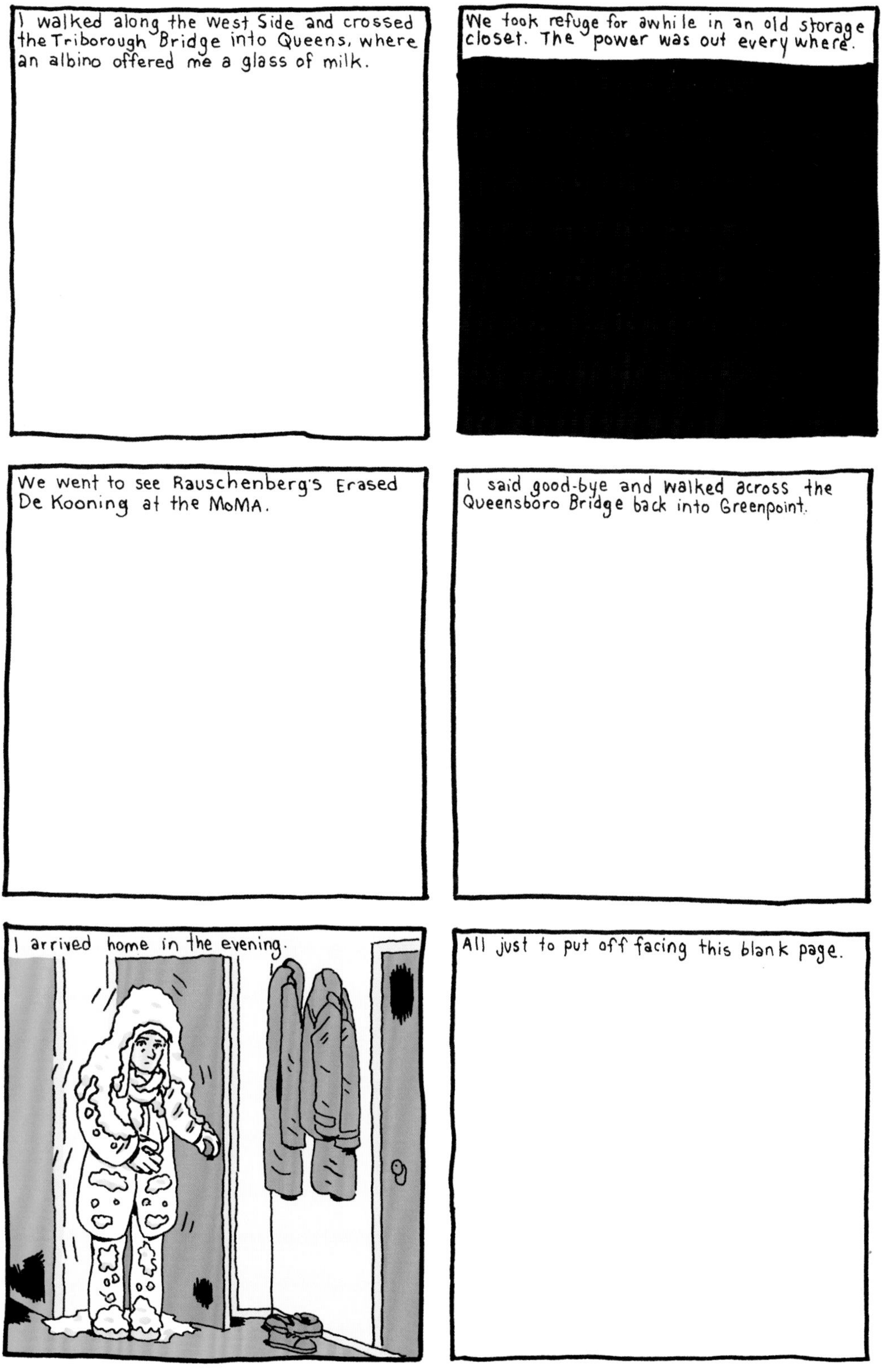
I walked along the West Side and crossed the Triborough Bridge into Queens, where an albino offered me a glass of milk.
We took refuge for awhile in an old storage closet. The power was out everywhere.
We went to see Rauschenberg's Erased De Kooning at the MoMA.
I said good-bye and walked across the Queensboro Bridge back into Greenpoint.
I arrived home in the evening.
All just to put off facing this blank page.

# How I Make My Comics

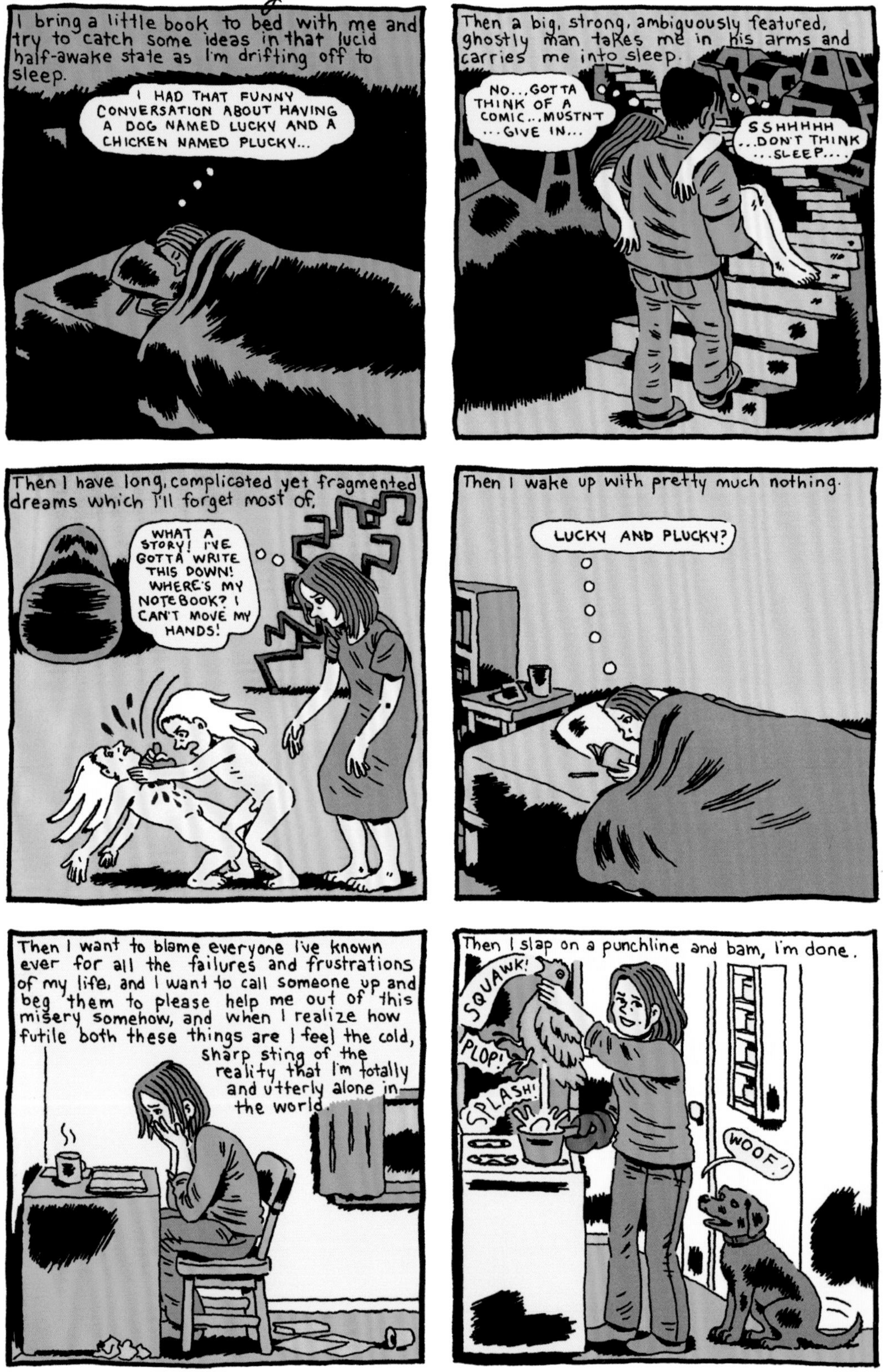
I bring a little book to bed with me and try to catch some ideas in that lucid half-awake state as I'm drifting off to sleep.
I HAD THAT FUNNY CONVERSATION ABOUT HAVING A DOG NAMED LUCKY AND A CHICKEN NAMED PLUCKY...
Then a big, strong, ambiguously featured, ghostly man takes me in his arms and carries me into sleep.
NO...GOTTA THINK OF A COMIC...MUSTN'T ...GIVE IN...
SSHHHHH ...DON'T THINK ...SLEEP....
Then I have long, complicated yet fragmented dreams which I'll forget most of.
WHAT A STORY! I'VE GOTTA WRITE THIS DOWN! WHERE'S MY NOTEBOOK? I CAN'T MOVE MY HANDS!
Then I wake up with pretty much nothing.
LUCKY AND PLUCKY?
Then I want to blame everyone I've known ever for all the failures and frustrations of my life, and I want to call someone up and beg them to please help me out of this misery somehow, and when I realize how futile both these things are I feel the cold, sharp sting of the reality that I'm totally and utterly alone in the world.
Then I slap on a punchline and bam, I'm done.
SQUAWK!
PLOP!
SPLASH!
WOOF!

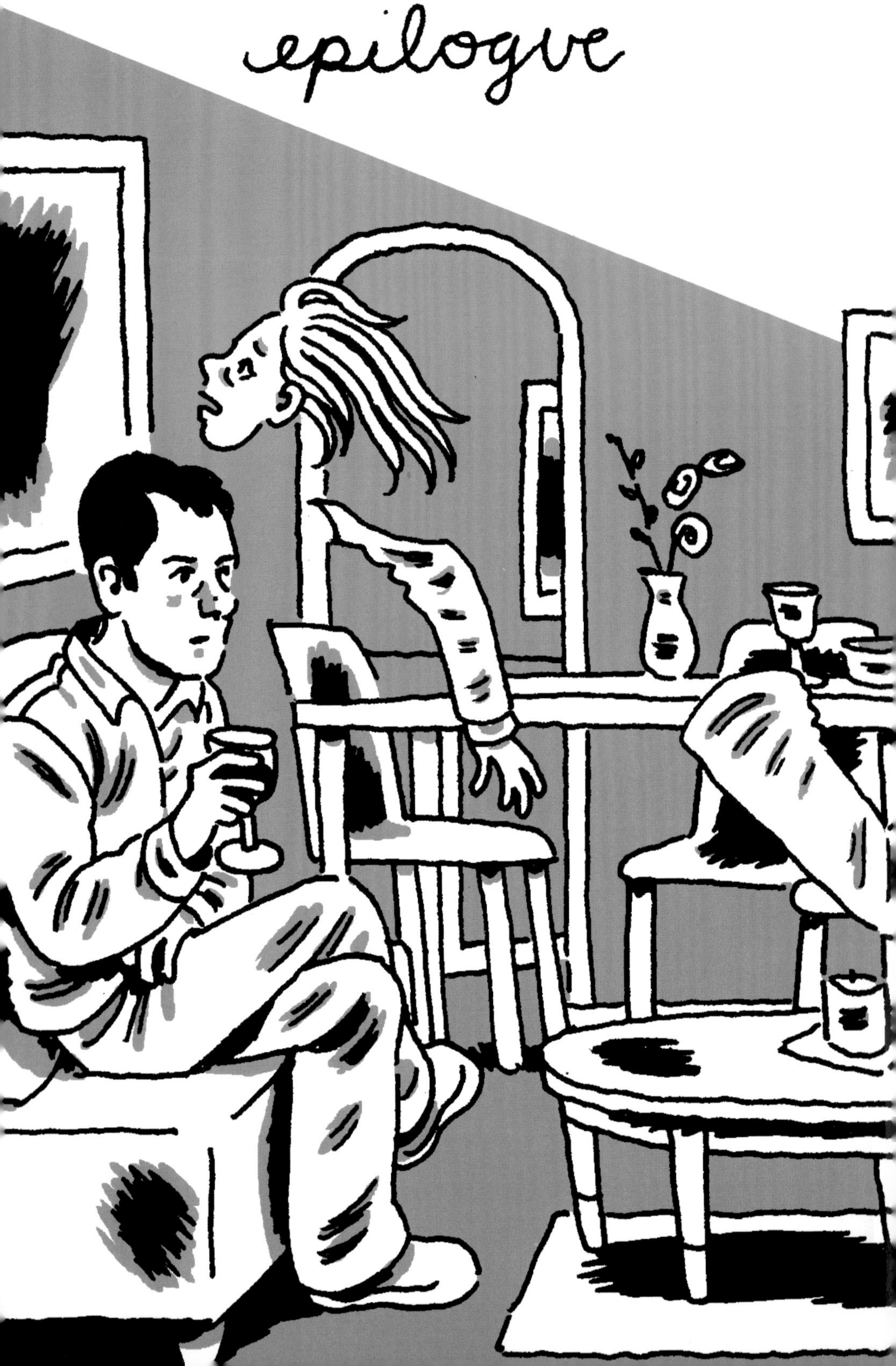
epilogue

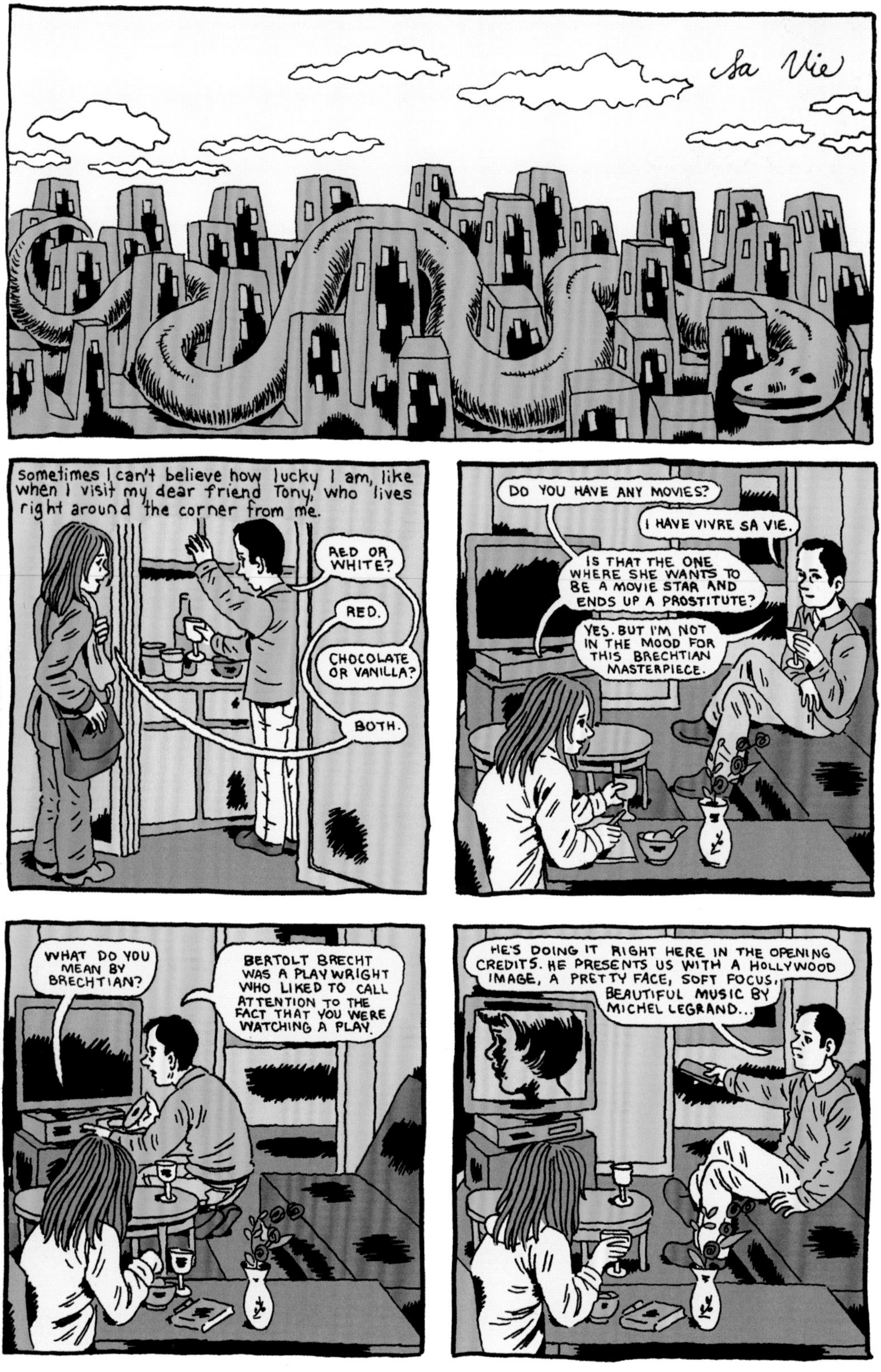
Sa Vie
sometimes I can't believe how lucky I am, like when I visit my dear friend Tony, who lives right around the corner from me.
RED OR WHITE?
RED.
CHOCOLATE OR VANILLA?
BOTH.
DO YOU HAVE ANY MOVIES?
I HAVE VIVRE SA VIE.
IS THAT THE ONE WHERE SHE WANTS TO BE A MOVIE STAR AND ENDS UP A PROSTITUTE?
YES. BUT I'M NOT IN THE MOOD FOR THIS BRECHTIAN MASTERPIECE.
WHAT DO YOU MEAN BY BRECHTIAN?
BERTOLT BRECHT WAS A PLAYWRIGHT WHO LIKED TO CALL ATTENTION TO THE FACT THAT YOU WERE WATCHING A PLAY.
HE'S DOING IT RIGHT HERE IN THE OPENING CREDITS. HE PRESENTS US WITH A HOLLYWOOD IMAGE, A PRETTY FACE, SOFT FOCUS, BEAUTIFUL MUSIC BY MICHEL LEGRAND...

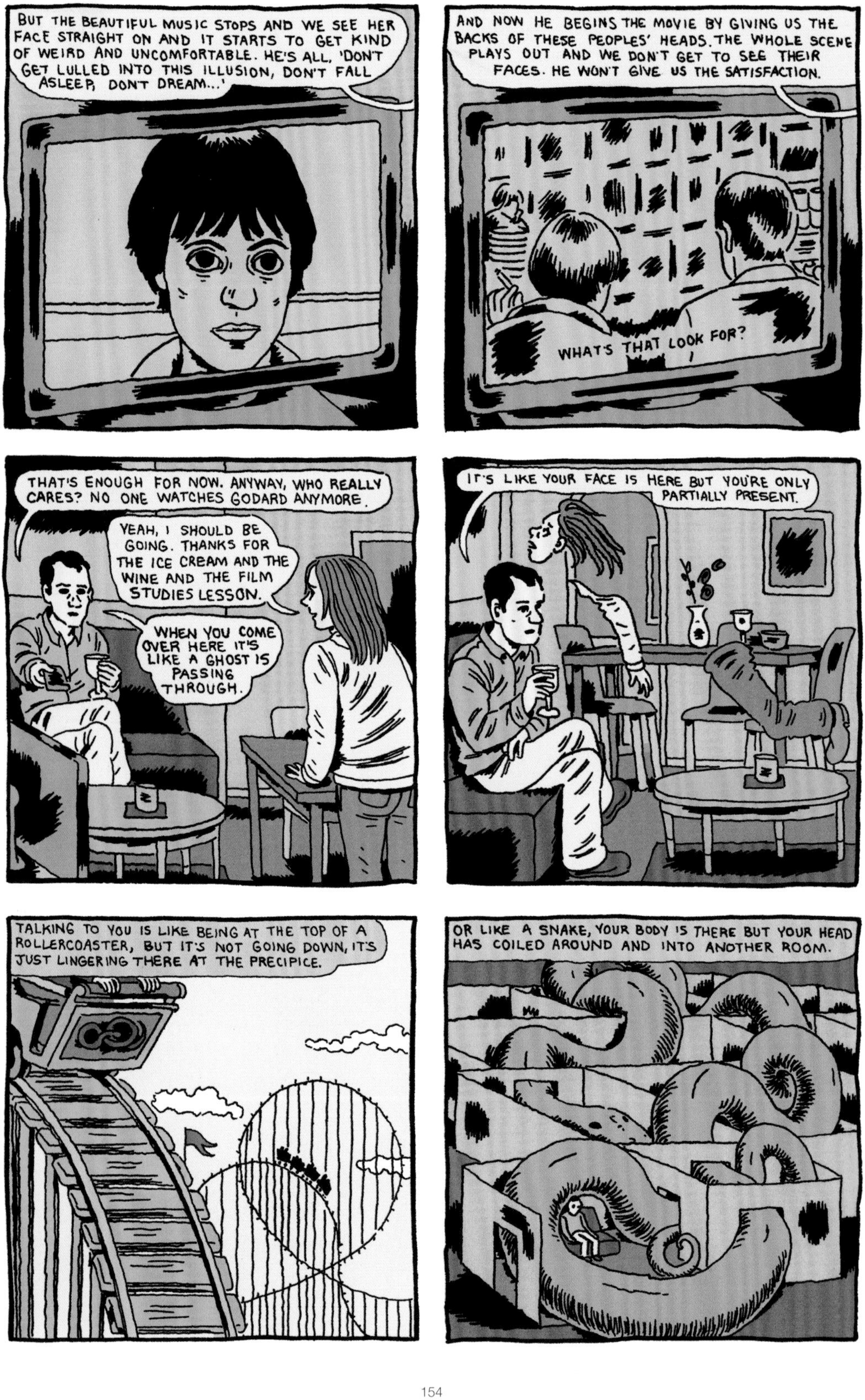
BUT THE BEAUTIFUL MUSIC STOPS AND WE SEE HER FACE STRAIGHT ON AND IT STARTS TO GET KIND OF WEIRD AND UNCOMFORTABLE. HE'S ALL, 'DON'T GET LULLED INTO THIS ILLUSION, DON'T FALL ASLEEP, DON'T DREAM...'
AND NOW HE BEGINS THE MOVIE BY GIVING US THE BACKS OF THESE PEOPLES' HEADS. THE WHOLE SCENE PLAYS OUT AND WE DON'T GET TO SEE THEIR FACES. HE WON'T GIVE US THE SATISFACTION.
WHAT'S THAT LOOK FOR?
THAT'S ENOUGH FOR NOW. ANYWAY, WHO REALLY CARES? NO ONE WATCHES GODARD ANYMORE.
YEAH, I SHOULD BE GOING. THANKS FOR THE ICE CREAM AND THE WINE AND THE FILM STUDIES LESSON.
WHEN YOU COME OVER HERE IT'S LIKE A GHOST IS PASSING THROUGH.
IT'S LIKE YOUR FACE IS HERE BUT YOU'RE ONLY PARTIALLY PRESENT.
TALKING TO YOU IS LIKE BEING AT THE TOP OF A ROLLERCOASTER, BUT IT'S NOT GOING DOWN, IT'S JUST LINGERING THERE AT THE PRECIPICE.
OR LIKE A SNAKE, YOUR BODY IS THERE BUT YOUR HEAD HAS COILED AROUND AND INTO ANOTHER ROOM.

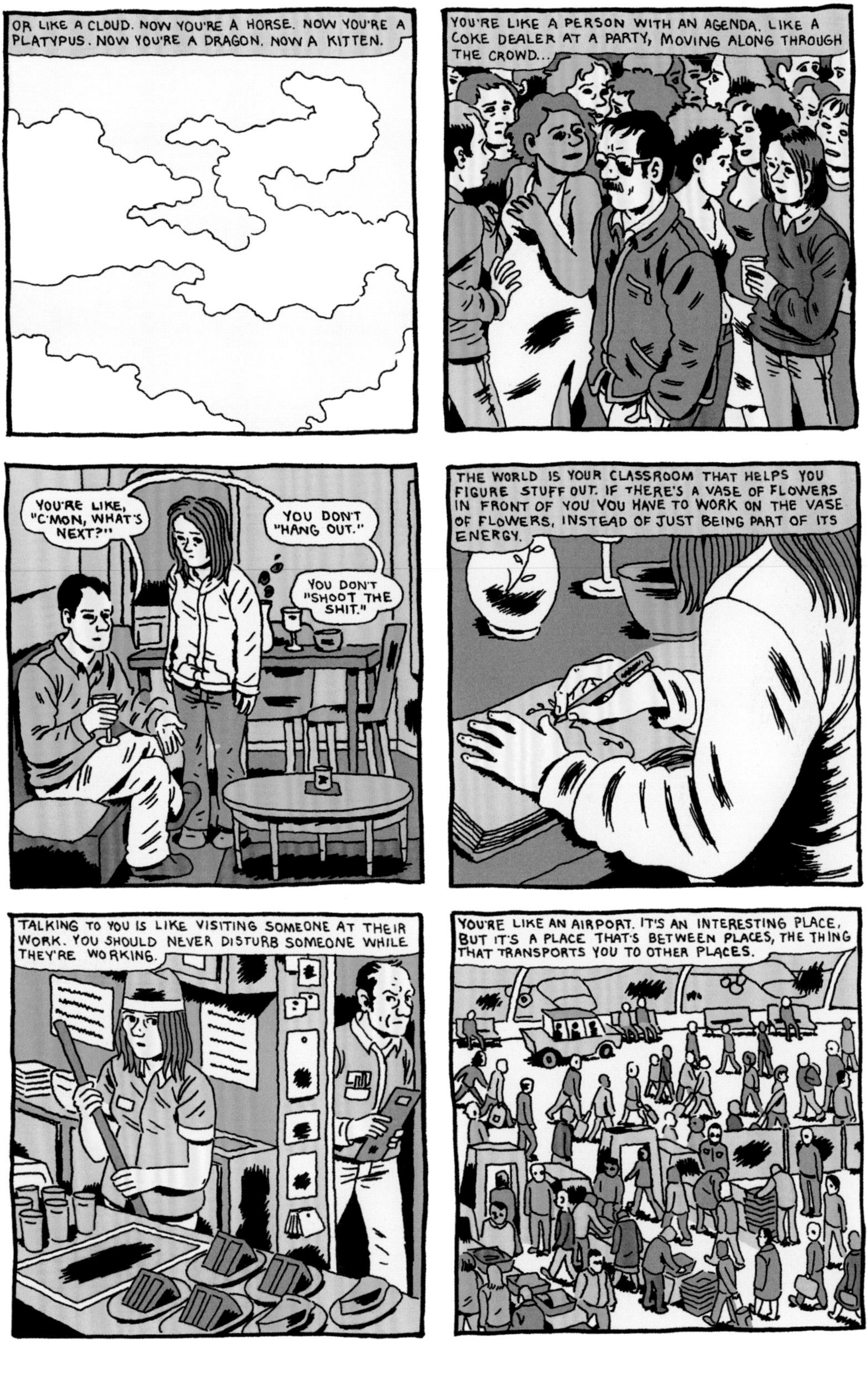
OR LIKE A CLOUD. NOW YOU'RE A HORSE. NOW YOU'RE A PLATYPUS. NOW YOU'RE A DRAGON. NOW A KITTEN.
YOU'RE LIKE A PERSON WITH AN AGENDA. LIKE A COKE DEALER AT A PARTY, MOVING ALONG THROUGH THE CROWD...
YOU'RE LIKE, "C'MON, WHAT'S NEXT?"
YOU DON'T "HANG OUT."
YOU DON'T "SHOOT THE SHIT."
THE WORLD IS YOUR CLASSROOM THAT HELPS YOU FIGURE STUFF OUT. IF THERE'S A VASE OF FLOWERS IN FRONT OF YOU YOU HAVE TO WORK ON THE VASE OF FLOWERS, INSTEAD OF JUST BEING PART OF ITS ENERGY.
TALKING TO YOU IS LIKE VISITING SOMEONE AT THEIR WORK. YOU SHOULD NEVER DISTURB SOMEONE WHILE THEY'RE WORKING.
YOU'RE LIKE AN AIRPORT. IT'S AN INTERESTING PLACE, BUT IT'S A PLACE THAT'S BETWEEN PLACES, THE THING THAT TRANSPORTS YOU TO OTHER PLACES.

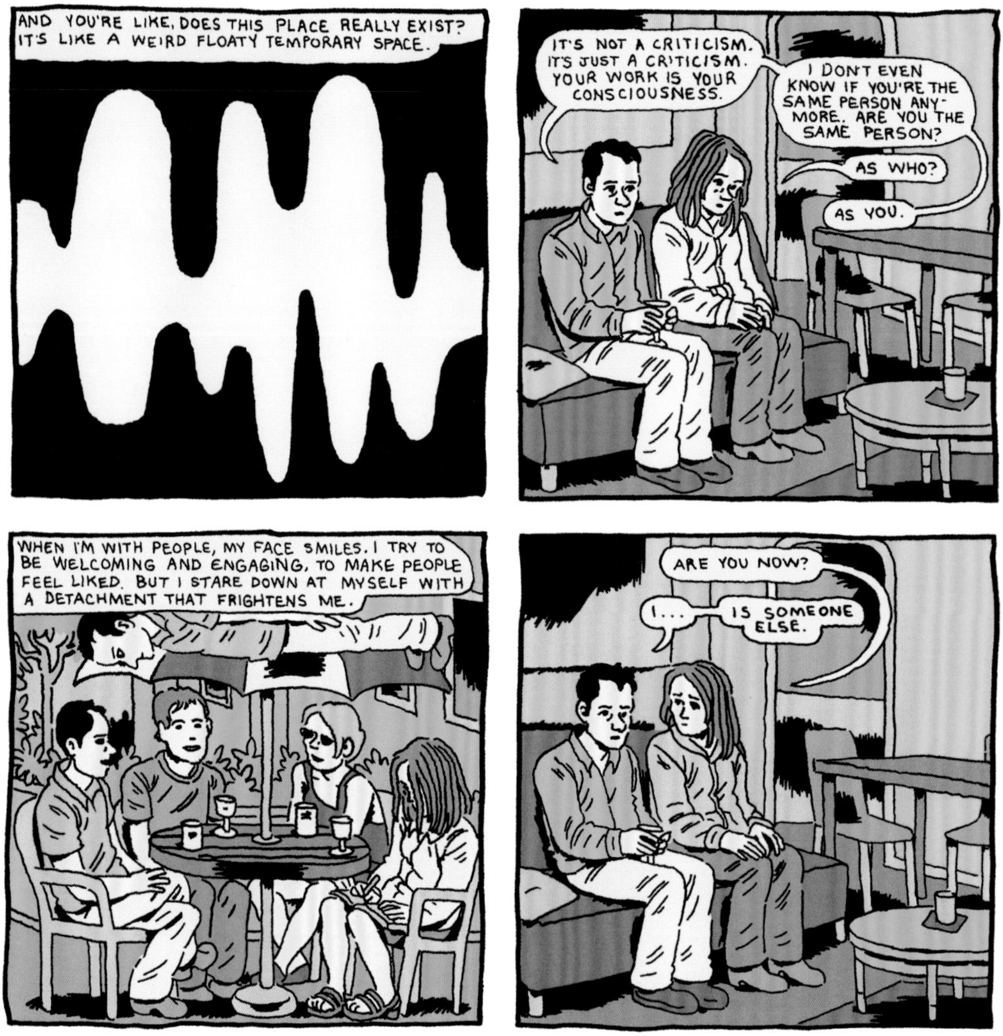
AND YOU'RE LIKE, DOES THIS PLACE REALLY EXIST? IT'S LIKE A WEIRD FLOATY TEMPORARY SPACE.
IT'S NOT A CRITICISM. IT'S JUST A CRITICISM. YOUR WORK IS YOUR CONSCIOUSNESS.
I DON'T EVEN KNOW IF YOU'RE THE SAME PERSON ANY-MORE. ARE YOU THE SAME PERSON?
AS WHO?
AS YOU.
WHEN I'M WITH PEOPLE, MY FACE SMILES. I TRY TO BE WELCOMING AND ENGAGING, TO MAKE PEOPLE FEEL LIKED. BUT I STARE DOWN AT MYSELF WITH A DETACHMENT THAT FRIGHTENS ME.
ARE YOU NOW?
I...
IS SOMEONE ELSE.

**Gabrielle Bell**'s work has been selected for the 2007, 2009, 2010 and 2011 Houghton-Mifflin *Best American Comics* and the *Yale Anthology of Graphic Fiction*, and has been featured in McSweeney's, The Believer, Bookforum and Vice magazines. "Cecil and Jordan In New York," the title story of her most recent book, was adapted for the screen by Bell and director Michel Gondry in the film anthology *Tokyo*! She lives in Brooklyn.

**Thank you:**
Tom Kaczynski, Tony Groutsis,
Larry Livermore, Ariel Schrag, Ron Rege Jr, Karen Sneider,
Michel Gondry, Richard Mcguire, Aaron Renier, Aaron Cometbus, Francoise Mouly,
Alison Bechdel, Chris Ware, Joe Matt, Victoria Kraus, Daryl Seitchik,
Bill Kartalopoulis, Shannon O' Leary, Dash Shaw, Naho Yamamoto,
Sharon Pan & The Big Issue Taiwan, Drawn & Quarterly,
San Diego Comic-Con, and always,
Margaret Hayes